SOMETHING ABOUT THE AUTHOR®

Something about
the Author *was named
an "Outstanding
Reference Source,"*
the highest honor given
by the American
Library Association
Reference and Adult
Services Division.

ISSN 0276-816X

SOMETHING ABOUT THE AUTHOR®

Facts and Pictures about Authors
and Illustrators of Books for Young People

volume 188

GALE
CENGAGE Learning™

Detroit • New York • San Francisco • New Haven, Conn • Waterville, Maine • London

GALE
CENGAGE Learning™

LSL
ReF
PN
451
.S6
v.188

Something about the Author, Volume 188

Project Editor: Lisa Kumar

Editorial: Dana Ferguson, Amy Elisabeth Fuller, Michelle Kazensky, Jennifer Mossman, Joseph Palmisano, Mary Ruby, Amanda D. Sams, Marie Toft

Permissions: Beth Beaufore, Jackie Jones, Jhanay Williams

Imaging and Multimedia: Leitha Etheridge-Sims, Lezlie Light

Composition and Electronic Capture: Amy Darga

Manufacturing: Drew Kalasky

Product Manager: Janet Witalec

For product information and technology assistance, contact us at
Gale Customer Support, 1-800-877-4253.
For permission to use material from this text or product,
submit all requests online at **www.cengage.com/permissions.**
Further permissions questions can be emailed to
permissionrequest@cengage.com

While every effort has been made to ensure the reliability of the information presented in this publication, Gale, a part of Cengage Learning, does not guarantee the accuracy of the data contained herein. Gale accepts no payment for listing; and inclusion in the publication of any organization, agency, institution, publication, service, or individual does not imply endorsement of the editors or publisher. Errors brought to the attention of the publisher and verified to the satisfaction of the publisher will be corrected in future editions.

EDITORIAL DATA PRIVACY POLICY: Does this publication contain information about you as an individual? If so, for more information about our editorial data privacy policies, please see our Privacy Statement at www.gale.cengage.com.

Gale
27500 Drake Rd.
Farmington Hills, MI, 48331-3535

LIBRARY OF CONGRESS CATALOG CARD NUMBER 62-52046

ISBN-13: 978-0-7876-9937-6
ISBN-10: 0-7876-9937-3

ISSN 0276-816X

This title is also available as an e-book.
ISBN-13: 978-1-4144-3840-5
ISBN-10: 1-4144-3840-0
Contact your Gale sales representative for ordering information.

Printed in the United States of America
1 2 3 4 5 6 7 12 11 10 09 08

Contents

Authors in Forthcoming Volumes vii

Introduction ix

SATA Product Advisory Board xi

A

Allsopp, Sophie 1

Armstrong, Matthew 1975- 1

Armstrong, Matthew S.
   See Armstrong, Matthew 1

Azore, Barbara 1934- 2

B

Baum, Maxie 5

Bee, William 5

Bley, Anette 1967- 7

Bolden, Tonya 1959- 8

Bolden, Tonya Wilyce
   See Bolden, Tonya 8

Brashares, Ann 1967- 13

C

Chamberlain, Barbara A.
   See Azore, Barbara 2

Cheaney, Janie B.
   See Cheaney, J.B. 18

Cheaney, J.B. 1950- 18

Clement-Moore, Rosemary 19

Cotten, Cynthia 20

Crisler, Curtis L. 1965- 22

Curie, Eve 1904-2007
   Obituary Notice 23

D

DeSaix, Deborah Durland 24

Dibley, Glin 25

Donnio, Sylviane 26

E

Emmett, Jonathan 1965- 28

F

Fields, Bryan W. 1958(?)- 32

Fleischner, Jennifer 1956- 33

Fox, Christyan 34

Fox, Diane 35

Franco, Betsy 1947- 37

G

Gershator, Phillis 1942- 41

Gévry, Claudine 46

Golding, Julia 1969- 48

Graff, Lisa 1981- 49

Gutman, Dan 1955- 50

H

Haining, Peter 1940-2007
   Obituary Notice 56

Haining, Peter Alexander
   See Haining, Peter 56

Hanson, Mary Elizabeth 56

Hawkins, Jimmy 1941- 57

High, Linda Oatman 1958- 57
   Autobiography Feature 63

Hill, Kirkpatrick 1938- 75

Howarth, Daniel 78

J

Jenkins, Steve 1952- 79

Johnson, Angela 1961- 87

Johnston, Jeffry W. 93

K

Kanzler, John 1963- 95

Keaney, Brian 1954- 96

Kent, Rose 100

Kerr, Anne Louise
See Mackey, Weezie Kerr 120

Krensky, Stephen 1953- 101

Krensky, Stephen Alan
See Krensky, Stephen 101

Kulka, Joe 1965(?)- 110

L

Labouisse, Eve Curie
See Curie, Eve 23

Labouisse, Eve Denise
See Curie, Eve 23

Leeds, Contance 112

Long, Loren 1966(?)- 113

Love, Judith Dufour
See Love, Judy 116

Love, Judy 116

Lyne, Alison Davis 118

M

Mackey, Weezie Kerr 120

Makhijani, Pooja 121

Martin, Jacqueline Briggs 1945- 123

Menchin, Scott 129

Miles, Victoria 1966- 130

Mowll, Joshua 1970(?)- 132

N

Nadimi, Suzan 135

Nickel, Barbara 1966- 136

O

O'Connor, Ian 1965- 138

P

Perkins, Mitali 1963- 139

Perl, Erica S. 141

Pinkwater, Jill 142

Prince, Joshua 146

R

Rabb, Margo 1972- 148

Rabb, M.E.
See Rabb, Margo 148

Reeve, Rosie 149

Rocco, John 1967- 150

Russo, Marisabina 1950- 151

S

Santat, Dan 159

Scannel, John Vernon
See Scannell, Vernon 160

Scannell, Vernon 1922-2007
Obituary Notice 160

Shea, Bob 161

Solomon, Heather M. 161

Stead, Rebecca 1968(?)- 162

Swinburne, Stephen R. 1952- 163

T

Tinkham, Kelly A. 169

Tong, Paul 170

Tripp, Jenny 171

Turner, Ann 1945- 172
Autobiography Feature 177

Turner, Ann Warren
See Turner, Ann 172

U

Umansky, Kaye 1946- 192

V

Vidrine, Beverly Barras 1938- 197

Vincent, Erin 1969- 198

W

Walden, Mark 1952- 200

Wallace, Karen 1951- 201

Weldin, Frauke 1969- 208

Y

Yamada, Utako 1963- 208

Young, Janet 1957- 209

Young, Janet Ruth
See Young, Janet 209

Authors in Forthcoming Volumes

Below are some of the authors and illustrators that will be featured in upcoming volumes of *SATA*. These include new entries on the swiftly rising stars of the field, as well as completely revised and updated entries (indicated with *) on some of the most notable and best-loved creators of books for children.

*Jim Arnosky ▮ Winner of the 2005 Key Lifetime Achievement Award for Excellence from the American Association of Science Teachers, Arnosky is an inveterate naturalist and artist who creates picture books about wildlife and nature. His engaging nonfiction texts pair with detailed illustrations to produce unique "how-to" books focusing on outdoor skills and animal identification, while in works such as *Exploring the Coast* he presents readers with new ways of seeing and participating in the out of doors. Arnosky's popular grandfatherly Crinkleroot character introduces a multitude of animal facts to young readers, while his award-winning *Drawing from Nature* and *Drawing Life in Motion* inspired a PBS television series.

Bret Bertholf ▮ A man of many talents—he is a painter, writer, musician, and featured yodeler in the country & western band Halden Wofford & the Hi Beams— Bertholf has contributed illustrations to children's books by by authors such as Allen Kurzweil and Paul Bajoria. He combines his many talents in his debut picture book, *The Long Gone Lonesome History of Country Music,* a humorous back-porch guide to the many people and traditions that make up America's unique musical genre.

Shane W. Evans ▮ A widely awarded illustrator, Evans has produced dozens of books, from the "Shanna" book series by Jean Marzollo to historical fiction by authors such as Alan Govenar, Doreen Rappaport, and Catherine Clinton. Based in Missouri, Evans has also created Dream Studio, which serves as a working studio, gallery, and gathering place for the surrounding community. In 2002, Evans was invited by First Lady Laura Bush to participate in the National Book Festival, and his other awards include the *Boston Globe/Horn Book* Award and the Orbis Pictus Award for Outstanding Nonfiction for Children.

Jason Hightman ▮ Beginning his career as a screenwriter and award-winning film director, Hightman eventually decided to pursue a longstanding interest in fantasy fiction. The result, *The Saint of Dragons,* was inspired in part by 9/11 and the realization that evil exists in the world. In the novel, a contemporary teen learns of his destiny as a dragon slayer just as the creatures he opposes learn of his existence, resulting in an action-filled race to seek out and slay the dragons before they can achieve their goal of destroying humanity.

*Suzy Kline ▮ An award-winning educator, Kline is perhaps best known as a writer of elementary-grade chapter books that inspire young children with a love of reading. Her books are noted for their humorous plots and engaging characters such as third grader Herbie Jones, second-grade stutterer Mary Marony, and Horrible Harry, a rambunctious second grader whose lighthearted hijinks make him the unwitting nemesis of even the most patient teacher. Critics have consistently complimented Kline's books as useful for the classroom and for encouraging reading, particularly among young boys.

Lydia Monks ▮ A prolific illustrator based in England, Monks creates collage art that has earned her several prestigious awards for illustration. Trained at Kingston University, she worked as a commercial illustrator for several years until her first original picture book, *I Wish I Were a Dog,* won the Bronze Smarties Prize in 1999. In addition to producing other original self-illustrated stories such as *Aaargh, Spider!,* Monks has also created artwork for texts by Roger McGough, Carol Ann Duffy, and Julia Donaldson.

*Gary Paulsen ▮ The author of acclaimed young-adult novels and nonfiction whose works are published around the world, Paulsen has earned Newbery Medal honors for his books *Dogsong, Hatchet,* and *The Winter Room.* His perennially popular stories are often set in wilderness or rural areas and focus on teen characters growing in maturity as they confront challenging tests for survival. In addition to writing for teens, Paulsen has produced picture books, children's nonfiction, and many works for adult readers.

V.A. Richardson ▮ Richardson's "Windjammer" novels take readers back to Holland's Golden Age, a time during the 1600s when Dutch ships traveled the world and Amsterdam was abloom with colorful tulips and a rich culture. A British writer with a strong grounding in history, Richardson entertains teen readers with *House of Windjammer* and *The Moneylender's Daughter,* novels that follow the fortunes of a wealthy trading family as its young scion attempts to save the family fortune, reputation, and ancestral home by searching for the rarest of treasures: a dusky tulip known as the Black Pearl.

Jackie Urbanovic ▮ Based in Maryland, Urbanovic is the author and illustrator of humorous picture books such as *Duck at the Door* and *Duck Soup.* Known for creating engaging animal characters, Urbanovic has also created artwork for award-winning picture books by Teresa Bateman and Jackie French Koller. *Duck at the Door* and *Duck Soup* have become childhood bestsellers on the strength of their fun-loving, slapstick plots and their whimsical watercolor-and-pencil art.

*Jacqueline Woodson ▮ The recipient of numerous honors, including a Coretta Scott King award, several Lambda Literary awards, a *Los Angeles Times* Book award, and a National Book Award nomination, Woodson focuses her fiction on young characters living in the shadows of mainstream America. While her stories work to correct derogatory stereotypes and labels, they also celebrate people's differences and individuality rather than support one minority group over another. The plight of three orphaned brothers is the focus of Woodson's award-winning novel *Miracle's Boys,* while *Hush* explores the loss of a child's identity when her family must enter the witness protection program.

Introduction

Something about the Author (*SATA*) is an ongoing reference series that examines the lives and works of authors and illustrators of books for children. *SATA* includes not only well-known writers and artists but also less prominent individuals whose works are just coming to be recognized. This series is often the only readily available information source on emerging authors and illustrators. You'll find *SATA* informative and entertaining, whether you are a student, a librarian, an English teacher, a parent, or simply an adult who enjoys children's literature.

What's Inside *SATA*

SATA provides detailed information about authors and illustrators who span the full time range of children's literature, from early figures like John Newbery and L. Frank Baum to contemporary figures like Judy Blume and Richard Peck. Authors in the series represent primarily English-speaking countries, particularly the United States, Canada, and the United Kingdom. Also included, however, are authors from around the world whose works are available in English translation. The writings represented in *SATA* include those created intentionally for children and young adults as well as those written for a general audience and known to interest younger readers. These writings cover the entire spectrum of children's literature, including picture books, humor, folk and fairy tales, animal stories, mystery and adventure, science fiction and fantasy, historical fiction, poetry and nonsense verse, drama, biography, and nonfiction. Obituaries are also included in *SATA* and are intended not only as death notices but also as concise overviews of people's lives and work. Additionally, each edition features newly revised and updated entries for a selection of *SATA* listees who remain of interest to today's readers and who have been active enough to require extensive revisions of their earlier biographies.

Autobiography Feature

Beginning with Volume 103, many volumes of *SATA* feature one or more specially commissioned autobiographical essays. These unique essays, averaging about ten thousand words in length and illustrated with an abundance of personal photos, present an entertaining and informative first-person perspective on the lives and careers of prominent authors and illustrators profiled in *SATA*.

Two Convenient Indexes

In response to suggestions from librarians, *SATA* indexes no longer appear in every volume but are included in alternate (odd-numbered) volumes of the series, beginning with Volume 57.

SATA continues to include two indexes that cumulate with each alternate volume: the Illustrations Index, arranged by the name of the illustrator, gives the number of the volume and page where the illustrator's work appears in the current volume as well as all preceding volumes in the series; the Author Index gives the number of the volume in which a person's biographical sketch, autobiographical essay, or obituary appears in the current volume as well as all preceding volumes in the series.

These indexes also include references to authors and illustrators who appear in *Gale's Yesterday's Authors of Books for Children, Children's Literature Review,* and *Something about the Author Autobiography Series.*

Easy-to-Use Entry Format

Whether you're already familiar with the *SATA* series or just getting acquainted, you will want to be aware of the kind of information that an entry provides. In every *SATA* entry the editors attempt to give as complete a picture of the person's life and work as possible. A typical entry in *SATA* includes the following clearly labeled information sections:

PERSONAL: date and place of birth and death, parents' names and occupations, name of spouse, date of marriage, names of children, educational institutions attended, degrees received, religious and political affiliations, hobbies and other interests.

ADDRESSES: complete home, office, electronic mail, and agent addresses, whenever available.

CAREER: name of employer, position, and dates for each career post; art exhibitions; military service; memberships and offices held in professional and civic organizations.

MEMBER: professional, civic, and other association memberships and any official posts held.

AWARDS, HONORS: literary and professional awards received.

WRITINGS: title-by-title chronological bibliography of books written and/or illustrated, listed by genre when known; lists of other notable publications, such as plays, screenplays, and periodical contributions.

ADAPTATIONS: a list of films, television programs, plays, CD-ROMs, recordings, and other media presentations that have been adapted from the author's work.

WORK IN PROGRESS: description of projects in progress.

SIDELIGHTS: a biographical portrait of the author or illustrator's development, either directly from the biographee—and often written specifically for the *SATA* entry—or gathered from diaries, letters, interviews, or other published sources.

BIOGRAPHICAL AND CRITICAL SOURCES: cites sources quoted in "Sidelights" along with references for further reading.

EXTENSIVE ILLUSTRATIONS: photographs, movie stills, book illustrations, and other interesting visual materials supplement the text.

How a *SATA* Entry Is Compiled

SATA editors examine a wide variety of published sources to gather information for an entry. Biographical and bibliographic sources are consulted, as are book reviews, feature articles, published interviews, and material sometimes obtained from the biographee's family, publishers, agent, or other associates. Whenever possible, the author or illustrator is sent a copy of the entry to check for accuracy and completeness.

Entries that have not been verified by the biographees or their representatives are marked with an asterisk (*).

Contact the Editor

We encourage our readers to examine the entire *SATA* series. Please write and tell us if we can make *SATA* even more helpful to you. Give your comments and suggestions to the editor:

Editor
Something about the Author
Gale, Cengage Learning
27500 Drake Rd.
Farmington Hills MI 48331-3535

Toll-free: 800-877-GALE
Fax: 248-699-8070

Something about the Author Product Advisory Board

The editors of *Something about the Author* are dedicated to maintaining a high standard of excellence by publishing comprehensive, accurate, and highly readable entries on a wide array of writers for children and young adults. In addition to the quality of the content, the editors take pride in the graphic design of the series, which is intended to be orderly yet inviting, allowing readers to utilize the pages of *SATA* easily and with efficiency. Despite the longevity of the *SATA* print series, and the success of its format, we are mindful that the vitality of a literary reference product is dependent on its ability to serve its users over time. As literature, and attitudes about literature, constantly evolve, so do the reference needs of students, teachers, scholars, journalists, researchers, and book club members. To be certain that we continue to keep pace with the expectations of our customers, the editors of *SATA* listen carefully to their comments regarding the value, utility, and quality of the series. Librarians, who have firsthand knowledge of the needs of library users, are a valuable resource for us. The *Something about the Author* Product Advisory Board, made up of school, public, and academic librarians, is a forum to promote focused feedback about *SATA* on a regular basis. The nine-member advisory board includes the following individuals, whom the editors wish to thank for sharing their expertise:

Eva M. Davis
Youth Department Manager,
Ann Arbor District Library,
Ann Arbor, Michigan

Joan B. Eisenberg
Lower School Librarian,
Milton Academy,
Milton, Massachusetts

Francisca Goldsmith
Teen Services Librarian,
Berkeley Public Library,
Berkeley, California

Susan Dove Lempke
Children's Services Supervisor,
Niles Public Library District,
Niles, Illinois

Robyn Lupa
Head of Children's Services,
Jefferson County Public Library,
Lakewood, Colorado

Victor L. Schill
Assistant Branch Librarian/Children's Librarian,
Harris County Public Library/Fairbanks Branch,
Houston, Texas

Caryn Sipos
Community Librarian,
Three Creeks Community Library,
Vancouver, Washington

Steven Weiner
Director,
Maynard Public Library,
Maynard, Massachusetts

SOMETHING ABOUT THE AUTHOR

ALLSOPP, Sophie

Personal

Born in England; children: one son. *Hobbies and other interests:* Making oak furniture.

Addresses

Home—South England. *E-mail*—allsopp@thorogood. net.

Career

Professional illustrator.

Illustrator

Stella Gurney, *The Hot Pepper Queen and Mango Babies,* Ginn & Company (Aylesbury, England), 1994.

Caroline Walsh, *The Little Book of Christmas,* Kingfisher (London, England), 1996.

Stella Gurney, *Dear God . . . ,* Templar (Dorking, England), 2005.

Stella Gurney, *Princess: A Glittering Guide for Young Ladies,* Candlewick Press (Cambridge, MA), 2006.

Virginia L. Kroll, *Everybody Has a Teddy,* Sterling (New York, NY), 2007.

Lois Rock, *The First Christmas,* Lion Hudson (Oxford, England), 2007.

Biographical and Critical Sources

PERIODICALS

Booklist, March 15, 2007, Gillian Engberg, review of *Everybody Has a Teddy,* p. 53.
School Library Journal, May, 2007, Linda Ludke, review of *Everybody Has a Teddy,* p. 102.

ONLINE

Childrensillustrators.com, http://www2.childrensillustrators.com/ (March 15, 2008), "Sophie Allsopp."*

*   *   *

ARMSTRONG, Matthew 1975-
(Matthew S. Armstrong)

Personal

Born June 9, 1975; married; children: one.

Addresses

Home and office—UT. *E-mail*—zebo_powertron@ yahoo.com.

Career

Illustrator. Worked variously as a comic-book artist, portrait painter, and artist for advertising and video-game industry; Incognito Entertainment (subsidiary of Sony Computer Entertainment, Inc.), conceptual artist and writer.

Illustrator

C.S. Lewis, *The Return to Narnia: The Rescue of Prince Caspian,* HarperCollins (New York, NY), 2006.

Jeremy Strong, *Stuff: The Life of a Cool Demented Dude,* HarperTempest (New York, NY), 2007.

Sidelights

Matthew Armstrong has been an illustrator of one sort or another since he was a young child; as he noted on his home page, in elementary school his teachers would often reprimand him because of his constant drawing. As a teen, Armstrong filled his head with comic-book stories, animes, and video games, and as a grown up he channels his creativity into the same entertainments he loved as a child, including comic books and video games. In addition to these media, Armstrong's black-and-white pencil drawings have been featured in two young-adult novels: *The Return to Narnia: The Rescue of Prince Caspian* and *Stuff: The Life of a Cool Demented Dude.*

A novel by British author Jeremy Strong, *Stuff* centers on a fourteen-year-old artist wannabe who is known as "Stuff." Stuff has several difficulties to deal with, including a new stepmother and a stepsister he dislikes; a girlfriend he is no longer infatuated with; and a new crush on Sky, a beautiful new girl at school. Stuff uses his personal dramas as fodder for the comic strip he anonymously publishes in his school magazine. The illustrations Armstrong contributes to Strong's novel have been recognized by critics for their ability to add dimension to the story, a *Publishers Weekly* critic noting that *Stuff* is "enhanced" by the illustrator's "manga-influenced" art. In *Kirkus Reviews* a critic credited Armstrong's comic-book illustrations for providing "a great look into the fantasy life and mind of an artist as a young boy."

Biographical and Critical Sources

PERIODICALS

Bulletin of the Center for Children's Books, April, 2007, April Spisak, review of *Stuff: The Life of a Cool Demented Dude,* p. 344.

Kirkus Reviews, February 1, 2007, review of *Stuff,* p. 129.

Publishers Weekly, March 12, 2007, review of *Stuff,* p. 59.

School Library Journal, July, 2007, Heather M. Campbell, review of *Stuff,* p. 111.

Voice of Youth Advocates, June, 2007, Jeff Mann, review of *Stuff,* p. 154.

ONLINE

Dark Inventions Web site, http://www.darkinventions.com/ (February 26, 2008), "Matthew Armstrong."

Matthew Armstrong Home Page, http://www.matthewart. com (February 26, 2008).*

*   *   *

ARMSTRONG, Matthew S. See ARMSTRONG, Matthew

*   *   *

AZORE, Barbara 1934- [A pseudonym] (Barbara A. Chamberlain)

Personal

Born August 12, 1934, in Hounslow, Middlesex, England; immigrated to Canada, 1967; married (divorced); children: Martin, Andrew, Katherine. *Education:* University of London, diploma of sociology, 1958. *Hobbies and other interests:* Fold dancing, theater, watercolor painting, travel, reading, playing Scrabble.

Addresses

Home—Canada. *E-mail*—azore@telus.net.

Career

Edmonton Public Schools, Edmonton, Alberta, Canada, laboratory aide and library aide, 1970-97. Edmonton Childbirth Education Association, founder and president, 1968-84; WECAM Food Co-operative, volunteer, 2000—.

Member

Canadian Children's Book Centre, Writers Guild of Alberta, Young Alberta Book Society.

Awards, Honors

Included in Best of the Best list, Edmonton Public Schools, 2005, for *Wanda and the Wild Hair.*

Writings

Wanda and the Wild Hair (juvenile), illustrated by Georgia Graham, Tundra Books (Toronto, Ontario, Canada), 2005.

Wanda and the Frogs (juvenile), illustrated by Georgia Graham, Tundra Books of Northern New York (Plattsburgh, NY), 2007.

Poetry represented in anthologies. Contributor to periodicals, including *Birth Issues* and *Edmonton Journal.* Editor, *ECEA Newsletter,* 1968-76, and *University of Alberta Volunteers Newsletter,* c. 1980s.

Author's work has been translated into Chinese.

Sidelights

As the creator of Wanda, an engaging fictional character with an unruly mop of curly hair, Barbara Azore shares her imagination and sense of fun with young children. Wanda makes her first appearance in *Wanda and the Wild Hair,* as her unruly tangle of hair attracts comments from her family, and even several stray objects. Although the girl finally agrees to let a hairdresser tame her unruly coiffure, she ultimately decides that letting her locks decide their own style suits her just fine. In *Resource Links,* Lorie Lavallee noted that Azore's tale incorporates "themes of self-esteem and identity, responsibility," and "problem solving," all of which "are cleverly enmeshed in a series of comical misadventures."

Wanda makes a second appearance in *Wanda and the Frogs,* once again brought to life in what *Resource Links* contributor Linda Berezowski described as "charming chalk pastel illustrations" created by artist Gloria Graham. In *Wanda and the Frogs* Wanda locates some tadpoles on her walk to school and, over the weeks that follow, she and her classmates watch as the tiny creatures grow and develop. When they reach frog stage, Wanda's teacher announces that the creatures must be returned to nature, but the mop-headed girl has other ideas. Berezowski praised Azore's picture-book sequel as "delightful," adding that the story ends with "a touching moral about compassion." The "substantial text" in *Wanda and the Frogs* "palatably folds in a bit of educational information," observed a *Kirkus Review* writer, while in *School Library Journal* Maura Bresnahan dubbed Azore's story as "perfect for a read-aloud tie-in to a . . . frog-themed storyhour."

"I did not start writing children's stories until 1987, the year after my first grandchild was born," Azore once commented. "I knitted him picture sweaters and, to go with them, wrote and illustrated stories about the pictures. As four more grandchildren came along, I did the same for them and later for a great-niece and nephew. None of these stories were intended for publication."

Barbara Azore introduces readers to a likeable young mop-head in a series of picture books that include **Wanda and the Frogs.** (Illustration copyright © 2007 by Georgia Graham. All rights reserved. Reproduced by permission.)

"I was five years old when World War II began, and when my grandson reached his fifth birthday I wrote and illustrated a picture book for him about my experiences as a child during the war. A copy has been given to each grandchild on his or her fifth birthday. There is also a copy of the story in the archives of the Second World War Experience Centre in Leeds, England.

"*Wanda and the Wild Hair* was written for my great-niece in 1997. It was published as a result of my entering a new story in the Writers' Union of Canada Writing for Children competition in 1999. I was later informed that my story, 'A Chicken for Christmas,' had placed second out of more than 800 entries, but there was no second prize. However, one of the readers asked if she could take the story to Kathy Lowinger at Tundra Books. Ms. Lowinger asked me if I had any other stories. *Wanda and the Wild Hair* was the last story I had written and was already on the computer, and it was this story that was accepted for publication. I like to think of Wanda as the child I would have liked to be and wasn't. Edmonton public schools have put *Wanda and the Wild Hair* on the list of resource books for their elementary social-studies curriculum. Teachers in the Edmonton public schools are using *Wanda and the Frogs* in the Life Cycles section of the Grade 3 science curriculum.

"Children often ask how I go about writing a story, and I have to admit that I do most of my 'writing' in bed. The idea (or inspiration) comes first. In the case of *Wanda and the Wild Hair,* it was a small wooden pin that I picked up at a garage sale for twenty-five cents. It was a round disc with a happy-type face on it and a bunch of hair sticking out of the top. Other ideas have come from my memories of my own children and now grandchildren, from experiences with children in general, and from my own childhood."

Biographical and Critical Sources

PERIODICALS

Canadian Book Review Annual, 2005, Anne Hutchings, review of *Wanda and the Wild Hair,* p. 440.

Kirkus Reviews, February 15, 2007, review of *Wanda and the Frogs.*

Resource Links, April, 2005, Lori Lavallee, review of *Wanda and the Wild Hair,* p. 2; April, 2007, Linda Berezowski, review of *Wanda and the Frogs,* p. 1.

School Library Journal, March, 2007, Maura Bresnahan, review of *Wanda and the Frogs,* p. 150.

B

BAUM, Maxie

Personal

Female.

Career

Children's book author.

Writings

I Have a Little Dreidel, illustrated by Julie Paschkis, Cartwheel Books (New York, NY), 2006.

Sidelights

In *I Have a Little Dreidel,* Maxie Baum adapts a traditional Hanukkah song for new listeners. Praised by several reviewers for its family-centered focus, the book follows a large, extended family as they gather to celebrate the traditional Jewish holiday by making and eating latkes (recipe included), light the menorah, and play the dreidel game that is the focus of the song. Baum incorporates the traditional song as the refrain for original verses that present "a homey articulation of Jewish tradition and continuity," according to a *Publishers Weekly* contributor. The book's illustrations—colorful, folk-style paintings by artist Julie Paschkis—also attracted positive attention, a *Kirkus Reviews* writer noting that their bold shapes include "enough detail to encourage lots of visual study by younger listeners." Paschkis's illustrations, which include stylized Jewish cultural motifs and symbols, reflects Baum's "cheery little song" and make *I Have a Little Dreidel* "a standout."

Biographical and Critical Sources

PERIODICALS

Booklist, September 15, 2006, Ilene Cooper, review of *I Have a Little Dreidel,* p. 60.

Horn Book, November-December, 2006, Rachel L. Smith, review of *I Have a Little Dreidel,* p. 688.
Kirkus Reviews, November 1, 2006, review of *I Have a Little Dreidel,* p. 1126.
Publishers Weekly, September 25, 2006, review of *I Have a Little Dreidel,* p. 68.
School Library Journal, October, 2006, Teri Markson, review of *I Have a Little Dreidel,* p. 94.*

*   *   *

BEE, William

Personal

Born in England. *Hobbies and other interests:* Gardening, skiing, racing vintage cars.

Addresses

Home and office—England.

Career

Author.

Writings

Whatever, Candlewick Press (Cambridge, MA), 2005.
And the Train Goes . . ., Candlewick Press (Cambridge, MA), 2007.
Beware of the Frog, Candlewick Press (Cambridge, MA), 2008.

Sidelights

Author and illustrator William Bee creates colorful children's books that entertain with a humorous flair. Bee has self-illustrated several titles, including *Whatever, And the Train Goes . . .,* and *Beware of the Frog.*

Critics have acknowledged Bee for creating digital renderings that are chock full of bright colors and bold

William Bee's unique self-illustrated picture books include And the Train Goes . . . ***and*** Whatever. (Copyright © 2005 by William Bee. Reproduced by permission of the publisher Candlewick Press, Inc., Cambridge, MA on behalf of Walker Books Ltd., London, England.)

patterns. Bee's first picture book for children, *Whatever,* is an updated remake of Maurice Sendak's *Pierre.* The story focuses on an unappreciative little boy and his father, a man who is determined to get a response from his stoic son. Bee reinvents the story through his digitally enhanced illustrations, which feature short, stocky characters. In *School Library Journal* Piper L. Nyman commented that Bee's images "engage the audience and mirror the humor" of the Sendak-inspired tale. A *Publishers Weekly* reviewer noted that Bee's new illustrations are "eye-pleasing" and "go a long way toward injecting some fun into the book."

Bee's second self-illustrated picture book, *And the Train Goes . . .,* incorporates the many sounds that can be heard on a passenger train, including the noises made by the train's engine and the chatter of the many pas-

sengers and crew. A critic for *Publishers Weekly* acknowledged Bee's illustrations for their ability to add a sensory energy to the simple text. His artful depictions "heighten the sense that readers are moving through the busy train cars as they advance through the book," the critic noted. In *Kirkus Reviews,* a contributor dubbed *And the Train Goes . . .* "a fresh, visually arresting read-aloud with a lovely old-time feel."

Biographical and Critical Sources

PERIODICALS

Bulletin of the Center for Children's Books, December, 2005, review of *Whatever,* p. 170; September, 2007, Deborah Stevenson, review of *And the Train Goes . . .,* p. 7.

Horn Book, July-August, 2007, Nell Beram, review of *And the Train Goes . . .,* p. 376.

Independent (London, England), April 20, 2007, "Trains, Tigers, and Swallows."

Kirkus Reviews, November 1, 2005, review of *Whatever,* p. 1181; April 1, 2007, review of *And the Train Goes. . . .*

New York Times Book Review, November 13, 2005, Lemony Snicket, "Folks of Few Words," p. L23.

Publishers Weekly, October 15, 2005, review of *Whatever,* p. 67; April 30, 2007, review of *And the Train Goes . . .,* p. 159.

School Librarian, summer, 2007, Trevor Dickinson, review of *And the Train Goes . . .,* p. 73.

School Library Journal, January, 2006, Piper L. Nyman, review of *Whatever,* p. 90; June, 2007, Linda M. Kenton, review of *And the Train Goes . . .,* p. 92.

Times Educational Supplement, February 24, 2006, Jane Doonan, review of *Whatever,* p. 18.

Washington Post Book World, July 15, 2007, Elizabeth Ward, review of *And the Train Goes . . .,* p. 12.

ONLINE

Children's Bookwatch Web site, http://www.midwestbook review.com/ (April 1, 2007), review of *And the Train Goes . . . .*

William Bee Home Page, http://www.williambee.com (February 28, 2008).*

* * *

BLEY, Anette 1967-

Personal

Born 1967, in Tübingen, Germany. *Education:* Educated in United States and Germany; Akademie der Bildenden Künste (Munich, Germany), degree, 1996.

Addresses

Home—Munich, Germany.

Career

Author and illustrator of books for children, and sculptor. Teacher of art; freelance author and illustrator, beginning 1990.

Awards, Honors

Children's Book Sense Pick, 2007, for *And What Comes after a Thousand?*

Writings

SELF-ILLUSTRATED

Den Papa hab'ich lieb, Ars Edition (Munich, Germany), 1997.

Sophia und die Gruselgeister, Ars Edition (Munich, Germany), 1998.

Und was kommt nach Tausend?, Ravensburger (Ravensburg, Germany), 2005, translation published as *And What Comes after a Thousand?,* Kane/Miller (La Jolla, CA), 2007.

Und Ich will Flieger sein!, Ravensburger (Ravensburg, Germany), 2006.

Ein Stern strahlt um die Welt. Kinder feiern Weihnachten hier bei uns und anderswo, Loewe (Bindlach, Germany), 2006.

ILLUSTRATOR

Nathan Zimelman, *Melwins Stern. Eine wihnachtliche Geschichte,* Ars Edition (Munich, Germany), 1994.

Frauke Nahrgang, *Der Ferienfeind,* Heinrich Ellermann (Hamburg, Germany), 1995.

Katrin Lauer, *Das kummervolle Kuscheltier,* Ars Edition (Munich, Germany), 1996.

Barbara Zoschke, *Hell leuchtet uns ein Stern,* Ars Edition (Munich, Germany), 1997.

Ulrike, Gerold and Wolfram Hänel, *Jetzt will Ich aber schlafen: zwei Gutenachtgeschichten,* Aare (Aarau, Germany), 1998.

Elisabeth Zöller, *Und wenn ich zurückhaue?,* Bertelsmann (Gütersloh, Germany), 1998.

Wilhelm Gruber, *Wihnachtsegeschichte: Nicholas auf dem Glatteis,* Aare by Sauerländer (Oberentfelden, Switzerland), 1999.

Gerda Wagener. *Indianergeschichten,* Edition Bücherbauer, 2002.

Jutta Langreuter, *Da bist du ja, kleiner Ole!,* Ars Edition (Munich, Germany), 2004.

Elisabeth Zöller, *Jetzt bist du fällig! Geschichten gegen Gewalt,* Loewe (Bindlach, Germany), 2005.

Pia Sandmann, *Nicht mit mir!,* Ravensburger (Ravensburg, Germany), 2005.

Judith Sixel, *Bleib bei mir, klenier Engel,* Herder, Freiburg (Freiburg, Germany), 2008.

Rudolf Herfurtner, adaptor, *Romeo und Julia. Das Ballett nach Sergei Prokofjew,* Betz (Vienna, Austria), 2008.

Also illustrator of advent calendars.

Sidelights

Artist and author Anette Bley has been praised for her watercolor-tinted drawings, which appear alongside her own stories as well as with those by many other picture-book authors in her native Germany. In addition to books, her artwork has decorated advent calendars, a popular tradition among young children celebrating the coming of Christmas. Bley studied drawing and painting, as well as graphic design, in both Germany and the United States, and trained closely with illustrator Robin Page until 1996. In addition her work in children's books, Bley is a sculptor and also teaches classes and workshops on creating picture-book art.

Bley's first published illustrations appeared in 1994, in Nathan Zimelman's *Melwins Stern. Eine wihnachtliche Geschichte.* Her first original story, *Den Papa hab'ich lieb,* was published three years later, and has been followed by several more self-illustrated books, among them *Sophia und die Gruselgeister, Und Ich will Flieger sein!,* and *Und was kommt nach Tausend?* A poignant intergenerational story, *Und was kommt nach Tausend?* has been translated into English as *And What Comes after a Thousand?*

In *And What Comes after a Thousand?* a young girl named Lisa is very close to Otto, an elderly man who lives on a nearby farm. While other grownups often have little time to devote to the girl, Otto dotes on Lisa, sharing stories and cookies, helping her count stars in the night sky. He also encourages her when she gets frustrated learning to aim her slingshot. Then the elderly man grows ill and ultimately dies, leaving the girl alone and angry. After the funeral, Lisa's feelings of loss make way for understanding as she learns that, despite death, her beloved Otto still lives in her heart. Praising Bley's "heartfelt pastel illustrations," a *Kirkus Reviews* writer deemed *And What Comes after a Thousand?* a "touching" picture book that "offers a comforting lesson in loss." In *School Library Journal* Maryann H. Owen praised Bley's images as "wonderfully varied," as did a *Publishers Weekly* critic. Citing the author/illustrator's "velvety, emotionally acute pictures" for creating "a visual poetry," the critic predicted that young readers "will find much to savor in the book's radiant pictures and lyrical elusiveness."

Biographical and Critical Sources

PERIODICALS

Booklist, May 15, 2007, Hazel Rochman, review of *And What Comes after a Thousand?,* p. 49.
Kirkus Reviews, February 1, 2007, review of *And What Comes after a Thousand?,* p. 120.
Publishers Weekly, February 12, 2007, review of *And What Comes after a Thousand?,* p. 85.
School Library Journal, March, 2007, Maryann H. Owen, review of *And What Comes after a Thousand?,* p. 151.

ONLINE

Goethe Institute Web site, http://www.goethe.de/ (March 21, 2008), "Anette Bley."
Kane Miller Web site, http://www.kanemiller.com/ (March 21, 2008), "Anette Bley."*

*   *   *

BOLDEN, Tonya 1959-
(Tonya Wilyce Bolden)

Personal

Born March 1, 1959, in New York, NY; daughter of Willie J. (a garment center shipping manager) and Georgia C. (a homemaker) Bolden; married (divorced 1990).

Tonya Bolden (Reproduced by permission.)

Education: Princeton University, B.A. (Slavic languages and literatures/concentration Russian; magna cum laude), 1981; Columbia University, M.A. (Slavic languages and literatures/concentration Russian), 1985, Harriman Institute, certificate for the advanced study of the Soviet Union, 1985. *Politics:* "Independent." *Religion:* Christian.

Addresses

Home—Bronx, NY. *Agent*—Jennifer Lyons Literary Agency, 151 W. 19th St., 3rd Fl., New York, NY 10011. *E-mail*—tonbolden@aol.com.

Career

Charles Alan, Inc., New York, NY, salesperson et al., 1981-83; Raoulfilm, Inc., New York, NY, administrative assistant/office coordinator, 1985-87; research and editorial assistant to food and wine critic William E. Rice, 1987-88; Malcolm-King College, New York, NY, English instructor, 1988-89; College of New Rochelle School of New Resources, New York, NY, English instructor, 1989-90, 1996-2000. Editor, *HARKline* (quarterly newsletter of Harkhomes, a shelter for the homeless in Harlem), 1989-90; editor, *Quarterly Black Review of Books,* 1994-95. Editorial consultant to MTA Arts for Transit Office, 1987-88, and Harlem River Press/Writers & Readers Publishing, Inc., 1987-90; editor and project consultant, Maafa Cultural Heritage Enrichment Kit, Brooklyn, NY, 2001. Member of Westside Repertory Theatre, 1977-82.

Member

PEN American Center.

Awards, Honors

Book for the Teen Age designation, New York Public Library, 1993, for *Mama, I Want to Sing,* 1999, for *And Not Afraid to Dare,* 2000, for *Strong Men Keep Coming,* 2006, for both *Maritcha* and *Cause,* 2008, for *Take-off;* Best Books for Young Adults designation, American Library Association, 1999, for *Thirty-three Things Every Girl Should Know;* YALSA Best Book for Young Adults designation, 2005, for *Wake up Our Souls;* Coretta Scott King Author Honor Book designation, and James Madison Book Award, both 2006, both for *Maritcha;* Orbis Pictus Award, 2008, for *M.L.K.*

Writings

FOR CHILDREN AND YOUNG ADULTS

(Coauthor) Vy Higginsen, *Mama, I Want to Sing* (young-adult novel), Scholastic (New York, NY), 1992.

(Editor) *Rites of Passage: Stories about Growing up by Black Writers from around the World,* Hyperion (New York, NY), 1994.

Just Family, Cobblehill Books (New York, NY), 1996.

Through Loona's Door: A Tammy and Owen Adventure with Carter G. Woodson, illustrated by Luther Knox, Corporation for Cultural Literacy (Oakland, CA), 1997.

And Not Afraid to Dare: The Stories of Ten African-American Women, Scholastic (New York, NY), 1998.

(Editor) *Thirty-three Things Every Girl Should Know: Stories, Songs, Poems, and Smart Talk by Thirty-three Extraordinary Women,* Crown (New York, NY), 1998.

Rock of Ages: A Tribute to the Black Church, illustrated by R. Gregory Christie, Knopf (New York, NY), 2001.

Tell All the Children Our Story: Memories and Mementos of Being Young and Black in America, Harry N. Abrams (New York, NY), 2001.

(Editor) *Thirty-three Things Every Girl Should Know about Women's History: From Suffragettes to Skirt Lengths to the E.R.A.,* Crown (New York, NY), 2002.

(Adaptor) Gail Buckley, *American Patriots: The Story of Blacks in the Military from the Revolution to Desert Storm,* Crown (New York, NY), 2003.

Portraits of African-American Heroes, illustrated by Ansel Pitcairn, Dutton (New York, NY), 2003.

Wake up Our Souls: A Celebration of Black American Artists, Harry N. Abrams (New York, NY), 2004.

The Champ: The Story of Muhammad Ali, illustrated by R. Gregory Christie, Knopf (New York, NY), 2004.

Maritcha: A Nineteenth-Century American Girl, Harry N. Abrams (New York, NY), 2005.

Cause: Reconstruction America, 1863-1877, Knopf (New York, NY), 2005.

M.L.K.: Journey of a King, Abrams Books for Young Readers (New York, NY), 2007.

Take-off!: American All-Girl Bands during WWII, Knopf (New York, NY), 2007.

George Washington Carver, Abrams Books for Young Readers (New York, NY), 2008.

FOR ADULTS

The Family Heirloom Cookbook, Putnam (New York, NY), 1990.

Starting a Business from Your Home, Longmeadow Press (Stamford, CT), 1993.

Getting into the Mail-Order Business, Longmeadow Press (Stamford, CT), 1994.

Mail Order and Direct Response, Longmeadow Press (Stamford, CT), 1994.

The Book of African-American Women: 150 Crusaders, Creators, and Uplifters, Adams Media (Holbrook, MA), 1996.

(Coauthor) Mother Love, *Forgive or Forget: Never Underestimate the Power of Forgiveness,* HarperCollins (New York, NY), 1999.

Strong Men Keep Coming: The Book of African-American Men, Wiley (New York, NY), 1999.

(Coauthor) Eartha Kitt, *Rejuvenate!: It's Never Too Late,* Scribner (New York, NY), 2000.

(Coauthor) Chaka Khan, *Chaka!: Through the Fire,* St. Martin's Press (New York, NY), 2003.

(Coauthor) Mother Love, *Half the Mother, Twice the Love: My Journey to Better Health with Diabetes,* Atria Books (New York, NY), 2006.

Bolden takes readers on a swing through twentieth-century musical history in **Take-off: American All-Girl Bands during WWII.** (Jacket photographs courtesy of Culver Pictures; Special Collections/Archives, John B. Coleman Library, Prairie View A & M University; "DownBeat" magazine. Used by permission of Alfred A. Knopf, an imprint of Random House Children's Books, a division of Random House, Inc.)

(Coauthor) Diane Valentine, *Weddings Valentine Style: Rich Inspiration for Every Woman's Dream Day,* Atria Books (New York, NY), 2006.

Also contributor to books, including *African-American History,* Scholastic, 1990; *Black Arts Annual,* edited by Donald Bogle, Garland, 1990, 1992; *Hands On!: Thirty-three More Things Every Girl Should Know,* edited by Suzanne Harper, Random House, 2001; *Go Girl!: The Black Woman's Book of Travel and Adventure,* edited by Elaine Lee, Eighth Mountain Press, 1997; and *The Harlem Reader,* edited by Herb Boyd, Three Rivers Press, 2003. Contributor of book reviews and articles to *Amsterdam News, Black Enterprise, Essence, Excel, Focus, New York Times Book Review, Small Press,* and *YSB.* Author of study guides for Carter G. Woodson Foundation artists-in-the-schools program.

Sidelights

In her books for younger readers, Tonya Bolden draws from history to present modern readers with hopeful and positive life examples. While much of her work is nonfiction, Bolden ranges in genre from history to biography to self-help book, bringing her knowledge and fascination with African-American history and the development of Black American culture to bear in books that include *And Not Afraid to Dare: The Stories of Ten African-American Women, Wake up Our Souls: A Celebration of Black Artists, M.L.K.: Journey of a King,* and *Maritcha: A Nineteenth-Century Girl.* According to *National Catholic Reporter* contributor Arthur Jones, as a writer Bolden is "quirky" but "not boring." He characterized her as "a storyteller who editorializes along the way—as good storytellers can without offense."

Brave black women fill the pages of *And Not Afraid to Dare.* The subjects of this book include Ellen Craft, a light-skinned enslaved woman who traveled a thousand miles to freedom by posing as an ailing white man attended by an enslaved man who was really Craft's husband. Contemporary women such as writer Toni Morrison and athlete Jackie Joyner-Kersee are also profiled. Bolden "writes easily and confidently about her subjects . . . and her compelling stories read like fiction," remarked Lauren Peterson in *Booklist.*

Turning to cultural history, *Wake up Our Souls* introduces readers to over thirty professional black artists, beginning with Joshua Johnson and ranging through sculptor Augusta Savage, painter William H. Johnson, ceramicist Winnin Owens-Hart, and photographer Gordon Parks. Published in association with the Smithsonian American Art Museum, the book features photographs of many works by these men and women, as well as profiles of their lives. She presents her history in "simple, graceful language," wrote *Booklist* contributor Gillian Engberg, and places each artist within their historical epoch. Bolden's inclusion of information on professional arts organizations such as Spiral, which were formed to support the works of such pioneers, "is

particularly fascinating," Engberg added. In *School Library Journal,* Robin L. Gibson noted in particular the author's "notable" history of the development of the civil rights movement, going on to call *Wake up Our Souls* a "welcome addition to art history collections."

Inspirational stories are collected by Bolden in several books, including *M.L.K., Portraits of African-American Heroes,* and *Tell All the Children Our Story: Memories and Mementos of Being Young and Black in America.* In *Portraits of African-American Heroes* she joins with artist Ansel Pitcairn to share twenty tales about Americans from past and present—Frederick Douglass, Dizzy Gillespie, Charlayne Hunter-Gault, and Thurgood Marshall among them—who have overcome significant challenges and achieved a measure of greatness. Terry Glover had strong praise for Bolden's approach in her *Booklist* review, writing that the author provides readers with "keen insights into a subject's personality based on interviews and information drawn from personal memoirs." Noting Pitcairn's ability to "unerringly . . . capture . . . the souls of these remarkable people" in his sepia-toned art, a *Kirkus Reviews* critic praised *Portraits of African-American Heroes* "a fascinating and unique" volume.

M.L.K. focuses on perhaps the best-known American of color: Rev. Martin Luther King, Jr. The life of the civil rights leader is traced by Bolden and enhanced by numerous illustrations documenting his life and work to

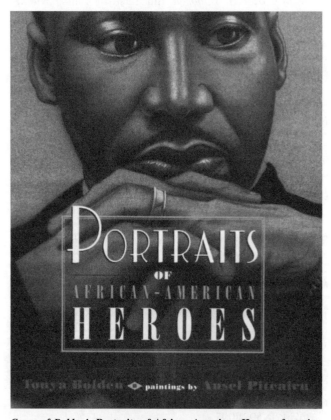

Cover of Bolden's Portraits of African-American Heroes, *featuring original paintings by Ansel Pitcairn.* (Puffin Books, 2003. Reproduced by permission of Puffin Books, a division of Penguin Putnam Books for Young Readers.)

bring about racial harmony. In *School Library Journal* John Peters noted that in her "eloquent, handsomely designed" volume, Bolden "looks past the public figure to bring the man, and his deeper vision . . . into focus," and "leave[s] readers with a strong, and perhaps inspiring, sense" of King's accomplishments. "Do libraries need another biography of King?," asked *Booklist* reviewer Hazel Rochman. "Yes, if it's as good as this one."

Among the people readers meet in *Tell All the Children Our Story* is Maritcha Remond Lyons, a black educator who grew up in southern Manhattan during a time when slavery still existed in the southern United States. Bolden bases her account of Lyons' life in *Maritcha* on the memoir set down by the woman herself. Along with vivid memories of her parents and the cultured black community they inhabited, as well as of her own childhood friendships and her recollections of attending the country's first World's Fair, Maritcha also recalls the 1863 riots that forced her to flee her home as well as her battle for education, a battle she won when she became the first African American to graduate from her Rhode Island high school. Bolden's well-researched text features "both an inspirational portrait of an individual and a piercing history" of the black experience in the wake of the U.S. Civil War, according to Engberg. Carolyn Janssen had a similar assessment in *School Library Journal,* writing that Bolden "skillfully presents interesting facts and a personal view of an often-overlooked segment of history." Containing numerous maps, photographs, and other images that bring the young woman's story to life, *Maritcha* was named a Coretta Scott King Author Honor Book. It was also awarded the 2006 James Madison Book Award, an honor established by Lynne Cheney to acknowledge "excellence in bringing knowledge and understanding of American history to children ages five to fourteen."

Turning her focus to contemporary girls who hope to accomplish great things, Bolden's *Thirty-three Things Every Girl Should Know: Stories, Songs, Poems, and Smart Talk by Thirty-three Extraordinary Women* gathers contributions from among writers, businesswomen, athletes, artists, and more, all of whom focus on the trials encountered while moving from childhood to adulthood. Communicating with boys, being true to oneself, and dealing with issues such as self-esteem and popularity are all treated. In *Booklist* Shelle Rosenfeld praised *Thirty-three Things Every Girl Should Know,* writing: "Astute, compassionate, sometimes witty, sometimes painfully honest, the pieces are highly readable, entertaining, and educational."

A related work, *Thirty-three Things Every Girl Should Know about Women's History: From Suffragettes to Skirt Lengths to the E.R.A,* contains what *Booklist* contributor Ilene Cooper described as "a cornucopia of information, some of which will surprise readers." Poems, journal entries, letters, essays, photographs, artwork, and a play make up the book's structure, with

Cover of Bolden's **Tell All the Children Our Story,** *which profiles the northern migration of a rural Southern family near the turn of the twentieth century.* (Copyright © 2001 by Harry N. Abrams. Reproduced by permission.)

such items as First Lady Abigail Adams's letter to her husband regarding women's rights, nineteenth-century feminist Charlotte Perkins Gilman's essay "The Yellow Wallpaper," and a modern rock critic's perspective on the girl groups of the 1960s among the many offerings. Bolden's work "demystifies" the term "feminist" according to Cooper, while in *Horn Book* Nell D. Beram noted that the fact that much of the book's content "tends toward the serviceable hardly mutes this resounding battle cry."

Bolden addresses younger children in several books that match her text with illustrations. Collaborating with artist R. Gregory Christie, she uses free verse to tell the story of one of the greatest boxers of all time in *The Champ: The Story of Muhammad Ali,* and presents a moving look at the unique role of churches in supporting a resilient spirit against oppression in *Rock of Ages: A Tribute to the Black Church.* Praising the author's "simple, clear, and lively text" in his *Booklist* review, John Green wrote that Bolden's biography of Ail follows the pugilist from his boyhood in Louisville when he was known as Cassius Clay through his Olympic victory, his refusal to fight in the Vietnam War, and his activism. Together with illustrations in which Christie brings to life Ali's "flamboyant personality," Bolden creates an energetic and "engaging text" appropriate for younger children, in the opinion of *School Library Journal* writer Anne M. Holcomb. In a text that a *Kirkus*

Cover of **Thirty-three Things Every Girl Should Know,** *an anthology edited by Bolden that features a cover photograph by Jim Cummins.* (Cover photograph copyright © 1997 by Jim Cummins/FPG International. Used by permission of Crown Publishers, an imprint of Random House Children's Books, a division of Random House, Inc.)

Reviews writer described as "clear and concise without being condescending," the author highlights one of Ali's most notable traits: "his fierce determination."

In addition to writing for children, Bolden has also written a number of books for adult readers, and has served as coauthor of autobiographical works by entertainer Eartha Kitt, singer Chaka Kahn and inspirational speaker and talk-show host Mother Love. In *Strong Men Keep Coming: The Book of African-American Men* she presents more than one hundred short biographies of admirable African Americans. Her subjects range from well-known people such as W.E.B. DuBois, Jesse Jackson, and Dred Scott to more obscure figures such as Dave Dinwiddie, a pioneer whose story stretches from Alabama to Oklahoma. *Strong Men Keep Coming* works both as "an informative read and a textbook," according to Jones, the critic concluding in *National Catholic Reporter:* "Bolden provided me with insights I didn't have, introduced me to people I didn't know, and the book ended all too soon."

Bolden once commented: "I've been a book lover ever since I was a child. However, I never thought seriously about becoming a writer as a child or young adult. But those who've long known me are not surprised that I've ended up with a writing life. It's the best of two glori-

ous worlds: teaching and lifelong learning." Asked to give advice to teens making choices regarding their own future, Bolden told *Buffalo News* interviewer Jean Westmoore: "Hone writing, speaking, and critical thinking skills. When you look into your future and think about what and who you want to be when you are an adult, give thought to living not for yourself alone."

Biographical and Critical Sources

PERIODICALS

American Visions, December, 1997, review of *Through Loona's Door: A Tammy and Owen Adventure with Carter G. Woodson,* p. 34.

Black Issues Book Review, January, 1999, review of *Thirty-three Things Every Girl Should Know: Stories, Songs, Poems, and Smart Talk by Thirty-three Extraordinary Women,* p. 56.

Booklist, February 15, 1996, Carolyn Phelan, review of *Just Family,* p. 1020; February 15, 1998, Lauren Peterson, review of *And Not Afraid to Dare: The Stories of Ten African-American Women,* p. 993; May 15, 1998, Shelle Rosenfeld, review of *Thirty-three Things Every Girl Should Know,* p. 1611; March 1, 2002, Ilene Cooper, review of *Thirty-three Things Every Girl Should Know about Women's History,* p. 1146; October 15, 2003, Vanessa Bush, review of *Chaka!: Through the Fire,* p. 374; February 15, 2004, Gillian Engberg, review of *Wake up Our Souls: A Celebration of Black American Artists,* p. 1065; March 15, 2004, Terry Glover, review of *Portraits of African-American Heroes,* p. 1301; November 15, 2004, John Green, review of *The Champ: The Story of Muhammad Ali,* p. 575; February 1, 2005, Gillian Engberg, review of *Maritcha: A Nineteenth-Century American Girl,* p. 970; October 15, 2005, Carolyn Phelan, review of *Cause: Reconstruction America,* p. 40; February 1, 2007, Hazel Rochman, review of *M.L.K.: Journey of a King,* p. 50; February 15, 2007, Ilene Cooper, review of *Take-off: American All-Girl Bands during WWII,* p. 87.

Book Report, September-October, 1996, Karen Sebesta, review of *Just Family,* p. 36; November-December, 1998, Melanie Scalpello, review of *Thirty-three Things Every Girl Should Know,* and Sandra B. Connell, review of *And Not Afraid to Dare,* both p. 82.

Buffalo News (Buffalo, NY), February 28, 2007, Jean Westmoore, interview with Boldon, p. N9.

Bulletin of the Center for Children's Books, May, 1998, review of *And Not Afraid to Dare,* p. 312; June, 1998, review of *Thirty-three Things Every Girl Should Know,* p. 353; September, 2004, Deborah Stevenson, review of *Wake up Our Souls,* p. 8; January, 2005, Elizabeth Bush, review of *The Champ,* p. 200; March, 2005, Elizabeth Bush, review of *Maritcha,* p. 282; January, 2006, Elizabeth Bush, review of *Cause,* p. 220; May, 2007, Elizabeth Bush, review of of *M.L.K.,* p. 360; June, 2007, Elizabeth Bush, review of *Take-off,* p. 405.

Crisis, May-June, 2007, Fern Gillespie, review of *M.L.K.,* p. 36.

Horn Book, July-August, 2002, review of *Thirty-three Things Every Girl Should Know about Women's History,* p. 483; January-February, 2005, Kathleen Isaacs, review of *The Champ,* p. 106, and Margaret A. Bush, review of *Maritcha,* p. 107.

Kirkus Reviews, December 1, 1995, review of *Just Family,* p. 1700; January 1, 1998, review of *And Not Afraid to Dare,* p. 54; March 1, 1998, review of *Thirty-three Things Every Girl Should Know,* p. 335; December 15, 2003, review of *Portraits of African-American Heroes,* p. 1446; December 15, 2004, reviews of *The Champ* and *Maritcha,* both p. 1198; November 15, 2005, review of *Cause,* p. 1230; April 15, 2007, review of *Take-off.*

Kliatt, November, 1995, review of *Rites of Passage,* p. 21; May, 1998, review of *Thirty-three Things Every Girl Should Know,* p. 27.

Library Journal, November 15, 1999, Lisa S. Wise, review of *Forgive or Forget: Never Underestimate the Power of Forgiveness,* p. 86.

National Catholic Reporter, January 28, 2000, Arthur Jones, review of *Strong Men Keep Coming: The Book of African-American Men,* p. 15.

Publishers Weekly, March 9, 1998, review of *Thirty-three Things Every Girl Should Know,* p. 69; October 4, 1999, review of *Forgive or Forget,* p. 55; March 11, 2002, review of *Tell All the Children Our Story,* p. 73; July 7, 2003, review of *Chaka!,* p. 59; January 3, 2005, review of *Maritcha,* p. 57; January 3, 2005, review of *The Champ,* p. 55.

School Library Journal, May, 1996, Susan W. Hunter, review of *Just Family,* p. 110; March, 1998, review of *And Not Afraid to Dare,* p. 228; May, 1998, review of *Thirty-three Things Every Girl Should Know,* p. 150; April, 2002, Lee Bock, review of *Thirty-three Things Every Girl Should Know about Women's History,* p. 164; January, 2004, Mary N. Oluonye, review of *Portraits of African-American Heroes,* p. 140; July, 2004, Robin L. Gibson, review of *Wake up Our Souls,* p. 117; January, 2005, Anne M. Holcomb, review of *The Champ,* p. 107; February, 2005, Carolyn Janssen, review of *Maritcha,* p. 145; November, 2005, Marianne Fitzgerald, review of *Cause,* p. 153; February, 2007, John Peters, review of *M.L.K.,* p. 131; June, 2007, Renee Steinberg, review of *Take-off,* p. 166.

Voice of Youth Advocates, October, 1996, review of *Just Family,* p. 205; June, 1998, review of *And Not Afraid to Dare,* p. 139; August, 1999, review of *Thirty-three Things Every Girl Should Know,* p. 165; August, 2004, review of *Wake up Our Souls,* p. 236; October, 2005, review of *Maritcha,* p. 332; April, 2007, Dotsy Harland, review of *M.L.K.,* p. 75.

Washington Post Book World, January 5, 1997, review of *The Book of African-American Women: 150 Crusaders, Creators, and Uplifters,* p. 13; July 4, 1999, review of *Strong Men Keep Coming,* p. 11.

ONLINE

Education World Web site, http://www.education-world. com/ (February 19, 2001), "Ten African-American Women Who 'Dared' to Make a Difference."

Tonya Bolden Web site, http://www.tonyabolden.com (March 20, 2008).

*   *   *

BOLDEN, Tonya Wilyce
See BOLDEN, Tonya

*   *   *

BRASHARES, Ann 1967-

Personal

Born 1967, in Chevy Chase, MD; married Jacob Collins (a portrait painter); children: Sam, Nathaniel, Susannah. *Education:* Barnard College, B.A. (philosophy).

Addresses

Home—Brooklyn, NY.

Career

Writer and editor. 17th Street Production (book packager), New York, NY, editor for ten years; Alloy Entertainment (book packager), New York, NY, former editor.

Awards, Honors

Best Book for Young Adults citation, American Library Association, and Book Sense Book of the Year designation, both 2002, both for *The Sisterhood of the Traveling Pants.*

Writings

The Sisterhood of the Traveling Pants (young-adult novel), Delacorte (New York, NY), 2001.

Linus Torvalds: Software Rebel (juvenile nonfiction; "Techies" series), Twenty-first Century Books (Brookfield, CT), 2001.

Steve Jobs: Think Different (juvenile nonfiction; "Techies" series), Twenty-first Century Books (Brookfield, CT), 2001.

The Second Summer of the Sisterhood (young-adult novel) Delacorte (New York, NY), 2003.

Girls in Pants: The Third Summer of the Sisterhood (young-adult novel) Delacorte (New York, NY), 2005.

Forever in Blue: The Fourth Summer of the Sisterhood (young-adult novel) Delacorte (New York, NY), 2007.

The Last Summer (of You and Me) (adult novel) Riverhead Books (New York, NY), 2007.

Contributor to periodicals, including *CosmoGirl!* and *Writer.*

Adaptations

The Sisterhood of the Traveling Pants was adapted for audiocassette by Listening Library, 2002, and adapted for film by Delia Ephron and Elizabeth Chandler,

Warner Bros., 2005. *Sisterhood of the Traveling Pants 2,* produced 2008, was also based on Brashares' novels. Film tie-ins include *The Sisterhood of the Traveling Pants: The Official Scrapbook* and *Keep in Touch: Letters, Notes, and More from The Sisterhood of the Traveling Pants,* both Delacorte, 2005.

Sidelights

Beginning her career as a book editor and the author of two juvenile biographies, Ann Brashares became a publishing phenomenon with her first young-adult novel, *The Sisterhood of the Traveling Pants.* Released in 2001, Brashares' first novel introduces four teen friends who agree to send a pair of secondhand jeans from friend to friend during the first summer they are to be separated. These traveling pants thus take on a metaphoric quality, uniting the best friends across the thousands of miles separating them.

One of four siblings, Brashares grew up in Chevy Chase, Maryland, where she and her three brothers attended Sidwell Friends, a Quaker school near Washington, DC. As a child, she was an avid reader, enjoying the works of Jane Austen, Charles Dickens, and other nineteenth-century writers. "When I was a kid, I had a scrapbook that I used to write letters in from places I wished I could have gone," Brashares recalled on Random House's *Sisterhood* Web site. "I would imagine being in Argentina and then write about all the incredible things I was seeing there."

Attending Barnard College, Brashares majored in philosophy and also met her future husband, artist Jacob Collins. After graduation, she took a year off before graduate school, planning to save money to pay for tuition. However, the job she took, working as an editor at a book packager, was such a good fit that Brashares never returned to school. Instead, she established a career in publishing, working in children's books.

As an extension of her editorial work, Brashares gained authorial experience on the biographies *Steve Jobs: Think Different* and *Linus Torvalds: Software Rebel.* "I hadn't at any point considered myself an author of nonfiction," she related to Dave Weich in a Powells.com interview. However, when the opportunity arose at work to create texts for two biographies, Brashares "decided to try it. I was wearing a certain hat to do that project, and it was really fun."

Part of Twenty-first Century Books' "Techies" series, Brashares' biographies briefly profile of well-known computer and software pioneers. *Steve Jobs* focuses on the man whose name is synonymous with Apple computers and Macintosh. Brashares traces Jobs's life from his youth traveling around the world to his collaboration with fellow techie Steve Wozniak in building prototype computers in a garage on the way to developing Apple Computers. *Linus Torvalds* introduces readers to the Finnish mastermind behind the open-source operat-

Ann Brashares became a publishing phenomenon with her first young-adult novel, **The Sisterhood of the Traveling Pants.** (Jacket photographs © 2005 Warner Bros. Entertainment Inc. All rights reserved. Used by permission of Dell Laurel-Leaf, an imprint of Random House Children's Books, a division of Random House, Inc.)

ing system known as Linux. Torvalds' teamwork approach to programming and the free access he allows to his operating system caused a revolution in computing. Reviewing *Steve Jobs* in *Voice of Youth Advocates,* Susan H. Levine praised the book's "breezy style, short length, large font, numerous photographs, and attractive page design." Similarly, Yapha Nussbaum Mason, writing in *School Library Journal,* called *Linus Torvalds* "fairly short and definitely accessible," and "appeal[ing] not only to report writers, but also to recreational readers."

Brashares' first novel was inspired by a story she heard from a coworker. One summer, when the woman was a teen, she and her friends had shared a pair of pants, although the pants were ultimately lost in Borneo. Brashares had her own experience with shared clothing, as she recalled on the *BookBrowse* Web site. When she was planning her marriage, the sister of a friend offered her own bridal gown. Brashares at first turned down the offer, especially as the woman's own marriage had not been successful. When this persistent donor came by with the wedding dress in question, Brashares discovered that it was the exact dress she had been dreaming of. She wore it at her own wedding, and subsequently loaned it to other friends, creating a sort of "bond of the bridal gown." Taking these experiences together and mixing in a measure of her own teenage angst and problems, Brashares came up with her story about a fictional pair of pants that fit every body type and make the wearer feel loved. She worked up a cast of characters to wear her magic pants, and an outline—a mixture of Greek myth and themes from movies such as *It's a Wonderful Life*—and then took the project to Random House, whose editors liked the idea.

The Sisterhood of the Traveling Pants recounts the adventures of Carmen, Lena, Bridget, and Tibby, fifteen year olds who decide to share a pair of jeans as a way of keeping their friendship alive during their first summer apart. The girls' mothers became friends while attending the same aerobics class and the four girls have become bosom buddies, meeting in the gym while their mothers attended class. This summer, the four teens will be separated for the first time: Carmen is planning to go to South Carolina and visit her divorced father; Lena is off to Greece to be with her grandparents; Bridget will be working out at a soccer camp in Baja California; and Tibby will remain at home in Washington, DC, working in the local Wallman's drugstore. Before departure, Carmen has purchased a pair of jeans at a local thrift shop. She decides to toss them. Then Tibby, Lena, and Bridget try on the pants, and they fit each in turn, even Carmen, who thinks she never looks good in anything. Because each has a distinctly different body type, the friends decide that these must be magic pants. The night before departure, they form the Sisterhood of the Traveling Pants, agreeing to a set of rules and behavior regarding the treatment and wearing of the pants. Each friend will wear the pants for a week, and then send them on to the next wearer. The pants become a link between the members of the sisterhood.

Although the thrift-store jeans seem magical at first, the four girls soon realize that they cannot help solve the problems each encounters that summer; such solutions must come from inner understanding. The pants, however, serve as a reminder that none of the friends are alone. Each girl learns to deal with individual problems, gaining elemental life lessons in the process. Carmen's dream of spending time alone with her dad is thwarted when she discovers he is on the verge of marrying into a brand new family in South Carolina. In Greece, Lena falls for Kostos, a family friend, but their relationship becomes marred when she mistakenly accuses him of spying on her while she is skinny dipping. Bridget also has romantic problems, falling in love with one of the camp counselors even though that is off-limits according to camp rules. Meanwhile, Tibby, who has stayed home, befriends a young girl named Bailey, who is suffering from leukemia. These two start making a documentary film about odd but interesting people, but when Bailey takes ill and is hospitalized, Tibby is confronted with the specter of death for the first time.

As Brashares noted on Random House's *Sisterhood* Web site, her fictional characters grew out of different parts of her own personality: "Carmen was the girl who said things I could never say and Bridget was the girl who did things I would never do." Speaking with Weich, she also noted that she wanted to use the idea of the pants as a "repository of friendship—love, hope, challenges, all of those things." She also remarked to Weich that stay-at-home Tibby is the one who seems to grow and learns the most about herself during this one turbulent summer. "She's the one who's shaken up the most," Brashares commented. "The idea that that can happen at home was something I wanted to present."

Brashares' unique coming-of-age novel won critical praise from *New York Times* reviewer Christine Leahy, who called the characters in *The Sisterhood of the Traveling Pants* "winning and precocious." The critic also praised Brashares' narrative pace, noting that the "story zips along, bouncing faster than the jeans from girl to girl." Linda Bindner, reviewing the title in *School Library Journal,* also noted the author's story-telling skills, remarking that she "deftly moves from narrative to narrative, weaving together themes from the mundane to the profoundly important." Bindner called *The Sisterhood of the Traveling Pants* a "complex book about a solid group of friends," while in *Horn Book* Jennifer M. Brabander praised the life lessons included in the "breezy feel-good" novel. In a review for *Publishers Weekly* a contributor concluded that Brashares' "outstanding and vivid book . . . will stay with readers for a long time."

Brashares' four heroines return in *The Second Summer of the Sisterhood.* Now sixteen, Bridget is heading to Alabama, Lena is still spending time with Kostos, Carmen dreads that her mother will make a fool of herself over a man, and Tibby takes a film course instead of spending another summer working at Wallman's. Writing in *Horn Book,* Jennifer M. Brabander suggested that "fans of the first book . . . will eagerly travel with the sisterhood again." Citing the author's ability to present a realistic, "hopeful book, easy to read and gentle in its important lessons," *Booklist* critic Frances Bradburn predicted that "readers will want" the girls to return for another season of shared sisterhood.

Like she did in her first novel, Brashares takes a light-hearted look at serious topics in *The Second Summer of the Sisterhood.* "I feel as though there are a lot of books trying very hard to deal with social issues—illness or social ills, all kinds of shocking things—and in some part of my mind I knew that I didn't want to do that," the author told Weich. "I wanted to write a book that wasn't insubstantial but wasn't really issues-driven,

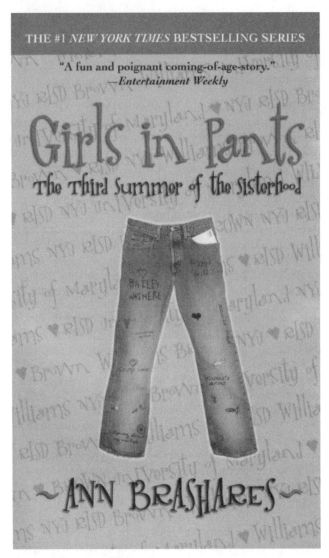

THE #1 *NEW YORK TIMES* BESTSELLING SERIES

"A fun and poignant coming-of-age-story."
—*Entertainment Weekly*

Girls in Pants
The Third Summer of the Sisterhood

~ANN BRASHARES~

The four teens in Brashares' series begin to go their separate ways as college approaches in Girls in Pants. *(Cover photograph copyright © 2006 by Barry David Marcus. All rights reserved. Used by permission of Dell Laurel-Leaf, an imprint of Random House Children's Books, a division of Random House, Inc.)*

either. I hope I did that." On the *Sisterhood* Web site, Brashares concluded of her teen novels that she hopes they are the sort to "stick with [readers] a bit, the way books I liked when I was that age stuck with me. If there's a message, I guess it's just this: love yourself and your friends unconditionally."

Carmen, Lena, Bridget, and Tibby reunite again, this time as high-school graduates, in *Girls in Pants: The Third Summer of the Sisterhood.* As they begin preparation for their first year at four different colleges, the "starring role . . . goes to those unbreakable bonds of Sisterhood that carry the girls through all kinds of family and boyfriend dramas," according to Brabander. Carmen's plans for college have to be downscaled when her mother becomes pregnant, Bridget links up with an old flame during summer soccer camp, Tibby feels responsible when her little sister takes a traumatic fall from an open window, and Lena struggles to pay for art school after her father balks at paying for lessons that

involve nude models. A good choice for "those wanting light fare," according to *School Library Journal* contributor Linda L. Plevak, *Girls in Pants* focuses primarily on romances that "end happily." Describing the series as "delightful," *Kliatt* contributor Claire Rosser added that the enjoyment comes from its cast; "each girl is . . . thoughtful, articulate, attractive," and inspired by a unique "set of talents and interests." Brashares "encourages her readers to look, feel, trust, and empathize" with the exploits of the novel's "fascinating" teen characters, according to *Booklist* contributor Frances Bradburn in a review of *Girls in Pants.*

The summer after their freshman year reunites the four friends for the last time in *Forever in Blue: The Fourth Summer of the Sisterhood.* Life is taking each of the young women in very different directions: While summering in Rhode Island, Lena is still emotionally tied to Kostos, even though she has been hurt by his infidelity; Carmen gains self-confidence when her job backstage during a Vermont theatre festival leads to a starring role; Tibby's romantic relationship ends in drama during a summer of acting classes; and Bridget is pursuing her interest in both archaeology and the handsome Eric while working on a dig in Turkey. The pants "play a more prominent role" in this concluding volume, serving as a catalyst as they pass from girl to girl. Their magic "fit" imbues the novel with a "fairytale spirit" that transforms the story into "an ode to love and friendship," according to a *Kirkus Reviews* writer. As Plevak wrote, "fans who already identify" with Brashares' teen heroines will enjoy "their latest exploits." In *Booklist,* Gillan Engberg dubbed *Forever in Blue* "a strong, satisfying conclusion that won't disappoint fans."

After the final installment in her "Sisterhood of the Traveling Pants" series, Brashares turned to older readers in *The Last Summer (of You and Me).* "A thoughtful coming-of-age story," according to *Library Journal* contributor Teresa L. Jacobsen, the novel focuses on twenty-one-year-old Alice and older sister Riley. The young women have a complex history with the handsome Paul, who has lived next door to their family's summer home on Fire Island since childhood. With the death of his father, Paul is now contemplating selling his family's house, thereby breaking his tie to the two sisters. As long-held summer traditions are threatened, romance, jealousy, conflicting loyalties, indifference, and mental instability all factor in a story that eventually leads to tragedy. As Brashares weaves a dual narrative around the novel's pivotal scene, she captures the three characters' "changing relationships" amid their upscale setting with a "spare" prose that evokes a "believable and easy familiarity."

Biographical and Critical Sources

PERIODICALS

Booklist, August, 2001, Frances Bradburn, review of *The Sisterhood of the Traveling Pants,* p. 2106; January 1,

2002, review of *The Sisterhood of the Traveling Pants,* p. 764; April 15, 2003, Frances Bradburn, review of *The Second Summer of Sisterhood,* p. 1461; December 15, 2004, Frances Bradburn, review of *Girls in Pants: The Third Summer of the Sisterhood,* p. 738; December 15, 2006, Gillian Engberg, review of *Forever in Blue: The Fourth Summer of the Sisterhood,* p. 48.

Bookseller, March 15, 2002, Jennifer Taylor, "Strong Contenders," p. S31.

Bulletin of the Center for Children's Books, March, 2005, Elizabeth Bush, review of *Girls in Pants,* p. 282; May, 2007, Elizabeth Bush, review of *Forever in Blue,* p. 361.

Entertainment Weekly, June 10, 2005, Jessica Shaw, "Forever in Blue Jeans: *The Sisterhood of the Traveling Pants . . .* Hopes to Find a Perfect Fit on the Big Screen," p. 40.

Horn Book, November-December, 2001, Jennifer M. Brabander, review of *The Sisterhood of the Traveling Pants,* pp. 741-742; May-June, 2003, Jennifer M. Brabander, review of *The Second Summer of Sisterhood,* p. 339; March-April, 2005, Jennifer M. Brabander, review of *Girls in Pants,* p. 198.

Journal of Adolescent and Adult Literacy, September, 2002, James Blasingame, review of *The Sisterhood of the Traveling Pants,* pp. 87-88.

Kirkus Reviews, August 1, 2001, review of *The Sisterhood of the Traveling Pants,* p. 1117; November 15, 2006, review of *The Fourth Summer of the Sisterhood,* p. 1172; April 15, 2007, review of *The Last Summer (of You and Me).*

Kliatt, March, 2003, Claire Rosser, review of *The Second Summer of the Sisterhood;* January, 2005, Claire Rosser, review of *Girls in Pants;* January, 2007, Claire Rosser, review of *Forever in Blue,* p. 10.

Library Journal, April 1, 2007, Teresa L. Jacobsen, review of *The Last Summer (of You and Me),* p. 78.

New York Times, March 10, 2002, Christine Leahy, review of *The Sisterhood of the Traveling Pants,* p. 7; January 4, 2007, Fred A. Bernstein, "Art above and Below, with Life in the Middle" (profile).

Publishers Weekly, July 16, 2001, review of *The Sisterhood of the Traveling Pants,* p. 182; December 24, 2001, Diane Roback, "Flying Starts," p. 30; March 25, 2002, Daisy Maryles, "A YA Debut Makes Five," p. 18; September 30, 2002, "Have Pants, Will Travel," p. 30; March 3, 2003, review of *The Second Summer of the Sisterhood,* p. 77; January, 2005, Linda L. Plevak, review of *Girls in Pants,* p. 122; November 20, 2006, review of *The Fourth Summer of the Sisterhood,* p. 60; February, 2007, Linda L. Plevak, review of *Forever in Blue,* p. 115; April 2, 2007, review of *The Last Summer (of You and Me),* p. 38.

School Library Journal, August, 2001, Linda Bindner, review of *The Sisterhood of the Traveling Pants,* p. 175; December, 2001, Yapha Nussbaum Mason, review of *Linus Torvalds: Software Rebel,* p. 153; May, 2003, Susan W. Hunter, review of *The Second Summer of Sisterhood,* p. 144.

U.S. News and World Report, May 12, 2003, Holly J. Morris, "Flying by the Seat of Her Pants," p. 8.

Voice of Youth Advocates, August, 2001, Susan H. Levine, review of *Steve Jobs: Think Different;* October, 2001, Deana Rutherford, review of *The Sisterhood of the Traveling Pants,* p. 272; August, 2003, review of *The Second Summer of the Sisterhood,* p. 217; February, 2007, Angie Hammond, review of *Forever in Blue,* p. 521.

Writer, August, 2007, Kara Gebhart Uhl, "One Leg at a Time" (interview), pp. 58-62.

ONLINE

Barnard College Alumna in Action Web site, http://alum.barnard.edu/ (May 23, 2005), interview with Brashares.

BookBrowse, http://www.bookbrowse.com/ (February 2, 2003), "Ann Brashares."

Powells.com, http://www.powells.com/ (September 7, 2001), Dave Weich, interview with Brashares.

Random House Sisterhood Web Site, http://www.randomhouse.com/teens/sisterhood/ (March 15, 2008), "Ann Brashares."*

C

CHAMBERLAIN, Barbara A.
See AZORE, Barbara

*   *   *

CHEANEY, Janie B.
See CHEANEY, J.B.

*   *   *

CHEANEY, J.B. 1950-
(Janie B. Cheaney)

Personal

Born 1950, in Dallas, TX; married 1971; children: Aquila, Tielman. *Education:* Attended Abilene Christian College (now Abilene Christian University).

Addresses

Office—P.O. Box 634, Bolivar, MO 65613.

Career

Writer.

Writings

The Room, Eldridge (Franklin, OH), 1992.
The Playmaker, Knopf (New York, NY), 2000.
The True Prince, Knopf (New York, NY), 2002.
My Friend the Enemy, Knopf (New York, NY), 2005.
The Middle of Somewhere, Knopf (New York, NY), 2007.

Regular contributor to *WORLD* magazine.

Sidelights

As a teen, J.B. Cheaney had a passion for theater. Because of an illness, she missed a year of public school, and when she entered high school as a freshman, she

had trouble making friends. "The next two years were miserable until I found my niche in high school: acting and singing," Cheaney recalled on her home page. In an interview on the *Semicolon Blog,* she admitted to an even earlier passion for the stage, and one that would eventually fuel her career as a novelist. "I was introduced to Shakespeare in my backyard, age ten," the author explained. "The best way to meet him is NOT by reading him, which can be deadly—the plays were meant to be performed."

Cheaney began writing while her daughter was an infant. After completing four adult novels that remain unpublished, she decided to try writing for a younger audience, and one of her children's novels draws on her love of theater. Set in Elizabethan England, *The Playmaker* introduces young Richard Malory, an actor who performs plays by "Master Will"—William Shakespeare. "Informed by solid historical and literary scholarship, this well-written adventure novel is a winner," wrote Starr E. Smith in *School Library Journal.* Noting the "breathless action" and period details in *The Playmaker,* Gillian Engberg wrote in *Booklist* that "most compelling are the highly detailed theater scenes, which beautifully articulate a young artist's struggles to master his craft." Mary M. Burns, reviewing *The Playmaker* for *Horn Book,* found the tale to be "an engrossing blend of intrigue and insight into the operation of a theater in Shakespeare's day."

Richard's adventures continue in *The True Prince,* during which a highway man, appearing as a new incarnation of Robin Hood, threatens the theater's livelihood. A *Kirkus Reviews* contributor called *The True Prince* "a fine addition to the growing body of literature about Shakespeare's world." A *Publishers Weekly* critic concluded that "only the dourest reader would pass up this breathless scramble of 16th-century London."

Leaving Elizabethan England behind, Cheaney has also written a tale set during World War II. *My Friend the Enemy* was inspired by her son's time working in Japan as well as by the events of 9/11, which she felt echoed the bombing of Pearl Harbor. In the novel, a girl named Hazel befriends fifteen-year-old Japanese-American Sogoji. Orphaned and cut off from his community, Sogoji works secretly on Hazel's neighbor's farm and ponders how to be both American and Japanese when the two nations are enemies. As tensions escalate against Japan in Hazel's community, she must choose to take a stand in defense of her new friend. "This powerful work deftly explores how war affects a community, when the identity of friend, enemy and hero is sometimes difficult to discern," wrote a contributor to *Kirkus Reviews* in a review of *My Friend the Enemy.*

The Middle of Somewhere is Cheaney's first contemporary novel. Set in small-town Kansas, it tells the story of Ronnie Sparks, who must take care of her brother as her mother recovers from knee surgery. The task becomes more challenging as Ronnie, her grandfather Pop, and little brother Gee make a road trip together. "The main characters are particularly well drawn and believable, and readers will root for both children as they attempt to overcome the obstacles placed in front of them," wrote Kay Weisman in *Booklist.* While finding some problems with the story's pacing, a *Kirkus Reviews* contributor complimented the "crafty, descriptive first-person narrative" Cheaney employs in *The Middle of Somewhere.*

Describing her writing process in an interview for *World Online,* Cheaney explained: "I start with a setting (time and place), a handful of characters, and a very vague idea of where I want to end up. The first draft is excruciating; it's like bulldozing a field of rocks uphill. Once the story is in place, I can look back and see a loamy plowed slope, ready to revise. Oh, joy! It's all downhill from there."

Biographical and Critical Sources

PERIODICALS

Booklist, November 1, 2000, Gillian Engberg, review of *The Playmaker,* p. 524; January 1, 2003, Gillian Engberg, review of *The True Prince,* p. 870; May 15, 2005, Carolyn Phelan, review of *My Friend the Enemy,* p. 1674; March 15, 2007, Kay Weisman, review of *The Middle of Somewhere,* p. 46.

Bulletin of the Center for Children's Books, October, 2000, review of *The Playmaker,* p. 56; December, 2002, review of *The True Prince,* p. 149; September, 2007, Karen Coats, review of *The Middle of Somewhere,* p. 11.

Horn Book, January, 2001, Mary M. Burns, review of *The Playmaker,* p. 88.

Kirkus Reviews, September 15, 2002, review of *The True Prince,* p. 1386; June 15, 2005, review of *My Friend, the Enemy,* p. 679; April 15, 2007, review of *The Middle of Somewhere.*

Kliatt, November, 2002, Michele Winship, review of *The True Prince,* p. 6.

Publishers Weekly, August 7, 2000, review of *The Playmaker,* p. 96; November 4, 2002, review of *The True Prince,* p. 85.

School Library Journal, December, 2000, Starr E. Smith, review of *The Playmaker,* p. 142; November, 2002, Starr E. Smith, review of *The True Prince,* p. 159; November, 2005, Ginny Gustin, review of *My Friend the Enemy,* p. 130; July, 2007, Miriam Lang Budin, review of *The Middle of Somewhere,* p. 99.

Voice of Youth Advocates, August, 2005, Melissa Moore, review of *My Friend the Enemy,* p. 213.

ONLINE

Cynsations Blog, http://cynthialeitichsmith.blogspot.com/ (March 9, 2008), Cynthia Leitich Smith, interview with Cheaney.

J.B. Cheaney Home Page, http://www.jbcheaney.com (March 5, 2008).

World Online, http://www.worldontheweb.com/ (September 20, 2007), Susan Olasky, interview with Cheaney.*

*   *   *

CLEMENT-MOORE, Rosemary

Personal

Married. *Education:* M.A. (communications). *Hobbies and other interests:* Reading, sewing, sailing, music, vintage embroidery.

Addresses

Home—TX. *E-mail*—rosemary@readrosemary.com.

Career

Writer. Former teacher and actress.

Writings

Prom Dates from Hell, Delacorte (New York, NY), 2007.
Hell Week, Delacorte (New York, NY), 2008.

Sidelights

Rosemary Clement-Moore is a Texas-based writer whose first novel, *Prom Dates from Hell,* is an entertaining story that mixes high-school life with the supernatural. In the novel, ace journalist and brainy senior Maggie Quinn has a passion, but it is not fellow student Stanley Dozer. When the uber-geeky Stanley asks Maggie to be his date for Avalon High's senior prom, she balks and unknowingly causes the humiliated young man to unleash an evil that only Maggie can stop. Harnessing her latent ESP abilities, Maggie dons the hated prom dress, runs the gauntlet of condescension formed by Avalon's ruling clique, and appears at prom on the elbow of college friend Justin, hoping to avert a demon-led disaster.

Teen readers "will have fun with this one," predicted *Kliatt* contributor Claire Rosser, "especially if they like rather crazy, humorous stories" and sharp-witted teen heroines. Noting that the humorous plot of *Prom Dates from Hell* Clement-Moore includes a touch of teen romance, Emily Rodriguez wrote in *School Library Journal* that "sharp writing and a satirical portrayal of the high school social scene make [*Prom Dates from Hell*] . . . an enjoyable read." "There is a lot to like in this story that takes on magic, romance and even clique politics," concluded a *Publishers Weekly* contributor.

In reviewing *Prom Dates from Hell*, critics have credited Clement-Moore's ability to create such a spunky and engaging heroine with the author's former career as an actor. Popular with teen readers, Maggie returns in *Hell Week* as an undercover stint draws her into the clutches of a sorority at her new college, where student mixers lead to secret meetings, bizarre pledging rituals, and a dark secret.

Biographical and Critical Sources

PERIODICALS

Bulletin of the Center for Children's Books, July-August, 2007, Karen Coats, review of *Prom Dates from Hell,* p. 457.

Horn Book, May-June, 2007, Christine M. Heppermann, review of *Prom Dates from Hell,* p. 297.

Kirkus Reviews, February 15, 2007, review of *Prom Dates from Hell.*

Kliatt, March, 2007, review of *Prom Dates from Hell,* p. 10.

Publishers Weekly, March 26, 2007, review of *Prom Dates from Hell,* p. 95.

School Library Journal, March, 2007, Emily Rodriguez, review of *Prom Dates from Hell,* p. 206.

Voice of Youth Advocates, April, 2007, Jennifer Rummel, review of *Prom Dates from Hell,* p. 63.

ONLINE

Rosemary Clement-Moore Home Page, http://www.rosemaryclementmoore.com (February 20, 2008).

Class of 2K7 Web site, http://classof2k7.com/ (March 15, 2008), "Rosemary Clement-Moore."*

* * *

COTTEN, Cynthia

Personal

Born in Lockport, NY; daughter of a high-school art teacher and painter; married 1975; children: Amanda, Christopher. *Education:* Vermont College, M.F.A.

Addresses

Home—Montclair, VA. *E-mail*—cynthia@cynthiacotten.com.

Career

Writer.

Writings

Snow Ponies, illustrated by Jason Cockcroft, Holt (New York, NY), 2001.

At the Edge of the Woods: A Counting Book, illustrated by Reg Cartwright, Holt (New York, NY), 2002.

Cover of Rosemary Clement-Moore's teen novel **Prom Dates from Hell,** *featuring artwork by Angela Carlino and Andy Smith.*

Abbie in Stitches, illustrated by Beth Peck, Farrar, Straus & Giroux (New York, NY), 2006.

This Is the Stable, illustrated by Delana Bettoli, Holt (New York, NY), 2006.

Some Babies Sleep, illustrated by Paul Tong, Philomel (New York, NY), 2007.

Fair Has Nothing to Do with It, Farrar, Straus & Giroux (New York, NY), 2007.

Rain Play, illustrated by Javaka Steptoe, Holt (New York, NY), 2008.

Sidelights

As a child, Cynthia Cotten had no intention of becoming a writer. "As I was growing up, I wanted to be a teacher, a marine biologist, a U.N. interpreter and a book translator," Cotton wrote on her home page. "I loved horses so much that, for a while, I even wanted to be a jockey." However, her mother decided that horseback riding was not a good idea, so Cotten comforted herself by reading and playing with words. She continued to enjoy reading throughout school, and following high school, she spent a year in Belgium as an international exchange student.

Cotten did not begin writing until 1981, when her own daughter was two years old. When the search for a simple retelling of the Christmas story for very young children met with no success, Cotten realized that she could probably write one. She took correspondence courses and joined a local writer's group, then attended Vermont College to earn her M.F.A. in writing for children. While still enrolled in that program, she published her first picture book, *Snow Ponies.*

Snow Ponies describes the day, each year, when Old Man Winter releases his snow ponies and brings winter to the world. Cotton's "brief text is rich with descriptive phrases of their antics," wrote Carol Schene of the book in a review for *School Library Journal.* A *Kirkus Reviews* contributor called the picture book "a magical read."

Cotten's next title, *At the Edge of the Woods: A Counting Book,* features a rhyming refrain that describes how animals, in pairs, then trios, and then larger groups, appear in succession as the sun rises over the woods. "Children will enjoy joining in on the refrain," predicted Jody McCoy in her *School Library Journal* review.

Cotton leaves animals behind and turns to historical fiction in *Abbie in Stitches.* Featuring artwork by Beth Peck, the story introduces a girl who, despite her proper upbringing in the 1800s, would much rather read than practice embroidery on her sampler. Margaret Bush called the book a "pleasant family story" and felt that it would appeal to "those who like reading about life in other times."

Cotton's intention to retell the Christmas story gained fruition in 2006. "Sometimes I get a phrase in my head," Cotten told Cynthia Leitich Smith on *Cynsations* on-line, "and it plays itself over and over until I do something about it. In this case, it was 'the stable, dusty and brown.'" Once she had that phrase, the rest of the story followed, and the process from writing, waiting for her publishers to choose an artist, and seeing the book published took three years. Reviewing *This Is the Stable,* Linda Israelson wrote in *School Library Journal* that Cotton's "seamless, thoughtful" text features a rhyme that "is sweet but never forced." According to *Booklist* contributor Gillian Engberg, "the pace is just right for participatory read-alouds." After finishing her Christmas tale, Cotten wrote the lullaby *Some Babies Sleep,* about which a *Kirkus Reviews* contributor commented that the author's use of "gentle rhymes make this perfect for bedtime."

In addition to picture books, Cotten is also the author of the children's novel *Fair Has Nothing to Do with It.* When readers first meet him, twelve-year-old Michael feels devastated. His beloved grandfather has died, and his father is too busy to pay attention to Michael's grief. Through an art project in school and the help of a grandfatherly neighbor, Michael finally is able to cope with his feelings of loss and sadness. *Fair Has Nothing to Do with It* "is touching and accurate in its portrayal of the grieving process," Nicki Clausen-Grace concluded in her *School Library Journal* review, while Hazel Rochman wrote in *Booklist* that Cotton's "dramatic portrayal of Michael's grief" is "true to the child's viewpoint."

Asked by Leitich Smith what advice she would offer to aspiring picture-book writers, Cotten replied: "Read picture books—stacks of them. Take some you like and type their texts out—it gives a feel for the rhythm and flow. Do a word count on the ones you've typed—you'll probably find they're a lot shorter than you thought. Then go read some more." On her home page, Cotten admitted that writing really is her dream job. "I love kids, I love books, I love writing—and while the words don't always come easily and there are days when I find myself looking for excuses not to sit down at my computer, there is really no other job I'd rather have."

Biographical and Critical Sources

PERIODICALS

Booklist, December 1, 2002, Helen Rosenberg, review of *At the Edge of the Woods: A Counting Book,* p. 672; September 1, 2006, Julie Cummins, review of *Abbie in Stitches,* p. 135; November 1, 2006, Gillian Engberg, review of *This Is the Stable,* p. 60; April 1, 2007, Hazel Rochman, review of *Fair Has Nothing to Do with It,* p. 44.

Bulletin of the Center for Children's Books, November, 2002, review of *At the Edge of the Woods,* p. 102; September, 2007, Hope Morrison, review of *Fair Has Nothing to Do with It,* p. 13.

Horn Book, November-December, 2006, Tanya D. Auger, review of *This Is the Stable*, p. 689.

Kirkus Reviews, October 15, 2001, review of *Snow Ponies*, p. 1481; July 1, 2002, review of *At the Edge of the Woods*, p. 952; August 1, 2006, review of *Abbie in Stitches*, p. 783; November 1, 2006, review of *This Is the Stable*, p. 1127; December 1, 2006, review of *Some Babies Sleep*, p. 1218; May 1, 2007, review of *Fair Has Nothing to Do with It*.

Publishers Weekly, August 26, 2002, review of *At the Edge of the Woods*, p. 66; September 25, 2006, review of *This Is the Stable*, p. 70.

School Library Journal, December, 2001, Carol Schene, review of *Snow Ponies*, p. 97; June, 2003, Jody Mc-Coy, review of *At the Edge of the Woods*, p. 98; September, 2006, Margaret Bush, review of *Abbie in Stitches*, p. 164; October, 2006, Linda Israelson, review of *This Is the Stable*, p. 95; June, 2007, Nicki Clausen-Grace, review of *Fair Has Nothing to Do with It*, p. 142.

ONLINE

Cynsations Web site, http://cynthialeitichsmith.blogspot.com/ (December 5, 2006), Cynthia Leitich Smith, interview with Cotten.

Cynthia Cotten Home Page, http://www.cynthiacotten.com (March 5, 2008).

*　　*　　*

CRISLER, Curtis L. 1965-

Personal

Born 1965. *Education:* Southern Illinois University-Carbondale, M.F.A. (creative writing).

Addresses

Home and office—Fort Wayne, IN.

Career

Author and instructor at Indiana University—Purdue University, Fort Wayne.

Member

NOMMO Literary Society.

Awards, Honors

Cave Canem fellow, 2003.

Writings

Tough Boy Sonatas, illustrations by Floyd Cooper, Wordsong (Honesdale, PA), 2007.

Contributor to periodicals, including *Fourth River* and *Black Arts Quarterly* and to the anthology *The Sea Keeps: Poetry of the Tsunami.*

Sidelights

Poet and educator Curtis L. Crisler has published his poems in several journals, including *Fourth River* and *Black Arts Quarterly*. His children's book *Tough Boy Sonatas* incorporates his verses with the paintings of renowned artist Floyd Cooper. *Tough Boy Sonatas* presents a series of poems that explores the individual stories of young men growing up in Gary, Indiana. The verses capture the character of diverse individuals and convey the character of each young man in a manner considered "thought-provoking" by *Black Issues Book Review* critic Clarence V. Reynolds.

Gillian Engberg, reviewing *Tough Boy Sonatas* in *Booklist,* commented that Crisler incorporates a "skillful manipulation of sound, rhythm, and form" into his collection, adding that "the poems are filled with sophisticated imagery and graphic words." Engberg also acknowledged Crisler's work as "potent [and] hard-hitting," while a *School Library Journal* reviewer wrote

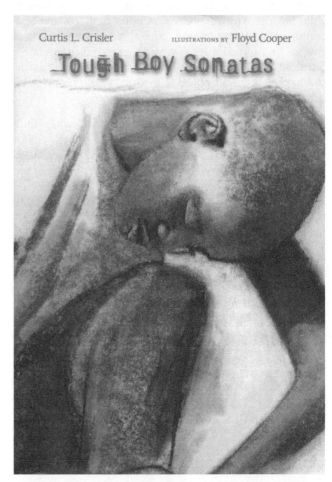

Curtis L. Crisler's young-adult verse novel Tough Boy Sonatas *features artwork by noted illustrator Floyd Cooper.* (Illustration copyright © 2007 by Floyd Cooper. All rights reserved. Reproduced by Wordsong, an imprint of Boyds Mills Press, Inc.)

that the author "palpably captures . . . the hopes and dreams" of Gary, Indiana's careworn young men. Also writing in *School Library Journal,* Susan Moorhead surmised Crisler's collection of poems as "muscular and vivid, fierce with the sound and force of language."

Biographical and Critical Sources

PERIODICALS

Black Issues Book Review, March-April, 2007, Clarence V. Reynolds, "Coming of Age—Free-Verse Style," p. 23.

Booklist, February 1, 2007, Gillian Engberg, review of *Tough Boy Sonatas,* p. 50.

Books, March 4, 2007, Mary Harris Russell, review of *Tough Boy Sonatas,* p. 7.

Bulletin of the Center for Children's Books, April, 2007, Deborah Stevenson, review of *Tough Boy Sonatas,* p. 326.

Publishers Weekly, March 5, 2007, "Rhyme Time," p. 64.

School Library Journal, March, 2007, Susan Moorhead, review of *Tough Boy Sonatas,* p. 225.

Voice of Youth Advocates, August, 2007, Mary Ann Harlan, review of *Tough Boy Sonatas,* p. 268.

ONLINE

Boyds Mills Press Web site, http://www.boydsmillspress. com/ (February 28, 2008).

Indiana University-Purdue University Fort Wayne Web site, http://www.ipfw.edu/ (February 28, 2008), "Curtis L. Crisler."

L'Intrigue Web site, http://www.lintrigue.org/ (February 28, 2008).*

*   *   *

CURIE, Eve 1904-2007
(Eve Curie Labouisse, Eve Denise Labouisse)

OBITUARY NOTICE—

See index for *SATA* sketch: Born December 6, 1904, in Paris, France; died October 22, 2007, in New York, NY.

Biographer, journalist, and musician. Curie is known primarily for her award-winning biography of her mother, scientist Marie Curie. *Madame Curie: A Biography,* first published in 1937, was a loving appreciation, so much so that it avoided mentioning a few negative elements of the elder Curie's life, even though they were common knowledge during her lifetime. The book became a classic in its genre. It was translated into many foreign languages and adapted into a film starring Greer Garson in the title role. Eve Curie was the only member of her family who did not pursue a scientific career—the only one, as she once confessed, who did not win a Nobel Prize. However, her biography earned the author a National Book Award for nonfiction as well as honors from her native land, including a croix de guerre and decoration as a chevalier of the French Legion of Honor. Despite the celebrity generated by her book, Curie lived a modest and quiet life. She trained as a concert pianist and performed throughout Europe. After the publication of *Madame Curie,* she lectured widely as well. Curie left France during the Nazi occupation, supported the French Resistance in exile, and worked as a war correspondent during World War II. Afterward she published an account of her travels, *Journey among Warriors* (1943). Following the war, Curie worked for a Paris newspaper until the early 1950s, when she married an American diplomat and United Nations executive. She settled in New York City, where she remained for the rest of her life.

OBITUARIES AND OTHER SOURCES:

BOOKS

Curie, Eve, *Journey among Warriors,* Doubleday, Doran (New York, NY), 1943.

PERIODICALS

Los Angeles Times, October 26, 2007, p. B9.

New York Times, October 25, 2007, p. A25.

Times (London, England), October 26, 2007, p. 78.

Washington Post, October 26, 2007, p. B7.

D

DeSAIX, Deborah Durland

Personal

Born in Miami, FL; married George Inge IV (an artist). *Education:* University of North Carolina, B.A. (art); School of Visual Arts, M.F.A. (illustration).

Addresses

Home and office—Asheville, NC. *E-mail*—karenanddeb@hotmail.com.

Career

Author and illustrator. School of Visual Arts, New York, NY, former instructor in illustration.

Member

Society of Children's Book Writers and Illustrators, Author's Guild, Author's League.

Writings

SELF-ILLUSTRATED

In the Back Seat, Farrar, Straus & Giroux (New York, NY), 1993.
Returning Nicholas, Farrar, Straus & Giroux (New York, NY), 1995.
(With Karen Gray Ruelle) *Hidden on the Mountain: Stories of Children Sheltered from the Nazis in Le Chambon,* Holiday House (New York, NY), 2007.

ILLUSTRATOR

Frank DeSaix, *Hilary and the Lions,* Farrar, Straus & Giroux (New York, NY), 1990.
Frank DeSaix, *The Girl Who Danced with Dolphins,* Farrar, Straus & Giroux (New York, NY), 1991.

Lisa Westberg Peters, *Meg and Dad Discover Treasure in the Air,* Henry Holt (New York, NY), 1995.
Nancy Taylor, reteller, *Daniel and the Lions' Den,* Time-Life for Children (Alexandria, VA), 1996.

At the start of her illustration career, Deborah Durland DeSaix created cover art for novels such as Michael Delaney's middle-grade adventure **The Great Sockathon.** (Illustration copyright © 2004 by Deborah Durland DeSaix. Reproduced by permission of Dutton Children's Books, a division of Penguin Putnam Books for Young Readers.)

Aileen Fisher, *Know What I Saw?*, Roaring Brook Press (New Milford, CT), 2005.

Karen Gray Ruelle, *The Tree*, Holiday House (New York, NY), 2009.

Sidelights

Deborah Durland DeSaix grew up in North Carolina and by age eight she knew she would become an artist. Studying art and illustration during her college years, she went on to contribute illustrations to several children's books. DeSaix has also illustrated several original children's stories, including *Returning Nicholas* and *In the Back Seat*. In 2007 she collaborated with writer Karen Gray Ruelle to coauthor *Hidden on the Mountain: Stories of Children Sheltered from the Nazis in Le Chambon*. DeSaix first met Ruelle when Ruelle enrolled in a class in illustration that she was teaching at New York City's School of Visual Arts. The two women have since worked together on a second children's book.

Hidden on the Mountain pairs a photo-essay with a nonfiction text that recounts the stories of the refugee children who took shelter in the mountains of Le Chambon-sur-Lignon, France and were therefore protected from Holocaust atrocities. DeSaix and Ruelle tell the various and individual tales of the surviving children through interviews they reinterpret as first-person diary entries. Adding to the book's coverage of a complex period of history, the coauthors include maps, a chronology of events, and a bibliography including resources that will further inspire young researchers.

Several reviewers acknowledged the extensive research that DeSaix and Ruelle consulted and which contributed to the book's authenticity. In *School Library Journal* Rachel Kamin commented that *Hidden on the Mountain* serves as an "invaluable resource for Holocaust educators," and also noted that "many of the children's narratives would read beautifully out loud." Hazel Rochman, in her critique of the book for *Booklist*, deemed DeSaix and Ruelle's collaborative work an "inspiring photo-essay" that "tell[s] an amazing rescue story."

Biographical and Critical Sources

PERIODICALS

Booklist, September 1, 1993, Denia Hester, review of *In the Back Seat,* p. 67; September 15, 2005, Jennifer Mattson, review of *Know What I Saw?,* p. 72; December 1, 1995, April Judge, review of *Meg and Dad Discover Treasure in the Air,* p. 630; March 15, 2007, Hazel Rochman, review of *Hidden on the Mountain: Stories of Children Sheltered from the Nazis in Le Chambon,* p. 42.

Bulletin of the Center for Children's Books, September, 2007, Hope Morrison, review of *Hidden on the Mountain,* p. 16.

DeSaix teamed up with Karen Gray Ruelle to bring to life a dramatic story of refugee children during World War II in **Hidden on the Mountain.** (Holiday House, 2007. Reproduced by permission of Holiday House, Inc.)

Kirkus Reviews, July 1, 2005, review of *Know What I Saw?,* p. 734; April 1, 2007, review of *Hidden on the Mountain.*

Publishers Weekly, June 14, 1993, review of *In the Back Seat,* p. 69; October 30, 1995, review of *Returning Nicholas,* p. 61; September 2, 1996, review of *Hilary and the Lions,* p. 133.

School Library Journal, August, 1993, George Delalis, review of *In the Back Seat,* p. 140; January, 1996, Kate McClelland, review of *Returning Nicholas,* p. 77; January, 1996, Diane Nunn, review of *Meg and Dad Discover Treasure in the Air,* p. 92; September, 2005, Teresa Pfeifer, review of *Know What I Saw?,* p. 169; May, 2007, Rachel Kamin, review of *Hidden on the Mountain,* p. 152.

ONLINE

Children's Bookwatch Web site, http://www.midwestbook review.com/ (October 1, 2005), review of *Know What I Saw?*

Hidden on the Mountain Web site, http://www.hiddenonthe mountain.com/ (March 2, 2008), "Deborah Durland DeSaix."*

*   *   *

DIBLEY, Glin

Personal

Married; children: two daughters.

Addresses

Home and office—CA.

Career

Illustrator.

Illustrator

Margie Palatini, *Tub-Boo-Boo*, Simon & Schuster Books for Young Readers (New York, NY), 2001.

Steve Seskin and Allen Shamblin, *Don't Laugh at Me*, Tricycle Press (Berkeley, CA), 2002.

Dandi Daley Mackall, *Made for a Purpose*, Zonderkidz (Grand Rapids, MI), 2004.

Janice Repka, *The Stupendous Dodgeball Fiasco*, Dutton Children's Books (New York, NY), 2004.

Valerie Wheeler, *Yes, Please! No, Thank You!*, Sterling Publishing (New York, NY), 2005.

Mary Ellen Friday, *It's a Bad Day*, Rising Moon (Flagstaff, AZ), 2006.

Elizabeth Ficocelli, *Kid Tea*, Marshall Cavendish (Tarrytown, NY), 2007.

Sidelights

Glin Dibley is an illustrator whose work has appeared in magazines, in advertising, and in children's books. His book art debuted in the picture book *Tub-Boo-Boo*, featuring a text by popular writer Margie Palatini. *Tub-Boo-Boo* has a humorous flair and shows how all the members of a family gets stuck in a bath tub. Dibley's illustrations for the work are rendered in colorful acrylics and are large in size. *School Library Journal* reviewer Linda M. Kenton wrote that the artist's expansive "illustrations occupy the entire opposite page with occasional oozing over to the text page." Kathy Broderick, in her review of *Tub-Boo-Boo* for *Booklist*, concluded that Dibley's "spindly, crazily exaggerated characters blend well" with Palatini's outrageous storyline.

Dibley's illustrations for Elizabeth Ficocelli's *Kid Tea* follow a messy lead character as he becomes dirtier by the minute as he moves from painting to eating popsicles to playing in the mud. After each activity the child dunks in a tub, like a tea-bag, and clears all the current muck away. In *School Library Journal*, Susan E. Murray dubbed Dibley's illustrations "exuberant" and added that the artist's "bright colors, splotches, and dribbles add to the enjoyment of the tale." According to *Booklist* reviewer Ilene Cooper, Dibley's "Jell-O-like colors" serve as a "big, brightening attraction" to young readers.

Biographical and Critical Sources

PERIODICALS

Booklist, September 1, 2001, Kathy Broderick, review of *Tub-Boo-Boo*, p. 117; December 15, 2004, Todd Morning, review of *The Stupendous Dodgeball Fiasco*, p. 742; March 1, 2007, Ilene Cooper, review of *Kid Tea*, p. 88.

Bulletin of the Center for Children's Books, October, 2001, review of *Tub-Boo-Boo*, p. 70; March, 2005, Karen Coats, review of *The Stupendous Dodgeball Fiasco*, p. 304.

Kirkus Reviews, July 1, 2001, review of *Tub-Boo-Boo*, p. 945; September 15, 2002, review of *Don't Laugh at Me*, p. 1400; October 1, 2004, review of *The Stupendous Dodgeball Fiasco*, p. 967.

Library Media Connection, February, 2006, Daniel R. Beach, review of *Yes, Please! No, Thank You!*, p. 75.

Publishers Weekly, August 20, 2001, review of *Tub-Boo-Boo*, p. 79; October 21, 2002, review of *Don't Laugh at Me*, p. 74; June 20, 2005, review of *Yes, Please! No, Thank You!*, p. 76; March 19, 2007, review of *Kid Tea*, p. 62.

School Library Journal, October, 2001, Linda M. Kenton, review of *Tub-Boo-Boo*, p. 128; January, 2003, Jody McCoy, review of *Don't Laugh at Me*, p. 129; December, 2004, Caitlin Augusta, review of *The Stupendous Dodgeball Fiasco*, p. 152; August, 2005, Piper L. Nyman, review of *Yes, Please! No, Thank You!*, p. 108; May, 2007, Kristine M. Casper, review of *It's a Bad Day*, p. 91; May, 2007, Susan E. Murray, review of *Kid Tea*, p. 91.

ONLINE

Children's Bookwatch, http://www.midwestbookreview.com/ (October 1, 2006), review of *It's a Bad Day*.

Ten Speed Press Web site, http://www.tenspeedpress.com/ (March 3, 2008), "Glin Dibley."*

*   *   *

DONNIO, Sylviane

Personal

Female.

Addresses

Home—France.

Career

Children's book author.

Writings

Je mangerais bien un enfant, illustrated by Dorothée de Monfreid, Ecole des Loisirs (Paris, France), 2006, translation by Leslie Martin published as *I'd Really Like to Eat a Child*, Random House (New York, NY), 2007.

Sidelights

Luring young children with a title that both frightens and fascinates, Sylviane Donnio's picture book *I'd Really Like to Eat a Child* features droll artwork by

Dorothée de Monfreid. A hit among children in the author's native France under its original title, *Je mangerais bien un enfant,* the book was quickly translated into English for the entertainment of American readers, a surprising accomplishment considering that the text was Donnio's picture-book debut.

As brought to life in de Monfreid's cartoon art, the book is set in Africa and tells the story of a young crocodile named Achilles. Achilles wakes up one morning and decides that no other food but a human child will do. Turning down his morning banana, then sausage, then even chocolate cake, Achilles' resolve begins to concern his crocodile mother. The young reptile grows increasingly hungry, and eventually he decides to go in search of a tasty child himself. When he meets up with a little girl playing near a riverbank, the tables turn for the young croc. Although he has more teeth, the girl is bigger and proves to be more than his match; she treats Achilles like a toy, tickles him, and tosses him in the water, whereupon the humbled reptile swims back home for a lunch of bananas. Donnio's "appetizing mixture of domestic breakfast concerns and fierce child-eating monsters will leave children hungry for more," concluded a *Publishers Weekly* contributor in a review of *I'd Really Like to Eat a Child,* while a *Kirkus Reviews* writer dubbed the picture book "a nice addition to storytimes about finicky eaters." In *School Library Journal,* Blair Christolon commented in particular on de Monfreid's "sunny cartoon illustrations" while the *Kirkus Reviews* writer deemed them reminiscent of the work of Pulitzer Prize-winning cartoonist Jules Feiffer.

Biographical and Critical Sources

PERIODICALS

Kirkus Reviews, April 1, 2007, review of *I'd Really Like to Eat a Child.*

Publishers Weekly, April 23, 2007, review of *I'd Really Like to Eat a Child,* p. 49.

School Library Journal, April, 2007, Blair Christolon, review of *I'd Really Like to Eat a Child,* p. 98.*

E

EMMETT, Jonathan 1965-

Personal
Born December 10, 1965, in Leicester, England; son of Robert (a rig fitter) and Joyce (a teacher) Emmett; married Rachel Grover (an arts administrator), July 30, 1994; children: Max, Laura. *Education:* Nottingham University, B.A. (honors architecture), 1988, B. Arch. (honors architecture), 1993. *Hobbies and other interests:* "Walking, reading, furniture design, and tinkering with my Web site."

Addresses
Home—England. *Agent*—Caroline Walsh, David Hingham Associates, 5-8 Lower John St., Golden Square, London W1F 9HA, England. *E-mail*—sitemail@scribblestreet.co.uk.

Career
Writer, illustrator, and paper engineer. Worked for several years as an architect, mid-1990s.

Awards, Honors
Southampton Favourite Book to Share Award, 2003, for *A Turtle in the Toilet,* and 2006, for *Zoom!;* Kiekeboekprojs (Netherlands), 2003, for *Bringing Down the Moon;* Norfolk Libraries Children's Book Award, and Red House Children's Book Award, both 2006, both for *Pigs Might Fly!;* Richard and Judy's Best Kids' Books Award shortlist, for *Someone Bigger.*

Writings

FOR CHILDREN

Doohickey and the Robot, Oxford University Press (Oxford, England), 1999.

Jonathan Emmett (Photo courtesy of Jonathan Emmett.)

Ten Little Monsters: A Counting Book, illustrated by Ant Parker, Kingfisher, (New York, NY), 2000, with finger puppet set, Houghton Mifflin (Boston, MA), 2002.

Fox's New Coat, illustrated by Penny Ives, Viking (London, England), 2000.

Bringing down the Moon, illustrated by Vanessa Cabban, Candlewick Press (Cambridge, MA), 2001.

Dinosaurs after Dark, illustrated by Curtis Jobling, Golden Books (New York, NY), 2001.

Cosmo for Captain, illustrated by Peter Rutherford, Oxford University Press (Oxford, England), 2002, published as *Dino Boulder Ball,* illustrated by Peter Rutherford, Picture Window (Minneapolis, MN), 2007.

A Turtle in the Toilet, illustrated by Caroline Jayne Church, Tiger Tales Books (Wilton, CT), 2002.

A Mouse inside the Marmalade, illustrated by Caroline Jayne Church, Tiger Tales Books (Wilton, CT), 2002.

Terry Takes Off, illustrated by Peter Rutherford, Oxford University Press (Oxford, England), 2003.

Through the Heart of the Jungle, illustrated by Elena Gomez, Tiger Tales Books (Wilton, CT), 2003.

Someone Bigger, illustrated by Adrian Reynolds, Oxford University Press (Oxford, England), 2003.

What Friends Do Best, illustrated by Nathan Reed, HarperCollins (London, England), 2004.

Creatures Colours (pop-up book), Gullane Children's (London, England), 2004.

Robots, HarperCollins (London, England), 2004.

Once upon a Time upon a Nest, illustrated by Rebecca Harry, Macmillan Children's Books (London, England), 2004, published as *Ruby in Her Own Time,* Scholastic (New York, NY), 2004 published as *Ruby Flew Too!,* Macmillan Children's Books, 2005.

Someone Bigger, illustrated by Adrian Reynolds, Clarion Books (New York, NY), 2004.

No Place like Home, illustrated by Vanessa Cabban, Candlewick Press (Cambridge, MA), 2005.

Safari Shapes (pop-up book), Gullane Children's (London, England), 2005.

Pigs Might Fly: The Further Adventures of the Three Little Pigs, illustrated by Steve Cox, Puffin (London, England), 2005.

Zoom!, illustrated by Christyan Fox, Macmillan Children's (London, England), 2005.

Diamond in the Snow, illustrated by Vanessa Cabban, Candlewick Press (Cambridge, MA), 2006.

Rabbit's Day Off!, illustrated by Thomas Taylor, Gullane Children's (London, England), 2006.

Captain Comet and the Purple Planet, illustrated by Andy Parker, Oxford University Press (Oxford, England), 2006.

If We Had a Sailboat, illustrated by Adrian Reynolds, Oxford University Press (Oxford, England), 2006.

Dig It, Build It!, illustrated by Christyan Fox, Macmillan Children's (London, England), 2006.

This Way, Ruby!, illustrated by Rebecca Harry, Macmillan (London, England), 2006, Scholastic (New York, NY), 2007.

I Love You Always and Forever, illustrated by Daniel Howarth, Scholastic (New York, NY), 2007.

Terry Takes Off, illustrated by Peter Rutherford, Picture Window Books (Minneapolis, MN), 2007.

(Reteller) *She'll Be Coming 'round the Mountain,* illustrated by Deborah Allwright, Atheneum (New York, NY), 2007.

Captain Comet and the Dog Star, illustrated by Andy Parker, Oxford University Press (Oxford, England), 2007.

Author's books have been translated into other languages, including French, German, Danish, Finish, Slovenian, Swedish, and Friesian.

"CONJUROR'S COOKBOOK" SERIES

Goblin Stew, illustrated by Colin Paine, Bloomsbury Children's Books (London, England), 2000.

Serpent Soup, illustrated by Colin Paine, Bloomsbury Children's Books (London, England), 2000.

Ghostly Goulash, illustrated by Colin Paine, Bloomsbury Children's Books (London, England), 2000.

Fairy Cake, Bloomsbury Children's Books (London, England), 2000.

Sidelights

Wanting to write children's books, Jonathan Emmett itched to leave his job as an architect, but he didn't dare, even though his wife Rachel offered to support the family. "I couldn't face the possibility of giving up a steady job and then failing to get anything published," he once told *SATA.* Finally he got a push in 1995 when he was laid off. Within three months, he had found a literary agent and even sold a pop-up book called *Scraposaurus Wrecks.* Although that book was never published, it led Emmett to other opportunities, as he recalled: "Although this was a big disappointment, the fact that I had sold the story, and been commissioned to illustrate and paper-engineer it, gave me the confidence to continue working on children's books."

Emmett's interest in books dates from childhood, when as a young boy he made a spare bedroom into a library for his parents' books, arranging them by color and size. He once told *SATA,* "I can remember visiting our local library as a toddler. The books that we borrowed then, including *Where the Wild Things Are* by Maurice Sendak, *The Cat in the Hat* by Dr. Seuss, and *Harold and the Purple Crayon* by Crockett Johnson, have a great influence on the picture book stories that I now write. The first 'proper' book that I read for myself was *The Folk of the Faraway Tree* by Enid Blyton. I went on to read other popular children's authors like C.S. Lewis, but like many children of my generation, the author who made the biggest impression on my early childhood was Roald Dahl." While in grade school Emmett wrote a weekly serial instead of the assigned short stories.

"It wasn't until I was about fourteen years old that it occurred to me that I might write for a living," he explained to *SATA.* As a student he elaborately decorated his school notebook covers to look like the book jackets of novels, complete with publishers' blurbs. Ultimately, however, Emmett studied architecture in college. The urge to write still simmered within him, however; as he recalled to *SATA,* "It was while I was at college that I first started developing my skills as a writer and illustrator." Joining a few friends and attempting to start a band, he started writing song lyrics. "Then one day, I decided to try and do an illustration to accompany the lyrics to one of the songs. I was pleased with the result, so I illustrated some of my poems, spending more and more time on each picture."

Meanwhile, earning his architecture degree in 1988, Emmett joined an architecture firm and worked on projects that included an art gallery, a theater, and an airport check-in building. Losing this job, he finally gave himself the permission to reach for his dream. "My first three children's books (a chapter fiction, a novel and a pop-up book) got nowhere," he explained on his home page, "but they whetted my appetite for creating children's books and my fourth book was accepted by a publisher in 1996." Since then, Emmett has published picture books, mostly illustrated by other artists, as well as pop-up books and early chapter books geared to children aged seven to nine.

Although paper engineering is now taught in technical schools in Great Britain, at the time Emmett entered the pop-up-book field, he had to teach himself the rudiments. "I learnt all of my paper engineering by trial and error and by studying mechanisms from existing books and adapting them," he explained. To help others, Emmett provides tips and refers future paper engineers to some useful handbooks via his home page. He also answers the perennial question: Where do you get your ideas? "Anywhere and everywhere—books, television, cinema, real life. Working on one book will often throw out an idea for another. I jot the new idea down and come back to it later. Sometimes I can't get an idea to work well as a story the first time I look at it, but if I put it to one side and come back to it a few months (or even a few years) later, I'm often able to finish it off."

Among Emmett's many books for children are the "Conjuror's Cookbook" series of early chapter books, featuring such delectable titles as *Goblin Stew* and *Serpent Soup*. Other works include the pop-up books *Ten Little Monsters: A Counting Book* and *Safari Shapes*, and picture books such as *Dinosaurs after Dark*, *Bringing down the Moon*, *Pigs Might Fly: The Further Adventures of the Three Little Pigs*, and *I Love You Always and Forever*. In a slight change of pace, his retelling of an American folk song in *She'll Be Coming 'round the Mountain*, with its high-energy, fold-out artwork by Deborah Allwright, presents storytime audiences with an "uproarious" read in which Emmett "encourages kids to participate in joyful, silly actions," according to *Booklist* critic Hazel Rochman.

Bringing down the Moon, about a mole who tries to touch the moon and fears he has broken it, was highly praised for its artwork by Vanessa Cabban, as well as its ambiance and "unadorned gentle prose," to quote a *Publishers Weekly* writer. According to *School Library Journal* contributor Anne Knickerbocker, Emmett's use of onomatopoeia adds to the book's read-aloud appeal. In *Booklist* Connie Fletcher dubbed *Bringing down the Moon* "comical" and "thought-provoking," while a *Kirkus Reviews* writer described the author's simple story as a "sweet lesson in not getting what you want."

Cabban and Emmett team up again for *No Place like Home*, in which Mole asks each of his animal friends to help him find the perfect cozy new burrow, and *Diamond in the Snow*, where Mole experiences his first winter. "Children will love" the book's "cozy characters," predicted Kelley Rae Unger in her review of *No Place like Home* for *School Library Journal*. Noting that Cabban's "cartoonlike animals portray the playfulness and rambunctiousness" typical of toddlers, Jessica Lamarre concluded in the same periodical that in *Diamond in the Snow* Emmett successfully "capture[s] the magic and curiosity" of young children.

I Love You Always and Forever features artwork by Daniel Howarth and is classic Emmett in its gentle story about father and daughter fieldmice. After a day spent playing in a sunny field, the father, Longtail, reassures his young offspring, Littletail, that, although many things may change, his love will always remain strong. Praising Howarth's realistic illustrations, Linda Staskus described Emmett's story as "a simple, heartwarming tale of companionship and a parent's unconditional love," while a *Kirkus Reviews* writer called the book "one of those standouts where text and illustrations are in perfect unison." A flock of ducklings are the focus of another family-centered story in *Ruby in Her Own Time*, one of several collaborations with artist Rebecca Harry that *Booklist* contributor Stephanie Zvirin dubbed "a winning read."

Brought to life in illustrations by Elena Gomez, *Through the Heart of the Jungle* features Emmett's cumulative rhyme about a buzzing fly that is gobbled up by a spider, which in turn is swallowed by a frog, and so in before the food chain is finally broken by the arrival of a large lion. Readers can follow a trip of a different but equally exotic nature in *Dinosaurs after Dark*. Describing the latter book, in which Emmett takes readers along on a midnight jaunt down a dinosaur-filled street, Carol L. MacKay wrote in *School Library Journal* that the picture book should hold a special fascination for little boys. "Dino stories have huge appeal," the critic noted, "and Emmett's offering is no exception."

On his inventive home page, which the author has named "Scribble Street," Emmett gives would-be writers and illustrators some friendly advice: 1. "Get stuck in!" (meaning get going and "don't be disappointed if the first things you write are not as impressive as you'd hoped"); 2. "Think ahead!" (meaning make an outline); 3. "Always use the POINTY end of the pencil! You'll find it's much easier to write with."

Biographical and Critical Sources

PERIODICALS

Booklist, February 1, 2002, Connie Fletcher, review of *Bringing down the Moon*, p. 946; February 15, 2004, Stephanie Zvirin, review of *Ruby in Her Own Time*, p. 1062; March 1, 2004, Lauren Peterson, review of *Someone Bigger*, p. 1193; December 15, 2006,

Stephanie Zvirin, review of *This Way, Ruby!*, p. 51; April 1, 2007, Hazel Rochman, review of *She'll Be Coming 'round the Mountain*, p. 54.

Bulletin of the Center for Children's Books, July-August, 2007, Hope Morrison, review of *She'll Be Coming 'round the Mountain*, p. 464.

Kirkus Reviews, September 15, 2001, review of *Bringing down the Moon*, p. 1357; January 1, 2002, review of *Dinosaurs after Dark*, p. 45; January 1, 2004, review of *Ruby in Her Own Time*, p. 36; February 15, 2004, review of *Someone Bigger*, p. 176; March 1, 2005, review of *No Place like Home*, p. 285; January 1, 2006, review of *What Friends Do Best*, p. 40; December 1, 2006, review of *I Love You Always and Forever*, p. 1219; April 1, 2007, review of *She'll Be Coming 'round the Mountain*.

Publishers Weekly, November 5, 2001, review of *Bringing down the Moon*, p. 66; December 24, 2001, review of *Dinosaurs after Dark*, p. 62; March 24, 2003, review of *Through the Heart of the Jungle*, p. 74; February 23, 2004, review of *Someone Bigger*, p. 74.

School Library Journal, January, 2002, Anne Knickerbocker, review of *Bringing down the Moon*, p. 98; June, 2002, Carol L. MacKay, review of *Dinosaurs after Dark*, pp. 92-93; September, 2003, Wanda Meyers-Hines, review of *Through the Heart of the Jungle*, p. 177; March, 2004, Sawn Brommer, review of *Ruby in Her Own Time*, p. 156; May, 2004, G. Alyssa Parkinson, review of *Someone Bigger*, p. 109; March, 2005, Kelley Rae Unger, review of *No Place like Home*, p. 170; February, 2007, Susan E. Murray, review of *This Way, Ruby!*, p. 86; March, 2007, Mary Jean Smith, review of *She'll Be Coming 'round the Mountain*, p. 160; April, 2007, Jessica Lamarre, review of *Diamond in the Snow,* and Linda Staskus, review of *I Love You Always and Forever*, both p. 98.

ONLINE

Jonathan Emmett Home Page, http://scribblestreet.co.uk (March 10, 2008).

F

FIELDS, Bryan W. 1958(?)-

Personal

Born c. 1958, in MO; married; wife's name Lesli; children: five.

Addresses

Home and office—Denton, TX.

Career

Author. Worked previously as a copy writer, customer-service representative, business manager, janitor, music teacher, and professional musician.

Member

Oklahoma Writers Federation, Lonestar Nightwriters.

Awards, Honors

Best Juvenile Book designation, Oklahoma Writers Federation, 2006, for *Lunchbox and the Aliens.*

Writings

Lunchbox and the Aliens, illustrated by Kevan J. Atteberry, Henry Holt (New York, NY), 2006.
Froonga Planet, illustrated by Kevan J. Atteberry, Henry Holt (New York, NY), 2008.

Contributor to periodicals, including *Denton Record-Chronicle, Absolutewrite.com, Writers Weekly, Writing for Dollars, Imperfect Parent,* and *Byline.*

Sidelights

Bryan W. Fields has dabbled in many different careers, including that of music teacher, copy writer, business manager, and professional musician. He has also lived in many different places, including Japan, New Mexico, Missouri, Colorado, Florida, Arizona, and Mississippi. Now based in Denton, Texas, Fields has also settled into a career as a freelance writer and author, and his first published children's book, *Lunchbox and the Aliens,* was published in 2006.

Labeled a "zany tale" by a *Children's Bookwatch* reviewer, Fields' eccentric story centers on a pup named Lunchbox who is abducted by two otherworldly beings. Frazz and Grunfloz are on a mission to find the food they need to survive. When the aliens discover that the garbage of Earthlings meets their dietary needs, they employ Lunchbox as their garbage scout. The dog is fitted with a special helmet which enhances his mental capabilities, and soon Lunchbox's owner, a boy named Nate, is also assisting in the garbage-scouting process. Their efforts yield a surprising result: as Nate and Lunchbox feed the aliens, they also help clean up the Earth. However, Fields also presents them with a few obstacles, including an antagonistic town mayor and some local bullies. In *School Library Journal,* Cynde Suite noted that *Lunchbox and the Aliens* includes a "fast-moving plot and satisfying conclusion" and added that the book is a prime selection for "any child who enjoys a good book about a boy and his dog."

Biographical and Critical Sources

PERIODICALS

School Library Journal, October, 2006, Cynde Suite, review of *Lunchbox and the Aliens,* p. 110.

ONLINE

Bryan W. Fields Home Page, http://www.bryanwfields. com (March 3, 2008).
Children's Bookwatch Web site, http://www.midwestbook review.com/ (November, 2006), review of *Lunchbox and the Aliens.**

FLEISCHNER, Jennifer 1956-

Personal

Born January 16, 1956, in New York, NY; daughter of Irwin (a high school principal) and Ruth Mintz Goodman Holman (co-director of a children's summer camp) Fleischner. *Education:* Williams College, B.A. (cum laude), 1977; Columbia University, M.A. (with highest honors), 1980, M.Phil. (with distinction), 1983, Ph.D., 1988; Columbia University Center for Psychoanalytic Training and Research, postdoctoral study, 1992-94; attended Training Institute of the National Psychological Association for Psychoanalysis, 1990-92.

Addresses

Home—New York, NY. *Office*—Department of English, Humanities Building, State University of New York at Albany, Albany, NY 12222. *E-mail*—jf007@ntr.net; fleischner@adelphi.edu.

Career

Educator and writer. Dover Publications, New York, NY, publicity director, 1977-78; State University of New York at Albany, lecturer, 1986-88, assistant professor, 1988-96, associate professor of English, 1996-2002, director of undergraduate studies, 1996-2000, director of honors program, 1997-99; Adelphi University, Garden City, NY, professor of English and chair of department, beginning 2002. Affiliated faculty member in women's studies, 1988—, Diversity Lecturer, 1995. College of Mount St. Vincent, visiting assistant professor, 1989-90; Hartwick College, Babcock Lecturer, 1992; Harvard University, Andrew W. Mellon faculty fellow in Afro-American studies, 1993-94; Columbia University, visiting scholar in English, 1994-95. Macmillan Publishing Co., Inc., managing editor of "Reading Theme" book series, 1993. Manhattan Reading Club, founder and director of book groups, 1992-93.

Awards, Honors

Faculty research awards, State University of New York at Albany, 1987, 1990, 1992, 1996; Andrew W. Mellon faculty fellowship, Harvard University, 1993-94; Nuala McGann Drescher Award, United University Professors, 1994-95.

Writings

FOR YOUNG READERS

The Apaches: People of the Southwest, Millbrook Press (Brookfield, CT), 1994.
The Inuit: People of the Arctic, Millbrook Press (Brookfield, CT), 1995.
The Dred Scott Case: Testing the Right to Live Free, Millbrook Press (Brookfield, CT), 1996.

"I Was Born a Slave": The Life of Harriet Jacobs as Told in Her Own Words, illustrated by Melanie K. Reim, Millbrook Press (Brookfield, CT), 1997.
Nobody's Boy, University of Missouri Press (St. Louis, MO), 2006.

Contributing editor to books, including *The American Experience,* Prentice-Hall (Englewood Cliffs, NJ), 1990; and *Scholastic Encyclopedia of American Presidents,* Agincourt (New York, NY), 1994.

FOR ADULTS

(Editor with Susan Ostrov Weisser, and contributor) *Feminist Nightmares: Women at Odds, Feminism and the Problem of Sisterhood,* New York University Press (New York, NY), 1994.
Book Group Guide to the Work of Barbara Kingsolver, HarperCollins (New York, NY), 1994.
Book Group Guide to the Work of Louise Erdrich, HarperCollins (New York, NY), 1995.
Book Group Guide to the Work of Doris Lessing, HarperCollins (New York, NY), 1995.
Mastering Slavery: Memory, Family, and Identity in Women's Slave Narratives, New York University Press (New York, NY), 1996.
Mrs. Lincoln and Mrs. Keckly: The Remarkable Story of the Friendship between a First Lady and a Former Slave, Broadway Books (New York, NY), 2003.

Contributor to books, including *Recasting Intellectual History: African American Cultural Studies,* edited by Walter Jackson, Oxford University Press, 1996. Contributor of articles and reviews to magazines, including *American Imago, American Literature, Journal of the History of Sexuality, Studies in the Novel, Nineteenth-Century Literature,* and *Scottish Literary Journal.*

Sidelights

Jennifer Fleischner is an educator, writer, and historian whose books for children and adults focus on the role of African Americans during the nineteenth century. In *"I Was Born a Slave": The Life of Harriet Jacobs as Told in Her Own Words,* for example, Fleischner retells a well-known slave narrative by focusing on the woman who fled mistreatment at the hands of her master and spent several years as a fugitive slave before achieving freedom.

In *Mrs. Lincoln and Mrs. Keckly: The Remarkable Story of the Friendship between a First Lady and a Former Slave,* Fleischner explores the provocative intersection between two lives: that of First Lady Mary Todd Lincoln and a Washington, DC, dressmaker named Elizabeth Keckly. Dubbing the book "an essential read" in *Library Journal,* Randall M. Miller wrote that the work's "beauty comes from Fleischner's exquisite control of the narrative as she writes a dual biography of two women" and demonstrates an understanding of both "the people and the age." Played out amid the U.S.

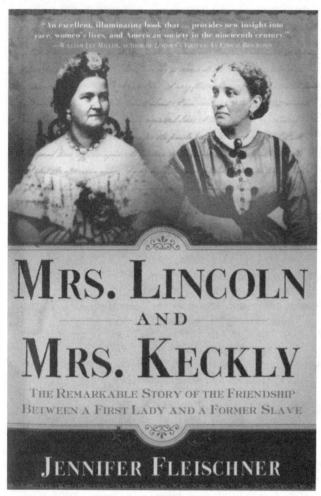

Cover of Jennifer Fleischner's Civil War-era biography Mrs. Lincoln and Mrs. Keckley, *which focuses on the strong friendship between two unique women.* (Photographs courtesy of the Granger Collection (Mary Todd Lincoln) and The Lincoln Museum (Beth Keckly). Used by permission of Broadway Books, a division of Random House, Inc.)

Civil War, *Mrs. Lincoln and Mrs. Keckly* offers readers a "glimpse into a friendship that defied convention . . . during an age when social associations between the races were feared," according to *Booklist* contributor Margaret Flanagan. Fleischner's "almost conversational writing style will keep readers engrossed," concluded Peggy Bercher in *School Library Journal.*

Turning to fiction, *Nobody's Boy* again draws on the life of dressmaker Keckly, this time by telling the story of George Kirkland, Keckly's real-life son. In this middle-grade novel, George is the property of an attorney working on the *Dred Scott* case. He lives in St. Louis, Missouri, with his hard-working dressmaker mother. After Mrs. Keckly purchases her family's freedom, the light-skinned George helps a darker friend escape and ultimately makes it to the free state of Illinois. When the Civil War breaks out, George has become a student at Wilberforce University. He leaves school to join the First Missouri Volunteers, a decision that is both noble and ultimately tragic. "Skillfully and sensitively written," *Nobody's Boy* tells a story that "should appeal to all younger teens," predicted *Kliatt* reviewer Patricia Moore.

Fleischner once told *SATA:* "As a child I was a passionate reader. I loved books, and some of my fondest memories are of sitting somewhere private and alone, reading a book. There were four children in my family, and it seemed like you could never be alone. Reading a book was like having a secret life that no one could touch. Now when I think about being a writer, I can hardly believe it. It's what I always wanted to do."

Biographical and Critical Sources

PERIODICALS

Black Issues Book Review, July-August, 2003, Angela P. Dodson, review of *Mrs. Lincoln and Mrs. Keckly: The Remarkable Story of the Friendship between a First Lady and a Former Slave,* p. 59.
Booklist, December 15, 1994, p. 94; September 15, 1997, GraceAnne A. DeCandido, review of *"I Was Born a Slave": The Life of Harriet Jacobs as Told in Her Own Words,* p. 225; March 1, 2003, Margaret Flanagan, review of *Mrs. Lincoln and Mrs. Keckly,* p. 1139; February 1, 2007, Hazel Rochman, review of *Nobody's Boy,* p. 57.
Bulletin of the Center for Children's Books, December, 1997, review of *"I Was Born a Slave,"* p. 124.
Kirkus Reviews, February 1, 2003, review of *Mrs. Lincoln and Mrs. Keckly,* p. 203; December 1, 2006, review of *Nobody's Boy,* p. 1219.
Kliatt, July, 2007, Patricia Moore, review of *Nobody's Boy,* p. 24.
Library Journal, February 15, 2002, Randall M. Miller, review of *Mrs. Lincoln and Mrs. Keckly,* p. 149.
Publishers Weekly, January 20, 2003, review of *Mrs. Lincoln and Mrs. Keckly,* p. 64.
School Library Journal, January, 1998, Debbie Feulner, review of *"I Was Born a Slave,"* p. 123; December, 2003, Peggy Bercher, review of *Mrs. Lincoln and Mrs. Keckly,* p. 177.
Voice of Youth Advocates, August, 1998, review of *"I Was Born a Slave,"* p. 177.
Washington Post Book World, January 28, 2007, Elizabeth Ward, review of *Nobody's Boy,* p. 12.
Washington Times, May 25, 2003, Erin Mendell, "Was Former Slave Her True Friend?," p. B7.

ONLINE

Adelphi University Web site, http://www.adelphi.edu/ (March 15, 2008), "Jennifer Fleischner."
University of Missouri Press Web site, http://press.umsystem.edu/ (March 15, 2008), "Jennifer Fleischner."*

*   *   *

FOX, Christyan

Personal

Born in England; married; wife's name Diane (an author).

Addresses

Home—Thames Ditton, Surrey, England. *E-mail*—christyan@christyanfox.co.uk.

Career

Illustrator.

Awards, Honors

Southampton Favourite Book to Share Award, 2006, for *Zoom!* by Jonathan Emmett.

Illustrator

Rebecca Treays, *Understanding Your Body,* Usborne (London, England), 1995.

Harriet Castor, *Milly of the Rovers,* Viking (London, England), 1996.

Rebecca Treays, *Understanding Your Senses,* Usborne (London, England), 1997.

Rebecca Treays, *Understanding Your Muscles and Bones,* Usborne (London, England), 1997, Scholastic (New York, NY), 2004.

Katherine Starke, *Cats and Kittens,* photographs by Jane Burton, Usborne (London, England), 1998, Scholastic (New York, NY), 2004.

Harriet Castor, *Milly's Golden Goal,* Viking (London, England), 1998.

Lesley Sims, *A Visitor's Guide to Ancient Rome,* Usborne (London, England), 1999.

Susan Meredith, *Hamsters,* Usborne (London, England), 1999, Scholastic (New York, NY), 2004.

Mark Wallace and Philippa Wingate, *The Usborne Guide to E-Mail,* Usborne (London, England), 2000.

(With Jacqui Thomas) David Ross and Harriet Castor, *The Big Book of Football Stories,* Viking (London, England), 2000.

Helen Paiba, compiler, *Funny Stories for Five Years Olds,* Macmillan Children's Books (London, England), 2000.

Diane Fox, *Goodnight, PiggyWiggy,* Handprint Books (Brooklyn, NY), 2000.

Diane Fox, *Count to Ten, PiggyWiggy!,* Handprint Books (Brooklyn, NY), 2001.

Diane Fox, *Cat and Mouse: The Hole Story,* Handprint Books (Brooklyn, NY), 2001.

Diane Fox, *Fire Fighter PiggyWiggy,* Handprint Books (Brooklyn, NY), 2001, published as *Fireman Piggy-Wiggy,* Little Tiger (London, England), 2001.

Diane Fox, *Bathtime PiggyWiggy,* Handprint Books (Brooklyn, NY), 2001.

Diane Fox, *What Color Is That, PiggyWiggy?,* Handprint Books (Brooklyn, NY), 2001.

Katie Daynes, *Trucks,* Usborne (London, England), 2002, new edition, 2007.

Diane Fox, *Around the World PiggyWiggy,* Handprint Books (New York, NY), 2002.

Diane Fox, *What Shape Is That, PiggyWiggy?,* Handprint Books (New York, NY), 2002.

Diane Fox, *Astronaut PiggyWiggy,* Handprint Books (New York, NY), 2002, published as *Spaceman PiggyWiggy,* Little Tiger (London, England), 2002.

Diane Fox, *What's the Opposite, PiggyWiggy?,* Handprint Books (New York, NY), 2002.

Russell Punter, *Stories of Pirates,* Usborne (London, England), 2003.

Sue Nicholson, *Traffic Jamboree,* Campbell (London, England), 2003.

Diane Fox, *Pirate PiggyWiggy,* Handprint Books (New York, NY), 2003.

Katherine Starke, *Dogs and Puppies,* Scholastic (New York, NY), 2004.

Katie Daynes, *Firefighters,* Usborne (London, England), 2004, Scholastic (New York, NY), 2006.

Diane Fox, *Jungle Street Hide-and-Seek,* Campbell (London, England), 2005.

Bill Gillham, *How Many Sharks in the Bath?,* Frances Lincoln (London, England), 2005.

Laura Howell, *Gerbils,* Usborne (London, England), 2005.

(With Patrizia Donaera) Laura Howell, *Guinea Pigs,* Usborne (London, England), 2005.

Diane Fox, *Tyson the Terrible,* Bloomsbury Children's Books (New York, NY), 2006.

Jonathan Emmett, *Zoom!,* Macmillan Children's (London, England), 2006.

Anna Milbourne, *Cats,* Usborne (London, England), 2007.

Biographical and Critical Sources

PERIODICALS

Booklist, April 1, 2001, Shelley Townsend-Hudson, reviews of *What Color Is That, PiggyWiggy?* and *Count to Ten, PiggyWiggy!,* p. 1478; May 1, 2001, Ilene Cooper, review of *Fire Fighter PiggyWiggy,* p. 1689; February 1, 2002, Stephanie Zvirin, review of *Bathtime PiggyWiggy,* p. 946.

Bulletin of the Center for Children's Books, June, 2002, review of *What's the Opposite, PiggyWiggy?,* p. 364.

Kirkus Reviews, October 15, 2001, review of *Bathtime, PiggyWiggy,* p. 1483; December 1, 2006, review of *Tyson the Terrible,* p. 1219.

School Library Journal, December, 2000, JoAnn Jonas, review of *Goodnight PiggyWiggy,* p. 108; May, 2001, Linda M. Kenton, review of *Fire Fighter PiggyWiggy,* p. 115; August, 2001, Sally Bates Goodroe, reviews of *What Color Is That, PiggyWiggy?* and *Count to Ten, PiggyWiggy!,* p. 146; December, 2001, Melinda Piehler, review of *Cat and Mouse: The Hole Story,* p. 100; January, 2002, Melinda Piehler, review of *Bathtime PiggyWiggy,* p. 98; June, 2002, Lisa Smith, review of *What Shape Is That, PiggyWiggy?,* p. 94; July, 2002, Linda Ludke, review of *Astronaut Piggy-Wiggy,* p. 90; June, 2003, Melinda Piehler, review of *Pirate PiggyWiggy,* p. 99; January, 2006, Linda Zeilstra Sawyer, review of *How Many Sharks in the Bath?,* p. 97; February, 2007, Lynne Mattern, review of *Tyson the Terrible,* p. 86.*

*   *   *

FOX, Diane

Personal

Born in England; married Christyan Fox (an illustrator).

Addresses

Home—Thames Ditton, Surrey, England.

Career

Children's book author.

Writings

Goodnight, PiggyWiggy, illustrated by Christyan Fox, Handprint Books (Brooklyn, NY), 2000.

Count to Ten, PiggyWiggy!, illustrated by Christyan Fox, Handprint Books (Brooklyn, NY), 2001.

Cat and Mouse: The Hole Story, illustrated by Christyan Fox, Handprint Books (Brooklyn, NY), 2001.

Fire Fighter PiggyWiggy, illustrated by Christyan Fox, Handprint Books (Brooklyn, NY), 2001, published as *Fireman PiggyWiggy,* Little Tiger (London, England), 2001.

Bathtime PiggyWiggy, illustrated by Christyan Fox, Handprint Books (Brooklyn, NY), 2001.

What Color Is That, PiggyWiggy?, illustrated by Christyan Fox, Handprint Books (Brooklyn, NY), 2001.

Around the World PiggyWiggy, illustrated by Christyan Fox, Handprint Books (New York, NY), 2002.

What Shape Is That, PiggyWiggy?, illustrated by Christyan Fox, Handprint Books (New York, NY), 2002.

Astronaut PiggyWiggy, illustrated by Christyan Fox, Handprint Books (New York, NY), 2002, published as *Spaceman PiggyWiggy,* Little Tiger (London, England), 2002.

What's the Opposite, PiggyWiggy?, illustrated by Christyan Fox, Handprint Books (New York, NY), 2002.

Pirate PiggyWiggy, illustrated by Christyan Fox, Handprint Books (New York, NY), 2003.

Jungle Street Hide-and-Seek, illustrated by Christyan Fox, Campbell (London, England), 2005.

Tyson the Terrible, illustrated by Christyan Fox, Bloomsbury Children's Books (New York, NY), 2006.

Sidelights

Husband-and-wife team Diane and Christyan Fox are the talents behind numerous picture books for children, among them the popular interactive "PiggyWiggy" series. Readers meet the Foxes' engaging porker in books such *Goodnight, PiggyWiggy, Bathtime PiggyWiggy,* and *What Shape Is That, PiggyWiggy?,* all which feature lift-the-flap elements that bring to life a simple concept via Christyan Fox's cartoon art. It is time for bed as PiggyWiggy imagines growing up to become everything from a fireman to a pirate in *Goodnight PiggyWiggy,* while *Bathtime PiggyWiggy* finds the pig taking another imaginative voyage while watching his toy boat in the tub. A globe transports the imaginative character in *Around the World PiggyWiggy,* where the career possibilities span both time and geography: from a Roman gladiator to a climber tackling Mount Everest. Simple concepts are the focus of *What's the Opposite, Piggy-Wiggy?, What Shape Is That, PiggyWiggy?,* and *What*

Christyan Fox illustrates the stories he and wife Diane Fox write for younger readers, producing books such as Tyson the Terrible.

Color Is That, PiggyWiggy?, all of which feature both PiggyWiggy and his beloved teddy bear. Citing Diane Fox's use of "relatively challenging vocabulary," a *Kirkus Reviews* contributor praised *Bathtime Piggy-Wiggy* for its "simple, crayon-drawn forms, and saturated colors." "There's a sense of joyous abandon as PiggyWiggy lives out his dreams," Stephanie Zvirin observed of the same title in *Booklist,* while Sally Bates Goodroe concluded in *School Library Journal* that *Count to Ten, PiggyWiggy!* is "clever and fun for the toddler crowd."

In addition to their "PiggyWiggy" books, the Foxes have also created several stand-alone picture books. In *Tyson the Terrible* a trio of young dinosaurs is fearful at the crashing sounds of an approaching Tyrannosaurus until they meet up with the lumbering creature and realize that Tyson is actually lonely. Citing the book's "kid-friendly format, cheerful colors, and laugh-aloud ending," *School Library Journal* critic Lynne Mattern praised *Tyson the Terrible* as "a definite crowd pleaser," while a *Kirkus Reviews* writer dubbed it "a bouncy little tale with a winning finale." Another stand-alone board-covered book by Fox and Fox, *Cat and Mouse: The Hole Story,* mixes die-cut pages with a humorous tale of a mouse escaping from a chubby kitty, serving up "an entertaining choice" for the story-hour set, according to *School Library Journal* contributor Melinda Piehler.

Biographical and Critical Sources

PERIODICALS

Booklist, April 1, 2001, Shelley Townsend-Hudson, reviews of *What Color Is That, PiggyWiggy?* and *Count to Ten, PiggyWiggy!,* p. 1478; May 1, 2001, Ilene Cooper, review of *Fire Fighter PiggyWiggy,* p. 1689; February 1, 2002, Stephanie Zvirin, review of *Bathtime PiggyWiggy,* p. 946.
Bulletin of the Center for Children's Books, June, 2002, review of *What's the Opposite, PiggyWiggy?,* p. 364.
Kirkus Reviews, October 15, 2001, review of *Bathtime, PiggyWiggy,* p. 1483; December 1, 2006, review of *Tyson the Terrible,* p. 1219.
School Library Journal, December, 2000, JoAnn Jonas, review of *Goodnight PiggyWiggy,* p. 108; May, 2001, Linda M. Kenton, review of *Fire Fighter PiggyWiggy,* p. 115; August, 2001, Sally Bates Goodroe, reviews of *What Color Is That, PiggyWiggy?* and *Count to Ten, PiggyWiggy!,* p. 146; December, 2001, Melinda Piehler, review of *Cat and Mouse: The Hole Story,* p. 100; January, 2002, Melinda Piehler, review of *Bathtime PiggyWiggy,* p. 98; June, 2002, Lisa Smith, review of *What Shape Is That, PiggyWiggy?,* p. 94; July, 2002, Linda Ludke, review of *Astronaut Piggy-Wiggy,* p. 90; June, 2003, Melinda Piehler, review of *Pirate PiggyWiggy,* p. 99; February, 2007, Lynne Mattern, review of *Tyson the Terrible,* p. 86.*

*   *   *

FRANCO, Betsy 1947-

Personal

Born 1947; married; husband's name Douglas; children: James, Thomas, David. *Education:* Stanford University, B.A.; Lesley College, M.Ed.

Addresses

Office—P.O. Box 60487, Palo Alto, CA 94306. *E-mail*—francobe@aol.com.

Career

Writer and editor for children and adults; creator of educational materials.

Member

Authors Guild, Authors League.

Writings

Japan, illustrated by Jo Supancich, Evan-Moor, 1993.
Mexico, illustrated by Jo Supancich, Evan-Moor, 1993.
Russia, illustrated by Jo Supancich, Evan-Moor, 1993.
India, illustrated by Jo Supancich, Evan-Moor, 1994.
Nigeria, illustrated by Jo Supancich, Evan-Moor, 1994.
China, illustrated by Jo Supancich, Evan-Moor, 1994.
Brazil, illustrated by Cheryl Kirk Noll, Evan-Moor, 1995.
South Korea, illustrated by Cheryl Kirk Noll, Evan-Moor, 1995.
Italy, illustrated by Susan O'Neill, Evan-Moor, 1995.
Quiet Elegance: Japan through the Eyes of Nine American Artists, Charles E. Tuttle (Boston, MA), 1997.
Sorting All Sorts of Socks, illustrated by Sheila Lucas, Creative Publications (Mountain View, CA), 1997.
Fourscore and Seven, Good Year Books (Glenview, IL), 1999.
Grandpa's Quilt, illustrated by Linda A. Bild, Children's Press (New York, NY), 1999.
Write and Read Math Story Books, Scholastic (New York, NY), 1999.
Unfolding Mathematics with Unit Origami, Key Curriculum, 1999.
Shells, illustrated by Kristin Sorra, Children's Press (New York, NY), 2000.
Why the Frog Has Big Eyes, illustrated by Joung Un Kim, Harcourt, Brace (San Diego, CA), 2000.
Caring, Sharing, and Getting Along, Scholastic (New York, NY), 2000.
Thematic Poetry: On the Farm, Scholastic (New York, NY), 2000.
Twenty Marvelous Math Tales, Scholastic (New York, NY), 2000.
Thematic Poetry: Neighborhoods and Communities, Scholastic (New York, NY), 2000.
Thematic Poetry: Creepy Crawlies, Scholastic (New York, NY), 2000.
201 Thematic Riddle Poems to Build Literacy, Scholastic (New York, NY), 2000.
Thematic Poetry: All about Me!, Scholastic (New York, NY), 2000.
The Tortoise Who Bragged: A Chinese Tale with Trigrams, illustrated by Ann-Marie Perks, Stokes Publishing (Sunnyvale, CA), 2000.
My Pinkie Finger, illustrated by Margeaux Lucas, Children's Press (New York, NY), 2001.
Instant Poetry Frames for Primary Poets, Scholastic (New York, NY), 2001.
Fifteen Wonderful Writing Prompt Mini-Books, Scholastic (New York, NY), 2001.
Clever Calculator Cat, illustrated by Ann-Marie Perks, Stokes Publishing (Sunnyvale, CA), 2001.
Funny Fairy Tale Math, Scholastic (New York, NY), 2001.
Thematic Poetry: Transportation, Scholastic (New York, NY), 2001.
Clever Calculations about Cats and Other Cool Creatures (teacher resource book), Stokes Publishing (Sunnyvale, CA), 2001.
Adding Alligators and Other Easy-to-Read Math Stories, Scholastic (New York, NY), 2001.
Five-Minute Math Problem of the Day for Young Learners, Scholastic (New York, NY), 2001.
Twelve Genre Mini-Books, Scholastic (New York, NY), 2002.
Instant Math Practice Pages for Homework—or Anytime!, Scholastic (New York, NY), 2002.
Six Silly Seals, and Other Read-Aloud Story Skits, Teaching Resources, 2002.

Amazing Animals, illustrated by Jesse Reisch, Children's Press (New York, NY), 2002.

Pocket Poetry Mini-Books, Scholastic (New York, NY), 2002.

Silly Sally, illustrated by Stacey Lamb, Children's Press (New York, NY), 2002.

Jake's Cake Mistake, illustrated by Paul Harvey, Scholastic (New York, NY), 2002.

(With Claudine Jellison and Johanna Kaufman) *Subtraction Fun,* Pebble Books, 2002.

(With Denise Dauler) *Math in Motion: Wiggle, Gallop, and Leap with Numbers,* Creative Teaching Press, 2002.

Many Ways to 100, Yellow Umbrella Books (Mankato, MN), 2002.

A Bat Named Pat, illustrated by Bari Weissman, Scholastic (New York, NY), 2002.

Time to Estimate, Yellow Umbrella Books (Mankato, MN), 2002.

Marvelous Math Word Problem Mini-Books, Scholastic (New York, NY), 2002.

What's Zero?, Yellow Umbrella Books (Mankato, MN), 2002.

Going to Grandma's Farm, illustrated by Claudia Rueda, Children's Press (New York, NY), 2003.

Word Families: Guess-Me Poems and Puzzles, Scholastic (New York, NY), 2003.

Mathematickles!, illustrated by Steven Salerno, Margaret K. McElderry Books (New York, NY), 2003.

Amoeba Hop, illustrated by Christine Lavin, Puddle Jump Press, 2003.

Alphabet: Guess-Me Poems and Puzzles, Scholastic (New York, NY), 2003.

Counting Our Way to the 100th Day!: 100 Poems and 100 Pictures to Celebrate the 100th Day of School, illustrated by Steven Salerno, Margaret K. McElderry Books (New York, NY), 2004.

Conversations with a Poet: Inviting Poetry into K-12 Classrooms, Richard C. Owen (Katonah, NY), 2005.

Birdsongs: A Backwards Counting Book, illustrated by Steve Jenkins, Margaret K. McElderry (New York, NY), 2006.

Math Poetry: Linking Language and Math in a Fresh Way, Good Year Books (Tucson, AZ), 2006.

Summer Beat, illustrated by Charlotte Middleton, Margaret K. McElderry Books (New York, NY), 2007.

Bees, Snails, and Peacock Tails: Shapes—Naturally, illustrated by Steve Jenkins, Margaret K. McElderry Books (New York, NY), 2008.

Author of numerous workbooks, easy-level readers, easy mathematics resource books, and science resource books.

EDITOR

You Hear Me?: Poems and Writing by Teenage Boys, Candlewick Press (Cambridge, MA), 2000.

Things I Have to Tell You: Poems and Writing by Teenage Girls, photographs by Nina Nickles, Candlewick Press (Cambridge, MA), 2001.

(With Annette Ochoa and Traci Gourdine) *Night Is Gone, Day Is Still Coming: Stories and Poems by American Indian Teenagers and Young Adults,* Candlewick Press (Cambridge, MA), 2003.

Falling Hard: Teenagers in Love, Candlewick Press (Cambridge, MA), 2008.

Sidelights

Betsy Franco's many projects for children range widely across the educational and entertainment spectrums, from easy-level readers and books that use games and projects to teach basic skills to picture books to edited anthologies of poetry by teens. The poetry she collects in *You Hear Me?: Poems and Writing by Teenage Boys, Things I Have to Tell You: Poems and Writing by Teenage Girls, Night Is Gone, Day Is Still Coming: Stories and Poems by American Indian Teenagers and Young Adults,* and *Falling Hard: Teenagers in Love* reveal the authentic voices of contemporary Americans wrestling with typical issues, feelings, and challenges and share with readers what it feels like to come of age in a challenging and uncertain time.

Although she has gained prominence as an author, Franco initially studied to be a fine artist, and she still loves to paint. When her children were born, however, she realized that she could not spare the time needed for her visual art, so she channeled her creativity into writing. In her books for younger children, one of her first—and favorite—challenges was finding ways to make learning math fun; as she noted on her home page, "I particularly love to show how exciting, sassy, and creative math can be." In books such as *Clever Calculator Cat,* and *Many Ways to 100,* students can sharpen math skills through activities and riddles, while *Marvelous Math Word Problem Mini-Books* takes the challenge factor up a notch. With its lighthearted approach, Franco's *Mathematickles!* incorporates common math signs such as plus, minus, and parentheses in word poems about the seasons and the outdoor world. Noting Steven Salerno's colorful art, a *Publishers Weekly* critic praised *Mathematickles!* as a "nimble brain teaser" that "elevates basic mathematical concepts plus wordplay to the level of inspiration."

Franco and Salerno team up again for *Counting Our Way to the 100th Day!: 100 Poems and 100 Pictures to Celebrate the 100th Day of School.* Ranging from what *Booklist* contributor Gillian Engberg described as "whimsical arithmetic exercises" to "reassuring" verses designed to quell the fears of new students, the book is enhanced by Salerno's "stylish, cheerful gouache paintings." A more popular part of a child's year is the focus of *Summer Beat,* in which Franco uses alliteration and rhyme to chronicle the many activities that fill up summer vacation. Enhanced by Charlotte Middleton's digitally enhanced art, the poet's verses serve up "an energetic tribute to the sensations of summer," according to a *Kirkus Reviews* contributor.

YOU HEAR ME?

poems and writing by teenage boys

edited by Betsy Franco

Cover of the teen poetry anthology You Hear Me?, *edited by Betsy Franco.* (Copyright © 2000 by Candlewick Press. Reproduced by permission of the publisher Candlewick Press, Inc., Cambridge, MA.)

In *Birdsongs,* a picture book featuring cut-paper collages by award-winning artist Steve Jenkins, Franco "spins a nature lesson in lucid language," according to *Booklist* contributor GraceAnne A. DeCandido. "The writing is lyrical and engaging," wrote Teresa Pfeifer in *School Library Journal,* the critic concluding that the "lavishly illustrated" *Birdsongs* "will engender a love for birds and an awareness of their unique music."

Franco's first edited anthology was inspired by her own teenage sons. When she decided to solicit poetry written by young men, some worried that she would not receive enough submissions to fill an entire book. Surprisingly, Franco received more manuscripts than she could use, and in *You Hear Me?* she assembles frank and honest verses on topics of importance to these teen poets, from homosexuality and dating to self-image, family and neighborhood issues, aspirations, and creativity. Sharon Korbeck, reviewing *You Hear Me?* for *School Library Journal,* cited the book's "fresh approach to hearing what today's youths have to say." In

Booklist Hazel Rochman wrote that the poems have "more urgency than many YA novels," and concluded: "Many teens will recognize their search for themselves."

Things I Have to Tell You collects the poetry of teenage girls. A *Horn Book* reviewer wrote of the book that, "varying in tone, style, and degree of polish," the verses collected in *Things I Have to Tell You* "convey moments of strength and weakness, of anger, fear, and joy, commanding our attention from beginning to end."

Voices of both young men and young women are represented in Franco's *Night Is Gone, Day Is Still Coming* and *Falling Hard,* the first a collection of Native-American voices and the second a reflection of the ups and downs of first love. In her *School Library Journal* review of *Night Is Gone, Day Is Still Coming,* Sharon Korbek observed of the book's contributors: "Whether they feel oppressed, cheated, or inspired, these young people write from the depths of their souls."

In an online interview for *Teenreads,* Franco had some advice for aspiring authors. "You have things to say that no one else can say," she commented. "Just don't give up. Half of being a writer is being stubborn and believing in yourself, not so much in a self-esteem way, but knowing you have something to say. . . . In my case, I found I had to write all kinds of different types of books to make a living, from poetry to nonfiction, from adults to young children. Work very hard."

Biographical and Critical Sources

PERIODICALS

Booklist, October 1, 2000, Hazel Rochman, review of *You Hear Me?: Poems and Writing by Teenage Boys,* p. 330; August, 2004, Gillian Engberg, review of *Counting Our Way to the 100th Day!: 100 Poems and 100 Picture to Celebrate the 100th Day of School,* p. 1947; January 1, 2007, GraceAnne A. DeCandido, review of *Birdsongs: A Backwards Counting Book,* p. 114; May 15, 2007, Carolyn Phelan, review of *Summer Beat,* p. 53.

Bulletin of the Center for Children's Books, May, 2007, Deborah Stevenson, review of *Birdsongs,* p. 366; September, 2007, Hope Morrison, review of *Summer Beat,* p. 22.

Horn Book, May, 2001, review of *Things I Have to Tell You: Poems and Writing by Teenage Girls,* p. 343; July-August, 2003, Susan Dove Lempke, review of *Mathematickles!,* p. 472.

Kirkus Reviews, June 1, 2003, Betsy Franco, review of *Mathematickles!,* p. 803; July 1, 2003, review of *Night Is Gone, Day Is Still Coming: Stories and Poems by American Indian Teens and Young Adults,* p. 912; June 15, 2004, review of *Counting Our Way to the 100th Day!,* p. 576; December 1, 2006, review of *Birdsongs,* p. 1220; May 1, 2007, review of *Summer Beat.*

Publishers Weekly, June 16, 2003, review of *Mathematick-les!,* p. 70; December 11, 2006, review of *Birdsongs,* p. 68.

School Library Journal, October, 2000, Sharon Korbeck, review of *You Hear Me?,* p. 183; May, 2001, Sharon Korbeck, review of *Things I Have to Tell You,* p. 164; August, 2003, Sharon Korbeck, review of *Night Is Gone, Day Is Still Coming,* p. 184; July, 2004, Lisa Gangemi Kropp, review of *Counting Our Way to the 100th Day!,* p. 93; September, 2006, Cris Reidel, review of *Conversations with a Poet: Inviting Poetry into K-12 Classrooms,* p. 252; January, 2007, Teresa Pfeifer, review of *Birdsongs,* p. 94; May, 2007, Gloria Koster, review of *Summer Beat,* p. 91.

Voice of Youth Advocates, October, 2001, review of *Things I Have to Tell You,* p. 308.

ONLINE

Betsy Franco Home Page, http://www.betsyfranco.com (March 10, 2008).

Candlewick Press Web site, http://www.candlewick.com/ (December 12, 2003), "Betsy Franco."

Teenreads.com, http://www.teenreads.com/ (December 12, 2003), interview with Franco.*

G

GERSHATOR, Phillis 1942-

Personal

Born July 8, 1942, in New York, NY; daughter of Morton Dimondstein (an artist) and Miriam Green (an artist); married David Gershator (an author) October 19, 1962; children: Yonah, Daniel. *Education:* Attended University of California, Berkeley, 1959-63; Douglass College, B.A., 1966; Pratt Institute, M.L.S., 1975. *Hobbies and other interests:* Reading, gardening, cooking.

Addresses

Home—P.O. Box 303353, St. Thomas, Virgin Islands 00803-3353. *E-mail*—phillis@gershator.com.

Career

St. Thomas Public Library, St. Thomas, Virgin Islands, librarian, 1974-75, 1988-89; Enid M. Baa and Leonard Dober Elementary School libraries, Brooklyn, NY, children's librarian, 1977-84; Department of Education, St. Thomas, children's librarian, 1984-86. Has also worked as a secretary and in library promotion for various New York City publishers. Reading Is Fundamental volunteer in St. Thomas, 1984—; secretary of Friends of the Library, St. Thomas, 1985-95.

Member

Society of Children's Book Writers and Illustrators, American Civil Liberties Union.

Awards, Honors

Cooperative Children's Book Center of the University of Wisconsin choice book, Children's Book of the Year, Bank Street's Child Study Children's Book Committee, American Children's and Young Adult literature Award commended title, Consortium of Latin American Studies Programs, and Blue Ribbon Book, *Bulletin of the Center for Children's Books,* all 1994, all for *Tukama*

Phillis Gershator (Photograph by Joshua Dimondstein reproduced by permission of Phillis Gershator.)

Tootles the Flute; Best Children's Book of the Year designation, Bank Street's Child Study Children's Book Committee, 1994, for *The Iroko-Man,* 2001, for *Only One Cowry,* and 2005, for *The Babysitter Sings;* National Council of Teachers of English Notable Trade Book in the Language Arts, and Best Black History for Young People designation, *Booklist,* both 1995, both for *Rata-pata-scata-fata; Bulletin of the Center for Chil-*

dren's Books Choice designation, 1999, for *When It Starts to Snow;* Anne Izard Storyteller's Choice Award, 2000, for *ZZZng! ZZZng! ZZZng!*

Writings

FOR CHILDREN

Honi and His Magic Circle, Jewish Publications Society of America (Philadelphia, PA), 1979 revised edition published as *Honi's Circle of Trees,* illustrated by Mim Green, 1994.

Rata-pata-scata-fata: A Caribbean Story, illustrated by Holly Meade, Little, Brown (Boston, MA), 1994.

(Reteller) *Tukama Tootles the Flute: A Tale from the Antilles,* illustrated by Synthia St. James, Orchard Books (New York, NY), 1994.

(Reteller) *The Iroko-Man: A Yoruba Folktale,* illustrated by Holly Kim, Orchard Books (New York, NY), 1994.

Sambalena Show-off, illustrated by Leonard Jenkins, Macmillan Books for Young Readers (New York, NY), 1995.

(With husband, David Gershator) *Bread Is for Eating,* illustrated by Emma Shaw-Smith, Holt (New York, NY), 1995.

Sweet, Sweet Fig Banana, illustrated by Fritz Millevoix, Albert Whitman (Morton Grove, IL), 1996.

(With David Gershator) *Palampam Day,* illustrated by Enrique O. Sánchez, 1997.

Sugar Cakes Cyril, Mondo (Greenvale, NY), 1997.

(With David Gershator) *Greetings, Sun,* illustrated by Synthia St. James, DK Ink (New York, NY), 1998.

Zzzng! Zzzng! Zzzng!: A Yoruba Tale, illustrated by Theresa Smith, Orchard Books (New York, NY), 1998.

When It Starts to Snow, illustrated by Martin Matje, Holt (New York, NY), 1998.

Tiny and Bigman, illustrated by Lynne Cravath, Marshall Cavendish (New York, NY), 1999.

Only One Cowry: A Dahomean Tale, illustrated by David Soman, Orchard Books (New York, NY), 2000.

Someday Cyril, Mondo (Greenvale, NY), 2000.

(With David Gershator) *Moon Rooster,* Marshall Cavendish (New York, NY), 2001.

The Babysitter Sings, illustrated by Melisande Potter, Holt (New York, NY), 2004.

(Reteller) *Wise and Not So Wise: Ten Tales from the Rabbis,* illustrated by Alexa Ginsburg, Jewish Publication Society (Philadelphia, PA), 2004.

(With David Gershator) *Kallaloo!: A Caribbean Tale,* illustrated by Diane Greenseid, Marshall Cavendish (New York, NY), 2005.

(With David Gershator) *Summer Is Summer,* illustrated by Sophie Blackall, Henry Holt (New York, NY), 2006.

Sky Sweeper, illustrated by Holly Meade, Farrar, Straus & Giroux (New York, NY), 2007.

(Adaptor) *This Is the Day!,* illustrated by Marjorie Priceman, Houghton Mifflin (Boston, MA), 2007.

Listen, Listen, illustrated by Alison Jay, Barefoot Books (Cambridge, MA), 2008.

Old House, New House, illustrated by Katherine Potter, Marshall Cavendish (New York, NY), 2008.

OTHER

A Bibliographic Guide to the Literature of Contemporary American Poetry, 1970-1975, Scarecrow Press (Metuchen, NJ), 1976.

Contributor of poems, stories, and book reviews to periodicals, including *Cricket, Highlights for Children, Ladybug, Spider, Home Planet News,* and *Caribbean Writer.*

Author's works have been translated into Japanese, French, and Spanish.

Sidelights

Phillis Gershator is the author of award-winning picture books that are often grounded in the folkloric traditions of such places as the Caribbean and Africa. Her works range from original tales, as in *Rata-pata-scata-fata: A Caribbean Story* and *Sky Sweeper,* to retellings of folk tales and songs, as in *Tukama Tootles the Flute: A Tale from the Antilles* and *This Is the Day!,* the latter an adaptation of a century-old popular song.

Having spent her entire life surrounded by books, it is not surprising that Gershator's career path eventually led her to become an author. "[My] family was in the book business in New York," she explained in a *Junior Library Guild* article, adding that she often received books as gifts. In fact, the young Gershator read so much that her mother often had to insist that she go outside to play and get some exercise. After graduating from Douglas College, she worked in a library on the island of St. Thomas, where she and her husband, writer David Gershator, moved after leaving New York City in 1969. The sun-filled skies around Gershator's Caribbean home have inspired for many of her books, including *Rata-pata-scata-fata,* and *Tukama Tootles the Flute.*

Returning to the United States, Gershator earned a degree in library science, then working for several years at libraries and publishing companies in New York City. She and her family returned to St. Thomas in 1988, and continue to make their home there. Gleaning much satisfaction through her library work and as a Reading Is Fundamental (RIF) volunteer, she wanted to contribute even more to children by writing her own stories. Although career and family kept Gershator from spending much time on her writing, she published her first book, *Honi and His Magic Circle,* in 1979. It was not until the mid-1990s that her career really took off, however. In 1993 and 1994 she published three very successful books, *Rata-pata-scata-fata, Tukama Tootles the Flute,* and *The Iroko-Man: A Yoruba Tale,* all of which have won awards.

In *Rata-pata-scata-fata* a young St. Thomas boy named Junjun tries to avoid household chores by chanting gibberish in the hope that his tasks will be completed by magic. Although luck, not magic, smiles on Junjun and grants all his wishes, the boy attributes everything to his gobbledygook. A *Kirkus Reviews* critic called *Rata-pata-scata-fata* "an engagingly cadenced story that will be just right for sharing aloud." "Gershator has a light and lively sense of language," declared *Bulletin of the Center for Children's Books* contributor Betsy Hearne, the critic adding that the author's prose possesses "a storytelling rhythm that shows experience with keeping young listeners involved."

In a vein similar to *Rata-pata-scata-fata*, *Tukama Tootles the Flute* is about another St. Thomas boy who is unreliable in his chores. In this yarn, young Tukama loves to play his flute so much that he does not help his grandmother as he should, even when she warns him that his disobedient ways might one day cause him to wind up in the stomach of a local two-headed giant. The elderly woman's words prove prophetic when the boy is captured by the giant, but he manages to escape by playing his flute for the giant's wife. The frightening experience teaches Tukama a lesson, however: thereafter he postpones his playing until his chores are done. Pointing out the similarities between this story and "Jack and the Beanstalk," *School Library Journal* reviewer Lyn Miller-Lachman commented that *Tukama Tootles the Flute* "offers an opportunity to observe similarities and differences in folklore around the world." Like the Caribbean children in these early stories, Gershator considers herself to be very lucky. "Wishes do, once in a while, "come true," she wrote in her *Junior*

Phillis Gershator retells an African folktale in* Only One Cowry, *a picture book featuring an illustration by David Soman. (Illustration copyright © 2000 by David Soman. Reprinted by permission of Orchard Books, an imprint of Scholastic, Inc.)

Library Guild article, "so I don't consider *Rata-pata-scata-fata* a fairy tale, and oddly enough, that little boy seems very familiar."

Gershator tells a love story in *Tiny and Bigman*. Miss Tiny is a large woman who is told by the men of her Caribbean island home that she is so strong that she makes them feel weak. However, when the frail Mr. Bigman arrives on the island, he finds Miss Tiny to be perfect and the unlikely pair gets married. When a hurricane hits the island just as Tiny is going to give birth to their child, Mr. Bigman must fight to keep the roof from blowing off the couple's house. Shelle Rosenfeld, writing in *Booklist*, called *Tiny and Bigman* "an inventive, appealing love story," while a critic for *Publishers Weekly* described it as a "sunny picture book."

In *Only One Cowry: A Dahomean Tale* Gershator turns from the Caribbean to Africa in recounting the tale of a miserly king who wishes to only pay one seashell as a dowry for a bride. Yo, the king's clever assistant, goes in search of a family willing to allow their daughter to marry the king in exchange for such a small dowry. Along the way, he manages to trade the seashell for more useful and valuable items, eventually assembling an amount worthy to be a king's dowry. When the bride Yo locates learns that her royal suitor adjudged her worth at only a single seashell, she exacts her own price for the match. Grace Oliff, reviewing *Only One Cowry* in *School Library Journal*, wrote that "Gershator brings her considerable storytelling skills" to the story. Writing in *Booklist*, John Peters predicted that "young readers and listeners will laugh" at the tale and *Horn Book* critic Jennifer M. Brabander admired "Gershator's thoughtful attention to the story's oral roots."

Gershator takes readers to Japan in *Sky Sweeper*, in which a boy named Takeboki works as a gardener at a Zen temple. Although his family complains that the job is not worthy, and the monks take his work for granted, Takeboki dedicates his life to the task of keeping the monastery grounds orderly and beautiful. After death he rises to create a new garden in the night sky, whereupon all appreciate his efforts. Although *Booklist* critic Gillian Engberg described *Sky Sweeper* as a "complex, challenging story" due to its themes about "sense of purpose and personal reward," the critic also praised Gershator's gentle message and "philosophical themes." Praising Holly Meade's "pleasing" collage and watercolor illustrations, Margaret Bush added in *School Library Journal* that *Sky Sweeper* would be a good choice for story times due to its "satisfying progression" and themes that "might prompt reflective discussion." "Infused with a Buddhist sensibility" and enhanced by Gershator's "clear, minimalist" text, the book presents "an original fable not to be missed," in the opinion of a *Kirkus Reviews* writer.

Gershator drawing readers back into a more familiar world in picture books such as *When It Starts to Snow*, *Listen, Listen*, and *The Babysitter Sings*. A little boy asks a number of different animals to describe their reactions to the year's first snowfall in *When It Starts to Snow*. A bear explains that snow means that it is time for him to go to sleep; a mouse says that it is time for him to hide in a house to escape the cold; and a fish describes how he must lie at the bottom of his pond to stay warm. Noting that the book features "words that roll off the tongue, pictures of charming woodland inhabitants and a dash of science," a *Publishers Weekly* critic added that *When It Starts to Snow* "will have readers raving to go on a snow quest of their own."

Animals and nature are also the focus of *Listen, Listen*, as Gershator captures the sounds and sights of the seasons in a rhyming text. The lazy buzz of the bumble bee in summer, the crisp crackle of fall leaves, and other music emanating from a country village are evoked in engaging folk-art-style paintings by Alison Jay, creating a picture book that Linda Ludke praised in *School Library Journal* for "provid[ing] . . . a smooth transition between the seasons. Gershator's "rhyming, onomatopoeic text wraps around the busy scenes," Ludke added, creating a warmhearted "ode to the seasons." In *Booklist* Jesse Karp noted the strong balance between art and text, citing Gershator's "simple, evocative rhyming imagery" and Jay's "stylized pictures," which possess "the texture of ancient frescos." *Listen, Listen* is a "jewel of a book," concluded the critic.

In a scenario familiar to many young children, *The Babysitter Sings* finds a baby crying because his parents have left for the day. The infant's desperate babysitter sings a variety of songs based on traditional lullabies from the Caribbean and Africa in an effort to quiet the unhappy child. The baby finally stops crying and falls asleep just in time for his parents' return. According to Lauren Adams in *Horn Book*, in *The Babysitter Sings* "Gershator smoothly integrates bits of traditional lullabies . . . into original verse in this tribute to babysitters." "The text's reassuring tone and the dazzling artwork make this offering a gem to share with little ones," Ajoke T.I. Kokodoko wrote in *School Library Journal*, and a *Kirkus Reviews* critic praised *The Babysitter Sings* as a "reassuring rhythmical tale."

In *This Is the Day!* Gershator teams up with award-winning illustrator Marjorie Priceman to produce what *School Library Journal* contributor Martha Simpson described as a "cheery adaptation" of a song about infant orphans who are bundled off to loving new homes. As the days of the week fly by, so do young babies, one on Monday, two on Tuesday, and so on, their departure "creat[ing] a lyrical, joyous, and somewhat silly mood," according to Simpson. Gershator's retelling "retains a buoyant musical quality" that is in keeping with her story's roots, noted a *Kirkus Reviews* writer, and in *Booklist* Jennifer Mattson wrote that the author's "fanciful verses" pair well with Priceman's "effervescent paintings." Another whimsical story is served up by Gershator in *Old House, New House* as a young child

Noted illustrator Marjorie Priceman brings to life Gershator's joyous story in **This Is the Day!** (Illustration copyright © 2007 by Marjorie Priceman. Reprinted by permission of Houghton Mifflin Harcourt Publishing Company. All rights reserved.)

enjoys a summer in the country in a rambling house where the frisky mice that enliven the place make up for the lack of modern conveniences.

In addition to her original stories, Gershator has collaborated with husband David Gershator on several picture books. In *Kallaloo!: A Caribbean Tale,* they team up to present an island version of the classic folk tale "Stone Soup," as an elderly woman announces that she has discovered a magic shell that can make a popular Caribbean gumbo called Kallaloo. In *Moon Rooster* the couple present what *School Library Journal* contributor

Susan Hepler described as a "humorous, tongue-in-cheek" tale about a rooster that believes that its nocturnal crowing calls forth the waxing moon. *Summer Is Summer,* the Gershators' picture-book celebration of that most favorite season, features warm-toned artwork by Sophie Blackall that brings to life the activities of four children enjoying each fun-filled day. The coauthors' "rhyming text is bouncy and brief," wrote Marge Loch-Wouters in her *School Library Journal* assessment, the critic adding that *Summer Is Summer* "captures the exhilaration of . . . seemingly endless days and opportunities for fun." "The simple, joyful sounds and sunny artwork will appeal to young listeners," concluded Hazel Rochman in her *Booklist* review of the picture book.

Biographical and Critical Sources

PERIODICALS

Booklist, April 15, 1994, review of *Rata-pata-scata-fata: A Caribbean Story,* p. 1541; May 1, 1994, review of *Tukama Tootles the Flute: A Tale from the Antilles,* p. 1603; May 15, 1994, review of *The Iroko-Man: A Yoruba Folktale,* p. 1676; November 15, 1998, John Peters, review of *When It Starts to Snow,* p. 595; October 15, 1999, review of *Tiny and Bigman,* p. 452; October 15, 2000, John Peters review of *Only One Cowry,* p. 442; April 15, 2006, Hazel Rochman, review of *Summer Is Summer,* p. 51; March 15, 2007, Gillian Engberg, review of *Sky Sweeper,* p. 53; November 15, 2007, Jesse Karp, review of *Listen, Listen,* p. 46; February 15, 2008, Jennifer Mattson, review of *This Is the Day!,* p. 84.
Bulletin of the Center for Children's Books, April, 1994, Betsy Hearne, review of *Rata-pata-scata-fata,* p. 257; April, 1998, review of *Greetings, Sun,* p. 279; December, 1998, review of *When It Starts to Snow,* p. 130; January, 2001, review of *Only One Cowry,* p. 181; September, 2007, Deborah Stevenson, review of *Sky Sweeper,* p. 25.
Horn Book, May-June, 1994, Mary M. Burns, review of *Tukama Tootles the Flute,* p. 326; September-October, 1994, Ellen Fader, review of *Rata-pata-scata-fata,* p. 574; November, 2000, Jennifer M. Brabander, review of *Only One Cowry,* p. 764; May-June, 2004, Lauren Adams, review of *The Babysitter Sings,* p. 313; May-June, 2007, Joanna Rudge Long, review of *Sky Sweeper,* p. 264.
Junior Library Guild, April-September, 1994, interview with Gershator, p. 14.
Kirkus Reviews, May 1, 1994, review of *Rata-pata-scata-fata,* p. 629; April 15, 2004, review of *The Baby Sitter Sings,* p. 393; May 15, 2006, review of *Summer Is Summer,* p. 518; March 1, 2007, review of *Sky Sweeper,* p. 221; September 1, 2007, review of *This Is the Day!*
Publishers Weekly, January 10, 1994, review of *Tukama Tootles the Flute,* p. 60; April 4, 1994, review of *Rata-pata-scata-fata,* p. 79; November 9, 1998, review of *When It Starts to Snow,* p. 75; October 11, 1999, review of *Tiny and Bigman,* p. 75; May 14, 2007, review of *Sky Sweeper,* p. 53; September 24, 2007, review of *Listen, Listen,* p. 71; October 29, 2007, review of *This Is the Day!,* p. 54.
School Librarian, November, 1994, review of *Rata-pata-scata-fata,* p. 145.
School Library Journal, April, 1994, Lyn Miller-Lachman, review of *Tukama Tootles the Flute,* p. 118; July, 1995, review of *Rata-pata-scata-fata,* p. 27; September, 1995, Marcia W. Posner, review of *Honi's Circle of Trees,* p. 194; September, 2000, Grace Oliff, review of *Only One Cowry,* p. 216; December, 2001, Susan Hepler, review of *Moon Rooster,* p. 102; July, 2004, Ajoke T.I. Kokodoko, review of *The Babysitter Sings,* p. 75; January, 2005, Teri Markson and Stephen Samuel Wise, review of *Wise . . . and Not So Wise: Ten Tales from the Rabbis,* p. 109; June, 2006, Marge Loch-Wouters, review of *Summer Is Summer,* p. 112; April, 2007, Margaret Bush, review of *Sky Sweeper,* p. 106; November, 2007, Linda Ludke, review of *Listen, Listen,* p. 92, and Martha Simpson, review of *This Is the Day!,* p. 106.
Teacher Librarian, November, 1998, Shirley Lewis, review of *When It Starts to Snow,* p. 49.

ONLINE

Phillis Gershator Home Page, http://phillis.gershator.com (March 21, 2008).*

*   *   *

GÉVRY, Claudine

Personal

Born in Canada. *Education:* University of Quebec, B.A. (graphic design). *Hobbies and other interests:* Designing jewelry, furniture, and clothing.

Addresses

Home—Montreal, Quebec, Canada. *Agent*—Mela Bolinao, MB Artists, 10 E. 29th St., Ste. 40G, New York, NY 10016. *E-mail*—cloe@mac.com.

Career

Illustrator, designer, and animator. Film Board of Canada, currently works as an art director.

Member

Society of Children's Book Writers and Illustrators, Association des Illustrateurs du Québec.

Illustrator

Mary Packard, *Spring Is Here!,* Scholastic (New York, NY), 2002.
Jocelyn Jamison, *Hoppy Feet,* Price Stern Sloan (New York, NY), 2003.
Tanya Lee Stone, *M Is for Mistletoe: A Christmas Alphabet Book,* Price Stern Sloan (New York, NY), 2003.
Deck the Halls: A Holiday Fun Sticker Book, Candlewick Press (Cambridge, MA), 2003.
Susan Hood, *Caterpillar Spring, Butterfly Summer,* Readers Digest Books, 2003.
AnnMarie Harris, *Countdown to Easter,* Price Stern Sloan (New York, NY), 2004.
Crystal Bowman, *My 1-2-3 Bible; My 1-2-3 Bible Promises,* Baker Books (Grand Rapids, MI), 2004.

Crystal Bowman, *My Color Bible; My Color Praises,* Baker Books (Grand Rapids, MI), 2004.

Alexandra Cooper, *Spin the Dreidel!,* Little Simon (New York, NY), 2004.

Allia Zobel Nolan, *The Littlest Princess,* Reader's Digest Books, 2004.

Treesha Runnells, *Spin and Spell: A Book and Game in One!,* Piggy Toes Press (Los Angeles, CA), 2004.

Allia Zobel Nolan, *Big Book of Bible Fiery Tales,* Kregel Kidzone, 2004.

Mara Van Fleet, *Mama Loves Me,* Readers Digest Books, 2005.

Dandi Daley Mackall, *Praying Jesus' Way,* Standard Publishing (Cincinnati, OH), 2005.

Crystal Bowman, *J Is for Jesus: The Sweetest Story Ever Told,* Zonderkidz (Grand Rapids, MI), 2005.

Crystal Bowman, *Jesus, Me, and My Christmas Tree,* Zonderkidz (Grand Rapids, MI), 2005.

Roberta Edwards, *Funny Bunny Feet,* Price Stern Sloan (New York, NY), 2005.

Karen Hill, *A Special Thanks,* Little Simon Inspirations (New York, NY), 2005.

Dandi Daley Mackall, *The Best Thing Is Love,* Standard Publishing (Cincinnati, OH), 2005.

Margaret Wang, *When I Grow Up,* Piggy Toes Press (Inglewood, CA), 2005.

Allia Zobel Nolan, *Little Cricket's Song of Praise,* Kregel Kidzone, 2005.

Dandi Daley Mackall, *God Shows the Way,* Standard Publishing (Cincinnati, OH), 2006.

Crystal Bowman, *A Star for Jesus,* Zonderkidz (Grand Rapids, MI), 2006.

Beth Engelman Berner, *Follow That Bee!,* Piggy Toes Press (Inglewood, CA), 2006.

Lissa Rovetch, *1, 2, 3 Octopus and Me,* Kindermusik International (Greensboro, NC), 2006.

Crystal Bowman, *My Christmas Stocking: Filled with God's Love,* Zonderkidz (Grand Rapids, MI), 2006.

Dandi Daley Mackall, *Seeing Stars,* Little Simon (New York, NY), 2006.

Crystal Bowman, *An Easter Gift for Me,* Zonderkidz (Grand Rapids, MI), 2007.

Megan McDonald, *Daisy Jane, Best-ever Flower Girl,* Random House (New York, NY), 2007.

Crystal Bowman, *My Valentine Story: Giving My Heart to God,* Zonderkidz (Grand Rapids, MI), 2007.

Dorothy Deprisco, *Little School of Fishes,* Piggy Toes Press (Inglewood, CA), 2007.

Alicia Zadrozny, *Little Dino's Egg,* Readers Digest Books, 2008.

Joanne Barkan, *Frogs and Friends,* Readers Digest Books, 2008.

Sidelights

A Canadian picture-book illustrator, Claudine Gévry studied graphic design at the University of Quebec, and then briefly worked as a designer for television before finding her niche in children's books. Her use of bright colors and cozy, round shapes, as well as her creation of endearing characters, give her art instant toddler appeal, and her illustration projects include many board-book titles. In addition to her work as a picture-book illustrator, where her images have been paired with

Claudine Gévry's colorful and whimsical art effectively complements Susan Hood's text in the picture book **Caterpillar Spring, Butterfly Summer.**

simple texts by writers such as Crystal Bowman, Dandi Daley Mackall, and Allia Zobel Nolan, Gévry serves as an art director for animation at the Film Board of Canada and also enjoys designing furniture and jewelry.

Calling Gévry's illustrations "richly colored" and noting her incorporation of foil accents within the pages, Carolyn Phelan wrote in her *Booklist* review of Mackall's *Seeing Stars* that "warm colors, simplified shapes, and rounded lines give . . . [the book's] outdoor scenes a cozy look." Megan McDonald's *Daisy Jane, Best-ever Flower Girl,* an easy reader about a girl whose dream of participating in a real wedding finally comes true, features "rounded forms and warm colors [that] give the pages an inviting look," according to Phelan. Another book featuring Gévry's art, Tanya Lee Stone's holiday abecederium *M Is for Mistletoe: A Christmas Alphabet Book* contains "softly textured pictures with cozy appeal," according to *School Library Journal* contributor Susan Patron.

Biographical and Critical Sources

PERIODICALS

Booklist, May 1, 2006, Carolyn Phelan, review of *Seeing Stars,* p. 86; February 15, 2007, Carolyn Phelan, review of *Daisy Jane, Best-ever Flower Girl,* p. 84.
School Library Journal, October, 2003, Susan Patron, review of *M Is for Mistletoe: A Christmas Alphabet Book,* p. 49.

ONLINE

Claudine Gévry Home Page, http://homepage.mac.com/cloe (March 15, 2008), "Catherine Gévry."
MB Portfolio Web site, http://www.hkporfolio.com/ (March 15, 2008), "Catherine Gévry."*

*   *   *

GOLDING, Julia 1969-

Personal

Born 1969, in England; married; children: three. *Education:* Cambridge University (English); Oxford University, Ph.D. (literature).

Addresses

Home and office—Oxford, England.

Career

Author. Worked previously as a diplomat for the British Foreign Office and as a lobbyist for Oxfam.

Awards, Honors

Waterstone's Children's Book Prize, Nestlé Children's Book Prize, British Book Trust, and Costa Coffee Children's Book Award shortlist, all 2006, all for *The Diamond of Drury Lane.*

Writings

Ringmaster, Egmont (London, England), 2007.
The Ship between the Worlds, Oxford University Press (Oxford, England), 2007.

"CAT ROYAL" SERIES

Cat among the Pigeons, Egmont (London, England), 2006.
Den of Thieves, Egmont (London, England), 2007.
Cat o' Nine Tails, Egmont (London, England), 2007.
Black Heart of Jamaica, Egmont (London, England), 2008.
The Diamond of Drury Lane, Roaring Brook Press (New York, NY), 2008.

"COMPANIONS QUARTET" SERIES

Secret of the Sirens, illustrated by David Wyatt, Marshall Cavendish (New York, NY), 2007.
The Gorgon's Gaze, illustrated by David Wyatt, Marshall Cavendish (New York, NY), 2007.
Mines of the Minotaur, illustrated by David Wyatt, Marshall Cavendish (New York, NY), 2008.

Cover of Julia Golding's teen novel Secret of the Sirens, *featuring artwork by David Wyatt.* (Marshall Cavendish, 2007. Jacket illustration © 2006 by David Cooper. All rights reserved. Reproduced by permission.)

The Chimera's Curse, illustrated by David Wyatt, Marshall Cavendish (New York, NY), 2008.

Sidelights

Julia Golding is a former British diplomat and a lobbyist who has advocated on behalf of people living in war zones. Now a full-time writer, she is the author of the popular "Cat Royal" children's novel series as well as the "Companions Quartet." As Golding noted for *Contemporary Writers* online, her purpose in writing is "to tell stories." Admitting the excitement that writing brings to her, she added that she writes her stories for one special audience: her own children. Asked by these home-grown fans what is going to happen next in a work in process, "the exciting thing is—I DON'T KNOW!," Golding explained.

Adventure is the plot-driving factor in Golding's first "Companions Quartet" novel, *Secret of the Sirens.* Subseqiemt to causing a series of strange animal-related mishaps, eleven-year-old Connie is sent to live with her eccentric Aunt Evelyn. After moving in, Connie learns that her aunt is a member of a secret society that defends and aids the mythical creatures of the world. The girl also discovers that she herself possesses a unique and extraordinary gift: the ability to communicate with all creatures. This power makes her a "Universal." Connie then joins the secret society, and as Golding's story unfolds she must help save the sirens from the demise of an oil company and the predations of Kullervo, a malicious spirit. A *Publishers Weekly* critic commented on Golding's incorporation of eco-friendly themes and remarked that *Secret of the Sirens* "packs a serious environmental message, yet never feels heavy-handed." Lisa Marie Williams, in her review of the novel for *School Library Journal,* wrote that Golding spins a "strong fantasy filled with fantastic mythical creatures and companions alike." In *Kirkus Reviews* a critic acknowledged Golding's middle-grade novel as "structurally epic but gentle in aura," making it "an easily accessible tale for readers."

Biographical and Critical Sources

PERIODICALS

Booklist, January 1, 2008, Diana Tixier Herald, review of *The Gorgon's Gaze,* p. 76.

Bookseller, August 26, 2005, "Diplomat Tells Secret," p. 9; November 18, 2005, Nicholas Clee, "Modernising Myths," p. 34; June 1, 2007, "Twice Struck Golding," p. 8.

Bulletin of the Center for Children's Books, April, 2007, Cindy Welch, review of *Secret of the Sirens,* p. 328.

Evening Standard (London, England), January 27, 2006, "Diplomat's 1,000-Pound Book Prize," p. 10.

Guardian (London, England), June 12, 2007, review of *The Ship between the Worlds,* p. 7.

Kirkus Reviews, March 15, 2007, review of *Secret of the Sirens;* September 1, 2007, review of *The Gorgon's Gaze.*

Magpies, November, 2006, Rayma Turton, review of *Cat among the Pigeons,* p. 36.

Publishers Weekly, May 7, 2007, review of *Secret of the Sirens,* p. 60.

School Librarian, summer, 2006, Janet Fisher, review of *The Diamond of Drury Lane,* p. 98; summer, 2006, Valerie Caless, review of *Secret of the Sirens,* p. 98; winter, 2006, Robert Dunbar, review of *The Gorgon's Gaze,* p. 206; winter, 2006, Valerie Caless, review of *Cat among the Pigeons,* p. 188; summer, 2007, Chris Brown, review of *Den of Thieves,* p. 89.

School Library Journal, January, 2008, Lisa Marie Williams, review of *Secret of the Sirens,* p. 118.

Times Educational Supplement, March 3, 2006, Fiona Lafferty, "Tales of Deferring-Do Past and Present," p. 13; April 14, 2006, Huw Thomas, "Worlds Apart," p. 25.

ONLINE

Children's Bookwatch, http://www.midwestbookreview.com/ (September 1, 2007), review of *Secret of the Sirens.*

Contemporary Writers Web site, http://www.contemporarywriters.com/ (March 4, 2008), "Julia Golding."

Julia Golding Home Page, http://www.juliagolding.co.uk (March 4, 2008).

Kidzworld Web site, http://www.kidzworld.com/ (March 4, 2008), interview with Golding.*

*   *   *

GRAFF, Lisa 1981-

Personal

Born 1981. *Education:* Attended University of California, Berkeley; New School University, M.F.A. (creative writing for children). *Hobbies and other interests:* Reading, writing, playing board games.

Addresses

Home and office—New York, NY. *E-mail*—graff.lisa@yahoo.com.

Career

Writer and editor. Farrar, Straus & Giroux Books for Young Readers, New York, NY, assistant editor.

Member

Society of Children's Book Writers and Illustrators.

Writings

The Thing about Georgie, Laura Geringer Books (New York, NY), 2006.

Bernetta Wallflower, Laura Geringer Books (New York, NY), 2007.

Sidelights

In addition her work in publishing, Lisa Graff has established a second career as an author of children's fiction. In the middle-grade novel *The Thing about Georgie* Graff shines the spotlight on an unusual young protagonist. While nine-year-old Georgie deals with the same things as many other children his age—including struggles with sibling rivalry, issues with his best-friend Andy, and problems at school when the teacher assigns him to write a book report with the class bully—he also has do deal with being a dwarf.

Graff weaves the challenges of dealing with an oversized world into *The Thing about Georgie* in such a way that readers gain compassion for the boy and begin to understand and appreciate his physical limitations. Susan Dove Lempke, reviewing the novel for *Horn Book,* wrote that Graff inspires reader "empathy with [a] . . . character who in many ways faces the same challenges they do." A critic for *Kirkus Reviews* called

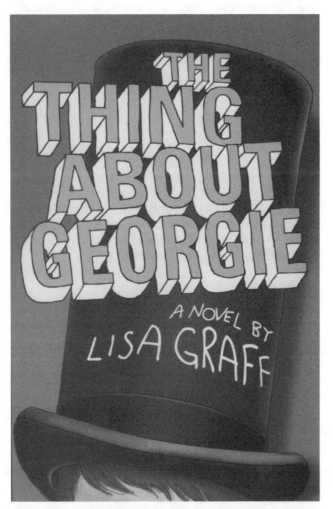

Cover of Lisa Graff's middle-grade novel The Thing about Georgie, *featuring artwork by Amy Ryan.*

Georgie "a likable hero" who "is realistically drawn" and dubbed *The Thing about Georgie* "a compelling portrayal of dwarfism, differences and growing up." In *Booklist,* Kay Weisman remarked on Graff's ability to introduce the difficulties of dwarfism to readers, praising the author's ability to portray, with humor, "what it means to celebrate one's skills rather than lamenting one's limitations."

Biographical and Critical Sources

PERIODICALS

Booklist, January 1, 2007, Kay Weisman, review of *The Thing about Georgie,* p. 100.

Bulletin of the Center for Children's Books, April, 2007, Hope Morrison, review of *The Thing about Georgie,* p. 329.

Horn Book, Susan Dove Lempke, review of *The Thing about Georgie,* p. 193.

Kirkus Reviews, December 15, 2006, review of *The Thing about Georgie,* p. 1268.

School Library Journal, February, 2007, Tina Zubak, review of *The Thing about Georgie,* p. 116.

ONLINE

Arkansas Chapter Society of Children's Book Writers and Illustrators Web site, http://members.aol.com/ddpatti son/scbwi/ (March 5, 2008).

Lisa Graff Home Page, http://www.lisagraff.com (March 5, 2008).*

*   *   *

GUTMAN, Dan 1955-

Personal

Born October 19, 1955, in New York, NY; son of Sidney J. Gutman (in advertising) and Adeline Berlin (a homemaker); married Nina Wallace (an illustrator), September 25, 1983; children: Sam, Emma. *Education:* Rutgers University, B.A., 1977. *Hobbies and other interests:* Travel, history, technology, sports, pop culture, movies.

Addresses

Office—224 Euclid Ave., Haddonfield, NJ 08033. *E-mail*—dangut@comcast.net.

Career

Video Review Publications, coeditor of *Electronic Fun* magazine, 1982-83; Carnegie Publications, founder and editor-in-chief of *Video Games Player* (later named *Computer Games*) magazine, 1983-84; freelance writer, 1984—.

Member

Society of Children's Book Writers and Illustrators, Society for American Baseball Research.

Awards, Honors

Volunteer State Book Award, Nutmeg Children's Book Award and Sequoyah Book Award, all 2000, Iowa Children's Choice Award and Maud Harte Lovelace Award, both 2001, and California Young Reader Medal, 2003, all for *The Million Dollar Shot;* California Young Reader Medal, 2001, for *Honus and Me;* Keystone to Reading Award, 2000, Black-eyed Susan Book Award, 2002, and Massachusetts Children's Book Award, 2004, all for *Jackie and Me;* Arizona Young Readers Award, and Nutmeg Children's Book Award, both 2003, both for *Babe and Me;* Black-eyed Susan Book Award, 2004, for *The Million Dollar Kick;* Flicker Tale Children's Book Award, 2007, for *Miss Daisy Is Crazy!*

Writings

FOR CHILDREN

Baseball's Biggest Bloopers: The Games That Got Away, Viking (New York, NY), 1993.

Baseball's Greatest Games, Viking (New York, NY), 1994.

World Series Classics, Viking (New York, NY), 1994.

They Came from Centerfield, Scholastic (New York, NY), 1995.

(With Vicki Van Meter) *Taking Flight: My Story,* Viking (New York, NY), 1995.

Ice Skating: From Axels to Zambonis, Viking (New York, NY), 1995, revised as *Ice Skating: An Inside Look at the Stars, the Sport, and the Spectacle,* 1997.

Gymnastics, Viking (New York, NY), 1996.

The Kid Who Ran for President, Scholastic (New York, NY), 1996.

The Pitcher Who Went Out of His Mind, Scholastic (New York, NY), 1997.

The Catcher Who Shocked the World, Scholastic (New York, NY), 1997.

The Green Monster in Left Field, Scholastic (New York, NY), 1997.

The Shortstop Who Knew Too Much, Scholastic (New York, NY), 1997.

The Million-Dollar Shot, Hyperion (New York, NY), 1997.

(With Keith Bowen) *Katy's Gift,* Running Press (Philadelphia, PA), 1998.

Virtually Perfect, Hyperion (New York, NY), 1998.

(Adaptor) Cal Ripken, Jr., and Mike Bryan, *Cal Ripken, Jr.: My Story,* Dial (New York, NY), 1999.

Funny Boy Meets the Airsick Alien from Andromeda, illustrated by John Dykes, Hyperion (New York, NY), 1999.

The Kid Who Became President, Scholastic (New York, NY), 1999.

Joe DiMaggio, Aladdin (New York, NY), 1999.

(Under pseudonym Herb Dunn) *Jackie Robinson,* Aladdin (New York, NY), 1999.

Funny Boy versus the Bubble-brained Barbers from the Big Bang, illustrated by Mike Dietz, Hyperion (New York, NY), 2000.

Landslide! A Kid's Guide to the U.S. Elections, Simon & Schuster (New York, NY), 2000.

Johnny Hangtime, HarperCollins (New York, NY), 2000.

The Million Dollar Kick, Hyperion (New York, NY), 2001.

Funny Boy Meets the Chit-chatting Cheese from Chattanooga, illustrated by Mike Dietz, Hyperion (New York, NY), 2001.

The Secret Life of Dr. Demented, Pocket Books (New York, NY), 2001.

Qwerty Stevens, Stuck in Time: The Edison Mystery, Simon & Schuster (New York, NY), 2001.

Qwerty Stevens, Stuck in Time with Benjamin Franklin, Simon & Schuster (New York, NY), 2002.

Babe Ruth and the Ice Cream Mess, illustrated by Elaine Garvin, Aladdin Paperbacks (New York, NY), 2003.

Race for the Sky: The Kitty Hawk Diaries of Johnny Moore, Simon & Schuster (New York, NY), 2003.

The Million Dollar Goal, Hyperion (New York, NY), 2003.

The Get Rich Quick Club, HarperCollins (New York, NY), 2004.

The Million Dollar Strike, Hyperion (New York, NY), 2004.

Jackie Robinson and the Big Game, illustrated by Elaine Garvin, Aladdin (New York, NY), 2006.

The Million Dollar Putt, Hyperion (New York, NY), 2006.

The Homework Machine, Simon & Schuster (New York, NY), 2006.

Getting Air, Simon & Schuster (New York, NY), 2007.

Casey Back at Bat (sequel to "Casey at the Bat" by Ernest Lawrence Thayer), illustrated by Steve Johnson and Lou Fancher, HarperCollins (New York, NY), 2007.

Nightmare at the Book Fair, Simon & Schuster (New York, NY), 2008.

"BASEBALL CARD ADVENTURE" SERIES; FOR CHILDREN

Honus and Me, Avon (New York, NY), 1997.

Jackie and Me, Avon (New York, NY), 1999.

Babe and Me, HarperCollins (New York, NY), 2000.

Shoeless Joe and Me, HarperCollins (New York, NY), 2002.

Mickey and Me, HarperCollins (New York, NY), 2002.

Abner and Me, HarperCollins (New York, NY), 2005.

Satch and Me, HarperCollins (New York, NY), 2006.

Jim and Me, HarperCollins (New York, NY), 2008.

"MY WEIRD SCHOOL" SERIES; FOR CHILDREN

Miss Daisy Is Crazy!, illustrated by Jim Paillot, HarperCollins (New York, NY), 2004.

Mr. Klutz Is Nuts!, illustrated by Jim Paillot, HarperCollins (New York, NY), 2004.

Mrs. Roopy Is Loopy!, illustrated by Jim Paillot, HarperCollins (New York, NY), 2004.

Miss Hannah Is Bananas!, illustrated by Jim Paillot, HarperCollins (New York, NY), 2005.

Miss Small Is Off the Wall!, illustrated by Jim Paillot, HarperCollins (New York, NY), 2005.

Mr. Hynde Is Out of His Mind!, illustrated by Jim Paillot, HarperCollins (New York, NY), 2005.

Mrs. Cooney Is Loony!, illustrated by Jim Paillot, HarperCollins (New York, NY), 2005.

Miss Lazar Is Bizarre!, illustrated by Jim Paillot, HarperCollins (New York, NY), 2005.

Ms. LaGrange Is Strange!, illustrated by Jim Paillot, HarperCollins (New York, NY), 2005.

Mr. Docker Is Off His Rocker!, illustrated by Jim Paillot, HarperCollins (New York, NY), 2006.

Ms. Kormel Is Not Normal!, illustrated by Jim Paillot, HarperCollins (New York, NY), 2006.

Ms. Todd Is Odd!, illustrated by Jim Paillot, HarperCollins (New York, NY), 2006.

Ms. Patty Is Batty!, illustrated by Jim Paillot, HarperCollins (New York, NY), 2006.

Ms. Holly Is Too Jolly!, illustrated by Jim Paillot, HarperCollins (New York, NY), 2006.

Mr. Macky Is Wacky!, illustrated by Jim Paillot, HarperCollins (New York, NY), 2007.

Ms. Suki Is Kooky!, illustrated by Jim Paillot, HarperCollins (New York, NY), 2007.

Ms. Coco Is Loco!, illustrated by Jim Paillot, HarperCollins (New York, NY), 2007.

Dr. Carbles Is Losing His Marbles!, illustrated by Jim Paillot, HarperCollins (New York, NY), 2007.

Mrs. Yonkers Is Bonkers!, illustrated by Jim Paillot, HarperCollins (New York, NY), 2007.

Mr. Louie Is Screwy!, illustrated by Jim Paillot, HarperCollins (New York, NY), 2007.

My Weird School Daze! (omnibus), HarperCollins (New York, NY), 2007.

FOR ADULTS

The Greatest Games, Compute Books (Greensboro, NC), 1985.

I Didn't Know You Could Do THAT with a Computer!, Compute Books (Greensboro, NC), 1986.

It Ain't Cheatin' If You Don't Get Caught, Penguin (New York, NY), 1990.

(Editor) Douglas J. Hermann, *SuperMemory*, Rodale Press (Emmaus, PA), 1991.

Baseball Babylon: From the Black Sox to Pete Rose; The Real Stories behind the Scandals That Rocked the Game, Penguin (New York, NY), 1992.

Banana Bats and Ding-Dong Balls: A Century of Baseball Invention, Macmillan (New York, NY), 1995.

The Way Baseball Works, Simon & Schuster (New York, NY), 1996.

Also author of self-syndicated column "Computer Report Today," 1983-90, and monthly column in *Success*. Contributor to periodicals, including *Esquire, Writer's Digest, Newsweek, Village Voice, Discover, Science Digest, Psychology Today*, and *USA Today*.

Sidelights

Dan Gutman is a prolific author whose favorite topic—baseball—often appears in the fiction and nonfiction he writes for children. Although he started his career pen-

ning nonfiction titles such as *World Series Classics, Baseball's Biggest Bloopers: The Games That Got Away,* and *Baseball Babylon,* Gutman has captured a loyal readership with his humorous middle-grade novels. Among Gutman's most popular books for younger readers include his time-travel "Baseball Card Adventure" books, his "My Weird School" series, and a sequence of books that includes *The Million Dollar Shot, The Million Dollar Putt,* and *The Million Dollar Strike. Casey Back at Bat,* a picture book featuring artwork by Steve Johnson and Lou Fancher, presents Gutman's sequel to a favorite American poem: "Casey at the Bat" by Ernest Lawrence Thayer. Once more facing the pitcher's mound at Mudville, Casey keeps keeps readers in suspense in a rhyming story that *Horn Book* critic Miriam Lang Budin described as a "clever mock-heroic ballad" that "finds exceptional partnership" in the illustrators' nostalgic-themed collage art.

Born in New York City, in 1955, Gutman was raised in nearby New Jersey and attended Rutgers University, where he earned a bachelor's degree in psychology in 1977. After two years of graduate school, he moved back to New York City, hoping to break into the field of humorous journalism established by writers such as Art Buchwald. Undaunted by the countless rejection letters he received, Gutman persisted, publishing the magazine *Video Games Player* in response to the growing popularity of games like Pac Man and Space Invaders. As editor, he was able to establish a healthy track record of published articles, and by the late 1980s he decided to once again submit his work to mainstream magazines. Sports being one of his main interests, Gutman decided that this would be his focus.

Gutman's success at publishing sports articles led him to author several books on baseball, among them *It Ain't Cheatin' If You Don't Get Caught,* which focuses on the unsportsmanlike side of America's favorite pastime. From there, encouragement from his young son inspired Gutman to write for children. *Baseball's Greatest Games* and *Baseball's Biggest Bloopers* were the immediate result of his nonfiction efforts, while his first book of juvenile fiction, *They Came from Centerfield,* deals with baseball while also showcasing Gutman's characteristic humor. With its mix of sports and alien invasion, the story appealed particularly to young boys, and Gutman found himself launched on a new career.

In Gutman's "Baseball Card Adventure" books the author plants interesting historical facts in entertaining stories about some of the greats of the sport. In *Honus and Me* readers meet Joe Stoshak, a preteen baseball fan and player-in-training who supplements his participation in the sport by collecting baseball cards. While earning money by cleaning out an elderly neighbor's attic, Joe finds an old baseball card that turns out to be the most valuable card in the world. The 1909 "Honus Wagner T-206" is more than just a collector's item, however, as Joe finds out when he is transported back

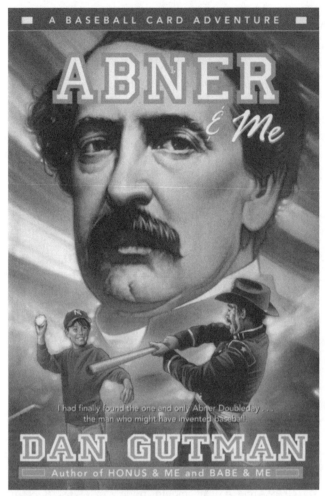

Part of Dan Gutman's "Baseball Card Adventure" series, **Abner and Me** *features artwork by Steve Chorney.* (Cover art © 2005 by Steve Chorney. All rights reserved. Used by permission of HarperCollins Publishers.)

in time to meet the actual baseball player and get a few pointers on his swing. Praising Gutman's "direct, no-frills writing style" and the inclusion of interesting trivia about the early game, a *Publishers Weekly* reviewer added that for readers looking for "a snappy plot along with the play-by-play, this novel hits at least a triple." A *Kirkus Reviews* critic praised *Honus and Me* as "a good fantasy for any baseball fanatic," while in *Booklist* Ilene Cooper maintained that "even readers not into sports will enjoy the fantasy elements."

Gutman continues the "Baseball Card Adventure" series with several more titles involving Joe's time travels to meet famous athletes. In *Jackie and Me* the boy takes a trip back to 1947 and visits with African-American baseball great Jackie Robinson; *Babe and Me* finds Joe and his divorced dad traveling to the year 1932 to take in a famous ball game in which Babe Ruth hits an historic home run; *Shoeless Joe and Me* lands Joe back in 1919, hoping to diffuse the scandal that would destroy the New York Black Sox and sully the reputation of "Shoeless Joe" Jackson; and *Satch and Me* follows the teen's efforts to clock Negro League pitcher Satchel Paige during the 1942 Negro League World Series.

Praising the series as "full of action," *School Library Journal* contributor Andrew Medlar predicted that *Jackie and Me* could "spark history discussions and be a good choice for . . . leisure reading." With its "light-hearted" approach, *Satch and Me* nonetheless addresses the racism that permeated both baseball and American society during the World War II era, according to Marilyn Tanaguchi in a review for the same periodical, while a *Kirkus Reviews* writer praised Gutman for creating "a delightful mix of humor, magic and history surrounded by the sheer joy of baseball."

Gutman moves from the baseball stadium to the political arena in his popular middle-grade novel *The Kid Who Ran for President.* In this novel, twelve-year-old Judson Moon decides to test the system and run for the highest office in the land. As his constituency, Judson marshals thousands of U.S. kids who force their parents to pass a constitutional amendment eliminating age restrictions for the office of president by threatening boycotts of household chores, bed-making, and dog-walking. Reviewing the novel for *Booklist,* Carol Phelan dubbed *The Kid Who Ran for President* "an entertaining romp through the political process" that contains "plenty of humor." In *School Library Journal,* Elisabeth Palmer Abarbanel deemed the book "humorous" as well as an "informative" introduction to the election process, and in *Publishers Weekly* a critic described it as a "snappy, lighthearted farce." In Gutman's sequel, *The Kid Who Became President,* Judson gains elected office and sets a decidedly new tone in Washington.

Other stand-alone novels that capture reader attention without the lure of sports include *Virtually Perfect, The Homework Machine, The Get Rich Quick Club,* and *Getting Air.* In *Virtually Perfect* twelve-year-old Yip, with access to his father's special-effects equipment, creates a "virtual actor" in his computer. Problems arise when the computer-generated, wisecracking teen thespian gains the power to leave the screen and enter reality; Yip has neglected to program the being to know the difference between right and wrong. Praising the novel as a "smoothly diverting "What if?" tale," a contributor for *Publishers Weekly* added that Gutman's "breezy dialogue" and ability to create a fast-paced plot "give this caper the scent of a smartly written sitcom." Noting that Yip's dilemma—whether or not to destroy the creature he has created—provides the story with an intriguing moral center, *School Library Journal* contributor Eunice Weech praised *Virtually Perfect* as "an amusing and thought-provoking novel."

The Homework Machine finds fifth graders Sam, Judy, Brenton, and Kelsey capitalizing on Brenton's computer program, which completes school assignments with no help from humans. Framed as a series of first-person narratives, Gutman's saga includes the perspective of each of the four students, as well as those of their classmates, their teacher, and even the local police chief as the scheme to gain good grades spins out of control. In *Booklist,* Phelan described *The Homework Machine* as a "fast-paced" and "entertaining" story in which the author weaves more serious topics such as "ethics and student computer use." *School Library Journal* contributor Elaine E. Knight praised Gutman's novel, writing that it intertwines "a dramatic and thought-provoking story with a strong message about honesty and friendship." Noting that the author's "over-the-top tale" ends with a compelling plot twist, a *Publishers Weekly* reviewer praised *The Homework Machine* as a "light, sprightly-paced" novel featuring an unique cast of middle-grade characters.

Another group of kids team up in *The Get Rich Quick Club,* as eleven-year-old Gina Turnolo leads four financially savvy schoolmates in a businesslike scheme to sell a story about alien visitors to a tabloid newspaper. Middle-grade readers "will chortle over Gutman's characteristically broad humor," predicted *Booklist* contributor Jennifer Mattson, praising *The Get Rich Quick Club* as a "tart, funny" satire of American avarice. In *School Library Journal,* Linda Zeilstra Sawyer noted the story's appeal to reluctant readers, and a *Kirkus Reviews* writer dubbed the book "believable, silly fun."

Geared for older readers, *Getting Air* trades humor for suspense as thirteen-year-old Jimmy and two friends board a plane to a California skateboarding championship, only to find that the flight is hijacked by terrorists. A battle for control of the plane results in a crash landing in the Canadian wilderness where Jimmy, his friends, and three other survivors must now face a new challenge. Calling *Getting Air* "a fast-paced adventure keyed to today's headlines," *Booklist* critic Carolyn Phelan also noted that Gutman's first young-adult novel maintains a slightly unsteady focus due to the author's effort to mix humor with more serious topics. Praising the "can-do attitude" of the young survivors, John Leighton wrote in *School Library Journal* that Gutman's novel features "a true adventure . . . with high-spirited and fundamentally good boys as the central characters."

Gutman once told *SATA:* "As a kid, I was a skinny, nerdy right fielder for the Galante Giants, a little league team sponsored by the Galante Funeral Home in Newark, New Jersey. I was terrible, but I loved baseball. It's a real thrill to be making a living writing about the game today." One of Gutman's favorite aspects of life as a writer is doing the research: "to dig into old newspapers to research classic ball games, and then re-create them so the readers feel like they're sitting in the stands watching."

Recognizing the popularity his books have among so-called reluctant readers, Gutman views his work as a contribution to building confidence among these young people. "I know that boys are often reluctant to read (I sure was). My hope is that they'll pick up my books because they like sports and then look up hours later to realize they've been *reading* the whole time. That would give me a lot of satisfaction."

Biographical and Critical Sources

PERIODICALS

Booklist, June 1, 1994, Carolyn Phelan, review of *Baseball's Greatest Games,* p. 1792; September 15, 1994, Chris Sherman, review of *World Series Classics,* p. 134; October 1, 1995, Chris Sherman, review of *Ice Skating: From Axels to Zambonis,* pp. 300-301; May 1, 1996, Chris Sherman, review of *Gymnastics,* p. 1500; July, 1996, Wes Lukowsky, review of *The Way Baseball Works,* p. 1795; November 1, 1996, Carolyn Phelan, review of *The Kid Who Ran for President,* p. 498; April 15, 1997, Ilene Cooper, review of *Honus and Me,* pp. 1428-1429; October 1, 1997, Lauren Peterson, review of *The Million-Dollar Shot,* p. 329; February 1, 1999, Karen Hutt, review of *Jackie and Me,* p. 974; February 1, 2000, Gillian Engberg, review of *Babe and Me,* p. 1023; JNovember 15, 2001, Anne O'Malley, review of *The Million Dollar Kick,* p. 571; January 1, 2002, Carolyn Phelan, review of *Shoeless Joe and Me,* p. 857; September 15, 2002, Carolyn Phelan, review of *Qwerty Stevens, Back in Time with Benjamin Franklin,* p. 235; January 1, 2004, Todd Morning, review of *Race for the Sky: The Kitty Hawk Diaries of Johnny Moore,* p. 856; August, 2004, Jennifer Mattson, review of *The Get Rich Quick Club,* p. 1934; September 1, 2004, John Green, review of *The Million Dollar Strike,* p. 111; March, 1, 2005, Anna Rich, review of *"My Weird School"* series, p.1218; February 1, 2006, Carolyn Phelan, review of *The Homework Machine,* p. 48; January 1, 2007, GraceAnne A. DeCandido, review of *Casey Back at Bat,* p. 114.

Family Life, February 1, 2001, Sara Nelson, review of *The Kid Who Became President,* p. 93.

Horn Book, May-June, 2007, Miriam Lang Budin, review of *Casey Back at Bat,* p. 265.

Kirkus Reviews, April 15, 1996, review of *Gymnastics,* p. 202; September 15, 1996, review of *The Kid Who Ran for President,* p. 1400; February 1, 1997, review of *Honus and Me,* p. 223; February 15, 2002, review of *Shoeless Joe and Me,* p. 257; July 1, 2004, review of *The Get Rich Quick Club,* p. 629; January 15, 2006, review of *Satch and Me,* p. 85; February 1, 2006, review of *The Homework Machine,* p. 131; April 15, 2007, review of *Getting Air.*

Publishers Weekly, November 11, 1996, review of *The Kid Who Ran for President,* p. 76; February 10, 1997, review of *Honus and Me,* p. 84; April 6, 1998, review of *Virtually Perfect,* p. 79; February 1, 1999, review of *Jackie and Me,* p. 87; January 31, 2000, review of *Babe and Me,* p. 108; August 27, 2001, review of *The Million Dollar Kick,* p. 86; March 18, 2002, review of *Babe and Me,* p. 106; January 27, 2003, review of *Honus and Me,* p. 262; September 6, 2004, review of *The Get Rich Quick Club,* p. 63; December 11, 2006, review of *Casey Back at the Bat,* p. 68.

School Library Journal, November, 1994, George Delalis, review of *World Series Classics,* pp. 125-126; August, 1996, Janice C. Hayes, review of *Gymnastics,* pp. 155-156; November, 1996, Elisabeth Palmer Abarbanel, review of *The Kid Who Ran for President,* p. 106; December, 1997, Denise E. Agosto, review of *The Million Dollar Shot,* p. 124; August, 1998, Eunice Weech, review of *Virtually Perfect,* p. 163; March, 1999, Andrew Medlar, review of *Jackie and Me,* pp. 209-210; January, 2001, Tim Wadham, review of *Johnny Hangtime,* p. 130; August, 2001, Lisa Prolman, review of *The Edison Mystery,* p. 182; December, 2001, Elaine E. Knight, review of *The Million Dollar Kick,* p. 134; March, 2002, Elaine E. Knight, review of *Shoeless Joe and Me,* p. 231; August, 2002, Doris Losey, review of *Qwerty Stevens, Back in Time with Benjamin Franklin,* p. 188; August, 2004, Linda Zeilstra Sawyer, review of *The Get Rich Quick Club,* p. 87; December, 2004, Taja Alkoriji, review of *The Million Dollar Strike,* p. 146; February, 2006, Marilyn Taniguchi, review of *Satch and Me,* p. 131; April, 2006, Elaine E. Knight, review of *The Homework Machine,* p. 140; January, 2007, Marilyn Taniguchi, review of *Casey Back at Bat,* p. 94; June, 2007, John Leighton, review of *Getting Air,* p. 145.

Voice of Youth Advocates, February, 1994, Florence H. Munat, review of *Baseball's Biggest Bloopers,* p. 395; April, 1995, Ian B. Lande, review of *World Series Classics,* pp. 45-46; February, 1996, Beth Karpas, review of *Ice Skating,* p. 395; December, 1996, Connie Allerton, review of *Gymnastics,* p. 287.

ONLINE

Dan Gutman Home Page, http://www.dangutman.com (March 15, 2008).

H

HAINING, Peter 1940-2007
(Peter Alexander Haining)

OBITUARY NOTICE—

See index for *SATA* sketch: Born April 2, 1940, in Enfield, Middlesex, England; died of a heart attack, November 19, 2007. Journalist, anthologist, editor, and author. Haining wrote dozens of books in his lifetime, mostly nonfiction, but his name is probably associated most often with the dozens of thematic anthologies of short stories he collected. Haining worked for a few years as a journalist, and the news stories that he uncovered led to his earliest books, from *Devil Worship in Britain* (1964) to *Sweeney Todd: The Real Story of the Demon Barber of Fleet Street* (1993). He spent nearly ten years on the editorial staff of the book publisher New English Library before turning to the freelance life, where he thrived. Haining's output over the next thirty-five years was prolific (more than 300 titles altogether) and wide-ranging. While he wrote about historical events, popular culture, film stars, pulp magazines, vampires, serial killers, television series, ancient myths and legends, and the miscellaneous and strange-but-true oddities that captured his fancy, he returned again and again to the occult, the supernatural, and the macabre. Whether his story collections were classified as horror, science fiction, mystery, or general fiction, Haining attempted, as he once explained, to present anthologies organized like novels, "with a beginning, middle, and end," and possessing a cohesive development of a central theme. He never seemed to run out of topics. One of his earliest collections was *The Gentlewomen of Evil: An Anthology of Rare Supernatural Stories from the Pens of Victorian Ladies* (1967); among the more recent are *The Wizard's Den: Spellbinding Stories of Magic and Magicians* (2001). Hundreds—perhaps thousands—of fiction writers living and dead are represented in his popular collections. Haining's own writings toward the end of his life seem to reflect an interest in World War II, as in *The Banzai Hunters: The Small Boat Operations That Defeated the Japanese, 1944-5* (2006).

OBITUARIES AND OTHER SOURCES:

BOOKS

Encyclopedia of Occultism & Parapsychology, 5th edition, Gale (Detroit, MI), 2001.

PERIODICALS

Times (London, England), January 5, 2008, p. 72.

*   *   *

HAINING, Peter Alexander
See HAINING, Peter

*   *   *

HANSON, Mary Elizabeth

Personal
Female.

Addresses
Home—Santa Barbara, CA.

Career
Children's author and librarian.

Writings

Foghorn, illustrated by Paul Orlando, Willowisp Press (St. Petersburg, FL), 1994.
Snug, illustrated by Cheryl Munro Taylor, Simon & Schuster Books for Young Readers (New York, NY), 1998.

The Old Man and the Flea, illustrated by David Webber Merrell, Rising Moon (Flagstaff, AZ), 2001.

The Difference between Babies and Cookies, illustrated by Debbie Tilley, Silver Whistle/Harcourt Trade Publications (San Diego, CA), 2002.

How to Save Your Tail: If You Are a Rat Nabbed by Cats Who Really Like Stories about Magic Spoons, Wolves with Snout-Warts, Big, Hairy Chimney Trolls—and Cookies Too, illustrated by John Hendrix, Schwartz & Wade Books (New York, NY), 2007.

Biographical and Critical Sources

PERIODICALS

Booklist, May 15, 1998, Hazel Rochman, review of *Snug,* p. 1632; March 1, 2002, Connie Fletcher, review of *The Difference between Babies and Cookies,* p. 1141; April 1, 2007, John Peters, review of *How to Save Your Tail: If You Are a Rat Nabbed by Cats Who Really Like Stories about Magic Spoons, Wolves with Snout-Warts, Big, Hairy Chimney Trolls—and Cookies Too,* p. 57.

Bulletin of the Center for Children's Books, September, 2007, Hope Morrison, review of *How to Save Your Tail,* p. 29.

Kirkus Reviews, April 22, 2002, review of *The Difference between Babies and Cookies,* p. 568; April 1, 2007, review of *How to Save Your Tail.*

Publishers Weekly, June 1, 1998, review of *Snug,* p. 48; January 8, 2001, review of *The Old Man and the Flea* p. 66; April 22, 2002, review of *The Difference between Babies and Cookies,* p. 68.

School Library Journal, October, 2001, Kathleen Whalin, review of *The Old Man and the Flea,* p. 119; May, 2002, Martha Topol, review of *The Difference between Babies and Cookies,* p. 116; June, 2007, Debbie Lewis O'Donnell, review of *How to Save Your Tail,* p. 107.*

*   *   *

HAWKINS, Jimmy 1941-

Personal

Born November 13, 1941, in Los Angeles, CA; married Lara Parker; children: Caitlin Elizabeth.

Addresses

Home—CA.

Career

Child actor, producer, and author. Actor in films, including (as Tommy Bailey) *It's a Wonderful Life,* Liberty Films, 1947; *Savage Frontier,* Republic Films, 1953; *Girl Happy,* Euterpe Films, 1965; and *Spinout,*

Metro-Goldwyn Mayer, 1966. Actor in television series, including (as Scotty) *The Donna Reed Show,* ABC Television, 1958-65; *Leave It to Beaver,* Gomalco Productions, 1961; (as Jimmy) *The Adventures of Ozzie and Harriet,* Stage Five Productions, 1961-65; *Petticoat Junction,* CBS Television, 1963-67; and *Gidget, My Three Sons,* and *Hitchcock Presents.* Producer of television films, including *Evel Knievel, Don't Look Back: The Life of Satchel Paige, A Time for Miracles, Love Leads the Way,* and *Scout's Honor.* Member of board of directors, Donna Reed Foundation for the Performing Arts and Jimmy Stewart Museum.

Awards, Honors

Voted into Academy of Motion Picture Arts and Sciences, 1961; Former Child Star Lifetime Achievement Award, 1994.

Writings

(Coauthor) Paul Petersen, *It's a Wonderful Life Trivia Book,* Crown Publishers (New York, NY), 1992.

It's a Wonderful Life: The Fiftieth Anniversary Scrapbook, Courage Books (Philadelphia, PA), 1996.

Wonderful Memories of It's a Wonderful Life (audiobook), Blackstone Audiobooks, 2002.

It's a Wonderful Life: Favorite Scenes from the Classic Film, Andrews McMeel Publishing (Kansas City, MO), 2003.

It's a Wonderful Life for Kids!, illustrated by Douglas B. Jones, Dutton Children's Books (New York, NY), 2006.

Biographical and Critical Sources

PERIODICALS

Booklist, September 15, 2006, Bill Ott, review of *It's a Wonderful Life for Kids!,* p. 96.

Kirkus Reviews, November 1, 2006, review of *It's a Wonderful Life for Kids!,* p. 1129.

School Library Journal, October, 2006, Teri Markson, review of *It's a Wonderful Life for Kids!,* p. 96.

ONLINE

Bullz-eye Web site, http://www.bullz-eye.com/ (December 15, 2006), Will Harris, interview with Hawkins.

Jimmy Hawkins Home Page, http://www.home.earthlink.net/~xka.*

*   *   *

HIGH, Linda Oatman 1958-

Personal

Born April 28, 1958, in Ephrata, PA; daughter of Robert (a miner) and Mary Myrna (an office worker) Haas; married Ken Oatman, June 10, 1978 (divorced); mar-

Linda Oatman High (Reproduced by permission.)

ried John High (a recycler); children: Justin Oatman, Zachary High; stepchildren: Kala High, J.D. High (son). *Ethnicity:* "Caucasian." *Religion:* Christian. *Hobbies and other interests:* Playing bass guitar in a band, reading, aerobics.

Addresses

Home and office—1209 Reading Rd., Narvon, PA 17555. *E-mail*—lohigh@frontiernet.com.

Career

News reporter and feature writer for newspapers in Ephrata, Coatesville, and Morgantown, PA. Has also worked as a waitress, lifeguard, and secretary.

Member

Society of Children's Book Writers and Illustrators, Pennwriters.

Awards, Honors

John Crane Memorial Scholarship, Highlights Foundation, 1993; work-in-progress grant, Society of Children's Book Writers and Illustrators, 1994; Notable Book in the Language Arts citation, National Council of Teachers of English, c. 1999, for *Barn Savers;* Blue Ribbon Book citation, *Bulletin of the Center for Children's Books,* and Best Books of the Year citation,

Parenting magazine, both 2001, both for *Under New York;* Great Lakes Book Award, Great Lakes Booksellers Association, Lee Bennett Hopkins Poetry Honor Book designation, and Notable Social Studies Book for Young People, National Council for the Social Studies/ Children's Book Council, all 2002, all for *A Humble Life.*

Writings

Maizie (young-adult novel), Holiday House (New York, NY), 1995.

Hound Heaven (young adult novel), Holiday House (New York, NY), 1995.

The Summer of the Great Divide (young adult novel), Holiday House (New York, NY), 1996.

A Stone's Throw from Paradise (young adult novel), William B. Eerdmans (Grand Rapids, MI), 1997.

A Christmas Star (picture book), illustrated by Ronald Himler, Holiday House (New York, NY), 1997.

Beekeepers (picture book), illustrated by Doug Chayka, Boyds Mills Press (Honesdale, PA), 1998.

Barn Savers (picture book), illustrated by Ted Lewin, Boyds Mills Press (Honesdale, PA), 1999.

Under New York (picture book), illustrated by Robert Rayevsky, Holiday House (New York, NY), 2001.

Winter Shoes for Shadow Horse (picture book), illustrated by Ted Lewin, Boyds Mills Press (Honesdale, PA), 2001.

The Last Chimney of Christmas Eve (picture book), illustrated by Kestutis Kasparavicius, Boyds Mills Press (Honesdale, PA), 2001.

A Humble Life: Plain Poems, William B. Eerdmans (Grand Rapids, MI), 2001.

Strum a Song of Angels: Poems about Music, Piano Press (Del Mar, CA), 2002.

The President's Puppy, illustrated by Steve Björkman, Scholastic (New York, NY), 2002.

The Girl on the High-diving Horse: An Adventure in Atlantic City, illustrated by Ted Lewin, Penguin Putnam (New York, NY), 2003.

Sister Slam and the Poetic Motormouth Road Trip, Bloomsbury (New York, NY), 2004.

City of Snow: The Great Blizzard of 1888, illustrated by Laura Francesca Filippucci, Walker & Co. (New York, NY), 2004.

The Cemetery Keepers of Gettysburg, illustrated by Laura Francesca Filippucci, Walker & Co. (New York, NY), 2006.

Cool Bopper's Choppers, illustrated by John O'Brien, Boyds Mills Press (Honesdale, PA), 2007.

The Hip Grandma's Handbook (adult nonfiction), Falls Media, 2007.

Contributor to anthologies, including *Soul Searching: Thirteen Stories of Faith and Belief,* edited by Lisa Rowe Fraustino, Simon & Schuster (New York, NY), 2002; and *Don't Cramp My Style: Stories about That Time of the Month,* edited by Fraustino, Simon & Schuster, 2004. Contributor to periodicals, including

Grit, Highlights, U.S. Kids, Child Life, and *Just for Women.* Author of weekly column "Jake's View," for local newspapers; author of weekly column for *Penny Saver News* (New Holland, PA).

Sidelights

Linda Oatman High is the author of young-adult novels, picture books, poetry, and other works for young readers. Her novels for young adults frequently feature spunky heroines whose unwillingness to give up their dreams, even in the face of unpleasant realities, helps ease the passage from childhood to adolescence. In *Maizie,* for instance, High's twelve-year-old central character has taken care of her alcoholic father and her four-year-old sister since her mother ran off with a vacuum-cleaner salesman. Maizie and little sister Grace keep their dreams alive by making "wish" books using pictures cut out of magazines. Maizie's most ardent wishes are for a horse of her own and a chance to see her mother again. In pursuit of these dreams, she takes a job at a nursing home to raise money to buy a horse, and writes to her mother.

High's characters "are fresh, and their dialogue is natural, with just a hint of mountain flavor," observed Elizabeth S. Watson in a review of *Maizie* for *Horn Book.* Several critics noted Maizie's ability to keep her spirits up, even when faced with seemingly insurmountable troubles. This feature of High's narrative "keeps the book from being dreary but makes [Maizie] unrealistically plucky," Susan Dove Lempke wrote in the *Bulletin of the Center for Children's Books,* although Lempke admitted that "overall, readers will find Maizie both likable and admirable." Maizie herself "is a character readers will not soon forget," Carrie Eldridge declared in *Voice of Youth Advocates,* adding that High's first effort deserves comparison to Vera Cleaver's classic tale about Mary Call, the strong female protagonist of *Where the Lilies Bloom.*

Like Maizie, Silver Nickles, the main character in *Hound Heaven,* lives in rural poverty on a mountain in the eastern United States. Silver has lived with her grandfather since the death of her parents and little sister in a car crash and only wishes she could have a dog to love, a thing she feels will soothe her aching sadness. "High creates a rich and at times humorous cast of characters around Silver," Jeanne M. McGlinn remarked in *Voice of Youth Advocates.* Others found that the plot of *Hound Heaven,* which includes a one-sided schoolboy crush with overtones of stalking and a beauty pageant, strains the story's credibility. But, according to a critic for *Kirkus Reviews,* "this quirky novel is satisfying despite its odd detachment from reality." *Bulletin of the Center for Children's Books* contributor Deborah Stevenson credited the ultimate success of *Hound Heaven* to Silver's first-person narration, which "is touching in its yearning and appealing in its gentle humor."

Also told in the first-person is *The Summer of the Great Divide,* High's third novel for young adults. Set in the turbulent 1960s, this novel finds a young teen spending the summer on her aunt and uncle's farm while her parents decide whether they should divorce. There, thirteen-year-old Wheezie is confronted by strange and physically demanding tasks connected with life on a farm, as well as with the necessity of making peace with a mentally challenged cousin and dealing with the onset of puberty and news of the ongoing war in Vietnam. Readers of *The Summer of the Great Divide* are likely to sympathize with Wheezie's problems, according to Leone McDermott in *Booklist,* and "the 1960s time frame gives an interesting twist to a familiar theme."

In *Sister Slam and the Poetic Motormouth Road Trip* eighteen-year-old Laura Crapper is tired of her life as a social outcast and school misfit. Determined to make a change, the brash teen starts calling herself Sister Slam and looks for fame and fortune as a slam poet. Together with best friend and rapper Twig, the mismatched pair (Sister Slam is overweight, while Twig is very skinny) climb into Laura's junker of a car and head off for a slam poetry competition in Tin Can, New Jersey. Just getting to the contest becomes an adventure, as they nearly kill a pig, get ticketed by the police, and manage to anger a person who turns out to be a judge in the poetry slam. When Laura gets into an accident and destroys her car, it turns out to be good luck. The other person in the crash is the charming and wealthy Jake, who invites the girls to stay with his family at the posh Waldorf Astoria hotel in New York. When a journalist overhears the slam poets perform at a fancy restaurant, their career shifts into high gear even as Laura and Jake find romance with each other. Throughout the book, High "creates events and people bigger than life, yet readers will find some very genuine emotions hidden beneath Laura's loud, cynical front," remarked a *Publishers Weekly* reviewer. High "makes everything work" in a "surprisingly sweet tale" that is "[e]xceedingly clever, if not complex," observed *Booklist* reviewer Frances Bradburn.

High addresses a slightly younger audience in *The Girl on the High-diving Horse: An Adventure in Atlantic City.* Set in the summer of 1936, *The Girl on the High-diving Horse* describes the spectacles of Atlantic City's Steel Pier—boxing kangaroos, surfing dogs, dancing tigers, and, of course, high-diving horses—through the eyes of eight-year-old Ivy Cordelia. Ivy is thrilled when she becomes friends with Arnette and Sonora, the sisters who ride the diving horses. She is allowed to help care for the horses, and at the end of the summer, Arnette takes Ivy on one single high dive before she must return home. "High tells her warm, nostalgic story in musical, well-paced language," Gillian Engberg wrote in *Booklist,* while a *Kirkus Reviews* contributor noted that "the immediacy of the first-person voice and the magnetic force of the scenes are totally engaging."

High's picture books for children include *A Christmas Star*. In this story, which is set during the Great Depression of the 1930s, a little girl and her family decorate their sleigh and their horse, Star, in preparation for a ride to church for the Christmas Eve service. The girl anticipates receiving a new pair of mittens, an orange, and some candy from the church's mitten tree, but when they arrive at the church they discover that the tree and the gifts have all been stolen. However, while the congregation is engrossed in creating their live Nativity scene, the girl catches a glimpse of St. Nicholas returning the stolen presents. High's "sensitive, well-paced tale brings the true meaning of Christmas to the fore," a reviewer commented in *Publishers Weekly*.

Other picture books by High focus on the warmer months of the year. The "spare, poetic descriptions" in *Beekeepers* "make it easy to imagine a dewy spring morning on the farm," a critic declared in *Publishers Weekly*. This book focuses on a girl and her grandfather, a farmer who raises bees. The two are working together one day to gather honey from the grandfather's hives when the girl must overcome her fear of the bees to deal safely with a swarm all by herself. This "personal triumph, sweet as honey" is "at the heart of the story," Stephanie Zvirin noted in a *Booklist* review of *Beekeepers*.

Barn Savers is "one of the few picture books to show rural life outside the farmyard," Carolyn Phelan wrote in *Booklist*. A century-old barn is about to be demolished, and rather than let its boards and beams go to waste, a boy and his father work to take the barn apart piece by piece. For an entire day, the father breaks the barn into single boards, and the son stacks them up. As they work, "the father passes on to his son a belief that the barn is a treasure . . . [that] deserves to be respectfully saved," a critic explained in *Kirkus Reviews*. At the end of the day, the boy takes the barn's old iron weathervane home to display in his room as a souvenir.

Winter Shoes for Shadow Horse is another father-son tale by High, this time about a blacksmith teaching his son how to shoe a horse. It is a story "about shared love and respect as one generation teaches another," John Peters related in *Booklist*. Describing the book as "memorable," *School Library Journal* critic Gay Lynn Van Vleck found *Winter Shoes for Shadow Horse* to be "remarkably rich in sensual elements."

Several of High's picture books are written in verse. *City of Snow: The Great Blizzard of 1888* is presented in a mix of rhyming poetry and free verse and tells the story of a young girl's experiences during the disastrous snowstorm that struck New York in the late nineteenth century. As the storm approaches, the girl and her family make preparations. The narrator notes the sights and sounds of the snowbound city, but life goes on even under the full force of winter as residents brave the weather to attend a circus performance in Madison Square. High offers an historical note explaining how the blizzard resulted in the city's public transportation and power systems being placed underground. She "offers a compelling picture of the disaster and its aftermath," remarked a *Kirkus Reviews* critic, while in *Booklist* Jennifer Mattson commented that "High conjures a snowbound Victorian New York through sharply etched details."

In *The Cemetery Keepers of Gettysburg* a family of graveyard caretakers provides a unique perspective on the famous U.S. Civil War battle held in rural Pennsylvania. In High's free-verse narrative seven-year-old Fred Thorn tells how his father left to fight for the Union Army while his pregnant mother and siblings have stayed behind to manage the graveyard. When the full force of the horrific battle erupts around them, the family has little choice but to dig in and endure the violence as best they can. When the fighting is over, the family emerges unharmed. Then, doing their duty, Thorn and his mother begin digging graves for the many dead soldiers. "High's sensitive verse creates a vivid yet restrained impression of the boy's experiences" during and after the war, commented Carolyn Phelan in *Booklist*. A *Kirkus Reviews* contributor predicted that "readers will be touched and sobered by this deeply felt glimpse of battle" and its tragic aftermath.

Under New York marks a change of pace for High. Rather than be set in her customary farm country, the book explores the vast slice of life existing underground in a big city like New York. Each spread shows a cutaway of the city, with the action above-ground contrasting with what is going on below. "This is a sensational idea for a children's book, as awesome as falling down a rabbit hole, as creepy as looking under a rock," Sam Swope wrote in a *New York Times Book Review* appraisal of *Under New York*. Alicia Eames commented in *School Library Journal* that "tidbits of history and curious facts of present-day life add to the adventure."

High once noted: "I was born and raised in Lancaster County, Pennsylvania, living in the boondocks on Swamp Road. Swamp Road was just a road like any other country road, with no swamp in sight. There were woods and trails and trees and creeks and relatives for neighbors. And there was me, wondering why in the world somebody named it Swamp Road when there was no swamp in sight. That wondering was probably one of the first signs that I'd be a writer. We writers spend lots of time thinking about titles and names and words and why people call things something they're not.

"So there I was, growing up on Swamp Road with two parents, one brother, and an assortment of pets. We had many pets: a nervous Chihuahua named Vester, who trembled whenever we looked his way; a yellow canary named Tweety-Bird, who threw birdseed all over my bedroom; an aquarium full of fish; a strawberry roan pony, Pedro the burro; a sheep named Lambchop who thought she was a dog; and Whitey, a fluffy Samoyed dog I loved with all my heart. It was my memory of the love I felt for Whitey that formed the backbone of *Hound Heaven*. . . . .

"I was a child who believed in everything: angels, fairies, ghosts, UFOs, Santa Claus, the Easter Bunny. Once, I swore I saw Rudolph the Red-nosed Reindeer through my bedroom window, and it wasn't anywhere near Christmas. Mom said that I had a crazy imagination, and Dad said I ate too many bananas before bed. You need a crazy imagination to write, but you don't necessarily need bananas.

"For first grade, I was lucky enough to attend California School. California School was a one-room school with a hill for sledding and the best spring water ever and a creek out back where I threw my bologna sandwiches. The teacher said that was why I was so skinny, but he never could explain why California School was on California Road, smack-dab in the center of Pennsylvania.

"My year in first grade—1964—was the last year of California School. The next year, I went to a brand-new school in a nearby town called Churchtown, which of course had lots of churches. The new school had unscratched desks, fresh paint, a cafeteria, a gym, and a black macadam playground with hoops and nets and hopscotch squares. The brand-new school had lots of rooms, but no creek for bologna sandwiches. No hill for sledding. No spring water. No coal stoves in the corners or creaking wooden floors. I thought they should have built another church instead.

"As a child, I had an obsessive fear of death, until I found faith in California Church that day. In *Hound Heaven*, Silver Nickles is dealing with the death of her mama and daddy and baby sister, and faith plays a large part in the novel. When I was in the tenth grade, I wrote an essay about the Fireman's Fair in a nearby town. I wrote about the greasy French fries and the hillbilly music and the spinning roulette wheels that steal your money away. I wrote the essay for a creative writing class taught by Mrs. Severs (who we secretly called by her first name, Susie). Mrs. Severs—Susie—loved my essay and hung it on the bulletin board for everybody to see. She raved and raved about my writing and said that I should be a writer. From that moment on, I was. That's all I needed: to hear the words out loud.

"I wasn't officially published until 1984, after my first child was born. I had quit my job as a secretary and wanted to stay home with my baby, while still bringing in some money. Writing fit in my plans perfectly, and I wrote feature articles for local newspapers until 1987, when I decided that I wanted to write from my heart and not my head, as I'd been doing with newspaper reporting.

"In 1987, Justin was four years old, and I was reading a lot of picture books to him, becoming very interested in children's literature in the process. That's when I began writing for magazines, selling some stories to *Highlights for Children, Hopscotch,* and *Children's Digest*. I loved writing fiction for magazines, but I had a dream. My dream was to write books—picture books, novels, chapter books. So I wrote and I wrote and I wrote, creating and submitting and collecting rejection slips as I acquired three more children: my stepchildren, J.D. and Kala, then Zachary.

"There were times when I almost gave up, because it was hard. The writing was hard, the waiting was hard, the competition was tough. I had lots of kids and little time for writing. I almost gave up, but not quite. In 1990, right after my son Zachary was born, I wrote a novel called *Maizie,* published by Holiday House in April of 1995. It was my first published book, and *Hound Heaven* was to follow, then *The Summer of the Great Divide*.

"My dream has come true, with a bit of faith, a dash of determination, and lots of hard work. In *Hound Heaven*, Silver Nickles never gives up. She has faith and determination, and she works hard toward her goal. I try to instill all my fictional characters with these very real attributes . . . they can make dreams come true! In giving advice to aspiring writers, I would quote Ben Franklin: 'Never, ever, ever, ever, ever give up.'"

Biographical and Critical Sources

PERIODICALS

Booklist, April 15, 1995, Frances Bradburn, review of *Maizie,* p. 1500; June 1, 1996, Leone McDermott, review of *The Summer of the Great Divide,* p. 1718; June 1, 1997, Shelley Townsend-Hudson, review of *A Stone's Throw from Paradise,* p. 1703; September 1, 1997, Hazel Rochman, review of *A Christmas Star,* p. 139; May 15, 1998, Stephanie Zvirin, review of *Beekeepers,* p. 1632; November 1, 1999, Carolyn Phelan, review of *Barn Savers,* p. 524; March 1, 2001, Gillian Engberg, review of *Under New York,* p. 1283; September 1, 2001, John Peters, review of *Winter Shoes for Shadow Horse,* p. 115; September 15, 2001, Ilene Cooper, review of *The Last Chimney of Christmas Eve,* p. 235; December 15, 2001, Susan Dove Lempke, review of *A Humble Life: Plain Poems,* p. 734; April 15, 2003, Gillian Engberg, review of *The Girl on the High-diving Horse: An Adventure in Atlantic City,* p. 1478; May 1, 2004, Frances Bradburn, review of *Sister Slam and the Poetic Motormouth Road Trip,* p. 1555; November 1, 2004, Jennifer Mattson, review of *City of Snow: The Great Blizzard of 1888,* p. 489; March 15, 2007, Carolyn Phelan, review of *The Cemetery Keepers of Gettysburg,* p. 45.

Book Report, November-December, 1996, Nancye Starkey, review of *The Summer of the Great Divide,* p. 41; January-February, 1998, Patricia Bender, review of *A Stone's Throw from Paradise,* pp. 32-33.

Bulletin of the Center for Children's Books, April, 1995, Susan Dove Lempke, review of *Maizie,* p. 277; December, 1995, Deborah Stevenson, review of *Hound Heaven,* p. 129; April, 1998, Pat Mathews, review of *Beekeepers,* p. 282.

Childhood Education, spring, 2002, Loline Saras, review of *Winter Shoes for Shadow Horse,* p. 173.

Horn Book, May-June, 1995, Elizabeth S. Watson, review of *Maizie,* p. 332; January-February, 1996, Maeve Visser Knoth, review of *Hound Heaven,* p. 74; July, 2001, review of *Under New York,* p. 439.

Kirkus Reviews, October 15, 1995, review of *Hound Heaven,* p. 1493; February 1, 1998, review of *Beekeepers,* p. 197; August 15, 1999, review of *Barn Savers,* p. 1311; September 1, 2001, review of *A Humble Life,* p. 1290; March 15, 2003, review of *The Girl on the High-diving Horse,* p. 468; April 1, 2004, review of *Sister Slam and the Poetic Motormouth Road Trip,* p. 331; September 15, 2004, review of *City of Snow,* p. 914; March 1, 2007, review of *The Cemetery Keepers of Gettysburg,* p. 223.

New York Times Book Review, May 20, 2001, Sam Swope, review of *Under New York,* p. 30.

Publishers Weekly, October 6, 1997, review of *A Christmas Star,* p. 55; February 2, 1998, review of *Beekeepers,* p. 90; February 26, 2001, review of *Under New York,* p. 86; September 24, 2001, review of *The Last Chimney of Christmas Eve,* p. 54; December 3, 2001, review of *A Humble Life,* p. 63; January 13, 2003, review of *The Girl on the High-diving Horse,* p. 60; March 29, 2004, review of *Sister Slam and the Poetic Motormouth Road Trip,* p. 63.

Reading Teacher, November, 1998, review of *A Christmas Star,* p. 280.

School Library Journal, April, 1995, Marie Orlando, review of *Maizie,* p. 132; November, 1995, Carol Schene, review of *Hound Heaven,* p. 100; April, 1996, Beth Tegart, review of *The Summer of the Great Divide,* pp. 134-135; October, 1997, Jane Marino, review of *A Christmas Star,* p. 42; December, 1997, Linda Binder, review of *A Stone's Throw from Paradise,* pp. 124-125; June, 1998, Evelyn Butrico, review of *Beekeepers,* p. 109; May, 2001, Alicia Eames, review of *Under New York,* p. 142; October, 2001, review of *The Last Chimney of Christmas Eve,* p. 65, and Gay Lynn Van Vleck, review of *Winter Shoes for Shadow Horse,* p. 120; February, 2003, Carol Schene, review of *The Girl on the High-diving Horse,* pp. 112-113; May, 2004, Nina Lindsay, review of *Sister Slam and the Poetic Motormouth Road Trip,* p. 148; November, 2004, Susan Lissim, review of *City of Snow,* p. 106.

Voice of Youth Advocates, October, 1995, Carrie Eldridge, review of *Maizie,* p. 220; February, 1996, Jeanne M. McGlinn, review of *Hound Heaven,* p. 372.

ONLINE

Authors Den Web site, http://www.authorsden.com/ (January 22, 2002), Linda Oatman High, "On the Edge of Pennsylvania Dutch Country"; (June 18, 2007) "Linda Oatman High."

Linda Oatman High Home Page, http://www.lindaoatman high.com (June 14, 2007).

Autobiography Feature

Linda Oatman High

Linda Oatman High contributed the following auto-biographical essay to *SATA:*

Once upon a time, there was Me: a baby named Linda Louise Haas.

Born on April 28th, 1958, I came way too close to entering this earth in a red 1955 Ford Crown Victoria. With my mother suffering labor pains and screaming, my father was speeding to the Ephrata Hospital in the hot red car he'd purchased right after returning home from serving the U.S. Army in the Korean War.

Dad was 28; Mom was 20. I was 0. The speedometer was over 100.

Dad heard sirens screaming along with my mom, and he saw in his rearview mirror the flashing lights of a Pennsylvania State Police officer.

"I can't stop," Dad said.

"Go!" Mom yelled.

"Stop!" the officer yelled as he overtook the Crown Victoria. Dad squealed to a halt and pointed at my mom.

"Go!" shouted the cop. So Dad did, with the officer leading the way at 105 miles per hour.

It was an auspicious beginning to my life. (I'm now 49. Mom's 69. Dad's 77. We don't know what happened to the red car or the Pennsylvania State Police officer.)

My parents and I were now a family, leaving from the Ephrata Hospital with Dad driving at a safe and legal speed. We went home to Loags Corner, Pennsylvania, where we lived in a tiny mobile home. My mother was a stay-at-home mom; Dad worked underground in the Grace Mines, where even the mules went blind from the constant dark. He worked hard to support us, and by the time I was two years old, Dad was building our new home. It was a 1960 green-painted "ranch house," the hippest suburban style on the market in those days. The house was built on a wooded lot, close to lots of Dad's relatives, on Swamp Road. There was no swamp; just trees and creeks and leaves that changed colors with the seasons.

My earliest memories include falling from my crib onto a metal toy camera (my parents confirm this memory, and so does a scar on my eye), playing with a sweet little beagle dog whose name nobody remembers, and staring warily at my brand-new baby brother Randy when he came home from the hospital, red-faced and squalling. Randy was new, our house was new, I was two.

The first book I can remember from my early years was a small Tell-a-Tale book titled *Happy* Written by Marion Borden. The story is one of a cat found under the hood of a school bus. Sweetly illustrated by Norma and Dan Garris, the book always stuck in my memory. It had a pink-checked border and a green-eyed smiling cat on the cover. My own *Happy* book was lost somewhere along the way, but I found one in an antique store a few years ago. It cost a dollar. I bought it, and it now sits on a file cabinet in my office, reminding me that books make me Happy.

Linda's "crazy baby picture" (Reproduced by permission.)

I spent a lot of time with my grandmothers. Emma Millard—my mother's mother—lived close to the mobile home in Loags Corner. Minnie Haas—my father's mother—lived close to the new ranch house. Emma—"Nana"—was (and still is, at the age of ninety-one) a good cook. Her special recipes include homemade Easter eggs, zucchini bread, and pies of any kind that you can imagine. Nana loves to work in her flower garden, and she adores cleaning her house, a big white farmhouse built in 1776. Nana plants strawberries and lettuce and tomatoes and beans, and she grows the tallest sunflowers you've ever seen.

Minnie—"Grammy"—died when I was nine. Grammy was a good cook, too, and she made the best meadow tea, using fresh mint picked from her fence row. Grammy's sugary meadow tea cured any ailment or bad mood. We called it "catnip tea," but I don't think it was really catnip. I think it was mint.

Grammy also loved gardening, flowers, and keeping her house sparkling clean. She planted corn, tomatoes, lettuce, green beans, and peas. She had a grape vine close to the house, with sour, purple-skinned grapes growing plump from the sun of Morgantown, Pennsylvania.

Grammy had chickens, and my brother and I loved to watch how they jumped around even after their heads were chopped off. It was frightening and strangely funny all at the same time. Of course, we didn't want to eat the steaming chicken soup, after having seen the butchering.

Grammy had given birth to sixteen children, the youngest being my dad. There had been twin boys, both of whom died of croup in my Grammy's arms. The babies were nine months old, and Grammy had thirteen other children. One of them—Jack—had to run across the fields to call for help from a neighbor's telephone. My Grammy had no phone in those early years.

Grammy had an outhouse: an outside wooden bathroom with two rough seats. The outhouse was scary at night, and there were spiders and mosquitoes and bees inside. I told my brother Randy that killer chickens lived under outhouses, and he was terrified.

I believe that the killer chickens were early signs of my wild writer's imagination. Other indications were that I totally believed in aliens, flying saucers, ghosts, and monsters, as well as in Rudolph the Red-nosed Reindeer. I used to sit for hours on Christmas Eve, staring through my window into the sky, looking for the elusive red light of the reindeer's nose.

I was a big dreamer as a kid: daydreaming and night dreaming. My favorite daydream was that I might grow up to become a cowgirl. I was a big fan of horses, and my favorite TV show was *Sally Starr,* a Philadelphia program that featured a sparkly cowgirl on a majestic white horse. I wanted to be Sally Starr. I also wanted to be Catwoman, Nancy Drew, a Roller Derby queen, or a rock star. I told you: I had big dreams.

My night dreams were full of detail and color. I frequently remembered my dreams, and very often they came true. Intuition is another quality that serves a writer well.

Living on Swamp Road near Morgantown, Pennsylvania, Randy and I played outside a lot. We made dams in the creeks; we caught turtles, "Daddy Longleggers" and fireflies; we climbed trees; we piled rocks. There were no video games in those days, so playing required lots of creativity.

I was an outdoors kind of girl; the kind of child that used to be called a "tomboy." Randy and I rode minibikes and three-wheelers and snowmobiles through the meadows and the wood trails. We had horses and dogs and fish and birds and a donkey and one sheep named Lambchop who thought she was a dog (we never had a monkey, despite the fact that I begged to get a tiny spider monkey like the one in Pippi Longstocking).

Lambchop followed our dog Whitey around the yard, trying to imitate her. Whitey would jump at our door when she wanted to come inside. One day, 200 pounds of sheep crashed up on two legs and into the door. That incident found its way into my first book, a middle-grade novel titled *Maizie.* I changed the sheep's name to Wooly Girl.

We writers sometimes change names and places and dates. It's fun: We get to be the bosses of our own universe. It's almost as good as being Catwoman.

When I was six years old, I started first grade (there was no kindergarten in our area in those days). I attended the California One Room School, on California Road, right in the middle of Pennsylvania. The California Schoolhouse had a coal stove and one line of books upon a shelf. There was a row of students for each grade: 1st through 6th. The teacher, Mr. Overly, would teach a row at a time. The grades not being instructed by Mr. Overly would read or work on assignments, and we learned how to focus and block out distractions. (This skill would serve me well in later years when I started writing while raising a houseful of kids!)

Mr. Overly was a patient teacher. He had a kind smile and a gentle voice. Mr. Overly loved to read, and he made sure that his students loved to read, too. I recall the excitement of learning words in the Dick and Jane storybooks, and I remember writing my name—LINDA—in crooked letters.

We had a sledding hill and a trickling creek at California School. We built forts in the woods. There was a spring across the road, with the coldest cleanest water in Pennsylvania. At recess and lunchtime, we'd cross the country road and fill our cups with water. Lunch was eaten on a little bridge over the creek in warm weather, and we ate at our desks on winter days. Once, we got snowed in by a blizzard.

My best friends were Bonnie Fink and Jimmy Hartranft. We toted our bologna sandwiches, bananas, apples, Tastykakes, and thermoses in metal lunchboxes. I had a Flintstones cartoon lunchbox, and I can still remember how it smelled when I opened it: like bologna and bananas. I was a skinny kid, and had a bad habit of not eating enough lunch. I'd either throw my bologna sandwiches in the creek, or give them to my friend Jimmy. I always ate my Tastykakes.

I wrote a story for *Hopscotch* magazine about California School. I like to say that my memories stick like bubblegum to my brain, and fall off onto the pages when I write.

For second grade, I moved on to the brand-new Caernarvon Elementary School. Caernarvon was built in the nearby village of Churchtown, and it was a beautiful school. There was a room for each grade, and some grades even had two rooms! There was a cafeteria and a gymnasium and a music room and the most magical place in the world: a library filled with books. I still remember how my heart lifted when I looked up at all those shelves and shelves of books.

To this day I continue to dream of that library, and in the dream there's a thick pink book. My heart gives a little squish at the sight. I think that the book may have been a Mary Poppins book. I remember reading lots of books in Caernarvon Elementary School, and being amazed at how an author could make something seem so real. I thought it was a miracle that twenty-six little letters of the alphabet could make a million different stories.

I loved to read the Wizard of Oz books, and I loved to read every Nancy Drew mystery that I could get my hands on. I read comic books and *Mad* magazine. As a teen, I devoured *Tiger Beat,* a magazine of movie stars. I read and read and read. My favorite book was *Baby Island* by Carol Ryrie Brink, and I also loved *A Tree Grows in Brooklyn* by Betty Smith.

I read so much that my parents couldn't keep up with my reading needs in the summertime, when the school library was closed. My Aunt Mary, who lived in the town of Goodville, would go to the Bookmobile each week, and she'd choose an armload of books for me to read. I was always so excited to see what Mary had found in the library on wheels.

My dad bought John Updike books for me, because Mr. Updike (a famous Pulitzer Prize-winning author) had lived nearby. His mother had been one of my dad's schoolteachers. I thought it was incredible that someone could be just a normal person living in the countryside of Pennsylvania, and grow up to become a well-known writer.

I read all of the John Updike books when I was probably too young to be reading his work. Some of the content was for more mature readers, but I liked the

Linda playing her guitar, 1972 (Reproduced by permission.)

feeling of reading "grown-up books." I also liked reading grown-up magazines, and would sneakily read *True Story* while my mom got her weekly hair perm at the beauty salon.

In addition to reading a lot, I also loved to watch television. My favorite programs were *Dark Shadows* (a daytime soap opera about a vampire), *The Brady Bunch,* and *The Partridge Family.* I had a crush on Keith Partridge, a character who was played by the very handsome actor David Cassidy. I used to imagine that David would pick me up for a date. He'd be riding in a shiny white limousine, carrying a bouquet of red roses, resplendent in a tuxedo. I'd be wearing the coolest black dress with real pearls. I'd kiss my arm at night, pretending that it was David Cassidy (my kids think that this was ridiculous, but I still think that kissing practice isn't a bad idea).

I had a vivid and colorful imagination, another quality that serves a writer well. I dream in color, I imagine in color, and I write in color. Writing is like art: it gets better with a lot of color.

My life as a teen was full of color: I drove a 1969 yellow Mustang, my bedroom was lilac-purple, and I played a candy-apple red 1969 electric Epiphone guitar. The grass in our neck of the woods was green; the sky was blue; the sunshine was yellow. Life was fun, and it was all about Me. (Isn't that how it is with every kid?!)

When I was in sixth grade, it was announced that there would be a Cow-Judging essay contest. (Hey; this was the 1960s, in Pennsylvania Dutch Country!) I was excited, and told my parents that I was going to win. They laughed.

"You go to school with Amish kids who live on farms," Dad said. "They know cows better than you. You know nothing about cows!"

He was right. I knew nothing about cows. But I was determined to learn, and so I researched and researched, studied and studied, wrote and wrote. With persistence, I finished that essay. I did my best, and guess what? I won the Cow-Judging essay contest at Caernarvon Elementary! I also won the school spelling bee, and I still have the prize thesaurus that I was awarded. It has served me well, and I still enjoy the challenge of research, though it's not always about cows.

I loved blizzards, and this fascination would stay with me as I wrote my book *City of Snow: The Great Blizzard of 1888*. I always suggest that people write about the things they love, as well as the things that scare them. Fear and love are powerful emotions, and you need lots of emotion in writing.

As a kid, I loved chocolate, Halloween, ice skating, bicycle riding, swimming, the ocean, and these musicians: a singer songwriter named Harry Chapin, the Rolling Stones, the Carpenters (people said that I looked like Karen Carpenter), John Denver, Olivia Newton-John, and the Monkees. I loved going to church at my little country church: California Church, just up the road from California School. My parents weren't church-goers, so I was happy to go there with my Aunt Julia and Uncle Dave. It was at California Church that I found faith, a theme that would later show up in several of my books. Fear of death had haunted me ever since I was a little girl, and finding faith helped me to deal with that fear.

At California Church, I met Tamie Braine, and we had lots of laughs when we were supposed to be praying. My antics with Tamie show up in several of my books, hidden under the fictional skin of my characters.

I was always big on laughing and on crying, and when I write a novel I hope that it makes my readers laugh a lot and cry a little. I could laugh or cry harder than anyone I knew. I often got in trouble in school for laughing. Sometimes my friends got in trouble, too. My biggest laughing friend was Lisa Lowry, who would make me laugh so hard that my sides hurt. My friends Rita Esch and Janet Fox, too, were my Partners in Hysteria. We would laugh so hard that we couldn't talk. Janet was a library volunteer, and the librarian would roll her eyes whenever I showed up in the library, because she knew it was going to turn into a Giggle Fest. (It was fun for me to bump into that librarian when I'd grown up, and to tell her that I was now an author.)

Funerals were very difficult for me. I would weep harder than anybody else, and I couldn't stop crying. When my Uncle Harry, Aunt Blanche, and neighbor Marie all died on the same day, there were three funerals. Marie's granddaughter Teresa was a good friend of mine, and we cried until our eyes puffed like the marshmallows in the Cocoa Puffs cereal we were always eating.

Teresa and I had liked to play tricks on Harry, Blanche, and Marie: three old people who got together for card games at least once a week. In warm weather, they'd put up a rickety card table and sit on the front porch of Marie's farmhouse. I can still hear the riffling of the cards as they were shuffled.

"Teresa!" Marie would call. "Make us some popcorn and Kool-Aid."

One day, Teresa and I had an idea that we thought was hilarious. We decided to put sugar on the popcorn, and salt in the Kool-Aid. Giggling uncontrollably, we peeked through the porch window.

Harry took a bite of popcorn. He grimaced.

Blanche took a swig of green Kool-Aid. She frowned.

Marie took a handful of popcorn. She screamed: "TERESA! LINDA!"

We were so busted.

Teresa and I created a little self-published newspaper about our escapades. The name of the paper was *The Secret Chicks*. We had no subscribers, but we had a lot of fun, and it was good preparation for my future career.

I can still recite every teacher I had through my five years at Caernarvon Elementary: Mrs. Reeser, Mrs. Weinhold, Mrs. Shirk, Mrs. Bretch, Mrs. Bretch. I had Mrs. Bretch for fifth grade, and then again for sixth. Mrs. Eloise Bretch recently passed away, and her daughter told me that she was always very proud that one of her students had grown up to become a writer. Mrs. Bretch will forever remain in my brain as "The Teacher Who Could Have Mortified Me But Didn't." This was during my infamous Toilet Shoes incident, the most embarrassing happening of 1969, my sixth-grade year.

My friend Darlene Kurtz was the instigator. Darlene was a beautiful blonde girl, a graceful cheerleader/ballerina type who was polite and well-behaved. She was a great student, and the teachers loved her. But Darlene wasn't as innocent as she seemed.

Darlene had discovered that if one stood upon a certain toilet in the Girls' Room of Caernarvon Elementary, there was a certain rusted metal grate that served as a walkie-talkie into the Boys' Room. Not only did it serve as a walkie-talkie, but it was also a Viewmaster, if a boy was standing in a certain spot by the sinks.

Darlene convinced me—clumsy Linda Haas—that I should climb up on this toilet and give it a try. I did. I was wearing brand-new Keds sneakers. I had only a moment of glory, shouting through the walkie-talkie into the Boys' Room, and then it happened. I fell. Slipping, splishing, splashing . . . my Keds sneaker-clad right foot was dripping with toilet water. I squished back to class in my Toilet Shoe, not quite sure what to do about my dilemma. Should I go to the Principal's Office and tell them that I had to call my mom and ask her to bring new shoes? No. That was not going to work. Should I take off my shoes? No. Against school rules. I didn't know what to do, so I just squished back into the classroom.

Mrs. Bretch looked at my shoe. She looked at me. "Why, Linda, what happened?" she asked.

"Um . . . my . . . my shoe got wet. It's . . . raining!"

Mrs. Bretch looked at my shoe. She looked through the window. It was a brilliantly sunny day. She looked at me. She smiled. She said nothing. I'm forever grateful to her for that.

The Toilet Shoes incident stuck to my brain like bubble gum, and it fell off onto the pages when I wrote a book titled *Cool Bopper's Choppers.* Cool Bopper is a jazz man, a baritone saxophonist, who loses his false teeth while playing his horn one night, one crazy old night. They land on the beehive wig of a be-boppin' lady, who drops them into the toilet.

We writers change details: a shoe becomes teeth. A sheep named Lambchop becomes Wooly Girl.

When I was eleven years old, my parents decided that my brother and I watched way too much T.V. In those days, we had only three channels (6, 8, and 10!), and in order to change those three channels we had to actually STAND UP AND WALK TO THE TV.! No remote control in those days. I know; it was crazy.

So anyway, one day my dad said to Randy and me: "You guys watch way too much TV., and all you do is listen to those Rock and Roll records all day long. It's not good for you. We're going on vacation to a little cabin in the Pocono Mountains, where there's no television and no record player. No telephone to call your friends, either. We'll just play Monopoly and take walks in the woods and cook on the campfire. It'll be fun."

My brother and I were bummed. We thought this trip to the mountains was going to be really boring. But it wasn't. It actually turned out to be fun.

We stayed in a rustic little cabin with a name plaque on the front porch. The sign read "Bark Shanty." Bark Shanty had no TV and no record player and no telephone. (In those days, we used phones that hung on the wall. They were almost always black, and they were dialed by sticking a finger in a hole over the number and actually moving the dial. I know. It was crazy.)

Bark Shanty had an outhouse, with spiders and bees and mosquitoes and quite possibly killer chickens. That outhouse, along with the two-seater one at my Grammy's house, stuck to my brain. They fell off onto the pages of my books *Hound Heaven* and *A Stone's Throw from Paradise.*

Hound Heaven takes place in rural West Virginia, in a little tarpaper shack. While writing the book, I had the idea to name the shack "Bark Shanty." I thought that I made up the name, and later found a photograph of me sitting on the porch of the cabin in the Pocono Mountains. The sign reading "Bark Shanty" hung over my head. I'd carried that cabin in my subconscious memory, and it was shook loose when I started writing a book set in the mountains. Writing really is mystical and magical at times, and nobody can really explain how it works.

In the summer before seventh grade, I had two terrible accidents. First of all, I dove too hard into three feet of water at the Morgantown Pool, hitting my face on the bottom of the pool. My two front teeth were horribly chipped. The dentist could do nothing until the "roots grew more," and so I walked around feeling like a vampire.

A few weeks after the Vampire Teeth incident, I was roughhousing with my brother in the backyard. Our roughhousing started as fun and games, and then it turned serious. Randy escaped from my clutches, and dashed away. He ran into the garage and slammed the door. I'd been running after him with outstretched hands—think Frankenstein—and when he slammed the door, my hands smashed through the glass.

"Linda!" gasped my brother. "You broke the window!"

I'd also broken through the skin on my right wrist. Blood was flowing from a huge gash, and tendons were literally hanging out of my arm. My left wrist was bleeding, too.

My cousin John, who lived next door, showed up right after the crash. He took one look, turned white, and hightailed it on home.

"Mom!" I screamed. "I need to go to the hospital!"

Mom came outside to see me standing on the green front porch, drenching it red. She went pale, and sank down to the ground, holding her head.

"Hurry!" I said. "Take me to the hospital!"

"Wait," Mom breathed. "Wait until Dad gets back." My Dad had gone on a motorcycle ride.

The next thing I remember is sitting in the backseat, Mom desperately pressing a tea towel tourniquet to my right wrist. Dad was speeding to the hospital. It must have been kind of like the scene when I was born, except there was no policeman and there was no 1955 Crown Victoria. We were in a beige Rambler, and I was dying. Or so I thought.

But I didn't die. The doctors stitched me up: twenty-six stitches in the right wrist and seven in the left.

I started junior high a week after that. I was taking pain medication, and my wrists were bandaged. I had to hold them mummy-like: upside-down and very, very still. My teeth were chipped.

It was horrific: I was a seventh-grade combination of a vampire, Frankenstein, a mummy, and a weirdo. I looked as though I'd been through a war. Blood leaked through the bandages on my hands, and people kept asking what had happened.

I couldn't participate in gym class, and I couldn't carry my books. (We had no backpacks in those days.) A boy from my homeroom, Russell Hackman, took it upon himself to help me. Without a word, he'd tote armfuls of books, write down homework assignments, and hang my jacket in the locker.

I was in absolute stammering awe of Russell Hackman, who seemed as if he towered at about six feet tall. I don't remember ever properly thanking him, or telling him how much his assistance meant to me. I'd just mumble an awkward "thanks," and be on my way, hoping that nobody noticed the girl with the chipped teeth and the bandaged hands.

Russell Hackman died in a car accident a few years after our high-school graduation. He left behind a wife and a baby boy. I told many people about Russell Hackman through the years: how much he'd helped me without even being asked, how much I wished that I could thank him, how I now tried really hard to express gratitude to people who did kind things.

Flash forward to 2005: my stepson's wedding. The reception was outside, and it was dark. Fireflies flittered and crickets chirped, and I was sitting on the porch chatting with a pony-tailed young man who played the guitar. I asked him his name.

"Phil Hackman," he said.

"Oh, I went to school with a Russell Hackman," I replied.

Phil caught his breath. "That was my dad," he said quietly.

Goosebumps prickled my arms, and tears sprung to my eyes. "You're Russell's baby boy," I said to this twenty-something young man. "Well, let me tell you a story about your dad."

By the time I finished, Phil and I were both weeping. "And I never even thanked him," I said.

Phil wiped his eyes. We hugged. "You just did," he said. "You have no idea how much that story meant to me."

It meant a lot to me, too. I included parts of it, fictionalized, in an adult novel I'm working on.

When I was thirteen years old, I was horse-crazy. The horse I wanted most was a strawberry roan pony. Mom and Dad responded to my wish with that favorite parental saying: "No way. You'd get tired of doing all the work, and we'll end up having to do it. No way."

My dad jokingly said, "If you want a pony, you earn the money and buy it." I took him seriously. I had a brilliant idea: I was going to collect money from my relatives and buy my own pony. My Aunt Dot and Aunt Mary came over a lot, so that my mom could give them home hair permanents. They played cards. I figured that in-between getting their hair permed and playing Rummy, my aunts could just throw some money into a Strawberry Roan Pony Donation Can. I used an old coffee can, and taped a sign onto it: *Linda's Strawberry Roan Fund. Contributions Greatly Appreciated.*

My dad didn't like the idea. He said that it was rude to ask my relatives—his sisters—for money. He threw my can in the trash. But I got him back: many years later I wrote a book *Maizie* about a girl who wants a strawberry roan pony. Maizie has a can just like mine.

I also got my dad back by writing a poem about his favorite saying, the one he said about my contribution coffee can. My dad's favorite saying is Pennsylvania Dutch, and it goes like this: "Don't Talk So Dumb." So here was my poem:

> "Don't Talk So Dumb"
> my Dad always said,
> my Dad always said
> wild cockeyed idea.
> "Where's Your Common Sense,"
> and "Use Your Head,"
> and "You Had No Business Making Up Stories."
> But,
> what Dad didn't know,
> was that someday,
> I'd use my head
> and make it my business
> to make up stories.

When I visit schools to talk about writing, I suggest that students think of one of their parents' favorite sayings, and try writing a poem about it. Poems can be very simple, and they don't have to rhyme. I also have the students write Road Poems, using the name of their road as the first line. Here's my Swamp Road poem:

> Swamp Road
> was just a road,
> like any other road,
> with no swamp in sight.
> Just houses and twists and turns,
> and a couple of creeks.
> There were woods and trails and trees,
> and there was Me . . .
> wondering why in the world
> they named it Swamp Road,
> when there was no swamp in sight!

That wondering, debating about names and places, is an early sign of a writer. We're always wondering.

When I write, I think of it as a recipe. It's like making chocolate chip cookies: you throw in flour and sugar and eggs and chips. Mix it up, and a new thing appears:

a cookie. Writing's recipe is wondering and thoughts and memories and dreams and wishes and pain and eavesdropping and curiosity. I throw all those things together, mix them up, and . . . TA-DA! A book appears.

When I was in the sixth grade, lots of things were happening, in addition to the Toilet Shoes incident. My cousin was in the Vietnam War. Mood rings were hot. We all watched the first man on the moon on our TV screens in July of 1969. I also watched a lot of *Sonny and Cher* shows, *Laugh-In,* and *American Bandstand.*

My parents were arguing a lot. They ultimately divorced when I was twenty-four years old, and even though I was grown up, my feelings were the same that a younger person has if parents divorce. I took my feelings and put them in a book titled *The Summer of the Great Divide.* Set in 1969, the book includes the Vietnam War and mood rings and the first moon walk. It's the story of Wheezie, whose parents are getting a divorce.

Writing doesn't have to be just about happy things: it can be about things that make you sad or mad or confused. When I created the character of Wheezie, I was suffering from serious allergies and asthma. I was wheezing, so hence the name.

When I created the character of Silver Nickles for my book *Hound Heaven* I gave her an annoying male character with whom to deal. He came directly from my real life, when an annoying kid named Roscoe had a big crush on me.

Another part of *Hound Heaven* that came from my real life was the "Painting the Toenails" incident. In the book, Silver's grandfather—Papaw—has his toenails painted pink on Easter Eve, by the alleged Easter Bunny who is losing his eyesight and paints toes instead of eggs. Here's the real-life story.

When our children were young, I would paint my husband John's toenails pink as he slept on Easter Eve. (John sleeps so soundly that we could paint his entire body and he wouldn't know it.) After painting John's toenails, I'd leave a note on our kitchen table that read: "Dear Mr. High: I am so sorry that I painted your toenails. As you know, my eyesight is failing and sometimes I mistake toenails for eggs. Please accept my apologies—The Easter Bunny."

John would wake up on Easter morning, see the pink toenails, grumble and promptly go for the nail polish remover. Except for the year that our son Zach was five, and believed in the Easter Bunny. That year, Zach cried and begged, "Please, Daddy. Please don't take it off. The Easter Bunny did it! Please leave it on, Daddy. Please leave it on for just one day. Please, Daddy!"

John gave in, and he said, "Just one day. Okay?"

Well, the next day John totally forgot about the polish. He headed off to work at his manly man job of being The Barn Saver. (I wrote a book about John's work,

Linda with her husband John and their kids J.D. (John David II), Justin, and Kala, 1980s (Reproduced by permission.)

titled *Barn Savers.* There's no pink polish in the book.) As The Barn Saver, John saves old barns from bulldozers. If a barn has to come down, to make way for new houses or stores or whatever, John takes it apart piece by piece. He makes a blueprint and tags the pieces so that the barn can be put back up somewhere else, living on for another hundred years.

So the day after Easter the year our son was five, John was working hard. It was a dusty and dirty morning. Lunchtime arrived, and the crew was sitting down in the barn to have lunch. John removed a boot and shook out the dust. He took off a sock. Every head in the barn dropped; every eye was riveted to John's foot. John looked down, and to his complete mortification, he saw five shiny pink toenails.

"But . . . but you don't understand," John stammered. "The Easter Bunny did it."

"Yeah, John. Sure. Right," replied the tattooed World War II veteran who owned the barn.

John made me promise to never again paint his toenails, but I didn't promise not to put it in a book. So I did.

I never thought of being a writer until I was in the eleventh grade. I was taking a creative writing class with a teacher named Mrs. Severs. Mrs. Severs was a genius, but she was a scatter-brained kind of genius. Her most famous day was when she accidentally tucked the back of her dress into the top of her stockings, and stood writing on the chalkboard with her ragged underwear in full view of the hysterical class.

For Mrs. Severs' class, I wrote an essay about the Morgantown Fair. It included details about greasy French fries and spinning roulette wheels and winning goldfish in tiny bowls. Mrs. Severs said to me two sentences that changed my entire life: "You're very creative. You should think about becoming a writer."

I am eternally thankful for those words. They planted the seed of the idea within my brain. I realized that I loved books more than just about anything in the world. I loved words. My friends Jim Hagey and Manny Regas and I had created another homemade newspaper in high school. Like the newspaper I'd written with Teresa, this one had no subscribers but it had us: The Writers. And that's all that mattered.

I took a few detours along the way to becoming a professional writer. I didn't pass "Go" and collect a degree in writing. I got married very young. On June 10th, 1978, at the age of twenty, I became Linda Oatman. Now married to Ken Oatman, Linda Haas was gone. For a few years, so was the girl who'd wanted to become a writer.

Linda Oatman was the girl who worked as an accounting department clerk at a nuclear power plant firm. It was there that I met a black girl named Helen: the first African American I'd ever known. Living in Lancaster County, Pennsylvania, was not a multicultural experience. Helen called me The Ivory Girl, because she said that I was naive, and that I looked like the fresh-faced woman in the soap commercial. Being friends with Helen helped to open my protected young eyes to the realities of life in the real world, where things could be tough.

Working at Gilbert Associates was my first step into real life. I gave up my dream of becoming a writer, or at least put it out of my mind. I focused upon making money, paying bills, being a wife. By the time my son Justin was born, when I was twenty-four, I'd almost totally forgotten that I was once Linda Louise Haas: the girl who wanted to write. I was now a wife and a mother.

I loved being a stay-at-home mom. I loved watching my son grow. I didn't miss working in an office, where I'd always felt as if I were somehow swimming against the stream. I never felt as if I fit in with the corporate world, even though I tried. I was always referred to as "The Little Hippie Girl" or "The Free Spirit."

When Justin was just a few months old, I saw an ad in a local weekly paper. They needed a feature writer. Something sparked inside of me: the smoldering ashes of what had once been a fire for writing. I applied for the job, and I got it. When my first article appeared with my byline (on the front page!), the fire was re-ignited. I remembered how much I'd loved putting words to paper.

I wrote feature after feature for that free paper in Morgantown, Pennsylvania. I took my son along on assignments: interviewing circus clowns, profiling cancer survivors, reporting on local tragedies, featuring tractor pulls and demolition derbies and bake sales and church charities. I interviewed nuns in a mansion, and they invited us to lunch. One-year-old Justin threw spaghetti all over the marble floor, and the nuns loved it. My world was expanding, and the experiences that writing gave me were fun for me and my son.

Reading lots of children's books to Justin, I was one day struck by the thought that maybe I could do this. Maybe I could write books for kids. I had no idea how to start.

I went through a difficult divorce when Justin was very small, and once again my writing dreams were put on the back burner. I worked at various jobs: attendant at an exercise salon where the motorized tables did all the work, lifeguard (where I never got to save anybody), convenience store clerk.

In 1986, I met John High, who had two children from his young marriage. We joined our families, which isn't as easy as *The Brady Bunch* made it seem.

Being a stepmother was the hardest job I ever had. I continued to work at odd jobs to earn some income, and I continued to write for local papers. I'd also started submitting stories to children's magazines, and to think about the goal of one day being able to write and publish a book for kids.

1989 was a horrible year. I had a car accident in which a drunk driver demolished my vehicle and left me with back and neck injuries. We suddenly got full custody of John's son, only six years old at the time his mother dumped him on our doorstep. I unexpectedly became pregnant, and contracted a form of the measles during the pregnancy. Having weekly ultrasounds to make sure that the baby was okay, I prayed for everything to work out fine. On the day before I was due to deliver, John was laid off from his job.

"I could give up this crazy dream of writing, and just get a job," I said to John.

"No; don't give up," John said. "You're going to do it."

Our son was born on August 4th, 1990: a beautiful and healthy baby that we named Zach. John stayed home with me for two weeks, and then saw an ad in the local paper: "Barn. Free for the taking down."

John took down the barn, and found that there was a market for all of the salvaged materials. It was then that his business of being The Barn Saver was born.

In 1993, I still hadn't broken into the world of books. Having published thousands of magazine and news articles, the desire to publish a children's book was still burning. I'd sold a few pieces to *Highlights for Children* magazine, as well as to *Hopscotch, New Moon for Girls,* and other publications.

I applied for a scholarship to attend the Highlights Foundation Writers Workshops at Chautauqua, and was elated when the phone call came that I was being awarded the John Crane Memorial Scholarship.

Attending the workshops in Chautauqua was a turning point in my career. It was there that I met Larry Rosler, editor of Boyds Mills Press. I told Larry about John's job of saving barns, and told him of how I wanted to write a picture book about it. Larry loved the idea, and we signed the book contract a month later. Ted Lewin illustrated *Barn Savers* and it was published in 1999.

Ted and I have since done two other books together: *Winter Shoes for Shadow Horse* and *The Girl on the High-diving Horse.* Ted and I share a passion for the Atlantic City of days past, where there were dancing tigers and boxing kangaroos and flagpole sitters and the high-diving horse act. As a child, I often went to Atlantic City with my family, and I was a fan of the brave girls who rode the high-diving horses, flying sixty feet from a platform into a tank of water. The high-diving horse act amazed and awed me. Amazement and awe are two things that a writer should always keep. We need to dive deep into our passions, interest, and curiosities in order to write.

Our writing sometimes seems like part of us. The writer is the words, and the words are the writer. The letters of the alphabet are my breath. Words are the beat of my heart: rhythmic, reliable, life giving. Sentences are the blood that runs through my veins; paragraphs the bones upon which my stories are built.

Writing, to me, is life. It is living; it is alive. My writing sustains me. It nourishes me, and soothes me, and excites me. It makes me nervous and it agitates me. It scares me to the core, and sometimes I'm bored by the chore of it. Writing is easy, and difficult, and everything in-between. It's fast and it's slow. Sometimes it flows; sometimes it doesn't.

My writing is like my child: sometimes I'm annoyed by it; sometimes I've overjoyed by it. I'm always proud of

Linda with her boys, 1993 (Reproduced by permission.)

it. It goes into the world and it does things without me. It takes on a life of its own, and I smile at its accomplishments. Writing is walking, except without feet, without legs. It is walking with fingers upon keyboard. It is walking with thoughts upon paper. It is running with stories.

Writing is faith; faith that a blank page will be transformed into something new and moving. My writing is me, and I am my writing. We are as one, until death, and then the writing will live on. It will outlive me, and my words will sit on shelves and resonate in the hearts and minds of my readers. My writing means dreams come true. Writing is my moon and stars and sun and sky. It's the place I reach high, and the place I go low. It's the only place I know that feels like dreaming. It's sleeping while awake, and flying while sitting still.

One of my characters looks as if she can fly: Granny Zook. She's a character in my middle-grade novel *A Stone's Throw from Paradise*. Granny Zook was real: she was my husband John's grandmother. She stars in the book, and also in a short story I wrote for an anthology titled *Soul Searching Stories*. Granny was born to parents who died of yellow fever shortly after her birth. Adopted by an Amish couple, she was raised as Nellie Zook, an Amish girl. Granny had an interesting and sad life, becoming pregnant out-of-wedlock and being sent to a "home for unwed mothers." Nellie died a few years ago, in her nineties, but she lives on in my memories and in my stories. When you're a writer, nobody ever has to die.

I always loved Christmas, and so of course I had to write a few Christmas books. The idea for *A Christmas Star* came from my Nana, who told me that she was happy if she received an orange, a piece of candy, and a pair of mittens for Christmas when she was a little girl. (This amazed my son Zach, whose Christmas lists were always very long and expensive!) I wrote the story *A Christmas Star* to help kids learn about holidays long ago, when there wasn't much money but lots of joy could be found.

My second Christmas book is *The Last Chimney of Christmas Eve*, illustrated by a Lithuanian artist named Kastutis Kasparavicius. Kastutus doesn't speak English, and his daughter translated my manuscript. He did an awesome job of illustrating the book in an Old-World European style, which suits the story perfectly. The tale of an orphaned chimney sweep named Nicholas who grows up to become Santa, *The Last Chimney of Christmas Eve* is a book that I'm proud to have written. People write letters to me stating that they love the message of kindness being passed along, and I love their kind letters.

A few years ago, my Nana casually mentioned that we are related to Abraham Lincoln. I couldn't believe it; why had nobody ever talked about this as I was growing up?!?! It would have been a great thing to brag about in school. I wasn't sure that Nana was correct

about the Millards being descendents of President Lincoln, and so I did some research. She was right! Abe Lincoln's great-great grandfather Mordecai Lincoln purchased 1,000 acres of land from my ancestor Thomas Millard in what is now Berks County, Pennsylvania. Thomas Millard's son Joseph later married Mordecai's daughter Hannah Lincoln. Hannah and Joseph (who would be my great-great-great-great something or other) had seven children before she died. So my Nana was right! I am proud to say that I'm related to Abe Lincoln.

Even before I learned this fascinating fact of ancestry, I'd been interested in Abe Lincoln. I wrote an easy-reader titled *The President's Puppy,* about Abe Lincoln's yellow dog Fido, who couldn't accompany him to Washington, DC, when he became president. I felt as if Abraham Lincoln was approving of the book, and I felt that way too during the writing of *The Cemetery Keepers of Gettysburg,* which ends with Lincoln giving the Gettysburg Address.

The Cemetery Keepers of Gettysburg is the story of Elizabeth Thorn. Elizabeth was the wife of Peter, cemetery keeper of the Evergreen Cemetery. Peter enlisted in the military in 1862, and went off to serve for the Union in the U.S. Civil War. Elizabeth promised to take care of the cemetery while her husband was gone. Little did she know that the horrific battle of Gettysburg would hit the town in July of 1863, leaving hundreds of casualties. In the week after the battle, Elizabeth (six months pregnant and with three little boys) buried more than one hundred soldiers. Her story intrigued me, and I'd wanted to write about her for a long time. I couldn't really figure out how to do it for a kid's book, though.

Finally the idea occurred to me that I could write it in the first-person voice of Fred, her oldest son. He was seven at the time of the battle, and he helped his mother to bury the soldiers. After that breakthrough idea, the book flowed.

I stopped at Evergreen Cemetery one day, on my way home from a school visit, and I talked to Elizabeth (silently, of course. I didn't want other cemetery tourists to think that I was completely out of my mind!) I said, "Elizabeth, I admire what you did. You were so strong and brave, and such an inspiration. I don't want you to be forgotten, and so I've written a book about you. It's been under consideration at various publishers for over three years, and I don't know if it'll ever be published. I did write it, though, and I admire what you did."

I drove home, and the phone was ringing as I walked in the door. It was editor Tim Travaglini, saying that he wanted to publish the book. Talk about serendipity and magic! There really are no coincidences in this mystical world of writing.

When I wrote *Sister Slam,* my teenage novel in verse, my house was filled with teenagers who loved to listen to rap music. The rhythm of rap (the word is an acronym that actually means "rhythm and poetry") was engrained in my brain, and it drained with no pain onto the pages. The main character is Laura Crapper, a large-sized girl whose stage name for performance poetry is "Sister Slam." Laura becomes a star, and she rises above hard circumstances in her life.

"I love that the fat girl gets the hot guy," emailed a teenage girl. "We need to have more books about normal-sized girls."

I agree. Our media-influenced culture has become obsessed with weight and appearance and image, to the point that many young girls are damaged. I'm honored that girls relate to my character, and feel empowered by her. I really felt as if I knew Laura/Sister when I was writing the book, and I almost felt like calling her when I got the contract offer.

Readers often ask me if I am my characters, and if my characters are me. Every character has bits and pieces of my soul. I'm a little bit of Sister and a little bit of Twig, her skinny best friend. The car they drive is a little bit of my first car: a yellow 1969 Ford Mustang with a hood scoop and a racing stripe.

I'm a little bit Silver Nickels and a little bit Maizie and a little bit Lizzie Zook and a little bit Wheezie Moore. I'm a little bit Ivy Cordelia, from *The Girl on the High-diving Horse* and a little bit of every other little boy or girl in my stories. I'm a little bit of every teenager, and a little bit of every adult. My heart and soul go into my books, and my books are my heart and soul.

Kids sometimes ask me: "Which of your books is your favorite?" That's like asking your mom who's her favorite kid, if she has more than one. It's hard to name a favorite, but I can say that when my books go out into the world and do something wonderful, I'm a proud parent.

If one of my books wins an honor or an award, I feel like a mom whose child brings home a blue ribbon from the spelling bee, or gets a trophy for MVP in a ballgame. Lots of my books have earned great honors: *Barn Savers* was lauded as a Best Picture Book of 1999; *Under New York* won a Nick Jr. award; *A Humble Life: Plain Poems* was a Lee Bennett Hopkins poetry honor award winner. I'm proud. My kids—my books that came from my body and my heart and my soul and my memories and my experiences—have done well for themselves.

I couldn't ask for more. I'm often asked what else I'd want to be, if I had not become a writer, and there's only one answer: a rock star. I still play the electric guitar, and my son Zach plays now, too. We have seven guitars between us, and my red electric Epiphone hangs on my kitchen wall. My dad bought it for me in 1969, and it's a shiny sight that reminds me of the music inside. I stopped playing during my too-busy child-rearing years, but got back to it in my forties. I played for five years with a wonderful band of guys: Clark,

Pierre, Perry, and Rob. We had so many good times, and shared so many songs. Clark flew away to play music with the angels a few years ago, and that band fell apart. I then played bass guitar with an all-woman band called Tickled Pink. I went on hiatus from playing guitar a few years ago, when I became a grandmother.

I babysit my spectacular grandson Connor, who was born on May 18th, 2004. Connor is with me two or three days a week, when I'm not traveling or doing school visits. He's one of my best friends, and I love being M'Mère. That's what Connor calls me: M'Mère. It's a French version of the word for grandmother. I'm not French, but I like the way it sounds: elegant and lighthearted and fun.

When I started babysitting the Con-Man, I researched like crazy. I wanted to know all about the best baby products and good nutrition and advice for raising happy babies. I wanted to find good educational toys and DVDs and books. I wanted to learn all the newest child-rearing theories, and I wanted to do the best job possible of helping to take care of this sweet little boy who came magically into my life.

All of that research is now being put to good use. I'm under contract for a book called *The Hip Grandma's Handbook*. It's a book of inspiration, tips, advice, and resources for the new breed of cool grandmother. We Baby Boomer grandmas don't rock; not in rocking

Linda playing her guitar (Reproduced by permission.)

Linda in Tuscany for a writing workshop (Reproduced by permission.)

chairs, anyway. We rock out at Rolling Stones concerts, and we like to dress hip. We're not the old traditional stereotype of a grandmother, and so there was a need for a book for grandmas like us. I'm writing it! The book will have a companion Web site, with Hip Grandmas Club membership. I'm in the process of forming a rock band of grandmothers. The publisher and I are hoping that Oprah Winfrey will notice. That's one of my goals: to be on *Oprah*. I'd also like to write a screenplay for a movie and a stage play (and have them produced). I'd like to have a tiny cameo role in my movie, and I'd like to have one of the songs I've written used in the soundtrack. I'd like to travel the world. Those are my goals.

A writer has to have goals.

I finally made it to Europe in July of 2006, at the age of forty-eight. I taught a writing workshop in Tuscany, Italy, for a company called Toscana Americana. The students and I stayed in a 1,000-year-old monastery on a hilltop. Roosters crowed in the valley below. The Tuscan food was incredibly delicious; the people were peaceful; the scenery divine. That trip filled my soul, and it fed my spirit. I'll be teaching for the same company again, and I hope that some of my readers will

think about attending. The details may be found on my Web site: www.lindaoatmanhigh.com.

Aren't Web sites wonderful? I never would have thought, back in my early writing career when I plugged away on a typewriter, that one day we'd have access to the whole world through our fingertips. With the click of a mouse and the flick of a keyboard, we can learn anything about almost anybody or anywhere or anything.

It's a great time to be alive. John and I took our first cruise in January, and it was a writing gig. The cruise was free, as I was writing an article.

When our children were all young, John and I could never afford to take them to Disney World. In October of 2006, though, we finally made it: John and Zach and I. The first sight of Cinderella's castle made me cry. We got free tickets to the park, due to the fact that I was writing an article. Sometimes I just can't believe this good fortune: Cruises! Disney! Italy! It's a tough job, but somebody has to do it.

Writing has nice benefits: it's helped me to travel outside of my usual walls.

Being in this business of writing books for kids has been a magnificent gift. I feel like Alice falling into Wonderland or like Dorothy being lifted into Oz. I truly feel as if I'm at home here in this magical world, and I'm grateful to be here. Sometimes I awaken at night, amazed and astonished that I have become what I always wanted to be: a writer.

My writing friends are many: Marty Crisp, Laurie Halse Anderson, David Lubar, Jennifer Bryant, Carolyn Magner, Lola Schaefer, Mary McIntosh, Jerry and Eileen Spinelli, Ted and Betsy Lewin, Michael Dooling, DyAnne DiSalvo Ryan, John O'Brien, John Rocco, Aileen Leitjen, Margery Cuyler . . . the list goes on and on and on. My agent Deborah Warren is a superb friend, and so are my editors. It's like I've skipped along the Yellow Brick Road, gathering fantastic people by my side to help me along this journey.

And what a journey it's been. The little girl who wanted to write has grown up (debatable to some) and become—TA-DA—a writer. I feel sometimes as if I've been sprinkled with fairy dust by one of the Disney pixies, granting me entrance into the Wonderful World of Publishing.

One of these days, I may get a tattoo. It'll be that of a fairy, waving her wand over the letters of the alphabet. Not all twenty-six of them (that's too much ink and pain), but maybe just A, B, C . . .

My life has not always been easy, but it's been consistently interesting. How did I get here, to this place? Hard work, determination, persistence, hope, faith, laughter, tears.

Find a dream, follow it, and never, ever, ever give up. That's my advice, and I'm sticking to it.

HILL, Kirkpatrick 1938-

Personal

Born April 30, 1938; daughter of William Clifton Hill (a mining engineer) and Isabel Stirling Matson (an office worker); married (divorced); children: Matt, Shannon, Kirk, Crystal, Mike, Sean. *Education:* Attended University of Alaska; Syracuse University, B.S., 1969. *Politics:* "Liberal." *Hobbies and other interests:* Music, art, history, cooking, books, animals, film.

Addresses

Home and office—Box 84435, Fairbanks, AK 99708. *E-mail*—kirkpatrick@mosquitonet.com.

Career

Author and educator. Elementary school teacher in Alaska, 1971-2001.

Awards, Honors

Blue Ribbon Award, *Bulletin of the Center for Children's Books,* 1991; Chicago Center for Children's Books Top Ten Books of the Year designation, and Children's Book Award Master List citations in Rhode Island, Alaska, and Kansas, 1993, all for *Toughboy and Sister;* Berlin Senate Commissioner for Foreigners' Affairs Award, 1997, for *Winter Camp; Smithsonian* magazine Notable Books for Children designation, and Once upon a World Book Award, Simon Wiesenthal Center, Museum of Tolerance, both 2001, both for *The Year of Miss Agnes;* Dorothy Canfield Fisher Award finalist, 2002; Jefferson Cup Title Worthy of Special Note designation, Virginia Library Association, 2003, for *Minuk;* nominations for Young Hoosier Award, William Allen White Children's Book Award, Rebecca Caudill Young Reader's Book Award, Dorothy Canfield Fisher Children's Book Award, Norma Klein Award, and Nebraska Golden Sower Award.

Writings

Toughboy and Sister, Margaret K. McElderry (New York, NY), 1990.

Winter Camp, Margaret K. McElderry (New York, NY), 1993.

The Year of Miss Agnes, Margaret K. McElderry (New York, NY), 2000.

Minuk: Ashes in the Pathway, illustrated by Patrick Faricy, Pleasant Company (Middleton, WI), 2002.

Dancing at the Odinochka, Margaret K. McElderry (New York, NY), 2005.

Do Not Pass Go, Margaret K. McElderry (New York, NY), 2007.

Hill's books have been translated into German, Danish, Italian, Japanese, Korean, and Braille.

Kirkpatrick Hill (Photo courtesy of Kirkpatrick Hill.)

Sidelights

An elementary teacher who worked in Alaska for over three decades, Kirkpatrick Hill is best known for writing novels that introduce younger readers to life in the Alaskan wilderness areas known as the "bush." In the middle-grade novels *Toughboy and Sister, The Winter Camp,* and *The Year of Miss Agnes,* as well as in the young-adult novels *Dancing at the Odinochka* and *Do Not Pass Go,* Hill "lets the audience live inside her story, and in fortifying her characters she fortifies readers too," according to Elizabeth Devereaux in the *New York Times Book Review.* Hill's novels are told entirely from a young protagonist's point of view, allowing readers to identify with the fear, grief, and resolve that her teen and preteen characters experience while surviving the harsh conditions of the Arctic region. "If good children's books got the attention they deserve, Kirkpatrick Hill would be a name known to everyone," Devereaux concluded.

Born in 1938, Hill spent her first years in a mining camp outside Fairbanks, Alaska. "We moved into Fairbanks so I could go to school," she once related to *SATA.* After graduating from high school, she enrolled at the University of Alaska, but left when she got married. Even with one, then two, then three children at home, Hill found the time to return to school to complete her studies, and she received her bachelor's degree from Syracuse University in 1969. Three more children followed, after Hill began a teaching career that took her back to the Alaskan bush.

Hill began writing during a year off from teaching, while she remained at home with her youngest child. "I decided [then] that it was the right time to write," she later recalled. "I was going to write the Great Alaskan Novel. There are Alaskan novels, of course, but most are romantic clichés, full of absurd situations which could never happen in Alaska. Jack London's stories of Alaska and the Yukon Territory are incredibly popular all over the world. But Jack was only here a year. He got some things right, but he got a whole lot wrong. For the next five months I wrote the Great Alaskan Novel. It was pretty terrible. So I thought I'd try a book for kids."

"Like all teachers, I read out loud every day," Hill told *SATA*. "When I read books about Alaska, my students and I would groan and roll our eyes when we came upon some bogus Alaskan myth. You know—bears that can be tamed by kindness; that water thrown in the air freezes solid before it reaches the ground; that a good lead dog will find the nearest state trooper when you're in trouble. So I decided I'd write a book for my Yukon River kids that was absolutely real. I was so determined that it be real that all the characters were real people and every situation had actually happened. This obsession with authenticity has become so ingrained, such a part of every book, that I worry that I have no imagination. Someday I'm going to try to write a book in which nothing is real, just to see if I can do it!"

Hill connected with an editor, Nachama Loechelle, who, the author recalled, "pointed out things in the book that would be obscure to a non-Alaskan kid, words we use differently, perhaps, or objects they'd never seen, like a fish-wheel or a kicker. But she let me leave in all the Yukon-ese, all the down-river speech patterns. That was very important to me because the speech has to be right if the book's going to be an authentic picture of our life."

With Loechelle's help, *Toughboy and Sister* was published in 1990. The book tells the story of two Athabascan Indian children who are forced to survive on their own after their mother dies during childbirth and their father—an alcoholic who cannot get over the loss of his wife—meets his death in a boating accident at a fishing camp on the Yukon River. Eleven-year-old John and his sister, nine-year-old Annie Laurie, find themselves abandoned in this remote area and forced to rely on their wits to survive. Calling *Toughboy and Sister* a "strong, satisfying short novel accessible to very young readers," Betty Levin added in the *New York Times Book Review* that "Hill has achieved a sense of a world that spans two cultures and a feeling for two children whose clear and convincing voices speak to us across the divide."

As she later told *SATA,* Hill was especially pleased that the publisher "didn't shy away from the grim aspects of *Toughboy and Sister.* There are a lot of bad things that happen to the children in this book and they didn't ask

me to water it down. Life in Alaskan villages is decidedly rough. We have the highest rate of alcoholism in the United States, the highest accident rate, and the highest infant mortality rate. You probably wouldn't believe some of the things our kids go through on a day-to-day basis. I want to write about those things honestly."

Toughboy and Sister return in Hill's second novel, *Winter Camp.* By now the siblings have found a new home with their neighbor, an elderly Alaskan woman named Natasha, who brings the children with her to her winter trapping camp during the month of October. Falls through the ice, attacks by moose, and the endless search for enough firewood to keep the trappers warm punctuate an experience during which Sister learns to abhor the cruelty of animal trapping. Praising *Winter Camp,* a *Kirkus Reviews* critic noted that Hill's "portrayal of these competent, courageous children battling the intense cold is compelling."

In *The Year of Miss Agnes* Hill transports readers to the 1940s and introduces ten-year-old Frederika. Fred's feelings about schoolwork change drastically after a new teacher named Miss Agnes comes to the small, one-room schoolhouse in Frederika's remote Abathascan village. While many teachers have come and gone—some lasting only a few weeks—Miss Agnes is here to stay, and inspires Fred and her friends with her creativity and excitement over learning. Told in what *Horn Book* reviewer Roger Sutton described as Fredrerika's "distinct and definite voice," Hill captivates her readers with "the anecdotes about Miss Agnes's masterful teaching methods," creating a novel Sutton dubbed "always true and involving." In *Booklist* Gillian Engberg praised *The Year of Miss Agnes* as "an uplifting portrait of a dedicated teacher."

Do Not Pass Go, Deet is a middle grader whose world comes crashing down when his stepfather, Charley, is arrested and sent to jail for possessing drugs. In addition to causing him to reevaluate his feelings toward Charley, Deet's reaction to having a parent in prison—including his self-absorbed worries about what his friends at school will think about *him*—gradually gives way to the realization that many of his assumptions about people are worth reexamining. In *Publishers Weekly* a critic praised *Do Not Pass Go* as a "quiet, insightful" novel featuring a "sensitive, courageous protagonist who is smart enough and open-minded enough to look past people's mistakes." In *Booklist,* Todd Morning was also enthusiastic, writing that "Hill is a master of the telling detail" and dubbing *Do Not Pass Go* "compelling."

Set in the mid-to-late nineteenth century, *Dancing at the Odinochka* follows a girl's coming of age as she grows up in the isolation of a Russian Alaskan trading post. Erinia Pavaloff lives on a cultural divide; her father is half Russian and half Tlingit while her mother is Athabascan, and her parents' trading post is located on the physical border between these same two worlds. A local murder threatens to inflame local cultural differences, and when the region is annexed to the United States, Erinia and her neighbors must learn to adapt to a third culture and become American Alaskans. Noting that Hill devotes much of the novel to bringing to life the small details about living in this northern region, Engberg concluded of *Dancing at the Odinochka* that "the central focus is on the family's closeness and the facts of survival" in a culture rarely captured in children's books. In *School Library Journal*, Denise Moore praised the novel, writing that "believable characters and good descriptions of the area allow readers to become a part of this time in history," and a *Kirkus Reviews* critic cited Hill for her "admirable research and attention to historical detail."

Turning again to history, Hill presents a contribution to Pleasant Company's popular "Girls of Many Lands" series in *Minuk: Ashes in the Pathway*. Featuring illustrations by Patrick Faricy, the middle-grade novel finds twelve-year-old Minuk watching as her family's Eskimo traditions give way to Western ways after Christian missionaries arrive in their Yup'ik village. The year is 1892, and Minuk is both intrigued and saddened as her language, lifestyle, and spiritual traditions confront those of America. Calling *Minuk* a "provocative book [that] will prompt thought and reflection" on the part of younger readers, Sue Sherif added in *School Library Journal* that Hill's short novel presents "a remarkably honest picture of [Eskimo] life . . . that pulls no punches" and is expanded in the book's well-researched afterword. "Minuk's story, and the skillful, involving manner in which it is told, should knock the socks off habitual readers of series historical fiction," concluded Martha V. Parravano in her *Horn Book* review of the novel.

As Hill told *SATA*, she "grew up in Alaska listening to the stories of the 'old timers'—the miners who had come north for gold, the women who came with them, and the old Indians who watched them come. I wish I'd had sense enough to write them down, but I didn't and of course I've forgotten half of them. On the Yukon River where I spent half my life the first Russians came in 1845 so there were old Athabascan people who remembered what their parents had to say about that first contact. My stepfather's mother told me about her mother, who remembered the first white men she'd ever seen. Since then I've always been interested in acculturation: the things that happen when one culture meets another.

"I didn't start writing until I was forty, so now I'm an old-timer myself. Old people live with a constant sense of impending loss. The old days, they old ways are melting away from all of us. We all think of the old days as better, more innocent. (In spite of the fact that people were dying of tuberculosis like flies, and if you had an accident out in the village you were pretty much a goner, but still. . . .) I wanted to capture life in the villages the way it was when I was a kid. Nothing makes me happier than when someone my age or older reads a book of mine and says, 'Yes, that's the way it was.' My first books were about those early days in Alaska and they're like scrapbooks or patchwork quits of memories: people I've known and the things that happened to them. A collage of old memories, old friends, old students, old places, old times. The way it used to be.

"I have six grandchildren in the Fairbanks area, so much of my time is spent with them. My house is always full of kids, toys, dogs, and cats. And in between I try to find a few hours to write. My youngest daughter and I spend as much of the summers as possible in our big cabin near the Yukon village of Ruby.

"I love getting letters from kids. I wish now I'd written to some of the writers I loved so much when I was a kid. But it never occurred to me that they were real people!"

Biographical and Critical Sources

PERIODICALS

Booklist, October 15, 2000, Gillian Engberg, review of *The Year of Miss Agnes,* p. 438; October 1, 2002, Kathleen Odean, review of *Minuk: Ashes in the Pathway,* p. 326; August, 2005, Gillian Engberg, review of *Dancing at the Odinochka,* p. 2028; December 15, 2006, Todd Morning, review of *Do Not Pass Go,* p. 41.

Bulletin of the Center for Children's Books, November, 1993, review of *Winter Camp,* p. 85; November, 2000, review of *The Year of Miss Agnes,* p. 105; September, 2005, Hope Morrison, review of *Dancing at the Odinochka,* p. 18; February, 2007, Deborah Stevenson, review of *Do Not Pass Go,* p. 241.

Horn Book, November, 2000, Roger Sutton, *The Year of Miss Agnes,* p. 755; February, 2003, Martha V. Parravano, review of *Minuk,* p. 73.

Kirkus Reviews, November 15, 1993, review of *Winter Camp,* p. 1461; June 15, 2005, review of *Dancing at the Odinochka,* p. 683; December 1, 2006, review of *Do Not Pass Go,* p. 1221.

Kliatt, July, 2005, Claire Rosser, review of *Dancing at the Odinochka,* p. 11.

New York Times Book Review, April 14, 1991, Betty Levin, review of *Toughboy and Sister,* p. 19; March 13, 1994, review of *Winter Camp,* p. 20; January 21, 2001, Elizabeth Devereaux, review of *The Year of Miss Agnes,* p. 24.

Publishers Weekly, August 26, 2002, review of *Minuk,* p. 69; August, 2005, Denise Moore, review of *Dancing at the Odinochka,* p. 128; January 15, 2007, review of *Do Not Pass Go,* p. 52.

School Library Journal, September, 2000, Kit Vaughn, review of *The Year of Miss Agnes,* p. 199; October, 2002, Sue Sherif, review of *Minuk,* p. 164; March, 2007, Kristin Anderson, review of *Do Not Pass Go,* p. 210.

Voice of Youth Advocates, December, 1993, review of *Winter Camp,* p. 292; February, 2003, review of *Minuk,* p. 476; October, 2005, review of *Dancing at the Odinochkha,* p. 18; April, 2007, Kevin Beach, review of *Do Not Pass Go,* p. 48.

* * *

HOWARTH, Daniel

Personal

Children: two. *Education:* Bristol University, B.A. (graphic design; with honors), 1994. *Hobbies and other interests:* Surfing, camping.

Addresses

Home and office—Devon, England.

Career

Illustrator. Worked previously at King Rollo Animation.

Writings

A Treasury for Five Year Olds: A Collection of Stories, Fairytales, and Nursery Rhymes, Marks & Spencer (London, England), 2001.

Keith Faulkner, *Guess Who? At the Zoo,* Barrons (Hauppauge, NY), 2002.

Emma Fischel, *Land of the Lost Teddies,* Usborne (London, England), 2002.

David Bedford, *What Are You Doing in My Bed?,* Little Tiger (London, England), 2003.

M. Christina Butler, *Who's Been Eating My Porridge?,* Tiger Tales (Wilton, CT), 2004.

The Chicken Who Saved Christmas, Sterling Publishing Company (New York, NY), 2004.

Sarah Nash, *The Cuddliest Cuddle in the World,* Gullane Children's (London, England), 2005.

Gillian Lobel, *Bertie Bunny's Big Adventure,* Igloo (Kettering, England), 2005.

Claire Freedman, *The Busy Busy Day,* Little Tiger (London, England), 2005.

M. Christina Butler, *Why I Love My Daddy,* HarperCollins (London, England), 2006.

Jonathan Emmett, *I Love You Always and Forever,* Scholastic (New York, NY), 2007.

Sarah Nash, *The Snuggliest Snuggle in the World,* Gingham Dog Press (Columbus, OH), 2007.

Gillian Lobel, *For Everyone to Share,* Good Books (Intercourse, PA), 2008.

Sidelights

British-born illustrator Daniel Howarth cultivated his skills as an artist at the University of Bristol. After graduating, Howarth went to work for King Rollo Animation, where he contributed to popular children's cartoon series such as *Spot* and *Maisy.* His animation work has also been presented on *The Bedtime Hour,* a children's television series broadcast in England. As a freelance illustrator, Howarth has created artwork for several children's books, among them Christina M. Butler's *Who's Been Eating My Porridge?* and Jonathan Emmett's *I Love You Always and Forever.*

Critics consistently characterize Howarth's book illustrations as gentle and often cite the artist's ability to incorporate realistic details within his images. In *School Library Journal* Andrea Tarr wrote that Howarth's illustrations for *Who's Been Eating My Porridge?*—a story of a little bear who is reluctant to eat his breakfast—" are gentle and sweet." Likewise, a *Kirkus Reviews* critic, reviewing the same title, remarked that Howarth's "sweet illustrations rendered in earthy tones depict" a little bear's attempt to solve a riddle posed by its mother. In *I Love You Always and Forever* a father reassures his downcast daughter that one day she will be able to do all the things he can do as an adult. Howarth's illustrations for Emmett's story are large in scale and capture the expressiveness of each character, a *Kirkus Reviews* contributor observed. The same critic went on to note that, in his picture-book illustrations, Howarth "achieves the ideal balance between cuteness and realistic detail."

Biographical and Critical Sources

PERIODICALS

Kirkus Reviews, August 1, 2004, review of *Who's Been Eating My Porridge?,* p. 738; December 1, 2006, review of *I Love You Always and Forever,* p. 1219.

Publishers Weekly, June 30, 2003, "A Moveable Feast for Preschoolers," p. 82.

School Librarian, summer, 2004, Peter Andrews, review of *Who's Been Eating My Porridge?,* p. 73.

School Library Journal, January, 2005, Andrea Tarr, review of *Who's Been Eating My Porridge?,* p. 88; April, 2007, Linda Staskus, review of *I Love You Always and Forever,* p. 98.

ONLINE

Daniel Howarth Home Page, http://www.danielhowarth.com (March 6, 2008).

Tide Mill Press Web site, http://www.tidemillpress.com/ (March 6, 2008), "Daniel Howarth."*

J

JENKINS, Steve 1952-

Personal
Born 1952, in Hickory, NC; son of Alvin (a physics professor) and Margaret (a bank employee and home-maker) Jenkins; married Robin Page (a graphic designer and author); children: Page, Alec, Jamie. *Education:* North Carolina State University, B.A. and M.A (graphic design).

Addresses
Home—Boulder, CO. *E-mail*—steve@jenkinspage.com.

Career
Graphic designer; illustrator and author. *Exhibitions:* Works exhibited in Society of Illustrators Original Art Show, 2004.

Awards, Honors
Scientific American Young Readers Book Award, 1996, for *Big and Little;* Outstanding Trade Book for Children citation, National Science Teachers Association, 1998, for *What Do You Do When Something Wants to Eat You?;* Recommended Books inclusion, National Council of Teachers of English (NCTE), 1998, for *Animal Dads;* Boston Globe/Horn Book Award for Nonfiction, and American Library Association (ALA) Notable Children's Book designation, both 2000, both for *The Top of the World;* Bank Street College of Education Best Children's Book of the Year selection, and Capitol Choice selection, both 2002, and NCTE Orbis Pictus Recommended Book citation, 2003, all for *Life on Earth;* (with Robin Page) Charlotte Zolotow Award Highly Commended honor, NCTE Notable Book in the Language Arts designation, and Caldecott Honor designation, all 2004, all for *What Do You Do with a Tail like This?;* Bank Street College of Education Best Children's Book of the Year, 2004, and Oppenheim Toy Portfolio Gold Award, 2005, both for *Next Stop, Nep-*

Steve Jenkins (Reproduced by permission of Houghton Mifflin Co.)

tune by Alvin Jenkins; Orbis Pictus Honor designation, New York Public Library 100 Titles for Reading and Sharing selection, Chicago Public Library Best-of-the-Best designation, and *Natural History* Best Book for Young Readers, all 2004, all for *Actual Size;* Bank Street College of Education Best Children's Book designation, 2004, and ALA Top Ten Sci-Tech Books for Youth designation, and International Reading Association Children's Choice, 2005, all for *I See a Kookaburra!;* New York Public Library 100 Titles for Reading and Sharing selection, and Parents' Choice Award, both 2005, and Oppenheim Toy Portfolio Gold Award, 2006, all for *Prehistoric Actual Size;* (with Page) New York Public Library 100 Titles for Reading and Sharing selection, *New York Times* Best Illustrated Children's Book of the Year, and *Parenting* magazine Book of the Year, all 2006, all for *Move!;* Orbis Pictus Recommended designation, and New York Public Library 100 Titles for Reading and Sharing selection, both 2008, both for *Living Color;* Theodor Seuss Geisel Honor designation, 2008, for *Vulture View.*

Writings

SELF-ILLUSTRATED

Duck's Breath and Mouse Pie: A Collection of Animal Superstitions, Ticknor & Fields (New York, NY), 1994.

Biggest, Strongest, Fastest, Ticknor & Fields (New York, NY), 1995.

Looking Down, Houghton Mifflin (Boston, MA), 1995.

Big and Little, Houghton Mifflin (Boston, MA), 1996.

What Do You Do When Something Wants to Eat You?, Houghton Mifflin (Boston, MA), 1997.

Hottest, Coldest, Highest, Deepest, Houghton Mifflin (Boston, MA), 1998.

The Top of the World: Climbing Mount Everest, Houghton Mifflin (Boston, MA), 1999.

Slap, Squeak, and Scatter: How Animals Communicate, Houghton Mifflin (Boston, MA), 2001.

(Coauthor with wife, Robin Page) *Animals in Flight,* Houghton Mifflin (Boston, MA), 2001.

Life on Earth: The Story of Evolution, Houghton Mifflin (Boston, MA), 2002.

(Coauthor with Robin Page) *What Do You Do with a Tail like This?,* Houghton Mifflin (Boston, MA), 2003.

Actual Size, Houghton Mifflin (Boston, MA), 2004.

Prehistoric Actual Size, Houghton Mifflin (Boston, MA), 2005.

(Coauthor with Robin Page) *I See a Kookaburra!: Discovering Animal Habitats around the World,* Houghton Mifflin (Boston, MA), 2005.

(Coauthor with Robin Page) *Move!,* Houghton Mifflin (Boston, MA), 2006.

Almost Gone: The World's Rarest Animals, HarperCollins (New York, NY), 2006.

Dogs and Cats (two stories, bound inverted), Houghton Mifflin (Boston, MA), 2007.

Living Color, Houghton Mifflin (Boston, MA), 2007.

(Coauthor with Robin Page) *Sisters and Brothers: Sibling Relationships in the Animal World,* Houghton Mifflin (Boston, MA), 2008.

ILLUSTRATOR

Janet Horowitz and Kathy Faggella, *My Dad,* Stewart, Tabori & Chang (New York, NY), 1991.

Janet Horowitz and Kathy Faggella, *My Mom,* Stewart, Tabori & Chang (New York, NY), 1991.

Janet Horowitz and Kathy Faggella, *My School,* Stewart, Tabori & Chang (New York, NY), 1991.

Janet Horowitz and Kathy Faggella, *My Town,* Stewart, Tabori & Chang (New York, NY), 1991.

Janet Horowitz and Kathy Faggella, *My Pet,* Stewart, Tabori & Chang (New York, NY), 1992.

Marc Robinson, *Cock-a-Doodle-Doo!: What Does It Sound like to You?,* Stewart, Tabori & Chang (New York, NY), 1993.

Linda Capus Riley, *Elephants Swim,* Houghton Mifflin (Boston, MA), 1995.

Sneed B. Collard, *Animal Dads,* Houghton Mifflin (Boston, MA), 1997.

Pat Mora, *This Big Sky,* Scholastic (New York, NY), 1998.

Sneed B. Collard, *Making Animal Babies,* Houghton Mifflin (Boston, MA), 2000.

Deborah Lee Rose, *Into the A, B, Sea: An Ocean Alphabet,* Scholastic Press (New York, NY), 2000.

Anne F. Rockwell, *Bugs Are Insects,* HarperCollins (New York, NY), 2001.

Deborah Lee Rose, *One Nighttime Sea,* Scholastic (New York, NY), 2003.

Wendy Pfeffer, *Wiggling Worms,* HarperCollins (New York, NY), 2004.

Brenda Z. Guiberson, *Rain, Rain, Rain Forest,* Henry Holt (New York, NY), 2004.

Alvin Jenkins, *Next Stop, Neptune: Experiencing the Solar System,* Houghton Mifflin (Boston, MA), 2004.

Betsy Franco, *Bird Songs: A Backwards Counting Book,* Margaret K. McElderry Books (New York, NY), 2006.

April Pulley Sayre, *Vulture View,* Henry Holt (New York, NY), 2007.

Valerie Worth, *Animal Poems,* Farrar, Straus & Giroux (New York, NY), 2007.

Betsy Franco, *Bees, Snails, and Peacock Tails: Shapes—Naturally,* Margaret K. McElderry Books (New York, NY), 2008.

Adaptations

A Braille version of *The Top of the World* was produced by National Braille Press (Boston, MA), 2000; a sound recording of *The Top of the World* was produced by Volunteer Services for the Visually Handicapped (Milwaukee, WI), 2000.

Sidelights

Steve Jenkins, an award-winning illustrator and author of children's books, is known for his ability to imbue his artwork with his fascination with the natural world. As he noted in his acceptance speech for the prestigious *Boston Globe/Horn Book* Award for Nonfiction: "In my books, I try to present straightforward information in a context that makes sense to children. Children don't need anyone to give them a sense of wonder; they already have that. But they do need a way to incorporate the various bits and pieces of knowledge they acquire into some logical picture of the world. For me, science provides the most elegant and satisfying way to construct this picture." In addition to *The Top of the World: Climbing Mount Everest,* the work that earned Jenkins

Jenkins' collage art is featured in Deborah Lee Rose's award-winning picture book **Into the A, B, Sea.** (Illustration copyright © 2000 by Steve Jenkins. Reprinted by permission of Scholastic, Inc.)

his *Boston Globe/Horn Book* honor, he is also the author/illustrator of books that include *What Do You Do When Something Wants to Eat You?, Life on Earth: The Story of Evolution,* and *I See a Kookaburra!: Discovering Animal Habitats around the World,* the last coauthored with Jenkins' wife, writer Robin Page.

Jenkins inherited his love of both science and art from his father, Alvin Jenkins, a physicist who was also, as the author/illustrator stated in his speech, a "frustrated artist." As a child, Jenkins was fascinated with science and nature and loved to draw and paint. The elder Jenkins encouraged his son in both pursuits, and father and son collaborated on many science projects. More recently, they collaborated on the book *Next Stop, Neptune: Experiencing the Solar System,* Alvin Jenkins writing the text that pairs with his son's dramatic art.

As a child, Jenkins believed that he would become a scientist. Then, while a student at North Carolina State University, he had a change of heart and decided, instead, to major in design. After marrying Page, whom he met during college, Jenkins moved to New York City, where he and his wife eventually established a graphic design firm. After twenty years working in design and raising two children, Jenkins "truly stumbled into making children's books," as he noted in his speech. For Jenkins, working as an illustrator has allowed him to "unite my early interest in science and my chosen career of creating art." As he recalled in an interview for the Children's Literature Web site: "While working on a book design project for Stewart, Tabori & Chang, I suggested to the editor that I also illustrate the books we were designing, and she agreed." It didn't take long for Jenkins to submit a proposal to another publisher, and his career as a children's book author and illustrator was launched. He credits his own curious children with inspiring many of his books for young people.

Jenkins' eye for design and his skilled use of paper collage has garnered wide acclaim. In their respective reviews of *Looking Down* and *Big and Little* for *School Library Journal,* John Peters and Caroline Ward made particular note of the unusual choice of medium. "Using neat, sharp-edged paper collages and pure, simple colors, Jenkins convincingly conveys, better than most aerial photography, both a sense of height and an almost vertiginous feeling of movement," wrote Peters, while Ward dubbed his "distinctive cut-paper collages . . . real showstoppers." In a review of *Actual Size* for *Horn Book,* Lauren E. Raece wrote that the author/illustrator's "signature cut-paper collages are once again amazing." Although explanations or additional important facts are often included, Jenkins incorporates such text in sidebars or closing paragraphs, allowing his visual theme to flow freely.

Jenkins is frequently hailed for the content and composition of his books for children. In *Looking Down,* for example, he combines the unusual with the factual in a wordless book that takes its audience on a ride from the outer reaches of space to spots on a ladybug's back as seen from the perspective of a child looking through a magnifying glass. Elizabeth S. Watson, writing in *Horn Book,* noted that, "set in the context of an astronaut viewing a rapidly approaching Earth, the book provides a perspective easily understood without a text" and will serve as "a welcome addition to the collections of young science enthusiasts." In *Kirkus Reviews* a critic wrote that, with its survey of planetary ecosystems, *Hottest, Coldest, Highest, Deepest* "provides jaw-dropping facts and extremely elegant paper collages to illustrate the amazing natural world." Reviewing the same book for *School Library Journal,* Anne Chapman Callaghan commented that Jenkins' "eye-catching introduction to geography" gives "young readers a full understanding of how amazing these natural wonders are."

Many of Jenkins' books deal with concepts, such as size, shape, and color. In *Big and Little, Actual Size,* and *Prehistoric Actual Size,* he uses creatures from the animal kingdom to illustrate concepts of relative size. Through contrasting, colorful, collage images—such as an ostrich and a hummingbird in the case of *Big and Little* or a plankton and a dinosaur in the case of *Prehistoric Actual Size*—and a spare text, he shows each animal in a perspective relative to another, providing the young reader with a cohesive concept. "As well as offering an inventive exploration of the concepts of big and little," Ward commented of *Big and Little* in *School Library Journal,* Jenkins' work "serves as an introduction to a group of animals, several of which are endangered." Calling Jenkins' decision to depict gigantic creatures through bits and pieces a "masterstroke," *Booklist* contributor Jennifer Mattson wrote that *Actual Size* constitutes "an unusual, unusually effective tool for connecting children to nature's astonishing variety." Dona

Jenkins' collage art features unique textures and contrasts, making books such as Slap, Squeak, and Scatter *picture-book stand-outs.* (Copyright © 2001 by Steve Jenkins. Reprinted by permission of Houghton Mifflin Harcourt Publishing Company. All rights reserved.)

Ratterree held a similar view, writing in *School Library Journal* that Jenkins' "beautiful book is an enticing way to . . . illustrate to budding scientists the importance of comparison, measurement, observation, and record keeping."

Distinguishing a rainbow of hues is the challenge at hand for young children in *Living Color,* and Jenkins' lush collage art reflects a rich spectrum. Set against a white background, his collage animals range over sixty creatures from sloths to stonefish to sea urchins, creatures for which color is a key to survival in their natural habitat. "Jenkins's design, always striking, reaches the heights of inspiration with this offering," concluded a *Kirkus Reviews* writer of the book, while in *Publishers Weekly* a critic exclaimed that the author/illustrator "once again astounds with his amazing lifelike" images.

In *Slap, Squeak, and Scatter: How Animals Communicate* Jenkins delves into animal behavior, and topics range from a honeybee's dance that tells her hive-mates where she has located food to what a cat is saying when it rubs its head on its owner's leg. "There are so many different ways and reasons why animals communicate," wrote Hazel Rochman in *Booklist.* "Each double-page spread could be expanded into a book of its own. Children will find this an exciting introduction to the wonder of zoology, and many will go from here to learn more."

In *Almost Gone: The World's Rarest Animals* and *Dogs and Cats* Jenkins ranges from the rare to the commonplace, finding magic in both. In *Almost Gone* he features twenty-one endangered animals, capturing each one in his cut-paper collage art and describing, in few words, its main characteristic or the reason it is threatened. Remarking on the texture created in his art, Stephanie Zvirin wrote in *Booklist* that the colored paper Jenkins selects for each image is "carefully matched to catch subtle variations of an animal's skin or a sense of the shagginess of its coat." In *School Library Journal* Gloria Koster praised *Almost Gone* as "informative as well as visually stunning," adding that Jenkins creates additional impact by noting the actual number of each creature still remaining on Earth. No such notation is needed for *Dogs and Cats,* a two-sided book that serves as what *Booklist* contributor Michael Cart described as "a delightful and insightful grab bag of facts about a human's best friends." On one side is *Dogs,* on the other is *Cats,* and both feature collage illustrations and information about the variety within each species. In his accompanying text, Jenkins discusses the way each animal found its way into man's life and heart, its evolution, and its unique habits and characteristics. Citing the book's "lively narrative," *School Library Journal* critic Kara Schaff Dean also deemed the collage art in *Dogs and Cats* "stunning" and full of "vitality," while a *Kirkus Reviews* writer praised Jenkins' "cleanly innovative design."

Jenkins takes a broad view in *Life on Earth,* presenting a guide to evolution that is geared for younger readers.

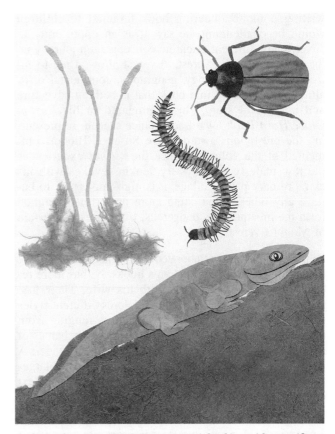

Jenkins takes on a sometimes-controversial subject with magnificent results in Life on Earth: The Story of Evolution. (Jacket art copyright © 2002 by Steve Jenkins. Reprinted by permission of Houghton Mifflin Harcourt Publishing Company. All rights reserved.)

To make this complex concept understandable, he begins with a time line showing how recently humans appeared relative to the history of Earth. He then goes on to cover basics such as fossil evidence and natural selection, while his illustrations show the diversity of the planet's plant and animal species. Jenkins' "explanations of science concepts are comprehensive and comprehensible, making good use of his excellent illustration," wrote Danielle J. Ford in her review for *Horn Book,* while a *Kirkus Reviews* critic considered the volume "a first-class foray into an often-neglected topic." Jenkins "illuminates another corner of the science world" according to a reviewer for *Publishers Weekly,* and Zvirin described *Life on Earth* as "clever, eyecatching, and extremely effective." Although *New York Times Book Review* contributor Christine Hepperman faulted Jenkins for avoiding the controversy surrounding evolutionary theory, in *School Library Journal,* Patricia Manning deemed the book "a polished exposition of a difficult, often controversial scientific concept." Overall, Hepperman concluded, *Life on Earth* is "an accessible introduction to a complex topic [that] taps into children's sense of wonder about the world, which is the great starting point for scientific exploration."

In *The Top of the World,* Jenkins leaves the animal kingdom to take readers on a trek through rugged terrain and a harsh environment. Although he realized that writing a mountaineering book targeted to children would be challenging, he saw it as an opportunity to cover many different scientific concepts on a journey up the side of Mount Everest. "Everest allowed me to introduce climate, geology, geography, continental drift, altitude, and history in a book that is both an adventure and a survival story," he commented in his *Boston Globe/Horn Book* Award acceptance speech. In presenting the prestigious award, judge Susan P. Bloom commented of the volume: "Once the viewer experiences the raw majesty and mystery Jenkins evokes with his extraordinary paper collage, it is nigh impossible to believe any other media could more powerfully summon forth the breathtaking, dangerous, truly awesome terrain of Mount Everest."

While Jenkins has collaborated with other authors since beginning his work in children's books, he has more recently begun collaborating with his wife. Their first joint venture, *Animals in Flight,* explores different styles of wings—those employed by creatures ranging from dragonflies to bats to birds—and the basic mechanics of animal flight. The book appeals to a range of reader: A large picture of each animal is accompanied by large-format text, while smaller pictures link to a smaller text containing more scientific detail. Although Gillian Eng-

berg noted in *Booklist* that the "smaller font often seems too small," she concluded that *Animals in Flight* is "an attractive, informative choice." Ellen Heath praised the book in *School Library Journal,* proclaiming Jenkins' illustrations to be "perfect for this exploration of wings," and a Children's Literature Web site reviewer dubbed the work "a fine introduction for a variety of age groups."

Page and Jenkins continue their collaboration with *What Do You Do with a Tail like This?* Here each page features an interesting, close-up feature of an animal's body part, followed by an illustration of the entire animal alongside a text that provides detailed animal facts. Tim Arnold, in his review for *Booklist,* called the title "another exceptional paper-cut science book from Jenkins." "Like [Jenkins'] previous books, it's a stunner," Arnold added. In *School Library Journal,* Wanda Meyer-Hines praised it as "yet another eye-opening" collaboration and a critic for *Kirkus Reviews* called the book a "display of genius." *What Do You Do with a Tail like This?* was named a Caldecott Honor Book in 2004.

Other collaborations between Page and Jenkins include *I See a Kookaburra!,* an exploration of diverse ecosystems, and *Move!,* which like *Animals in Flight* explores the variations in the way different creatures achieve motion. From swimming and flying to hopping, sliding, and waddling, *Move!* introduces a variety of creatures and provides basic information that explains the reason each form of transportation developed. Remarking on the "eye-popping" quality in Jenkins and Page's art, Susan Weitz noted in *School Library Journal* that *Move!* "is gorgeous and educational," while *Booklist* contributor GraceAnne A. DeCandido predicted that the "lively collaboration" will inspire young readers to imitate the actions explored. "Another intimate look at the natural world" can be found in *I See a Kookaburra!,* according to a *Publishers Weekly* contributor. Here Jenkins and Page transport readers from desert to jungle, savanna to forest, and tide pool to pond. The *Publishers Weekly* critic was impressed by the "straightforward language . . . and vivid, economical descriptions" linking the couple's characteristic attractive collages, while *School Library Journal* critic Joy Fleishhacker wrote that the book combines "clearly presented information with seek-and-find fun" via "breathtaking" double-spread collage art. "The bright and playful design will attract an enthusiastic audience," predicted Shelle Rosenfeld in her *Booklist* review of *I See a Kookaburra!*

Jenkins recreates an historic test of endurance in his 1999 picture book **The Top of the World: Climbing Mount Everest.**

In his interview on the Children's Literature Web site, Jenkins explained how the collaboration between him and Page works. "I'm more linear, and with the writing I always have to keep cutting away. My tendency is to keep adding information. She comes at it from the other end, keeping things simple and making intuitive connections. She does concept development, designs the pages, and works out how the book flows. When it gets down to the end her work is much more precise."

In **Animals in Flight** *Page and Jenkins present an accurate picture of nature, a world that includes both predator and prey.* (Art copyright © 2001 by Steve Jenkins. Reprinted by permission of Houghton Mifflin Harcourt Publishing Company. All rights reserved.)

Describing his own work process, Jenkins explained that he starts with photographs from books or those taken while visiting zoos or aquariums. Once he has established an overall plan, he begins putting things on paper. "I do an outline drawing based on the references and how I want them to look on the page. Then a quick color setting to figure out what paper I'm going to use in the collage. Finally I cut and tear," he told the online interviewer. He also explained part of the appeal of collage art for young readers: "They are filling in part of the information. So not only is it satisfying for me to find a piece of paper that is at the same time a hippopotamus's skin, but I think kids get the same satisfaction from filling in the details and making it into a hippo as well as a piece of paper."

Biographical and Critical Sources

PERIODICALS

Booklist, October 1, 1994, Chris Sherman, review of *Duck's Breath and Mouse Pie: A Collection of Animal Superstitions,* p. 330; February 1, 1995, Hazel Rochman, review of *Biggest, Strongest, Fastest,* p. 1003; October 1, 1996, Carolyn Phelan, review of *Big and Little,* p. 358; December 1, 1997, Hazel Rochman, review of *What Do You Do When Something Wants to Eat You?,* p. 633; August, 1998, Carolyn Phelan, review of *Hottest, Coldest, Highest, Deepest,* p. 201; April 1, 1999, Stephanie Zvirin, review of *The Top of the World: Climbing Mount Everest,* p. 1405; May 15, 2001, Hazel Rochman, review of *Slap, Squeak, and Scatter: How Animals Communicate,* p. 1754; December 15, 2001, Gillian Engberg, review of *Animals in Flight,* p. 735; December 15, 2002, Stephanie Zvirin, review of *Life on Earth: The Story of Evolution,* p. 759; February 15, 2003, Tim Arnold, review of *What Do You Do with a Tail like This?,* p. 1068; May 15, 2004, Jennifer Mattson, review of *Actual Size,* p. 1621; August, 2005, Shelle Rosenfeld, review of *I See a Kookaburra!: Discovering Animal Habitats around the World,* p. 2032; October 15, 2004, Diane Foote, review of *Prehistoric Actual Size,* p. 47; December 1, 2005, Stephanie Zvirin, review of *Almost Gone: The World's Rarest Animals,* p. 67; March 15, 2006, GraceAnne A. DeCandido, review of *Move!,* p. 50; May 1, 2007, Michael Cart, review of *Dogs and Cats,* p. 88; August, 2007, Jennifer Mattson, review of *Living Color,* p. 70.

Bulletin of the Center for Children's Books, June, 1995, Heather McCammonel-Watts, review of *Biggest, Strongest, Fastest,* p. 348; December, 1997, Elizabeth Bush, review of *What Do You Do When Something Wants to Eat You?,* p. 131; June, 1998, Deborah Stevenson, "Rising Star."; December, 2001, review of *Animals in Flight,* p. 143.

Horn Book, July-August, 1995, Ellen Fader, review of *Biggest, Strongest, Fastest,* p. 477; November, 1995, Elizabeth S. Watson, review of *Looking Down,* p. 734; March, 1999, Lilly Robinson, review of *The Top of the World,* p. 244; January, 2000, Steve Jenkins, transcript of *Boston Globe/Horn Book* Award acceptance speech, p. 51; September-October, 2002, Danielle J. Ford, review of *Life on Earth,* p. 595; May-June, 2004, Lauren E. Raece, review of *Actual Size,* p. 345; May-June, 2005, Danielle J. Ford, review of *I See a Kookaburra!,* p. 350; January-February, 2006, Daniel J. Ford, review of *Prehistoric Actual Size,* p. 101; March-April, 2006, Danielle J. Ford, review of *Almost Gone,* p. 206; May-June, 2006, Betty Carter, review of *Move!,* p. 344; May-June, 2007, Claire E. Gross, review of *Dogs and Cats,* p. 302.

Kirkus Reviews, September 15, 1997, review of *What Do You Do When Something Wants to Eat You?,* p. 1458; July 15, 1998, review of *Hottest, Coldest, Highest, Deepest,* p. 1036; October 15, 2001, review of *Animals in Flight,* p. 1485; October 1, 2002, review of *Life on Earth,* p. 1471; January 15, 2003, review of *What Do You Do with a Tail like This?,* p. 142; July 1, 2003, review of *One Nighttime Sea: An Ocean Counting Rhyme,* p. 913; May 1, 2004, review of *Actual Size,* p. 443; May 1, 2005, review of *I See a Kookaburra!,* p. 540; August 15, 2005, review of *Prehistoric Actual Size,* p. 916; January 1, 2006, review of *Almost Gone,* p. 42; April 1, 2006, review of *Move!,* p. 349; April 15, 2007, review of *Dogs and Cats;* July 15, 2007, review of *Living Color.*

New York Times Book Review, November 12, 1995, Patricia McCormick, review of *Looking Down,* p. 32; October 17, 1999, Christopher S. Wren, review of *The Top of the World,* p. 31; March 9, 2003, Christine Hepperman, "Evolution for Beginners," p. 24.

Publishers Weekly, November 10, 1997, review of *What Do You Do When Something Wants to Eat You?,* p. 73; May 10, 1999, review of *The Top of the World,* p. 68; November 11, 2002, review of *Life on Earth,* p.

Jenkins collaborates with wife and fellow artist Robin Page on several picture books, among them What Do You Do with a Tail like This? (Art copyright © 2003 by Steve Jenkins. Reprinted by permission of Houghton Mifflin Harcourt Publishing Company. All rights reserved.)

63; April 25, 2005, review of *I See a Kookaburra!,* p. 56; April 9, 2007, review of *Dogs and Cats,* p. 53; July 15, 2007, review of *Living Color,* p. 164; November 5, 2007, review of *Vulture View,* p. 63.

School Library Journal, September, 1994, Sandra Welzenbach, review of *Duck's Breath and Mouse Pie,* p. 208; September, 1995, John Peters, review of *Looking Down,* p. 179; October, 1996, Caroline Ward, review of *Big and Little,* p. 99; November, 1997, Sally Bates Goodroe, review of *What Do You Do When Something Wants to Eat You?,* p. 109; August, 1998, Anne Chapman Callaghan, review of *Hottest, Coldest, Highest, Deepest,* p. 151; May, 2001, Cynthia M. Sturgis, review of *Slap, Squeak, and Scatter,* p. 143; November, 2001, Ellen Heath, review of *Animals in Flight,* p. 146; December, 2002, Patricia Manning, review of *Life on Earth,* p. 124; March, 2003, Wanda Meyers-Hines, review of *What Do You Do with a Tail like This?,* p. 220; June, 2004, Dona Ratterree, review of *Actual Size,* p. 128; May, 2005, Joy Fleishhacker, review of *I See a Kookaburra!,* p. 108; December, 2005, Steven Engelfried, review of *Prehistoric Actual Size,* p. 128; February, 2006, Gloria Koster, review of *Almost Gone,* p. 120; June, 2006, Susan Weitz, review of *Move!,* p. 136; May, 2007, Kara Schaff Dean, review of *Dogs and Cats,* p. 118; December, 2007, Robin L. Gibson, review of *Vulture View,* p. 115.

Teaching Children Mathematics, April, 1997, Eunice Hendrix-Martin, "Students Use Their Bodies to Measure Animals," p. 426.

ONLINE

Children's Literature Web site, http://www.childrenslit.com/ (September 3, 2004), interview with Jenkins.
Steve Jenkins Home Page, http://www.stevejenkinsbooks.com (March 28, 2008).*

*   *   *

JOHNSON, Angela 1961-

Personal

Born June 18, 1961, in Tuskegee, AL; daughter of Arthur (an autoworker) and Truzetta (an accountant) Johnson. *Education:* Attended Kent State University.

Addresses

Home—Kent, OH.

Career

Volunteers in Service to America (VISTA), Ravenna, OH, child development worker, 1981-82; freelance writer of children's books, beginning 1989.

Member

Authors Guild, Authors League of America.

Angela Johnson (Photograph by David Massey. AP Images.)

Awards, Honors

Ezra Jack Keats New Writer Award, U.S. Board on Books for Young People, 1991; Coretta Scott King Honor Book designation, American Library Association Social Responsibilities Round Table, 1991, for *When I Am Old with You,* and 1998, for *The Other Side: Shorter Poems;* Coretta Scott King Author Award, 1993, for *Toning the Sweep,* and 1998, for *Heaven;* MacArthur Foundation grant, 2003; Coretta Scott King Award, and Michael J. Printz Award, both 2004, both for *The First Part Last.*

Writings

PICTURE BOOKS

Tell Me a Story, Mama, illustrated by David Soman, Orchard Books (New York, NY), 1989.
Do like Kyla, illustrated by James Ransome, Orchard Books (New York, NY), 1990.
When I Am Old with You, illustrated by David Soman, Orchard Books (New York, NY), 1990.
One of Three, illustrated by David Soman, Orchard Books (New York, NY), 1991.
The Leaving Morning, illustrated by David Soman, Orchard Books (New York, NY), 1992.
The Girl Who Wore Snakes, illustrated by James Ransome, Orchard Books (New York, NY), 1993.

Julius, illustrated by Dav Pilkey, Orchard Books (New York, NY), 1993.

Joshua by the Sea, illustrated by Rhonda Mitchell, Orchard Books (New York, NY), 1994.

Joshua's Night Whispers, illustrated by Rhonda Mitchell, Orchard Books (New York, NY), 1994.

Mama Bird, Baby Birds, illustrated by Rhonda Mitchell, Orchard Books (New York, NY), 1994.

Rain Feet, illustrated by Rhonda Mitchell, Orchard Books (New York, NY), 1994.

Shoes like Miss Alice's, illustrated by Ken Page, Orchard Books (New York, NY), 1995.

The Aunt in Our House, illustrated by David Soman, Orchard Books (New York, NY), 1996.

The Rolling Store, illustrated by Peter Catalanotto, Orchard Books (New York, NY), 1997.

Daddy Calls Me Man, illustrated by Rhonda Mitchell, Orchard Books (New York, NY), 1997.

Maniac Monkeys on Magnolia Street, illustrated by John Ward, Random House (New York, NY), 1999, bound with *When Mules Flew on Magnolia Street,* Yearling (New York, NY), 2005.

The Wedding, illustrated by David Soman, Orchard Books (New York, NY), 1999.

Those Building Men, illustrated by Mike Benny, Scholastic (New York, NY), 1999.

Down the Winding Road, illustrated by Shane W. Evans, DK Ink, 2000.

Rain Feet, illustrated by Rhonda Mitchell, Orchard Books (New York, NY), 2001.

When Mules Flew on Magnolia Street, illustrated by John Ward, Alfred A. Knopf (New York, NY), 2001, bound with *Maniac Monkeys on Magnolia Street,* Yearling (New York, NY), 2005.

I Dream of Trains, illustrated by Loren Long, Simon & Schuster (New York, NY), 2003.

Just like Josh Gibson, illustrated by Beth Peck, Simon & Schuster (New York, NY), 2003.

Violet's Music, illustrated by Laura Huliska-Beith, Dial Books (New York, NY), 2004.

A Sweet Smell of Roses, illustrated by Eric Velasquez, Simon & Schuster (New York, NY), 2005.

Lily Brown's Paintings, illustrated by E.B. Lewis, Orchard Books (New York, NY), 2007.

Wind Flyers, illustrated by Loren Long, Simon & Schuster (New York, NY), 2007.

OTHER

Toning the Sweep (novel), Orchard Books (New York, NY), 1993.

Humming Whispers (novel), Orchard Books (New York, NY), 1995.

Songs of Faith (novel), Orchard Books (New York, NY), 1998.

Heaven (novel), Simon & Schuster (New York, NY), 1998.

The Other Side: Shorter Poems, Orchard Books (New York, NY), 1998.

Gone from Home: Short Takes (stories), DK Children's (New York, NY), 1998.

Running back to Ludie (novel), Orchard Books (New York, NY), 2002.

Looking for Red (novel), Simon & Schuster (New York, NY), 2002.

A Cool Moonlight (novel), Dial Books (New York, NY), 2003.

The First Part Last (novel), Simon & Schuster (New York, NY), 2003.

Bird (novel), Dial Books (New York, NY), 2004.

Work included in anthologies, such as *In Daddy's Arms I Am Tall,* Simon & Schuster (New York, NY), 2003.

Adaptations

Many of Johnson's novels have been adapted for audiobook, including *Humming Whispers,* Recorded Books, 1997, and *The First Part Last,* Listening Library, 2004.

Sidelights

Angela Johnson first drew critical attention for creating picture books depicting African-American children and their warm, loving relationship to parents, grandparents, siblings, and friends. While Johnson's stories focus on black families, they also capture emotions and experiences that are familiar to young readers of all cultures. Her fiction for older children, which includes both short stories and novels such as *Running back to Ludie, The First Part Last,* and *Bird,* tackle difficult issues such as divorce, the death of a sibling, and chronic illness with an emphasis on learning to survive and thrive such dev-

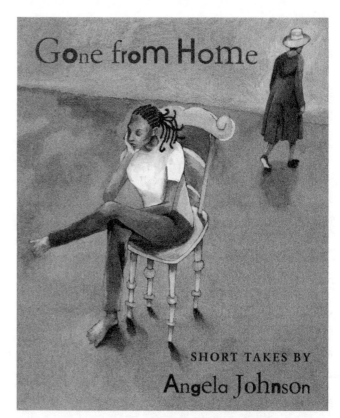

Cover of Johnson's short-story collection Gone from Home, *featuring artwork by Shane W. Evans.* (Jacket painting copyright © 1998 by Shane W. Evans. Reproduced by permission of DK Publishing, a division of Penguin Putnam Books for Young Readers.)

astating events. "Johnson is a master at representing human nature in various guises at different levels," asserted *Twentieth-Century Children's Writers* contributor Lucille H. Gregory. Rudine Sims Bishop, writing in *Horn Book,* maintained that Johnson's books "feature charming first-person narrators." These narrators "are distinct individuals," Bishop added, "but their emotions are ones shared across cultures."

In *Tell Me a Story, Mama,* which Bishop called an "impressive debut," a little girl asks her mother for a familiar bedtime story and ends up doing most of the storytelling herself as she reminds her mother of each favorite part. Another creative child is featured in *Lily Brown's Painting,* as a little girl is transported to amazing places through her art—and the illustrations created by noted illustrator E.B. White. In her *Horn Book* review of *Tell Me a Story, Mama* Maria Salvadore maintained that by "providing a glimpse of one African-American family, Johnson has validated other families' experiences, regardless of racial or ethnic background." Also transcending culture and race, *Lily Brown's Painting* will "inspire readers to don their painting smocks and create new worlds of their own," according to *School Library Journal* critic Marianne Saccardi.

Johnson features characters whose lives are enriched by familial affection and reassurance in books such as *One of Three, When I Am Old with You, Just like Josh Gibson,* and *Violet's Music.* In *Do Like Kyla,* a young narrator describes how she imitates her older sister all day, then at bedtime revels in the fact that "Kyla does like me." The young narrator of *One of Three* relates the fun she has being one of three sisters, as well as the frustration of not being able to join in some of the things her older siblings do. The Coretta Scott King Honor Book *When I Am Old with You* spotlights a boy who tells his grandfather the things they will do together when the boy catches up to him in age. Reviewing *One of Three,* a *Publishers Weekly* critic praised Johnson for her "perceptive and understated text," while Karen James, writing in *School Library Journal,* admired the way Johnson captures "the underlying love and strength of positive family relationships."

Just like Josh Gibson tells a story of empowerment as a young African-American girl repeats the family story of how her Grandma was trained to play baseball almost from birth. Growing up during the 1940s and 1950s and encouraged by her father to be as good a player as Negro League athlete Josh Gibson, Grandma was allowed to play with the local team only occasionally. The girl eventually shows off her skill when she pinch hits for an injured player and assures the all-male Maple Grove All-Stars a win. The story "has a baseball announcer's suspenseful rhythm," according to Engberg, and in an afterward Johnson includes a biography of the well-known real-life baseball player. While calling Johnson's story "slight," Susan Scheps concluded in *School Library Journal* that *Just like Josh Gibson* successfully communicates the message "that a girl can succeed at a

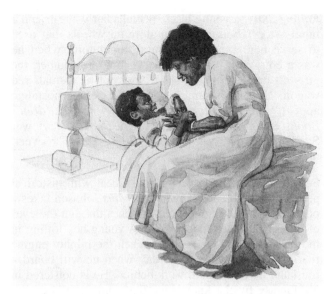

Johnson relates a gentle story about a loving parent-child relationship in **Tell Me a Story, Mama,** *illustrated by David Soman.* (Illustration copyright © 1989 by David Soman. All rights reserved. Reprinted by permission of Orchard Books, an imprint of Scholastic, Inc.)

'boy's game' if she sets her mind to it." "Johnson never disappoints," a *Kirkus Reviews* writer declared, describing *Just like Josh Gibson* "a sweetly powerful and slyly subversive tale."

A young girl wins like-minded friends through self-expression in *Violet's Music,* as Violet's love of making music is nurtured by her family until it blooms as a talent for playing guitar. Gillian Engberg praised Johnson's decision to depict Violet as upbeat and committed to following her muse rather than a lonesome outsider, writing in *Booklist* that the "repetitive phrases and . . . onomatopoeia" featured in *Violet's Music* "continue the story's cheerful energy and beat." Praising Johnson's "jazzy story," *School Library Journal* contributor Jane Marino added that the book "celebrates music as much as it applauds being true to what you love."

Unusual pets join the young protagonists in *The Girl Who Wore Snakes* and *Julius.* In the former, Ali's strong interest in snakes, which she wears as jewelry, surprises everyone in her family except her snake-loving aunt. *Julius,* illustrated by Dav Pilkey, features a young girl named Maya who receives Julius, an Alaskan pig, from her grandfather. Together, Maya and Julius teach each other new tricks and enjoy a variety of adventures. Betsy Hearne, writing in the *Bulletin of the Center for Children's Books,* called *Julius* a "gleeful celebration of silliness."

In *Shoes like Miss Alice's,* Sara is hesitant about being with a new babysitter. Her fears are quickly dispelled, however, and a bond is formed when Miss Alice changes into a different pair of shoes for each special activity they do together. "Tucked in the tale is a nice message about being open to new people walking into your life," noted *Booklist* reviewer Ilene Cooper. In *The*

Rolling Store, a young black girl tells her white friend a family story about a general store on wheels that used to serve her grandfather's rural community when he was a boy. With help from the visiting grandfather, the girls create their own mobile store out of a small red wagon. "Johnson's family story has a certain nostalgic appeal," noted *Bulletin of the Center for Children's Books* editor Janice M. Del Negro. *Booklist* reviewer Stephanie Zvirin deemed *The Rolling Store* "a sweet, upbeat story."

Several of Johnson's picture books deal with historical people or epochs. In *I Dream of Trains* Johnson takes a poignant look at engineer Casey Jones through the eyes of a fictional black field worker. A young boy toiling in the heat lives for the moment when the mighty engine roars by and dreams of the day when he will board a train and leave the hard work behind. He is bolstered in his fantasy by the knowledge that some of those who work with the mighty Casey Jones are black men. In *Black Issues Book Review* Suzanne Rust wrote: "Bold and provocative in prose, picture and content," *I Dream of Trains* is "a work worthy of any contemporary collection."

The civil rights movement is the focus of *A Sweet Smell of Roses,* which focuses on the children who became part of the struggle for racial equality led by Dr. Martin Luther King, Jr. In a text that pairs with illustrations by Eric Velasquez, two sisters witness the heckling Dr. King receives as he makes a speech in their town and ultimately decide to join the march. According to *Booklist* contributor Hazel Rochman, the older sister's "clear, first-person narrative draws on the language of the struggle," and in *School Library Journal* Mary N. Oluonye praised *A Sweet Smell of Roses* as a "quiet, gentle story" that makes "more real . . . this chapter of American history." A *Kirkus Reviews* contributor wrote that Velasquez's "marvelous" artwork provide Johnson's story with "extra punch and impact," dubbing the resulting fact-based picture book "powerful and moving."

In *Wind Flyers* Johnson pairs what Engberg described as "spare, poetic lines" with realistic artwork by Loren Long to share a boy's memories of his beloved great-great uncle, a pilot with the historic Tuskegee Airmen who flew during World War II. From the uncle's first rides in a barnstormer as a young boy, Johnson's verses move forward in time, focusing on the man's wartime service as part of the black air corps and his piloting following the war. "Long's acrylics beautifully extend the evocative words," concluded Engberg in her review of *Wind Flyers,* while in *School Library Journal* John Peters praised the work as a "soaring . . . tribute to both the . . . African-American pilots and to the profound longing to fly that impelled them." Johnson's text is "as light and graceful as the air in which the . . . [airmen] navigated their planes," wrote a *Publishers Weekly* critic, concluding that author and illustrator work together to "turn a quiet moment in history into a story that will send spirits soaring."

Cover of Johnson's award-winning young-adult novel Toning the Sweep, *featuring artwork by Synthia Saint James.* (Cover illustration © 1994 by Scholastic Inc. Reproduced by permission of Scholastic, Inc.)

In 1993, Johnson published her first novel for older children. In *Toning the Sweep* fourteen-year-old Emily participates in the final days of her cancer-stricken grandmother's life by videotaping the ailing woman as she visits with friends, recalling stories of the past. "Full of subtle nuance, the novel is overlaid with meaning about the connections of family and the power of friendship," maintained *School Library Journal* contributor Ellen Fader. *Booklist* reviewer Quraysh Ali lauded the work, asserting that, "with ingenuity and grace, Johnson captures the innocence, the vulnerability, and the love of human interaction as well as the melancholy, the self-discovery, and the introspection of adolescence." Mary M. Burns in *Horn Book,* cited of special note "the skill with which the author moves between times past and times present without sacrificing her main story line or diluting the emotional impact."

Humming Whispers focuses on Sophie, an aspiring dancer who worries that she is developing the schizophrenia that now afflicts her older sister. Rochman characterized the novel as "a bleak contemporary story of suffering, lit with the hope of people who take care of each other in the storm." *School Library Journal* contributor Carol Schene observed that, while "there are no easy answers" for the characters in the book, "the frailty and strength of the human spirit" displayed by each one makes the story memorable. Elizabeth Bush, writing in *Bulletin of the Center for Children's Books,* stated that the author "ably demonstrates the pervasive effects of mental illness on an entire family," and a *Kirkus Reviews* critic praised the way Johnson "carefully and richly fleshes out the characters."

Focusing on another medical condition, *A Cool Moonlight* tells the story of Lila, a child stricken with xeroderma pigmentosum, a rare over-sensitivity to sunlight. Forced to live a nocturnal lifestyle, Lila takes solace in imaginary friends until her ninth birthday, when she comes to terms with her individuality. In her *Horn Book* review of *A Cool Moonlight,* Joanna Rudge Long commended Johnson for her ability to include the "deft touches that make this spare portrait so effective."

The author drew particularly favorable reviews for her novel *Heaven.* Here fourteen-year-old Marley is the beloved only child in a happy family—until, by accident, she discovers that her parents are actually her uncle and aunt, and her real father is an itinerant "uncle" she hardly knows. This revelation leads Marley to investigate exactly what constitutes a family unit and how her identity is shaped by those who love her. Praising the book for its "plain, lyrical writing," *Booklist* contributor Rochman concluded that in *Heaven* the author "makes us see the power of loving kindness."

Readers first meet Bobby, the hero of *The First Part Last,* in *Heaven.* In *The First Part Last,* Johnson spins the story of Bobby's unexpected teenage parenthood, how it compromises his ambitions to be an artist but in return offers him the opportunity to love his infant daughter and connect with his parents. The responsibility for a helpless infant is scary—and at times frustrating—but Bobby is sustained by his fond memories of the past and moments of enjoyment in the present. In a *Publishers Weekly* review of *The First Part Last,* a critic praised the way Johnson "skillfully relates the hope in the midst of pain."

Difficult family situations inform both *Running back to Ludie* and *Looking for Red.* In *Running back to Ludie* a teen narrator explores the mixed emotions she experienced as she prepares to meet the mother who abandoned her to live in the woods. Long, writing in *Horn Book,* maintained that the free-verse style of the novel highlights the narrator's feelings of rejection and reconciliation. "Johnson's exploration of the process is subtle and beautifully wrought," the critic concluded. *Looking for Red* offers a more straightforward narrative with a dark secret at its core. Red's sister Mike is still reeling from grief in the wake of his disappearance, and

she receives small solace from Red's equally traumatized friends. Only as the story proceeds does the reader realize that Mike and Red's friends share some of the responsibility for his accidental death. "The strength of this story is the accurate portrayal of the surreal nature of grief laden with guilt," observed Jean Gaffney in *School Library Journal.* In *Horn Book* Long praised the "luminous ease" with which Johnson depicts the characters, "both their estrangement from reality and their eventual return toward it."

Described by a *Kirkus Reviews* writer as a "poignant tale" about "friendship, family, and human limitations," *Bird* finds Johnson's thirteen-year-old title character on the road as a runaway. Traveling from Ohio down to rural Alabama in the hope that she can convince her stepfather to return to her family, Bird meets interesting new friends along the way, including teens Ethan and Jay and elderly Mrs. Pritchard. As she becomes more receptive to others, the girl learns that even people who

Cover of Johnson's **Humming Whispers,** *in which a teen worries that she will inherit the same mental illness that cripples an older sister.*
(Copyright © 1995 by Scholastic Inc. Reprinted by permission of Scholastic, Inc.)

seem happy on the outside often carry sadness in their heart. Other narratives include those of Ethan and Jay, and their stories interweave with Bird's tale in surprising ways. Although a *Publishers Weekly* contributor found Johnson's narrators surprisingly mature for their age, the "overwhelming kindness" of all the characters in *Bird* allow readers to share in the "compassionate world" that allows Bird to learn and grow. In her "open-ended, interconnected" storylines, Johnson demonstrates "how small kindnesses can ease the grip of grief," Miriam Lang Budin wrote in *School Library Journal*, concluding that *Bird* reveals "many truths about human emotion."

Humorous in tone, *Maniac Monkeys on Magnolia Street* and its sequel, *When Mules Flew on Magnolia Street*, introduce Charlie, a girl who must adjust to new friends and new surroundings after moving to Magnolia Street. Told from Charlie's point of view, the two chapter books reveal how the youngster adapts to new situations by being "open to the small wonders around her," to quote Helen Rosenberg in *Booklist*. In her *Booklist* review of *When Mules Flew on Magnolia Street*, Denise Wilms likewise praised the "small slices of life" Johnson serves up for early readers.

Johnson once told *SATA*: "I don't believe the magic of listening to [my grade-school teacher] . . . read us stories after lunch will ever be repeated for me. Book people came to life. They sat beside me in Maple Grove School. That is when I knew. I asked for a diary that year and have not stopped writing. My family, especially my grandfather and father, are storytellers and those spoken words sit beside me too." In recognition of her work in children's literature, Johnson was honored with a 2003 MacArthur Foundation grant, a half-million-dollar prize awarded to a select few individuals working in the arts and sciences who make unique contributions to the betterment of society.

Biographical and Critical Sources

BOOKS

Children's Literature Review, Volume 33, Gale (Detroit, MI), 1994, pp. 93-96.
Twentieth-Century Children's Writers, 4th edition, St. James (Detroit, MI), 1995, pp. 493-494.

PERIODICALS

Black Issues Book Review, July-August, 2003, Suzanne Rust, review of *I Dream of Trains*, p. 65.
Booklist, April 1, 1993, Quraysh Ali, review of *Toning the Sweep*, p. 1432; February 15, 1995, Hazel Rochman, review of *Humming Whispers*, p. 1072; March 15, 1995, Ilene Cooper, review of *Shoes like Miss Alice's*, p. 1334; February 15, 1997, Stephanie Zvirin, review of *The Rolling Store*, p. 1026; September 15, 1998, Hazel Rochman, review of *Heaven*, p. 219; November 15, 1998, Helen Rosenberg, review of *The Other Side: Shorter Poems*, p. 579; January 1, 1999, Helen Rosenberg, review of *Maniac Monkeys on Magnolia Street*, p. 878; February 15, 2000, Michael Cart, review of *Down the Winding Road*, p. 1118; November 15, 2000, Anna Rich, review of *Heaven*, p. 657; January 1, 2001, Denise Wilms, review of *When Mules Flew on Magnolia Street*, p. 960; February 15, 2001, Henrietta M. Smith, review of *Rain Feet*, p. 1161; January 1, 2002, review of *Running back to Ludie*, p. 858; September 1, 2003, Hazel Rochman, review of *The First Part Last*, p. 122; October 1, 2003, Carolyn Phelan, review of *A Cool Moonlight*, p. 324; October 1, 2003, Gillian Engberg, review of *I Dream of Trains*, p. 328; February 15, 2004, Gillian Engberg, review of *Just like Josh Gibson*, p. 1077; March 15, 2004, Gillian Engberg, review of *Violet's Music*, p. 1308; February 1, 2005, Hazel Rochman, review of *A Sweet Smell of Roses*, p. 978; February 15, 2005, Brian Wilson, review of *The First Part Last*, p. 1988; December 1, 2006, Gillian Engberg, review of *Wind Flyers*, p. 52; February 1, 2007, Gillian Engberg, review of *Lily Brown's Paintings*, p. 60.
Bulletin of the Center for Children's Books, May, 1993, Betsy Hearne, review of *Julius*, p. 284; April, 1995, Elizabeth Bush, review of *Humming Whispers*, p. 278; May, 1997, Janice M. Del Negro, review of *The Rolling Store*, pp. 325-326; January, 2002, review of *Running back to Ludie*, p. 176; October, 2003, Karen Coats, review of *A Cool Moonlight*, p. 65; February, 2004, Janice Del Negro, review of *Violet's Music*, p. 236; March, 2004, Elizabeth Bush, review of *Just like Josh Gibson*, p. 280; December, 2004, Karen Coats, review of *Bird*, p. 172; February, 2005, Elizabeth Bush, review of *A Sweet Smell of Roses*, p. 254.
Horn Book, September-October, 1992, Rudine Sims Bishop, "Books from Parallel Cultures: New African-American Voices," p. 620; March-April, 1993, Ellen Fader, review of *Julius*, pp. 196-197; September-October, 1993, Mary M. Burns, review of *Toning the Sweep*, p. 603; March-April, 1995, Maria Salvadore, review of *Tell Me a Story, Mama*, p. 229; November, 1998, Nancy Vasilakis, review of *The Other Side*, p. 750; November-December, 2001, Joanna Rudge Long, review of *Running back to Ludie*, p. 766; July-August, 2002, Joanna Rudge Long, review of *Looking for Red*, p. 463; September-October, 2003, Joanna Rudge Long, review of *A Cool Moonlight*, p. 611; September-October, 2004, Christine M. Heppermann, review of *Bird*, p. 587; January-February, 2005, Martha V. Parravano, review of *A Sweet Smell of Roses*, p. 79.
Kirkus Reviews, April 1, 1995, review of *Humming Whispers*, p. 470; September 1, 2001, review of *Running back to Ludie*, p. 1292; September 1, 2003, review of *A Cool Moonlight*, p. 1125; December 15, 2003, reviews of *Just like Josh Gibson* and *Violet's Music*, p. 1450; July 15, 2004, review of *Bird*, p. 688; January 1, 2005, review of *A Sweet Smell of Roses*, p. 53; December 1, 2006, review of *Lily Brown's Paintings*, p. 1221; December 15, 2006, review of *Wind Flyers*, p. 1269.

New York Times Book Review, November 16, 2003, Marsha Wilson Chall, "One-Track Minds," p. 24.

Publishers Weekly, August 9, 1991, review of *One of Three,* p. 56; August 3, 1998, review of *Heaven,* p. 86; November 16, 1998, review of *The Other Side,* p. 76; November 23, 1998, review of *Maniac Monkeys on Magnolia Street,* p. 67; March 22, 1999, review of *The Wedding,* p. 91; March 6, 2000, review of *Down the Winding Road,* p. 109; May 27, 2002, review of *Looking for Red,* p. 60; June 16, 2003, review of *The First Part Last,* p. 73; October 20, 2003, review of *I Dream of Trains,* p. 53 and *A Cool Moonlight,* p. 55; January 12, 2004, reviews of *Violet's Music* and *Just like Josh Gibson,* p. 53; October 18, 2004, review of *Bird,* p. 65; January 3, 2005, review of *A Sweet Smell of Roses,* p. 55; November 20, 2006, review of *Wind Flyers,* p. 57; January 1, 2007, review of *Lily Brown's Paintings,* p. 49.

School Library Journal, October, 1991, Karen James, review of *One of Three,* p. 98; April, 1993, Ellen Fader, review of *Toning the Sweep,* p. 140; April, 1995, Carol Schene, review of *Humming Whispers,* p. 154; January, 2001, Maria B. Salvadore, review of *When Mules Flew on Magnolia Street,* p. 101; March, 2001, Susan Helper, review of *Those Building Men,* p. 236; December, 2001, Nina Lindsay, review of *Running back to Ludie,* p. 164; July, 2002, Jean Gaffney, review of *Looking for Red,* p. 120; September, 2003, Maria B. Salvadore, review of *A Cool Moonlight,* p. 215; October, 2003, Catherine Threadgill, review of *I Dream of Trains,* p. 126; February, 2004, Jane Marino, review of *Violet's Music,* p. 114; March, 2004, Susan Scheps, review of *Just like Josh Gibson,* p. 172; September, 2004, Miriam Lang Budin, review of *Bird,* p. 209; March, 2004, Mary N. Oluonye, review of *A Sweet Smell of Roses,* p. 174; January, 2007, John Peters, review of *Wind Flyers,* p. 98; February, 2007, Marianne Saccardi, review of *Lily Brown's Paintings,* p. 88.

ONLINE

African American Literature Book Club Web site, http://aalbc.com (March 28, 2008), "Angela Johnson."

Ohioana Authors Web site, http://www.ohioana-authors.org/ (March 28, 2008), "Angela Johnson."

Visiting Authors Web site, http://www.visitingauthors.com/ (March 28, 2008), "Angela Johnson."*

*   *   *

JOHNSTON, Jeffry W.

Personal

Married; children: one son.

Addresses

Home—Broomall, PA. *Agent*—Scott Treimell, 434 Lafayette St., New York, NY 10003. *E-mail*—jeff@jeffrywjohnston.com.

Career

Fiction writer, columnist, and journalist. *Globe Times,* Bethlehem, PA, former feature writer and reviewer.

Member

Society of Children's Book Writers and Illustrators.

Awards, Honors

Edgar Allen Poe Award nomination for Best Young-Adult Novel, and YALSA Quick Pick for Reluctant Readers designation, both 2008, both for *Fragments.*

Writings

Fragments, Simon Pulse (New York, NY), 2007.

Author of numerous short stories for children and adults. Contributor of film and theatre reviews to periodicals; author of monthly column for Rodale, Inc.

Sidelights

Jeffry W. Johnston is a freelance writer and journalist based in Pennsylvania. A former staff writer for the Bethlehem, Pennsylvania *Globe Times* and a columnist for Rodale, Inc., publishers, Johnston has also written a great deal of short fiction, including stories in the horror, mystery, and fantasy genres. His first young-adult novel, *Fragments,* was published in 2007 and a year later was nominated for the Edgar Allen Poe Award for Best Young-Adult Novel by the Mystery Writers of America.

Fragments focuses on Chase Farrell, a high school student whose life is turned upside down after the night he becomes the lone survivor of a car accident that kills three of his friends. Because his memories of the events of that fateful night disappear, Chase is haunted by guilt and fear. When these memories start to return in the form of flashbacks, they bring with them visions so terrible that the teen is soon haunted by new fears. As narrated by Chase, Johnston's novel brings to life the teen's torment through what *Kliatt* critic Jay Wise described as "short, staccato chapters" that build suspense. Chase is "the quintessential unreliable narrator," Wise added, noting that *Fragments* would serves as "powerful bibliotherapy" for older teens wrestling with dysfunctional or abusive relationships.

Biographical and Critical Sources

PERIODICALS

Bulletin of the Center for Children's Books, April, 2007, Karen Coats, review of *Fragments,* p. 332.

Kliatt, January, 2007, Jay Wise, review of *Fragments,* p. 23.

Voice of Youth Advocates, February, 2007, Rollie Welch, review of *Fragments,* p. 526.

ONLINE

Jeffry W. Johnston Home Page, http://jeffrywjohnston.com (February 15, 2008).

K

KANZLER, John 1963-

Personal

Born 1963; married; wife's name Diane. *Hobbies and other interests:* "Learning more about paleontology, archaeology, and astronomy."

Addresses

Home and office—Greenfield, MA. *E-mail*—john@johnkanzler.com.

Career

Illustrator.

Illustrator

Sherry Garland, *Goodnight, Cowboy,* Scholastic (New York, NY), 1999.

Anita Reith Stohs, *Hush, Little One: A Lullaby for God's Children,* Concordia (St. Louis, MO), 2002.

Frank Asch, *Class Pets: The Ghost of P.S. 42,* Simon & Schuster (New York, NY), 2002.

Frank Asch, *Survival School,* Simon & Schuster (New York, NY), 2003.

Frank Asch, *Battle in a Bottle,* Simon & Schuster (New York, NY), 2003.

The Big Rock Candy Mountain, Mondo (New York, NY), 2004.

Susan Ring, *Safari Sounds,* Innovative Kids, 2004.

Nina Hess, *Whose Feet?,* Random House (New York, NY), 2004.

Martha Hamilton and Mitch Weiss, *Priceless Gifts: A Folktale from Italy,* August House (Little Rock, AR), 2007.

Margaret Read MacDonald, *The Old Woman and Her Pig: An Appalachian Folktale,* HarperCollins (New York, NY), 2007.

"THE STORY OF DR. DOLITTLE" SERIES

Diane Namm, adapter, *Animal Talk* (also see below), Sterling (New York, NY), 2006.

Diane Namm, adapter, *The Circus Crocodile* (also see below), Sterling (New York, NY), 2006.

Diane Namm, adapter, *Doctor Dolittle's Great Adventure* (also see below), Sterling (New York, NY), 2006.

Diane Namm, adapter, *Doctor Dolittle's Magical Cure* (also see below), Sterling (New York, NY), 2006.

Diane Namm, adapter, *The Story of Doctor Dolittle* (omnibus; contains *Animal Talk, The Circus Crocodile, Doctor Dolittle's Great Adventure,* and *Doctor Dolittle's Magical Cure*), Spotlight (Edina, MN), 2008.

Sidelights

Drawing animals comes naturally to John Kanzler: he gains his inspiration from the critters of all sorts that he and his wife, Diane, care for on their farm in Greenfield, Massachusetts. Along with its resident sheep, llamas, and cats, the Kanzlers' farm is home to mice, woodchucks, foxes, and occasionally even brown bears. Although Kanzler often uses his fellow farm-dwellers as models for his illustration assignments, he sometimes has to go further afield, as in his work creating art for Margaret Read MacDonald's *The Old Woman and Her Pig: An Appalachian Folktale.* The Kanzler farm is not, in fact, home to swine.

Despite his affinity for drawing animals, Kanzler's first two illustration assignments—Sherry Garland's *Goodnight, Cowboy* and Anita Reith Stohs' *Hush, Little One: A Lullaby for God's Children*—feature human protagonists. However, animals reclaim the spotlight in Kanzler's work for Frank Asch's *Class Pets: The Ghosts of P.S. 42,* which finds two homeless mice setting up a new home in the walls of an elementary classroom. "Kanzler's charming sketches provid[e] . . . a mouse's-eye view," wrote a critic in appraising *Class Pets* for *Kirkus Reviews.* The illustrator's "softly shaded drawings . . . add atmospheric details that help cement the book's appeal for the elementary crowd," a *Publishers Weekly* critic concluded.

Another book featuring Kanzler's art, *The Big Rock Candy Mountain,* pairs the lyrics of a popular U.S. folk song with pictures that bring to life a candied landscape.

"The illustrations are definitely the most charming component here," wrote a *Kirkus Reviews* contributor, the critic citing as a favorite Kanzler's humorous depiction of a sugary sweet Mt. Rushmore. Humor is also an important element of Kanzler's art for *The Old Woman and Her Pig,* in which the illustrator's "textured paintings play up the expressions and sauciness of the old woman, her little boy and the animals," according to a *Kirkus Reviews* writer. Another traditional tale, Martha Hamilton and Mitch Weiss's retelling titled *Priceless Gifts: A Folktale from Italy,* prompted Jayne Damron to write in *School Library Journal* that "Kanzler's warm-hued paintings evoke traditional images." GraceAnne A. DeCandido, reviewing the same book for *Booklist,* enjoyed Kanzler's inclusion of "colorful fairy-tale effects" within his art.

In addition to picture books, Kanzler also illustrates books for beginning readers. Among these are *Whose Feet?* by Nina Hess, in which Kanzler portrays all sorts of animal feet, from those of moles to those of orangutans. He has also illustrated Diane Namm's series of easy-reader adaptations of Hugh Lofting's classic children's novel *Doctor Dolittle,* as well as a lift-the-flap book titled *Safari Sounds,* in which he matches humorous riddles by Susan Ring with pictures chock full of noisy animals.

Biographical and Critical Sources

PERIODICALS

Booklist, December 15, 2002, Gillian Engberg, review of *Class Pets: The Ghost of P.S. 42,* p. 759; June 1, 2003, Eva Mitnick, review of *Battle in a Bottle,* p. 1774.

Kirkus Reviews, August 1, 2002, review of *Class Pets,* p. 1121: June 1, 2003, review of *Battle in a Bottle,* p. 800; March 1, 2004, review of *The Big Rock Candy Mountain,* p. 224; December 1, 2006, review of *The Old Woman and Her Pig: An Appalachian Folktale,* p. 1223.

School Library Journal, October, 2002, Beth Tegart, review of *Class Pets,* p. 98; January, 2004, Teri Markson, review of *Survival School,* p. 87; May, 2004, Mary Elam, review of *The Big Rock Candy Mountain,* p. 133; February, 2007, Martha Simpson, review of *The Old Woman and Her Pig,* p. 110; June, 2007, Jayne Damron, review of *Priceless Gifts: A Folktale from Italy,* p. 133.

ONLINE

August House Web site, http://store.augusthouse.com/ (March 5, 2008), profile of Kanzler.

Harper Collins Web site, http://www.harpercollins.com/ (March 5, 2008), profile of Kanzler.

John Kanzler Home Page, http://johnkanzler.com (March 5, 2008).

Simon and Schuster Web site, http://www.simonsays.com/ (March 5, 2008), profile of Kanzler.*

*　　*　　*

KEANEY, Brian 1954-

Personal

Born January 10, 1954, in London, England; son of John (a boiler operator) and Kathleen (a homemaker) Keaney; married Rosemary Brownhill (a teacher), August 21, 1976; children: Emily Jane, Kathleen Maeve. *Education:* Attended St. Ignatius College London, 1965-72; University of Liverpool, B.A. (with honors), 1975; Liverpool Institute of Education, postgraduate certificate in education, 1976. *Politics:* "Left of center." *Religion:* "Cultural Catholic."

Addresses

Home and office—London, England. *Agent*—A.M. Heath & Co., 79 St. Martin's La., London WC2N 4AA, England.

Career

Educator and fiction writer. English teacher in London, England, 1976-86; writer-in-residence in Redbridge, England, 1988-90, and London, 1990-91; freelance writer, 1991—.

Member

Society of Authors, National Association of Writers in Education.

Awards, Honors

South Lanarkshire Book Award nomination, 2006, for *Jacob's Ladder.*

Writings

FOR CHILDREN

Don't Hang About (short stories), Oxford University Press (Oxford, England), 1985.

Some People Never Learn, Oxford University Press (Oxford, England), 1986.

No Need for Heroes, Oxford University Press (Oxford, England), 1989.

(Editor with Bill Lucas) *Girls' Talk, Boys' Talk* (short stories), Macmillan (Basingstoke, England), 1989.

(Editor with Bill Lucas) *Class Rules* (short stories), Macmillan (Basingstoke, England), 1990.

If This Is the Real World, Oxford University Press (Oxford, England), 1991.

Boys Don't Write Love Stories, Oxford University Press (Oxford, England), 1993.

Brian Keaney (Photo by Matt Jaime Photography. Courtesy of Brian Keaney.)

Family Secrets, Orchard Books (London, England), 1997.

The Private Life of Georgia Brown, Orchard Books (London, England), 1998.

Only Made of Wood (with teacher's guide), illustrated by Patrice Aggs, Forest Education Initiative (Cambridge, England), 1998.

Bitter Fruit, Orchard Books (London, England), 1999.

Balloon House, Orchard Books (London, England), 2000.

No Stone Unturned, Barrington Stoke (Edinburgh, Scotland), 2001.

Falling for Joshua, Orchard Books (London, England), 2001.

Where Mermaids Sing, Orchard Books (London, England), 2004.

Jacob's Ladder, Orchard (London, England), 2005, Candlewick Press (Cambridge, MA), 2006.

The Hollow People ("Promises of Dr. Sigmundus" series), illustrated by Nicoletta Ceccoli, Orchard (London, England), 2006, Knopf (New York, NY), 2007.

The Gallow Glass ("Promises of Dr. Sigmundus" series), Orchard (London, England), 2007, published as *The Cracked Mirror,* Knopf (New York, NY), 2008.

The Haunting of Nathaniel Wolfe, Orchard (London, England), 2008.

The Mendini Canticle ("Promises of Dr. Sigmundus" series), Orchard (London, England), 2008.

Also author of beginning readers for Oxford University Press, including *Every Picture Tells a Story.*

OTHER

(With Bill Lucas) *Making Sense of English,* Oxford University Press (Oxford, England), 1987.

(With Bill Lucas) *Talking Sense,* Oxford University Press (Oxford, England), 1987.

(Adaptor with Bill Lucas) Marjorie Darke, *A Question of Courage* (stage play), Oxford University (Oxford, England), 1990.

A Kiss from France (short play), Thornes (Leckhampton, England), 1990.

The Fat of the Land (short play), Thornes (Leckhampton, England), 1990.

Boycott (short play), Thornes (Leckhampton, England), 1991.

Between Two Shores (short play), Thornes (Leckhampton, England), 1991.

(With Bill Lucas) *Sharing Experiences,* Nelson (Walton-on-Thames, England), 1991.

(With Bill Lucas) *Taking Shape,* Nelson (Walton-on-Thames, England), 1991.

(With Bill Lucas) *Taking Sides* (short stories), Macmillan (Basingstoke, England), 1991.

(Editor with Bill Lucas) *The Outdoor Classroom,* Scholastic (Leamington Spa, England), 1992.

(Compiler with Bill Lucas) *Poetry in Practice,* Hodder & Stoughton (London, England), 1993.

(With Bill Lucas) *Looking at Language,* Cambridge University Press (Cambridge, England), 1994.

(With Claire Wright) *English Grammar,* Pearson (Cambridge, England), 1995.

Contributor of articles and reviews to periodicals, including *Times Educational Supplement.* Author of curriculum and testing materials.

Sidelights

Brian Keaney is the author of young-adult novels as well as short stories and teen fantasy fiction. His novels such as *Falling for Joshua, Bitter Fruit,* and *The Private Life of Georgia Brown* introduce contemporary heroines as they deal with typical adolescent problems with friends and family. With *No Stone Unturned,* Keaney turns to mystery in his story of a young woman hoping to escape a violent husband, and he explores fantasy in his "Promises of Dr. Sigmundus" series and his standalone novels *Jacob's Ladder* and *The Haunting of Nathaniel Wolfe.*

Keaney's story collection *Don't Hang About* centers on the author's experiences growing up in East London during the 1960s. In this work, he shares with young readers his own teenage problems, including conflicts with peers, parents, and teachers, as well as the prejudice he encountered as the son of Irish-Catholic immigrants. "The author speaks with a direct voice to his teenage audience and avoids any hint of patronising his readers," maintained *School Librarian* contributor Julia C. Marriage. As the critic added, "the strength of the book lies in the fact that the author writes from his own experience . . . in an imaginative manner." In *Junior Bookshelf* a contributor concluded of *Don't Hang About:* "If you want to know how it felt to be a minority in the 'Sixties, here it is."

If This Is the Real World offers teens "a mirror of contemporary life," according to a *Junior Bookshelf* reviewer. The novel details the plight of Danny as he searches for the father who abandoned him and his family some eight years earlier. "Keaney is excellent with colloquial conversation," maintained the *Junior Bookshelf* reviewer, commending the author's "skill . . . at detailing the domestic/school/urban community life-style, and . . . communicating a young person's emotions/hopes/fears." The reviewer also had high praise for the novel's "expertly envisaged" school settings and the "similarly genuine" scenes of home life depicted in the book. "The most attractive element" of *If This Is the Real World* "is in watching Danny grow," noted Robert Dunbar in *School Librarian.* According to the critic, in the course of the novel Keaney's teen hero "comes to appreciate the essential differences between the easy escape offered by dream worlds and the increasingly tough realities to be faced in having to accept some of life's harsher aspects."

The issue of a father's absence is also addressed in *Family Secrets.* Here Kate and her single mother Anne travel to Ireland, where Kate's grandmother has suffered a stroke. There, Kate finds her father, experiences her first love, and gains an understanding of the grandmother who, for years, had nothing to do with either

Cover of Keaney's young-adult novel Jacob's Ladder, *featuring a photograph by Kent Richardson.* (Jacket photograph copyright © 2007 by Ken Richardson. All rights reserved. Reproduced by permission of the publisher Candlewick Press, Inc., Cambridge, MA.)

Kate or her mom. Val Randall, writing in *Books for Keeps,* maintained that, in his story, Keaney "strenuously avoids the glibness of tying all ends neatly together but gives positive indications of a brighter future for all the protagonists." Calling *Family Secrets* "enjoyable," *School Librarian* contributor Audrey Baker also cited the optimism pervading the work, writing that "there is no complete resolution but there is a note of hope" at novel's end.

Thirteen-year-old Matthew writes to an imaginary female confidante in *Boys Don't Write Love Stories,* another of Keaney's well-received novels for young adults. The teen's narrative reflects on his frustrations with tensions at home and problems at school: Matthew's parents are confined to a loveless marriage and seem to prefer being away from home; his school-skipping older sister is an animal-rights fanatic who is threatening to do something criminal to advance her cause; and the teen himself is struggling with a bully at school. In *School Librarian,* Robert Dunbar claimed that in *Boy's Don't Write Love Stories* "a young teenager's awareness of an adult world which is hurtfully unfair and frequently absurd, is presented with some sharpness" through Keaney's "pared dialogue." A *Junior Bookshelf* contributor offered a commendation frequently voiced by critics in assessing Keaney's books, noting that "the school bits are well done."

Keaney continues to focus on the lives of contemporary teens in *Balloon House* and *Falling for Joshua,* but in *Jacob's Ladder* he shifts to a mélange of science fiction, fantasy, myth, and literary allusion. The novel begins as Jacob wakes up in the middle of a vast field, with no recollection of how he came to be there. Jacob can only recall his name; his past is gone. Woven in with classical myths and vignettes from Dante's *Divine Comedy* and the Bible, *Jacob's Ladder* follows the teen as he is taken to a city called Locus, where he and many other teens live a mind-numbing existence while working at repetitive physical labor. Together with a girl named Aysha, Jacob attempts to escape from this waking nightmare and his adventures result in a compelling read. In *School Library Journal,* Beth Wright called *Jacob's Ladder* an "intriguing" and "engrossing" novel, noting that Keaney's novel is "a good choice for struggling and proficient readers alike."

Also dark in theme, *The Hollow People* is the first novel in Keaney's "Promise of Dr. Sigmundus" series. The story takes place in a world called Tarnagar, where inhabitants agree to drug themselves with Ichor and live a placid life rather than take risks that might result in their future unhappiness. A young, uneducated teen named Dante, whose mother was reportedly insane and a suicide, works at a menial job when he meets Bea. Although she is taking Ichor, Bea still dreams, and she also begins to question the way of life on Tarnagar, where Dr. Sigmundus controls all. Soon Bea and Dante meet another free-minded person, the supposedly insane Ezekiel Semiramis, and together they escape the con-

Keaney's teen fantasy novel The Hollow People, *featuring artwork by Italian illustrator Nicoletta Ceccoli.* (Illustration copyright © 2007 by Nicoletta Ceccoli. All rights reserved. Used by permission of Alfred A. Knopf, an imprint of Random House Children's Books, a division of Random House, Inc.)

fines of the controlled community to join a group of rebels who value free will. Noting the novel's philosophical themes, Claire Rosser noted in *Kliatt* that Keaney "creates a suspenseful plot as he also helps readers think seriously about what it means to be free." Although Denise Ryan wrote in *School Library Journal* that the second half of the story seems "hurried," *The Hollow People* "will captivate readers with a taste for suspense or psychological thrills." The story's "brisk pace" was praised by a *Kirkus Reviews* writer, the critic noting that Keaney's "simple, sometimes terse sentence structure" provides momentum for the "heady" novel. The adventures of Dante and Bea—characters from the *Divine Comedy*—continue in *The Cracked Glass* and *The Mendini Canticle.*

Describing his own process of becoming a writer, Keaney recalled to *SATA:* "My parents were Irish immigrants. When they came to London in the 1940s there were signs in lodging houses that said 'No Irish Need Apply.' There was nothing for them but hard work and the support of their own community. As a consequence, I was brought up in a cultural bubble in the

heart of London, and I grew up feeling slightly at odds with my surroundings. This was one of the factors that made me a writer.

"The respect my parents had for books and learning, though they themselves were largely uneducated, was another important element. Equally influential was the spoken language I heard all around me every day. My mother was and is a great natural talker and storyteller, and hearing the priest's thundering sermons each Sunday in church also had its effect.

"Mine was an intense childhood, and not entirely carefree. My father held very strong opinions on most subjects, and there were often dreadful clashes of will between us. I sometimes think that I write for children because I am trying to return in my imagination to my own childhood in order to work out those conflicts."

Discussing his work as a young-adult novelist, Keaney commented: "My books are about young people who face problems that seem to them insoluble and the ways they find to deal with those difficulties. I believe the strategies we devise as children for our own survival create our identities, and it is identity above all that interests me." "I love what I do and, in my opinion, it's very important," he added on his home page. "Without children's authors there would be no new readers and the whole community of literature would slowly begin to collapse and die. That's why writing for young people is one of the most important jobs on the planet."

Biographical and Critical Sources

PERIODICALS

Booklist, November 1, 2007, Debbie Carton, review of *The Hollow People,* p. 40.
Books for Keeps, November, 1997, Val Randall, review of *Family Secrets,* p. 27.
Bulletin of the Center for Children's Books, April, 2007, April Spisak, review of *Jacob's Ladder,* p. 333.
Junior Bookshelf, April, 1986, review of *Don't Hang About,* p. 77; December, 1991, review of *If This Is the Real World,* p. 264; June, 1993, review of *Boys Don't Write Love Stories,* p. 105.
Kirkus Reviews, January 15, 2007, review of *Jacob's Ladder,* p. 120; August 15, 2007, review of *The Hollow People.*
Kliatt, September, 2007, Claire Rosser, review of *The Hollow People,* p. 14.
Magpies, November, 2006, review of *The Hollow People,* p. 11.
School Librarian, September, 1986, Julia C. Marriage, review of *Don't Hang About,* pp. 269-270; February, 1992, Robert Dunbar, review of *If This Is the Real World,* p. 31; August, 1993, Robert Dunbar, review of *Boys Don't Write Love Stories,* p. 122; November, 1997, Audrey Baker, review of *Family Secrets,* p. 213;

autumn, 1998, review of *Only Made of Wood,* p. 152; winter, 1999, review of *Bitter Fruit,* p. 213; winter, 2000, review of *Balloon House,* p. 212; spring, 2005, Ann G. Gay, review of *Where Mermaids Sing,* p. 47; winter, 2005, Andy Sawyer, review of *Jacob's Ladder,* p. 214; winter, 2006, Jackie Oates, review of *The Hollow People,* p. 208.

School Library Journal, November, 1997, review of *Family Secrets,* p. 213; February, 2007, Beth Wright, review of *Jacob's Ladder,* p. 120; January, 2008, Denise Ryan, review of *The Hollow People,* p. 120.

Voice of Youth Advocates, June, 2007, Mary E. Heslin, review of *Jacob's Ladder,* p. 162.

ONLINE

Brian Keaney Home Page, http://www.briankeaney.com (March 25, 2008).

Brian Keaney Web log, http://www.odyllicforce.blogspot.com (March 17, 2008).

Jubilee Books Web site, http://www.jubileebooks.co.uk/ (March 25, 2008), "Brian Keaney."

*   *   *

KENT, Rose

Personal

Born in NY; married; husband's name Tom; children: Connor, Theresa, four other children. *Education:* U.S. Naval Academy, graduate. *Hobbies and other interests:* Running.

Addresses

Home—Upstate NY.

Career

Children's book author. U.S. Navy, naval officer, served five years; former manager of a public-relations firm.

Member

Society of Children's Book Writers and Illustrators.

Writings

Kimchi and Calamari, HarperCollins (New York, NY), 2007.

Sidelights

Describing herself as "a hopeless foodie," upstate New York writer Rose Kent was inspired to write her first novel, *Kimchi and Calamari,* by her son Connor, who was adopted at birth from South Korea. The novel "came from a place where I was reflecting on family

and identity and race—and what happens when they all merge," Kent explained to *PaperTigers.org* interviewer Aline Pereira. "I chose to get to know a lovable, quirky boy named Joseph and tell his story. And as I got to know him better, the themes that matter to me appeared along the way."

In *Kimchi and Calamari,* readers meet fourteen-year-old Joseph Calderaro. Adopted at birth by American parents of Italian descent, Joseph is Korean, but his ethnic ancestry has never been the topic of much conversation in his busy family. However, when a social-studies teacher assigns the class a writing project that involves a discussion of cultural heritage, the teen has to think fast. Working on his essay in between drum lessons and band practice, homework assignments, a slowly budding romance, and activities with family and friends, Joseph decides to take a creative approach. He writes an essay that casts Olympic marathon runner Sohn Kee Chung in the role of his grandfather. When the ruse is revealed, however, it is back to the keyboard for Joseph, and through his own search he gradually discovers both his cultural roots and possible members of his birth family.

Rose Kent introduces an adopted teen making sense of his cultural heritage in **Kimchi and Calamari,** *a novel featuring cover art by Gina Triplett.* (Jacket art © 2007 by Gina Triplett. All rights reserved. Used by permission of HarperCollins Publishers.)

Reviewing *Kimchi and Calamari* for *Booklist,* Kay Weisman praised Kent's "humorous" text for bringing to life a typical eighth grader's search for self as well as for highlighting "questions about family roots that . . . are universal." Because the author addresses not only Joseph's dilemma, but also the mixed feelings of his parents as their own Italian traditions are rejected, a *Kirkus Reviews* writer observed that *Kimchi and Calamari* "does justice to complex issues," while Joseph works his magic as "a funny, engaging tour guide to the world of transcultural adoption." Praising the novel as among "the best" books to date dealing with adopted teens coming to terms with their cultural heritage, Deborah Vose concluded in *School Library Journal* that "Kent has done an excellent job of creating a likable protagonist whose confusion about his status is touching, and also funny." Calling the first-time novelist both upbeat and honest in her depiction of "the issues of international adoption," *Kliatt* writer Claire Rosser recommended *Kimchi and Calamari* "for middle-school students like Joseph who are searching for information to understand who they are."

Biographical and Critical Sources

PERIODICALS

Booklist, February 15, 2007, Kay Weisman, review of *Kimchi and Calamari,* p. 78.
Bulletin of the Center for Children's Books, June, 2007, Deborah Stevenson, review of *Kimchi and Calamari,* p. 425.
Kirkus Reviews, April 1, 2007, review of *Kimchi and Calamari.*
Kliatt, March, 2007, Claire Rosser, review of *Kimchi and Calamari,* p. 15.
School Library Journal, May, 2007, Deborah Vose, review of *Kimchi and Calamari,* p. 136.
Tribune Books (Chicago, IL), June 23, 2007, Mary Harris Russell, review of *Kimchi and Calamari,* p. 7.

ONLINE

Class of 2k7 Web site, http://classof2k7.com/ (March 28, 2008), "Rose Kent."
Cynsations, http://cynthialeitichsmith.blogspot.com/ (April 5, 2007), Cynthia Leitich Smith, interview with Kent.
Paper Tigers Web site, http://www.papertigers.org/ (May 1, 2007), Aline Pereira, interview with Kent.
Rose Kent Home Page, http://www.rosekent.com (March 25, 2008).*

*   *   *

KERR, Anne Louise
See MACKEY, Weezie Kerr

KRENSKY, Stephen 1953-
(Stephen Alan Krensky)

Personal

Born November 25, 1953, in Boston, MA; son of Paul David (a business executive) and Roselyn Krensky; married Joan Frongello (a textbook editor), April 7, 1984; children: Andrew, Peter. *Education:* Hamilton College, B.A., 1975.

Addresses

Home—Lexington, MA. *E-mail*—stephen.krensky@ verizon.net.

Career

Freelance writer and critic, 1975—.

Awards, Honors

Notable Book designation, American Library Association (ALA), 1982, for *Dinosaurs, Beware!,* and 1998, for *How Santa Got His Job;* Children's Books of the Year citation, Child Study Association of America, 1985, for *Maiden Voyage,* 1987, for *Lionel in the Fall,* 1993, for *Lionel and Louise* and *Christopher Columbus,* and 1995, for *Lionel in the Winter,* and 1999, for *Louise Goes Wild;* Pick of the Lists citation, American Booksellers Association, 1992, for *Lionel in the Spring,* 1994, for *Lionel in the Winter,* and 1996, for *Breaking into Print;* Children's Choice selection, International Reading Association, 1992, for *George Washington,* and 2005, for *There Once Was a Very Odd School;* Reading Magic award, *Parenting* magazine, 1996, for *Lionel and His Friends;* Notable Children's Trade Book in the Field of Social Studies designation, National Council for the Social Studies/Children's Book Council (NCSS/CBC), 1996, for *Breaking into Print,* 2003, for *Paul Revere's Midnight Ride,* and 2006, for *Dangerous Crossing;* Sydney Taylor Book Award, 2007, for *Hanukkah at Valley Forge.*

Writings

FOR YOUNG PEOPLE

A Big Day for Scepters, illustrated by Bruce Degen, Atheneum (New York, NY), 1977.
The Dragon Circle, illustrated by A. Delaney, Atheneum (New York, NY), 1977.
Woodland Crossing, illustrated by Jan Brett Bowler, Atheneum (New York, NY), 1978.
The Perils of Putney, illustrated by Jeurg Obrist, Atheneum (New York, NY), 1978.
Castles in the Air, and Other Tales, illustrated by Warren Lieberman, Atheneum (New York, NY), 1979.
A Troll in Passing, Atheneum (New York, NY), 1980.

Stephen Krensky (Reproduced by permission.)

My First Dictionary, Houghton (Boston, MA), 1980, published as *The American Heritage First Dictionary* and *Houghton Mifflin Primary Dictionary,* illustrated by George Ulrich, Houghton Mifflin (Boston, MA), 1986.

The Witching Hour, illustrated by A. Delaney, Atheneum (New York, NY), 1981.

Conqueror and Hero: The Search for Alexander, illustrated by Alexander Farquharson, Little, Brown (Boston, MA), 1981.

(With Marc Brown) *Dinosaurs, Beware!: A Safety Guide,* illustrated by Brown, Atlantic—Little, Brown (Boston, MA), 1982.

The Wilder Plot, Atheneum (New York, NY), 1982.

The Lion Upstairs, illustrated by Leigh Grant, Atheneum (New York, NY), 1983.

The Wilder Summer, Atheneum (New York, NY), 1983.

(With Marc Brown) *Perfect Pigs: An Introduction to Manners,* illustrated by Brown, Little, Brown (Boston, MA), 1984.

A Ghostly Business, Atheneum (New York, NY), 1984.

Maiden Voyage: The Story of the Statue of Liberty, illustrated by Richard Rosenblum, Atheneum (New York, NY), 1985.

Scoop after Scoop: A History of Ice Cream, illustrated by Richard Rosenblum, Atheneum (New York, NY), 1986.

Who Really Discovered America?, illustrated by Steve Sullivan, Hastings House, 1987.

Snow and Ice, Scholastic (New York, NY), 1989.

Witch Hunt: It Happened in Salem Village, illustrated by James Watling, Random House (New York, NY), 1989.

Big Time Bears, illustrated by Maryann Cocca-Leffler, Little, Brown (Boston, MA), 1989.

Christopher Columbus, illustrated by Norman Green, Random House (New York, NY), 1991.

The Missing Mother Goose, illustrated by Chris Demarest, Doubleday (New York, NY), 1991.

Children of the Earth and Sky, illustrated by James Watling, Scholastic (New York, NY), 1991.

George Washington: The Man Who Would Not Be King, Scholastic (New York, NY), 1991.

Four against the Odds: The Struggle to Save Our Environment, Scholastic (New York, NY), 1992.

The Pizza Book: Fun, Facts, a Recipe—the Works!, illustrated by R.W. Alley, Scholastic (New York, NY), 1992.

All about Magnets, Scholastic (New York, NY), 1993.

Fraidy Cats, illustrated by Betsy Lewin, Scholastic (New York, NY), 1993.

The Iron Dragon Never Sleeps, illustrated by John Fulweiler, Delacorte (New York, NY), 1994.

Children of the Wind and Water: Five Stories about Native American Children, illustrated by James Watling, Scholastic (New York, NY), 1994.

The Three Blind Mice Mystery, illustrated by Lynn Munsinger, Yearling (New York, NY), 1995.

The Printer's Apprentice, illustrated by Madeline Sorel, Delacorte (New York, NY), 1995.

Breaking into Print: Before and after the Invention of the Printing Press, illustrated by Bonnie Christensen, Little, Brown (Boston, MA), 1996.

My Teacher's Secret Life, illustrated by JoAnn Adinolfi, Simon & Schuster (New York, NY), 1996.

Striking It Rich: The Story of the California Gold Rush, illustrated by Ann DiVito, Simon & Schuster (New York, NY), 1996.

Pocahontas Official Game Book, Brady Computer Books, 1996.

A Good Knight's Sleep, illustrated by Renee Williams-Andriani, Candlewick Press (Cambridge, MA), 1996.

Sharks Never Sleep, Candlewick Press (Cambridge, MA), 1997.

We Just Moved!, illustrated by Larry Difiori, Scholastic (New York, NY), 1998.

Write Away!: One Author's Favorite Activities That Help Ordinary Writers Become Extraordinary Writers, Scholastic Professional Books (New York, NY), 1998.

How Santa Got His Job, illustrated by S.D. Schindler, Simon & Schuster Books for Young Readers (New York, NY), 1998.

My Loose Tooth, illustrated by Hideko Takahashi, Random House (New York, NY), 1999.

Bones, illustrated by Davy Jones, Random House (New York, NY), 1999.

The Youngest Fairy Godmother Ever, illustrated by Diana Cain Bluthenthal, Simon & Schuster Books for Young Readers (New York, NY), 1999.

Taking Flight: The Story of the Wright Brothers, illustrated by Larry Day, Simon & Schuster Books for Young Readers (New York, NY), 2000.

What a Mess!, illustrated by Joe Mathieu, Random House (New York, NY), 2001.

The Moon Robber, illustrated by Dean Morrissey, Harper-Collins (New York, NY), 2001.

Pearl Harbor, illustrated by Larry Day, Aladdin Paperbacks (New York, NY), 2001.

Egypt, Scholastic Reference (New York, NY), 2001.

(Adapter) Charles Dickens, *A Christmas Carol,* pictures by Dean Morrissey, HarperCollins (New York, NY), 2001.

Shooting for the Moon: The Amazing Life and Times of Annie Oakley, Melanie Kroupa Books (New York, NY), 2001.

(Adapter) A.A. Milne, *Eeyore Has a Birthday,* decorations by Ernest H. Shepard, Dutton Children's Books (New York, NY), 2001.

(Adapter) A.A. Milne, *Winnie-the-Pooh and Some Bees,* decorations by Ernest H. Shepard, Dutton Children's Books (New York, NY), 2001.

How Santa Lost His Job, illustrated by S.D. Schindler, Simon & Schuster Books for Young Readers (New York, NY), 2001.

The Winter King, pictures by Dean Morrissey, HarperCollins (New York, NY), 2002.

Paul Revere's Midnight Ride, illustrated by Greg Harlin, HarperCollins (New York, NY), 2002.

Abe Lincoln and the Muddy Pig, illustrated by Greshom Griffith, Aladdin (New York, NY), 2002.

Ben Franklin and His First Kite, illustrated by Bert Dodson, Aladdin (New York, NY), 2002.

Sacagawea and the Bravest Deed, illustrated by Diana Magnuson, Aladdin (New York, NY), 2002.

(Adapter) A.A. Milne, *Pooh Goes Visiting,* decorations by Ernest H. Shepard, Dutton Children's Books (New York, NY), 2002.

(Adapter) A.A. Milne, *Tigger Comes to the Forest,* decorations by Ernest H. Shepard, Dutton Children's Books (New York, NY), 2002.

(Adapter) A.A. Milne, *Christopher Robin Leads an Expedition,* decorations by Ernest H. Shepard, Dutton Children's Books (New York, NY), 2003.

(Adapter) A.A. Milne, *Pooh Invents a New Game,* decorations by Ernest H. Shepard, Dutton Children's Books (New York, NY), 2003.

Do Not Open This Crate!, illustrated by Aristides Ruiz, Random House (New York, NY), 2003.

Nellie Bly: A Name to Be Reckoned With, illustrated by Rebecca Guay, Aladdin (New York, NY), 2003.

(With Dean Morrissey) *The Monster Trap,* illustrated by Morrissey, HarperCollins (New York, NY), 2004.

There Once Was a Very Odd School, and Other Lunch-Box Limericks, illustrated by Tamara Petrosino, Dutton Children's Books (New York, NY), 2004.

My Dad Can Do Anything, illustrated by Mike Wohnoutka, Random House (New York, NY), 2004.

Davy Crockett: A Life on the Frontier, illustrated by Bob Dacey and Debra Bandelin, Aladdin (New York, NY), 2004.

Bubble Trouble, illustrated by Jimmy Pickering, Aladdin (New York, NY), 2004.

George Washington's First Victory, illustrated by Diane Dawson Hearn, Aladdin (New York, NY), 2005.

Dangerous Crossing: The Revolutionary Voyage of John and John Quincy Adams, illustrated by Greg Harlin, Dutton Children's Books (New York, NY), 2005.

(With Dean Morrissey) *The Crimson Comet,* illustrated by Morrissey, HarperCollins (New York, NY), 2006.

Milo the Really Big Bunny, illustrated by Melissa Suber, Simon & Schuster Books for Young Readers (New York, NY), 2006.

Hanukkah at Valley Forge, illustrated by Greg Harlin, Dutton Children's Books (New York, NY), 2006.

Benjamin Franklin, Dorling Kindersley (New York, NY), 2007.

Curious George Finds a Friend (lift-the-flap book; based on the television series), Houghton Mifflin (Boston, MA), 2007.

Curious George Cleans Up (based on the television series), Houghton Mifflin (Boston, MA), 2007.

Big Bad Wolves at School, illustrated by Brad Sneed, Simon & Schuster Books for Young Readers (New York, NY), 2007.

What's the Big Idea?: Four Centuries of Innovation in Boston, Charlesbridge/Boston History Collaborative (Watertown, MA), 2007.

Too Many Leprechauns; or, How That Pot o' Gold Got to the End of the Rainbow, illustrated by Dan Andreasen, Simon & Schuster Books for Young Readers (New York, NY), 2007.

Snack Attack, illustrated by Stacy Curtis, Aladdin (New York, NY), 2008.

Sisters of Scituate Light, illustrated by Stacey Schuett, Dutton Children's Books (New York, NY), 2008.

Jungle Gym: A Touch-and-Feel Counting Book, illustrated by Marsha Gray Carrington, Little Simon (New York, NY), 2008.

Spark the Firefighter, illustrated by Amanda Haley, Dutton Children's Books (New York, NY), 2008.

A Man for All Seasons: The Life of George Washington Carver, illustrated by Wil Clay, HarperCollins (New York, NY), 2008.

Comic Book Century: The History of American Comic Books, Twenty-first Century Books (Minneapolis, MN), 2008.

Noah's Bark, illustrated by Rogé, Carolrhoda (Minneapolis, MN), 2009.

Contributor of short stories to *Cricket* and reviews to magazines and newspapers, including *New York Times Book Review, New Republic,* and *Boston Globe.*

"ARTHUR" CHAPTER BOOK SERIES; BASED ON CHARACTERS BY MARC BROWN; ADAPTED FROM THE "ARTHUR" TELEVISION SERIES

Arthur's Mystery Envelope, illustrated by Marc Brown, Little, Brown (Boston, MA), 1998.

Arthur and the Scare-Your-Pants-off Club, illustrated by Marc Brown, Little, Brown (Boston, MA), 1998.

Arthur Makes the Team, illustrated by Marc Brown, Little, Brown (Boston, MA), 1998.

Arthur and the Crunch Cereal Contest, illustrated by Marc Brown, Little, Brown (Boston, MA), 1998.

Arthur Accused, illustrated by Marc Brown, Little, Brown (Boston, MA), 1998.

Locked in the Library, illustrated by Marc Brown, Little, Brown (Boston, MA), 1998.

Buster's Dino Dilemma, illustrated by Marc Brown, Little, Brown (Boston, MA), 1998.

The Mystery of the Stolen Bike, illustrated by Marc Brown, Little, Brown (Boston, MA), 1998.

Arthur and the Popularity Contest, illustrated by Marc Brown, Little, Brown (Boston, MA), 1998.

Arthur Rocks with Binky, illustrated by Marc Brown, Little, Brown (Boston, MA), 1998.

Arthur and the Lost Diary, illustrated by Marc Brown, Little, Brown (Boston, MA), 1998.

Who's in Love with Arthur?, illustrated by Marc Brown, Little, Brown (Boston, MA), 1998.

Arthur and the Cootie-Catcher, illustrated by Marc Brown, Little, Brown (Boston, MA), 1999.

Buster Makes the Grade, illustrated by Marc Brown, Little, Brown (Boston, MA), 1999.

King Arthur, illustrated by Marc Brown, Little, Brown (Boston, MA), 1999.

Francine, Believe It or Not, illustrated by Marc Brown, Little, Brown (Boston, MA), 1999.

Muffy's Secret Admirer, illustrated by Marc Brown, Little, Brown (Boston, MA), 1999.

Arthur and the Poetry Contest, illustrated by Marc Brown, Little, Brown (Boston, MA), 1999.

Buster Baxter, Cat Saver, illustrated by Marc Brown, Little, Brown (Boston, MA), 2000.

Buster's New Friend, illustrated by Marc Brown, Little, Brown (Boston, MA), 2000.

Arthur and the Big Blow-Up, illustrated by Marc Brown, Little, Brown (Boston, MA), 2000.

Francine the Superstar, illustrated by Marc Brown, Little, Brown (Boston, MA), 2000.

Arthur and the Perfect Brother, illustrated by Marc Brown, Little, Brown (Boston, MA), 2000.

Binky Rules, illustrated by Marc Brown, Little, Brown (Boston, MA), 2000.

Arthur and the Double Dare, illustrated by Marc Brown, Little, Brown (Boston, MA), 2002.

Arthur and the Comet Crisis, illustrated by Marc Brown, Little, Brown (Boston, MA), 2002.

Arthur Plays the Blues, illustrated by Marc Brown, Little, Brown (Boston, MA), 2003.

Arthur and the Bad-Luck Brain, illustrated by Marc Brown, Little, Brown (Boston, MA), 2003.

Arthur Loses His Marbles, illustrated by Marc Brown, Little, Brown (Boston, MA), 2004.

Arthur and the Nerves of Steal, illustrated by Marc Brown, Little, Brown (Boston, MA), 2004.

Arthur and the World Record, illustrated by Marc Brown, Little, Brown (Boston, MA), 2005.

Also adapter of ten traditional bedtime tales for *Arthur's Really Helpful Bedtime Stories* (based on the characters by Marc Brown), illustrated by Marc Brown, Random House (New York, NY).

"ARTHUR GOOD SPORTS" SERIES; WITH MARC BROWN

Arthur and the Race to Read, illustrated by Marc Brown, Little, Brown (Boston, MA), 2001.

Arthur and the Best Coach Ever, illustrated by Marc Brown, Little, Brown (Boston, MA), 2001.

Arthur and the Goalie Ghost, illustrated by Marc Brown, Little, Brown (Boston, MA), 2001.

Arthur and the Pen-Pal Playoff, illustrated by Marc Brown, Little, Brown (Boston, MA), 2001.

Arthur and the Recess Rookie, illustrated by Marc Brown, Little, Brown (Boston, MA), 2001.

Arthur and the Seventh-Inning Stretcher, illustrated by Marc Brown, Little, Brown (Boston, MA), 2001.

"LIONEL" SERIES

Lionel at Large, illustrated by Susanna Natti, Dial (New York, NY), 1986.

Lionel in the Fall, illustrated by Susanna Natti, Dial (New York, NY), 1987.

Lionel in the Spring, illustrated by Susanna Natti, Dial (New York, NY), 1990.

Lionel and Louise, illustrated by Susanna Natti, Dial (New York, NY), 1992.

Lionel in the Winter, illustrated by Susanna Natti, Dial (New York, NY), 1994.

Lionel and His Friends, illustrated by Susanna Natti, Dial (New York, NY), 1996.

Lionel in the Summer, illustrated by Susanna Natti, Dial (New York, NY), 1998.

Lionel at School, illustrated by Susanna Natti, Dial (New York, NY), 2000.

Lionel's Birthday, illustrated by Susanna Natti, Dial (New York, NY), 2003.

"LOUISE" SERIES

Louise Takes Charge, illustrated by Susanna Natti, Dial (New York, NY), 1998.

Louise Goes Wild, illustrated by Susanna Natti, Dial (New York, NY), 1999.

Louise, Soccer Star?, illustrated by Susanna Natti, Dial (New York, NY), 2000.

"MONSTER CHRONICLES" SERIES

The Mummy, Millbrook Press (Minneapolis, MN), 2007.

Frankenstein, Millbrook Press (Minneapolis, MN), 2007.

Dragons, Millbrook Press (Minneapolis, MN), 2007.

Bigfoot, Millbrook Press (Minneapolis, MN), 2007.

Werewolves, Millbrook Press (Minneapolis, MN), 2007.

Vampires, Millbrook Press (Minneapolis, MN), 2007.

Zombies, Millbrook Press (Minneapolis, MN), 2008.

Watchers in the Woods, Millbrook Press (Minneapolis, MN), 2008.

Ghosts, Millbrook Press (Minneapolis, MN), 2008.

Creatures from the Deep, Millbrook Press (Minneapolis, MN), 2008.

The Bogeyman, Millbrook Press (Minneapolis, MN), 2008.

ADAPTOR; "ON MY OWN FOLKLORE" SERIES

Pecos Bill, illustrated by Paul Tong, Millbrook Press (Minneapolis, MN), 2007.

Paul Bunyan, illustrated by Craig Orback, Millbrook Press (Minneapolis, MN), 2007.

Mike Fink, illustrated by Jeni Reeves, Millbrook Press (Minneapolis, MN), 2007.

John Henry, illustrated by Mark Didroyd, Millbrook Press (Minneapolis, MN), 2007.

Casey Jones, illustrated by Mark Schroder, Millbrook Press (Minneapolis, MN), 2007.

Calamity Jane, illustrated by Lisa Carlson, Millbrook Press (Minneapolis, MN), 2007.

Anansi and the Box of Stories, illustrated by Jeni Reeves, Millbrook Press (Minneapolis, MN), 2007.

The Lion and the Hare: An East African Folktale, illustrated by Jeni Reeves, Millbrook Press (Minneapolis, MN), 2008.

Bokuden and the Bully: A Japanese Folktale, illustrated by Cheryl Kirk Noll, Millbrook Press (Minneapolis, MN), 2008.

How Coyote Stole the Summer: A Native American Folktale, illustrated by Kelly Dupre, Millbrook Press (Minneapolis, MN), 2009.

Adaptations

Krensky adapted his novel *The Wilder Summer* into a special for Home Box Office (HBO) Family Playhouse; the film was produced by Learning Corporation of America, 1984. *Dinosaurs, Beware!* was adapted into a filmstrip with cassette, Random House/Miller-Brody, 1985; *Big Bad Wolves at School* was adapted into a partially animated DVD, Spoken Arts, 2008.

Sidelights

Stephen Krensky is the prolific and popular author of a wide range of books for children. His picture books, easy readers, fiction, and nonfiction reflect his eclectic interests as well as those of the primary and middle graders for whom he usually writes. Krensky has written about dinosaurs, summer camp, Alexander the Great, Native-American children, the history of Boston, zombies and vampires, the invention of the printing press, America's founding fathers, and Annie Oakley, among other subjects, and he has also written a dictionary for primary graders, created original limericks, and compiled a social history of ice cream. Noted for his appealing sense of humor and his clear, easy-to-read style, Krensky is perhaps best known for his beginning readers, particularly those volumes in the "Lionel" reader series and his collaboration with noted author and illustrator Marc Brown on books featuring Brown's popular Arthur character.

Born in Massachusetts in 1953, Krensky never considered becoming a writer while growing up, although he did develop an early interest in both fiction and illustrating. His earliest stories were not written; rather, they were bedtime games that involved making up stories, attempting to visualize favorite characters such as Robin Hood in his dreams. More comfortable with writing than drawing, Krensky eventually gravitated to the former, developing a businesslike approach to his craft. Rather than waiting to be struck by inspiration, he worked at writing every day and revised each work until he was satisfied. Unlike some authors, he never viewed children's books as a stepping stone to writing for adults.

Krensky's first book for young readers appeared in 1977, just two years after he left college. *A Big Day for Scepters* tells the story of Calendar, a young sorcerer and collector of magic who searches for and finds a mysterious scepter with his thirteen-year-old companion. His second book, the novel *The Dragon Circle,* also deals with fantasy and magic; in this case, the Wynd family gets involved with dragons that need help recovering a long-lost treasure. Notable in these early books is the tongue-in-cheek humor that prompted a *Kirkus Reviews* contributor to call the action in *A Big Day for Scepters* "trippingly related."

Krensky's early books set the tone for much of his children's fiction. His combination of humor and magic earned the author the title of "talented fabulist" from one *Publishers Weekly* critic for another of his books involving magic and fantasy, *A Troll in Passing.* In this work, the young troll Morgan has no love for the nocturnal pursuits of his brethren. Instead of spending his time mining, he would rather roam the countryside gathering mistletoe—a useless occupation, it would seem, until the day the fearsome trolls of the Simon clan attack Morgan's people and his mistletoe becomes their one defense. A *Bulletin of the Center for Children's Books* contributor cited Krensky's "fluent and sophisticated" writing style and deemed *A Troll in Passing* "a nicely crafted story that has pace, humor, and momentum."

Lionel at Large is the first book in the "Lionel" series of easy-to-read books. Featuring art by Susanna Natti, the book introduces the youthful protagonist and his family in five "warm, down-to-earth stories" that are by turns "humorous and touching," according to a *School Library Journal* critic. In Krensky's chapters, Lionel visits the doctor, refuses to eat his vegetables, and stays overnight with a friend. "There's quiet humor in the writing," noted a reviewer for the *Bulletin of the Center for Children's Books.*

The same gentle humor is featured in each of the series installments as Krensky presents short vignettes featuring Lionel and his family and friends. *Lionel in the Spring* finds Lionel busy with such seasonal activities as planting a garden and spring housecleaning. Carolyn K. Jenks, writing in *Horn Book,* noted that Lionel's "cheerful attitude" and the "amusing, believable situations" enhance Krensky's "well-written . . . series of

One of Krensky's most popular characters is brought to life in Susanna Natti's artwork for Lionel and Louise. (Illustration copyright © 1992 by Susanna Natti. All rights reserved. Reproduced by permission of Dial Books for Young Readers, a division of Penguin Putnam Books for Young Readers.)

stories for beginning readers." Other seasonal additions to the series include *Lionel in the Winter, Lionel in the Summer,* and *Lionel in the Fall. Lionel in the Winter,* in which Lionel explores his backyard Arctic, learns about New Year's resolutions, and keeps company with a snowman in separate easy-to-read stories, "will invite warm smiles on any day, cold or not," according to *Bulletin of the Center for Children's Books* critic Carol Fox.

Moving from the seasons, *Lionel's Birthday* focuses on another special day as the boy buries a time capsule, hints at his most favorite gift, and practices blowing out candles. In *Booklist,* Hazel Rochman deemed the book "a warm, funny collection" of easy-to-read chapters. *Lionel and Louise* finds Lionel experiencing new adventures with his older sister. He rescues Louise from a dragon(fly), builds a sand castle on the beach, cleans up a mess at home, and goes on a camping expedition in the backyard. Reviewing *Lionel and Louise* for *Booklist,* Julie Corsaro wrote that Krensky's stories are "warm and funny," and Sharron McElmeel concluded in *School Library Journal* that the book serves as an "entertaining addition to beginning-reader collections."

Krensky gives Lionel's indomitable sister her own series beginning with *Louise Takes Charge,* a chapter book also illustrated by Natti. In the debut story, Louise's first few days of the new school year are blighted by the sudden change in personality in her friend Jasper. After a summertime growth spurt, Jasper returns to become the class bully. One day Lionel tells Louise a story about knight and his apprentice, and this gives Louise an idea: she offers to serve as Jasper's apprentice, and soon others in her class follow suit. "The setup isn't entirely plausible, but the dialogue is snappy," wrote *Booklist* critic Susan Dove Lempke. The series continued with *Louise Goes Wild,* in which the little girl laments that she is too boring and predictable, and *Louise, Soccer Star?,* wherein the heroine dreams of greatness on the soccer field and becomes irate when a new schoolmate from England usurps her prominent position on the team. "Krensky creates believable characters," noted Lempke of the book, adding that the author "nicely depict[s] . . . realistic, not-always-pretty feelings with empathy."

Krensky presents young readers with a comic prequel to the Santa story in *How Santa Got His Job.* Here a very young Santa applies for several jobs that hint at his future vocation. When he works as a chimney sweeper, he remains clean. He finds a job at the post office, but prefers to deliver in the middle of the night. At the zoo, Santa befriends the reindeer, and then runs away to join the circus with them. All the runaways are rescued by a group of elves and ultimately find their new home and a new calling at the North Pole. As the pages turn, Krensky's protagonist ages into his familiar, white-haired, roly-poly self, courtesy of S.D. Schindler's humorous illustrations. "The story is smart and funny, and Schindler knows exactly how to make his artwork play off the humor," noted *Booklist* critic Ilene Cooper.

Krensky reteams with Schindler for *How Santa Lost His Job.* Here the Christmas stalwart suddenly realizes that Muckle the Elf is planning to make St. Nick obsolete with the help of a new machine called the Deliverator. Predictably, the contraption fails at the worst possible time, and Santa is saved from compulsory early retirement. In this book, noted a *Kirkus Reviews* contributor, Krensky "has crafted a tale with an obvious lesson" that "highlights the importance of personal attention and the 'little things' in the celebration of Christmas."

In *The Youngest Fairy Godmother Ever* Krensky's indomitable heroine is facing a challenge: Mavis wants desperately to be a fairy godmother, as in the Cinderella story. She tells her parents that she wants to make the wishes of others come true, to which they respond by noting that they wish she would take out the garbage. Mavis studies hard to perform magic and tries to make her own magic wand, but she is seemingly stymied in the realization of her career goal. At school, her attempt to turn a pet classroom mouse into a coachman leads to some minor chaos and causes her to notice a new class-mate: shabbily dressed Cindy, who lives with two mean stepsisters who order her about. When Mavis learns that Cindy does not have a Halloween costume, she decides to sew one for her, an act that makes her a fairy godmother. "As sympathetic as it is witty, this prince-less 'Cinderella' should charm its readers," noted a *Publishers Weekly* contributor.

Tiny, mischievous men in green are the focus of *Too Many Leprechauns; or, How That Pot o' Gold Got to the End of the Rainbow*, which features detailed oil paintings by Dan Andreasen. The story finds befuddled traveler Finn O'Finnegan returning to his home in Dingle to find the village overrun by leprechauns. In addition to making things topsy turvy, the tiny men have kept the villagers awake with their noisy craft: making fairy shoes. Hoping to drive them away, the clever Finn convinces the leprechauns that he has stolen their gold and will return it only if they promise to leave. A *Kirkus Reviews* contributor dubbed *Too Many Leprechauns* "a good read," and a *Publishers Weekly* reviewer explained that the mysterious relationship be-tween rainbows and a pot of gold is resolved via a "playful explanation courtesy of Krensky's original tale."

Another fairy tale is given a unique treatment in *Big Bad Wolves at School*, as artist Brad Sneed brings to life Krensky's humorous take on a traditional story. When a young wolf named Rufus is sent to the Big Bad Wolf Academy to perfect his huffing and puffing, he is a dismal failure; affecting a human disguise à la Red Riding Hood also proves difficult. Rufus would rather do really wolfy things, like howling at the moon and running through the woods. While he is singled out as a poor student at school, Rufus finally gains the respect of his classmates when he comes to the rescue and finds his true calling in the process. "Krensky's tale cleverly points out . . . the advantages of being true to one's own nature," Mary Jean Smith observed in *School Library Journal*. In *Publishers Weekly* a critic dubbed *Big Bad Wolves at School* "comical," adding that "read-ers familiar with wolf fables will best appreciate" its sly humor. In *Booklist,* Cooper had particular praise for Sneed's artwork, calling it "full of energy and extremely funny."

In his "On My Own Folklore" books, Krensky brings to life some of the characters from American tall tales, such as Paul Bunyan, Calamity Jane, Pecos Bill, and John Henry. He also recounts tales from other lands that focus on folktale archetypes, such as the trickster character, which is featured in *Anansi and the Box of Stories: A West African Folktale*. Turning to more fan-tastical—and creepy—fare, his "Monster Chronicles" chapter books introduce the literary roots of mummies, zombies, vampires, werewolves, and dwarves. In a re-view of *Anansi and the Box of Stories,* Marilyn Tanigu-chi praised Krensky's retelling as "simple and fast-moving." His "conversational writing style and tendency

toward speculation and sensationalism," as well as the inclusion "illustrations [that] are really frightening," make the "Monster Chronicles" books more entertain-ing than scholarly, concluded Marcia Kochel in the same periodical. In *Booklist* Gillian Engberg recom-mended the series for reluctant readers due to Kren-sky's "high-interest subject and conversational tone."

Geared for older readers, *The Wilder Plot* and *The Wilder Summer* are two of Krensky's longest works of fiction and both feature eighth grader Charlie Wilder. In *The Wilder Plot,* Charlie unwillingly gets the lead role in the student production of *A Midsummer Night's Dream* and spends much of the rest of the book at-tempting to get out of this uncomfortable situation be-fore being saved just before show time. Amy L. Cohn noted in *School Library Journal* that Krensky captured the intensity of school in "a novel of high-spirited good humor."

Set at summer camp, *The Wilder Summer* describes Charlie's attempts to get to know Lydia, with whom he falls in love at first sight, despite the endeavors of Ly-dia's jealous friend Willoughby. "Charlie's shy reluc-tance to approach Lydia leads to a string of humorous situations," commented a reviewer for *Voice of Youth Advocates,* and creates a book that "should appeal to the youngest YAs." The reviewers proved to be right about the book's popularity: *The Wilder Summer* was appealing enough to be adapted for an HBO television movie.

In addition to fiction, Krensky has also written nonfic-tion books noted for presenting accurate and thoroughly researched overviews of interesting subjects. In *Con-queror and Hero: The Search for Alexander* Krensky "offers a clear, concise account of the brilliant and enig-matic Macedonian leader," according to *Horn Book* contributor Ethel R. Twichell. A reviewer noted in the *Bulletin of the Center for Children's Books* that the conciseness of Krensky's text "may appeal to reluctant readers," and *School Library Journal* critic Elizabeth Holtze commented that when "readers put down this good book, they will want to learn more about its fasci-nating subject." Although *Maiden Voyage: The Story of the Statue of Liberty* was joined by many other books on its subject in honor of the statue's centennial year, it stands out from the rest, according to Elizabeth S. Wat-son in *Horn Book,* because of its "brevity and humor." Assessing *Breaking into Print: Before and after the In-vention of the Printing Press,* Krensky's overview of the printed word, a *Kirkus Reviews* writer concluded that the text and the artwokr by Bonnie Christensen work in tandem to create "a gorgeous format that does complete justice to the subject."

Among Krensky's books dealing with the history of North America are *Who Really Discovered America?, Striking It Rich: The Story of the California Gold Rush,* and *Dangerous Crossing: The Revolutionary Voyage of John and John Quincy Adams. Who Really Discovered*

America? details the sea voyages that preceded that of Christopher Columbus, including those of Asian nomads, Polynesians, Phoenicians, and Scandinavians. "Though Krensky treats his subject with respect and precision, his text is leavened with humor," noted a *Kirkus Reviews* contributor of the book. A more recent voyage across the Atlantic—that of John Adams and ten-year-old son John Quincy Adams in 1778—is the focus of *Dangerous Crossing,* as readers follow the sea sickness, the threats from Portuguese battle ships, and the stress of weeks at sea through Krensky's fictionalized history. Based on the diary of the older Adams, the book "offers a stirring account of life aboard ship" that is "spiced with details," according to *Booklist* contributor Carolyn Phelan. In *School Library Journal,* Lynda Ritterman praised the "masterful watercolor paintings" by Greg Harlin, adding that *Dangerous Crossing* is a work of "engaging historical fiction . . . that truly brings the story to life."

As in *Dangerous Crossing,* Krensky often frames moments from history within a compelling story. Taking place in 1735, *Printer's Apprentice* finds a young boy learning the importance of freedom of speech the hard way, while in *The Iron Dragon Never Sleeps,* Krensky brings to life the plight of the Chinese workers constructing the transcontinental railroad through his fictional story about the friendship between a white girl and a Chinese boy. Based on an actual incident, *Hanukkah at Valley Forge* finds General George Washington learning about the traditional Jewish holiday ritual from a Polish-born volunteer while the Continental Army endures a harsh winter. A *Kirkus Reviews* contributor noted that Krensky "makes good use of historical fact" in *The Printer's Apprentice,* and Teri Markson cited *Hanukkah at Valley Forge* for offering "an interesting perspective through which to view a familiar holiday story." Reviewing *The Iron Dragon Never Sleeps* for *Kirkus Reviews,* a critic dubbed the work an "interesting adjunct to the study of Westward expansion," and a *Publishers Weekly* critic concluded that Krensky avoids "a pat, happy ending" by presenting readers with "a bittersweet conclusion that renders his historically accurate story even more powerful."

Much of Krensky's nonfiction takes the form of biography. *Taking Flight: The Story of the Wright Brothers* recounts the achievements of brothers Orville and Wilbur Wright in their attempt to make and send aloft a "flying machine" in North Carolina in 1903. Nineteenth-century Ohioan and famed sharpshooter Annie Oakley is the focus of *Shooting for the Moon: The Amazing Life and Times of Annie Oakley,* while what Phelan deemed "a stimulating introduction" to the life of young Davy Crockett is the focus of *Davy Crockett: A Life on the Frontier.* A collective biography of environmentalists John Muir, Rachel Carson, Chico Mendes, and Lois Gibbs, Krensky's *Four against the Odds: The Struggle to Save Our Environment* was praised by *Voice of Youth Advocates* contributor Catherine M. Clancy as "an ex-

cellent introduction to the 'environmental issue,'" and Chris Sherman noted in his *Booklist* review of the work that "Krensky's style is very readable."

Krensky once told *SATA* where his books and ideas come from. "People often ask me how I can write something that twelve-year-olds or nine-year-olds will want to read," he explained. "I'm not sure, but I do know that the part of me that was once twelve and nine and six is not neatly boxed and tucked away in some dusty corner of my mind. It's spread throughout the place like crepe paper or bunting. So far I think it's given the place a festive air. If I'm lucky, it always will." Noting the discipline required to be such a prolific author, Krensky noted on his home page: "Writing is hard and fun at the same time, and writing children's books is the best job I can think of having. So if I didn't do it, I'd have to do something I'd like less. That certainly helps me keep focused."

Biographical and Critical Sources

PERIODICALS

Booklist, November 15, 1986, Ilene Cooper, review of *Scoop after Scoop: A History of Ice Cream,* p. 513; December 1, 1991, Julie Corsaro, review of *Lionel and Louise,* p. 709, and Carolyn Phelan, review of *Christopher Columbus,* p. 111; June 1, 1992, Chris Sherman, review of *Four against the Odds: The Struggle to Save Our Environment,* p. 1759; July, 1998, Carolyn Phelan, review of *We Just Moved!,* and *Lionel in the Summer,* p. 1890; September 1, 1998, Ilene Cooper, review of *How Santa Got His Job,* p. 112; October 1, 1998, Susan Dove Lempke, review of *Louise Takes Charge,* p. 330; March 15, 1999, Ilene Cooper, review of *My Loose Tooth,* p. 1337; July, 1999, Lauren Peterson, review of *Louise Goes Wild,* p. 1946; May 15, 2000, Carolyn Phelan, review of *Taking Flight: The Story of the Wright Brothers,* p. 1740; June 1, 2000, Carolyn Phelan, review of *Arthur and the Big Blow-Up,* p. 1894; July, 2000, Ilene Cooper, review of *The Youngest Fairy Godmother Ever,* p. 2040; October 1, 2000, Hazel Rochman, review of *Lionel at School,* p. 352; March 1, 2001, Susan Dove Lempke, review of *Louise, Soccer Star?,* p. 1278; April 15, 2001, Roger Leslie, review of *The Moon Robber,* p. 1559; May 15, 2001, Connie Fletcher, review of *Arthur and the Seventh-Inning Stretcher,* p. 1753; September 15, 2001, Stephanie Zvirin, review of *How Santa Lost His Job,* p. 235, and Carolyn Phelan, review of *Shooting for the Moon: The Amazing Life and Times of Annie Oakley,* p. 228; October 1, 2002, Carolyn Phelan, review of *Paul Revere's Midnight Ride,* p. 318; July, 2003, Hazel Rochman, review of *Lionel's Birthday,* p. 1899; September 1, 2004, Kay Weisman, review of *There Once Was a Very Odd School, and Other Lunch-Box Limericks,* p. 117; December 1, 2004, Carolyn Phelan, review of *Davy Crockett: A Life on the Frontier,* p. 656; March 1,

2005, Carolyn Phelan, review of *Dangerous Crossing: The Revolutionary Voyage of John and John Quincy Adams,* p. 1198; September 1, 2006, Kay Weisman, review of *Hanukkah at Valley Forge,* p. 137; October 15, 2006, Gillian Engberg, review of *Vampires,* p. 71; April 1, 2007, Ilene Cooper, review of *Big Bad Wolves at School,* p. 57; October 1, 2007, Jesse Karp, review of *Comic Book Century: The History of American Comic Books,* p. 50; March 1, 2008, Todd Morning, review of *What's the Big Idea?: Four Centuries of Innovation in Boston,* p. 67.

Bulletin of the Center for Children's Books, May, 1980, review of *A Troll in Passing,* p. 175; January, 1982, review of *Conqueror and Hero: The Search for Alexander,* p. 88; November, 1984, review of *A Ghostly Business,* p. 49; April, 1986, review of *Lionel at Large,* p. 113; February, 1987, Betsy Hearne, review of *Scoop after Scoop,* p. 111; February, 1994, Carol Fox, review of *Lionel in Winter,* pp. 190-191; January, 1997, review of *Breaking into Print: Before and after the Invention of the Printing Press,* p. 177; February, 1997, review of *Lionel and His Friends,* p. 212; September, 1998, review of *How Santa Got His Job,* p. 18; July, 2001, review of *Shooting for the Moon,* p. 412; March, 2007, Hope Morrison, review of *Too Many Leprechauns; or, How That Pot o' Gold Got to the End of the Rainbow,* p. 298.

Five Owls, September, 1991, review of *American Heritage First Dictionary,* p. 20.

Horn Book, December, 1981, Ethel R. Twichell, review of *Conqueror and Hero,* pp. 677-678; January-February, 1986, Elizabeth S. Watson, review of *Maiden Voyage: The Story of the Statue of Liberty,* pp. 76-77; July-August, 1990, Carolyn K. Jenks, review of *Lionel in the Spring,* p. 477; March, 1992, p. 219; March-April, 1994, Margaret A. Bush, review of *Lionel in the Winter,* p. 195; September-October, 1995, Margaret A. Bush, review of *The Printer's Apprentice,* pp. 600-601.

Kirkus Reviews, April 1, 1977, review of *A Big Day for Scepters,* p. 352; January 1, 1988, review of *Who Really Discovered America?,* p. 56; June 1, 1994, review of *The Iron Dragon Never Sleeps,* p. 776; June 15, 1995, review of *The Printer's Apprentice,* p. 858; July 15, 1996, review of *Breaking into Print,* p. 1051; September 15, 2001, review of *How Santa Lost His Job,* p. 1360; July 15, 2002, review of *Paul Revere's Midnight Ride,* p. 1035; January 1, 2005, review of *Dangerous Crossing,* p. 53; November 1, 2006, review of *Milo the Really Big Bunny,* p. 1323; November 1, 2006, review of *Hanukkah at Valley Forge,* p. 1130; December 1, 2006, review of *Too Many Leprechauns,* p. 1222; June 1, 2007, review of *Big Bad Wolves at School.*

New York Times Book Review, November 9, 1980, Richard Mitchell, review of *My First Dictionary,* p. 56; May 20, 1990, Ann M. Martin, review of *Perfect Pigs: An Introduction to Manners,* p. 46.

Publishers Weekly, June 13, 1980, review of *A Troll in Passing,* p. 72; June 27, 1986, review of *Lionel at Large,* p. 88; October 9, 1987, review of *Lionel in the Fall,* p. 86; May 2, 1994, review of *The Iron Dragon Never Sleeps,* p. 309; June 5, 2000, review of *The Youngest Fairy Godmother Ever,* p. 93; June 11, 2001, review of *The Moon Robber,* p. 86; October 8, 2001, review of *Shooting for the Moon,* p. 64; August 5, 2002, review of *Paul Revere's Midnight Ride,* p. 71; February 13, 2006, review of *Milo the Really Big Bunny,* p. 89; September 25, 2006, review of *Hanukkah at Valley Forge,* p. 68; October 2, 2006, review of *The Crimson Comet,* p. 63; January 1, 2007, review of *Too Many Leprechauns,* p. 48; July 9, 2007, review of *Big Bad Wolves at School,* p. 52.

School Arts, April, 1997, Kent Anderson and Ken Marantz, review of *Breaking into Print,* p. 63.

School Library Journal, April, 1977, Craighton Hippenhammer, review of *A Big Day for Scepters,* p. 68; October, 1977, Craighton Hippenhammer, review of *The Dragon Circle,* p. 115; November, 1981, Elizabeth Holtze, review of *Conqueror and Hero,* pp. 106-107; January, 1983, Amy L. Cohn, review of *The Wilder Plot,* p. 77; May, 1986, review of *Lionel at Large,* p. 113; April, 1992, Sharron McElmeel, review of *Lionel and Louise,* p. 95; February, 1993, Carolyn Jenks, review of *The Pizza Book: Fun, Facts, a Recipe—the Works!,* p. 100; June, 2000, Gay Lynn Van Vleck, review of *The Youngest Fairy Godmother Ever,* p. 118; August, 2000, Susan Knell, review of *Taking Flight,* p. 171; September, 2000, Helen Foster James, review of *Lionel at School,* p. 202; January, 2001, Blair Christolon, review of *Louise, Soccer Star?,* p. 102; July, 2001, Susan Lissim, review of *Pearl Harbor,* p. 95; September, 2001, Devon Gallagher, review of *The Moon Robber,* p. 200; October, 2001, review of *How Santa Lost His Job,* p. 67; October, 2003, Laura Scott, review of *Lionel's Birthday,* p. 129; August, 2004, Doris Losey, review of *There Once Was a Very Odd School,* p. 110; February, 2005, Lynda Ritterman, review of *Dangerous Crossing,* p. 104; February, 2006, Rachel G. Payne, review of *Milo the Really Big Bunny,* p. 106; October, 2006, Teri Markson, review of *Hanukkah at Valley Forge,* p. 97; December, 2006, Piper L. Nayman, review of *The Crimson Comet,* p. 110; February, 2007, Kirsten Cutler, review of *Too Many Leprechauns,* p. 90; June, 2007, Mary Jean Smith, review of *Big Bad Wolves at School,* p. 110; November, 2007, Marilyn Taniguchi, review of *Anansi and the Box of Stories: A West African Folktale,* p. 109, Marcia Kochel, review of *The Bogeyman,* p. 150, and Benjamin Russell, review of *Comic Book Century,* p. 151.

Voice of Youth Advocates, February, 1984, review of *The Wilder Summer,* p. 339; October, 1992, Catherine M. Clancy, review of *Four against the Odds,* p. 254.

Wilson Library Bulletin, February, 1992, review of *Christopher Columbus and His Voyage to the New World,* p. 83.

ONLINE

Stephen Krensky Home Page, http://www.stephenkrensky.com (March 28, 2008).

KRENSKY, Stephen Alan
See KRENSKY, Stephen

*   *   *

KULKA, Joe 1965(?)-

Personal

Born c. 1965; married; children: three. *Education:* University of Arts, B.F.A. (illustration), 1987.

Addresses

Home and office—Quakertown, PA. *E-mail*—joe@joekulka.com.

Career

Author and illustrator. Formerly worked as a medical textbook illustrator.

Member

Graphic Artists Guild, Picture Book Artists Association.

Writings

SELF-ILLUSTRATED

Wolf's Coming!, Carolrhoda Books (Minneapolis, MN), 2007.
The Rope, Pelican Publishing (Gretna, LA), 2008.

ILLUSTRATOR

Jackie Glassman, *Happy Birthday, Princess Lolly!* ("My First Game Reader: Candyland" series), Scholastic (New York, NY), 2000.
Jackie Glassman, *Have You Seen King Candy?* ("My First Game Reader: Candyland" series), Scholastic (New York, NY), 2000.
Francine Hughs, *Candyland: Sweets and Treats,* Scholastic (New York, NY), 2001.
Andrea Jones, *The Spitting Twins,* Frog (Berkeley, CA), 2004.
Dotti Enderle, *Granny Gert and the Bunion Brothers,* Pelican Publishing (Gretna, LA), 2006.
Larry Dane Brimner, *Monkey Math,* Children's Press (New York, NY), 2007.
Carol Murray, *Storytime Stickers: Pirate Treasure Hunt,* Sterling Publishing Company (New York, NY), 2007.
Marcy Brown and Dennis Haley, *Just Five More Minutes,* Treasure Bay (San Anselmo, CA), 2008.

Sidelights

Joe Kulka began his illustrating career as a medical textbook artist, spending much of his time drawing organs within the human body. It was not until Kulka

viewed Charles Santore's illustrations in *The Wizard of Oz* and saw the many picture books presented on public television's *Reading Rainbow* series that he realized the other creative avenues open to him. Jackie Glassman's *Happy Birthday, Princess Lolly!,* an easy reader based on the popular *Candyland* board game, was the first published book to feature Kulka's artwork; since that work was published in 2000, the artist has added several more illustration credits and also expanded his role to that of author/illustrator.

Wolf's Coming!, Kulka's first self-illustrated children's book, came about after he joined a writing group. With the group's help, he was able to fine-tune his writing skills and produce his first picture-book text. *Wolf's Coming!* was acknowledged by several reviewers for its ability to keep readers in suspense, and then surprise them at story's end. Hazel Rochman, reviewing the picture book for *Booklist,* noted of *Wolf's Coming!* that "kids will enjoy the mounting suspense, and feel smug about the happy ending." Featuring digital elements displaying feature vivid colors, Kulka's illustrations "grow progressively darker" as the pages turn, observed *School Library Journal* reviewer Debbie Lewis, and this technique "help[s] . . . to create and sustain the intended mood."

Joe Kulka captivates young readers with an exciting story and amusing artwork in his picture book **Wolf's Coming!** (Illustration copyright © 2007 by Joe Kulka. All rights reserved. Reproduced by Carolrhoda Books, a division of Lerner Publishing Group.)

Biographical and Critical Sources

PERIODICALS

Booklist, April 15, 2007, Hazel Rochman, review of *Wolf's Coming!,* p. 48.

School Library Journal, January, 2007, Marge Lock-Wouters, review of *Granny Gert and the Bunion Brothers,* p. 92; January, 2007, Colleen D. Bocka, review of *Monkey Math,* p. 88; July, 2007, Debbie Lewis, review of *Wolf's Coming!,* p. 80.

ONLINE

Joe Kulka Home Page, http://www.joekulka.com (March 9, 2008).*

L

LABOUISSE, Eve Curie
See CURIE, Eve

*   *   *

LABOUISSE, Eve Denise
See CURIE, Eve

*   *   *

LEEDS, Contance

Personal
Married (husband deceased, 2006); children: three. *Education:* Wellesley College, A.B.; Boston University, J.D.

Addresses
Home—Boston, MA. *E-mail*—constance.leeds@gmail.com.

Career
Author. Formerly worked as an attorney.

Member
Authors Guild, Society of Book Writers and Illustrators.

Awards, Honors
Sydney Taylor Award Notable Book for Older Readers designation, and International Reading Association Children's and Young-Adult Book Award for Intermediate Fiction, both 2008, both for *The Silver Cup.*

Writings

The Silver Cup, Viking (New York, NY), 2007.

Constance Leeds (Photo courtesy of Constance Leeds Bennett.)

Also author of "A Boy on Board Old Ironsides" (narrative), music by Larry Bell, produced by Boston Landmarks Orchestra.

Biographical and Critical Sources

PERIODICALS

Booklist, February 15, 2007, Jennifer Mattson, review of *The Silver Cup,* p. 87.
Kirkus Reviews, March 15, 2007, review of *The Silver Cup.*
School Library Journal, June, 2007, Rita Soltan, review of *The Silver Cup,* p. 152.

ONLINE

Constance Leeds Home Page, http://www.constanceleeds.com (February 15, 2008).

Class of 2k7 Web site, http://classof2k7.com/ (March 5, 2008), "Constance Leeds."

*   *   *

LONG, Loren 1966(?)-

Personal

Born c. 1966, in Joplin, MO; son of Bill Long; married Tracy Maines, 1993; children: Griffith, Graham. *Education:* University of Kentucky, B.A., 1987; graduate study at American Academy of Art (Chicago, IL). *Hobbies and other interests:* Baseball, kayaking.

Addresses

Office—P.O. Box 8377, West Chester, OH 45069.

Career

Gibson Greeting Cards, Cincinnati, OH, illustrator, 1988-92; freelance illustrator, beginning 1993. Northern Kentucky University, instructor in illustration. *Exhibitions:* Participant in group shows, including *Centro Cultura Recolata,* Buenos Aires, Argentina, 2001, and solo shows at Thurber House, Columbus, OH, 2004. Works included in permanent collections at Cincinnati Art Museum, U.S. Golf Association's Museum and Archives, and *Sports Illustrated.*

Awards, Honors

Two gold medals, Society of Illustrators; One Hundred Titles for Reading and Sharing citation, New York Public Library, and Golden Kite Award for Illustration, Society of Children's Book Writers and Illustrators, both 2003, both for *I Dream of Trains* by Angela Johnson; Cuffies Award, *Publishers Weekly,* 2007, for *Toy Boat* by Randall de Sève.

Writings

ILLUSTRATOR; FOR CHILDREN

Betsy Byars, Betsy Duffy, and Laurie Myers, *My Dog, My Hero,* Holt (New York, NY), 2000.

Gary D. Schmidt, *The Wonders of Donal O'Donnell: A Folktale of Ireland,* Holt (New York, NY), 2002.

Angela Johnson, *I Dream of Trains,* Simon & Schuster (New York, NY), 2003.

Frances Ward Weller, *The Day the Animals Came: A Story of Saint Francis Day,* Philomel Books (New York, NY), 2003.

Madonna, *Mr. Peabody's Apples,* Callaway (New York, NY), 2003.

Walt Whitman, *When I Heard the Learn'd Astronomer,* Simon & Schuster (New York, NY), 2004.

Loren Long (Reproduced by permission of Loren Long.)

Watty Piper, reteller, *The Little Engine That Could* (new edition), Philomel (New York, NY), 2005.

Angela Johnson, *Wind Flyers,* Simon & Schuster (New York, NY), 2007.

Frank McCourt, *Angela and the Baby Jesus,* Scribner (New York, NY), 2007.

Randall de Sève, *Toy Boat,* Philomel (New York, NY), 2007.

Contributor of illustrations to numerous periodicals, including *Time, Reader's Digest, Forbes, Wall Street Journal, Atlantic Monthly,* and *Sports Illustrated.*

"BARNSTORMERS; TALES OF THE TRAVELIN' NINE" NOVEL SERIES

(With Phil Bildner; and illustrator) *Game One: Three Kids, a Mystery, and a Magic Baseball,* Simon & Schuster (New York, NY), 2007.

(With Phil Bildner; and illustrator) *Game Two: Three Kids, a Letter, and Lots of Horsing Around,* Simon & Schuster (New York, NY), 2007.

(With Phil Bildner; and illustrator) *Game Three: Three Kids, a Villain, and Great Balls of Fire,* Simon & Schuster (New York, NY), 2008.

ILLUSTRATOR; "TRUCKTOWN" PICTURE BOOK SERIES

(With David Gordon and David Shannon) Jon Scieszka, *Snow Trucking!,* Aladdin (New York, NY), 2008.

(With David Gordon and David Shannon) Jon Scieszka, *Pete's Party,* Aladdin (New York, NY), 2008.

(With David Gordon and David Shannon) Jon Scieszka, *Zoom! Boom! Bully,* Aladdin (New York, NY), 2008.

(With David Gordon and David Shannon) Jon Scieszka, *Smash! Crash!,* Aladdin (New York, NY), 2008.

(With David Gordon and David Shannon) Jon Scieszka, *The Spooky Tire,* Aladdin (New York, NY), 2009.

(With David Gordon and David Shannon) Jon Scieszka, *The Big Noisy Book of Truckery Rhymes,* Aladdin (New York, NY), 2009.

Sidelights

Although Loren Long was catapulted to worldwide fame when pop star Madonna selected him to illustrate her picture book *Mr. Peabody's Apples,* the Ohio-based artist has built a strong line of steady successes in the picture-book field. After attending art school, he worked as an illustrator at a greeting-card company while also honing his distinctive style through freelance assignments. "I'm drawn to the work of the great WPA

Long's art can be found on covers of several novels, including Anne Quirk's Dancing with Great-Aunt Cornelia. (Jacket art © 1997 by Loren Long. Jacket © 1997 by HarperCollins Publishers. Used by permission of HarperCollins Publishers.)

[Works Progress Administration] muralists and American regionalists [of the 1930s] because there is a narrative quality to all their paintings. They were story tellers. That's why I like doing children's books," Long told *Cincinnati Post* interviewer Peggy Kreimer. In addition to his work for Madonna, Long has created illustrations for a variety of picture-book authors, including Jon Scieszka, Randall de Sève, and Angela Johnson, and has even produced new art for a childhood classic, Watty Piper's retelling of *The Little Engine That Could.* In 2007 Long paired illustration with writing by serving as coauthor alongside author Phil Bildner on the popular "Barnstormers" baseball-themed fantasy novels.

In fact, baseball is a theme that weaves its way throughout Long's body of work. In *Mr. Peabody's Apples,* for instance, Madonna's title character is a teacher who also serves as a Little League coach. One of his players, Tommy, notices that every week after the game, Mr. Peabody takes an apple from the local market without paying for it. Not knowing that the man pays for each apple in advance, the boy spreads the rumor that Mr. Peabody is a thief. To teach Tommy a lesson about the damage rumor-mongering can do, the coach asks the boy to bring his pillow to the baseball field. Then Mr. Peabody cuts it open and feathers fly everywhere. Asked by his coach to gather all the feathers back up, Tommy protests that this is impossible, whereupon he learns that the damage caused by a rumor is equally hard to undo. "Readers may be less than charmed by Mr. Peabody's self-righteous streak but Long's art is worth watching," a reviewer wrote in *Publishers Weekly.* In *Salon.com,* Emily Jenkins praised the book's "muscular, rubbery paintings," writing that Long's art reveals both "beautiful plays of light and a still, detailed beauty."

Other picture books featuring Long's art include Frances Ward Weller's *The Day the Animals Came: A Story of St. Francis Day,* Gary D. Schmidt's *The Wonders of Donal O'Donnell: A Folktale of Ireland,* and Frank McCourt's *Angela and the Baby Jesus.* In *Booklist* Ilene Cooper praised Long's work for the first-named title, which describes the Blessing of the Animals ceremony held annually at St. John the Divine Cathedral in New York City. The book's "acrylic paintings soar as Long looks at goings-on from many different perspectives," the critic noted.

Writing about *The Wonders of Donal O'Donnell* in *School Library Journal,* Marie Orlando noted that Long's "richly colored" images "successfully enhance the mood" of the story, which starts out dark as O'Donnell and his wife Sorcha cut themselves off from the community and mourn the death of their son. On one particularly brutal winter night, Sorcha relents and takes in three travelers who ask to come in and warm themselves by her home's fire. In return, Donal O'Sheary, Donal O'Neary, and Donal O'Leary each tell a story (adapted by Schmidt from traditional Irish folklore) about a boy who goes to Fairy Land but then returns.

As the night progresses, the O'Donnells realize that, while their son is gone, the stories they can tell about him will allow him to live on in their memories. Long's "somber" illustrations reflect the uplifting mood of the tale and "remind the reader of the darkened, candlelit atmosphere of the cottage," a critic commented in *Kirkus Reviews.*

Ireland is also the setting for *Angela and the Baby Jesus,* which takes place in Limerick, Ireland, in 1912. Although McCourt's story was intended for children, two illustrated versions of the book were published. Raul Colón created color illustrations for the children's version, while Long's interpretation of the story is more somber and his art more shadowed and suitable for general readers. In the story, a six-year-old girl sees the baby Jesus in a local parish church manger scene and decides that the Jesus figurine needs to be taken home and nestled up in a warm blanket.

In his artwork for *Toy Boat* by de Sève, Long inspires young readers while bringing to life the adventures of a homemade boat as it attempts to reunite with the young boy who made it. "Long's crisp acrylic illustrations . . . capture the drama" of the boat's adventure, wrote a *Kirkus Reviews* writer, while in *Booklist* Julie Cummins concluded that *Toy Boat* benefits from both "buoyant charm and imaginative artwork." In a story that takes to the air, *Wind Flyers* focuses on the Tuskegee Airmen and their bravery during World War II. "Long's acrylics beautifully extend the evocative words" of award-winning author Angela Johnson, noted Gillian Engberg in her *Booklist* review of *Wind Flyers.* Reviewing the same book for *School Library Journal,* John Peters wrote that Long's paintings, with their "misty look," "artfully evoke . . . that sense of remembered times" that is conjured up in Johnson's "lyrical . . . monologue." Long and Johnson also team up for *I Dream of Trains,* which finds a young farmer's son dreaming of riding the rails with the legendary engineer Casey Jones.

Working with fellow illustrators David Gordon and David Shannon, Long has also helped bring to life Scieszka's boy-friendly "Trucktown" beginning-readers series, which includes the books *Snow Trucking!, Smash! Crash!, Zoom! Boom! Bully,* and *The Spooky Tire.* Reviewing series installment *Smash! Crash!,* which finds an group of anthropomorphized big rigs staging their own demolition derby, *School Library Journal* contributor Lynn K. Vanca noted that the illustrators' "digital artwork adds plenty of personality" to Scieszka's diesel-powered protagonists "and perfectly suits the text." Dump Truck Dan and Jack Truck, the series' main characters, possess an "energy and zest [that] are perfectly captured by the trio of illustrators," concluded a *Kirkus Reviews* writer in reviewing another high-energy "Trucktown" installment.

In his first inning as coauthor, Long joined veteran writer Bildner to create the "Barnstormers" series of middle-grade novels. Planned as a sequence of six

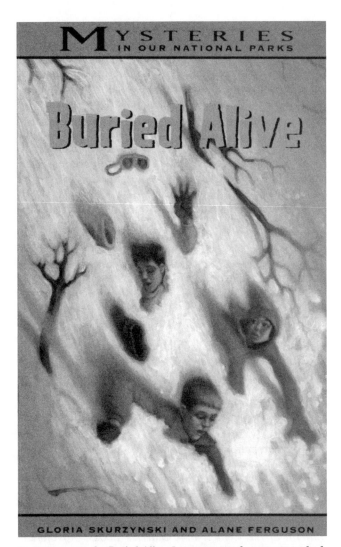

In his cover art for **Buried Alive,** *Long captures the urgency and adventure at the core of Alane Ferguston and Gloria Skurzynski's middle-grade novel.* (Cover illustration copyright © 2003 by Loren Long. Reproduced by permission.)

books, the series takes place in 1899 as the three Payne siblings join a group of traveling baseball players in the wake of their father's death. When their Uncle Owen Payne gives the boys a damaged baseball that their father once made, the children realize that this is no ordinary memento. In *Game One: Three Kids, a Mystery, and a Magic Baseball* Griffith, Graham, and Ruby Payne discover the baseball's magic power, while a mystery surrounding the Travelin' Nine Baseball Team continues to deepen in *Game Two: Three Kids, a Letter, and Lots of Horsing Around.* "There is no question that both Long and Bildner love baseball," wrote Kim Dare in a *School Library Journal* review of the series opener, the critic going on to call Long's pencil illustrations "breathtaking." While noting that the novel's plot is somewhat confusing, a *Kirkus Reviews* writer commented of *Game One* that the book features "an interesting cast of characters and lots of action." The score improves in *Game Two,* wrote another reviewer for the same periodical while praising the second installment as "better organized, with more fully developed structure and characters." *Game Three: Three Kids, a Villain, and Great Balls of Fire* also benefits from Long's artistic contribution, "unique pen-and-ink illustrations [that] are at once detailed, exaggerated and compelling," according to yet another *Kirkus Reviews* writer.

Although he has provided illustrations for many adult publications, Long prefers to work in the picture-book field. "The process of making a children's book from start to finish is very fulfilling," he told *Cincinnati Enquirer* interviewer Marilyn Bauer. "It's a way to touch children and to have an impact on American culture in general."

Biographical and Critical Sources

PERIODICALS

Black Issues Book Review, July-August, 2003, Suzanne Rust, review of *I Dream of Trains,* p. 65.

Booklist, October 1, 2003, Ilene Cooper, review of *The Day the Animals Came: A Story of Saint Francis Day,* p. 335; November 15, 2003, Ilene Cooper, review of *Mr. Peabody's Apples,* p. 601; November 15, 2004, Jennifer Mattson, review of *When I Heard the Learn'd Astronomer,* p. 585; September 1, 2005, Carolyn Phelan, review of *The Little Engine That Could,* p. 145; December 1, 2006, Gillian Engberg, review of *Wind Flyers,* p. 52; August, 2007, Julie Cummins, review of *Toy Boat,* p. 71; November 15, 2007, Hazel Rochman, review of *Smash! Crash!,* p. 51.

Bulletin of the Center for Children's Books, November, 2003, Janice Del Negro, review of *I Dream of Trains,* p. 108; January, 2007, Elizabeth Bush, review of *Wind Flyers,* p. 219; April, 2007, Elizabeth Bush, review of *Game One,* p. 335.

Cincinnati Enquirer (Cincinnati, OH), November 9, 2003, Marilyn Bauer, interview with Long.

Cincinnati Post (Cincinnati, OH), November 8, 2003, Peggy Kreimer, interview with Long.

Kirkus Reviews, November 15, 2002, review of *The Wonders of Donal O'Donnell: A Folktale of Ireland,* p. 1702; July 1, 2003, review of *The Day the Animals Came,* p. 916; September 1, 2003, review of *I Dream of Trains,* p. 1125; November 1, 2004, review of *When I Heard the Learn'd Astronomer,* p. 1047; August 15, 2005, review of *The Little Engine That Could,* p. 920; December 15, 2006, review of *Wind Flyers,* p. 1269; February 1, 2007, review of *Game One,* p. 125; August 1, 2007, review of *Toy Boat;* December 15, 2007, review of "Trucktown" series; February 15, 2008, review of *Three Kids, a Villain, and Great Balls of Fire.*

Lexington Herald-Leader (Lexington, KY), February 7, 2004, Mary Meehan, interview with Long.

New York Times Book Review, November 16, 2003, Tony Hiss, review of *I Dream of Trains,* p. 24.

Publishers Weekly, November 4, 2002, review of *The Wonders of Donal O'Donnell,* p. 84; September 29, 2003, review of *The Day the Animals Came,* p. 62; November 17, 2003, John F. Baker, "Madonna Artist in Big Kids' Deal," p. 12; December 15, 2003, review of *Mr. Peabody's Apples,* p. 73.

School Library Journal, January, 2001, Pat Leach, review of *My Dog, My Hero,* p. 92; December, 2002, Marie Orlando, review of *The Wonders of Donal O'Donnell,* p. 129; November, 2003, Susan Scheps, review of *The Day the Animals Came,* p. 118; September, 2005, Roxanne Burg, review of *The Little Engine That Could,* p. 184; January, 2007, John Peters, review of *Wind Flyers,* p. 98; April, 2007, Kim Dare, review of *Game One,* p. 110; September, 2007, Susan Moorhead, review of *Toy Boat,* p. 161; January, 2008, Lynn K. Vanca, review of *Smash! Crash!,* p. 97.

ONLINE

Loren Long Home Page, http://www.lorenlong.com (March 21, 2008).

Salon.com, http://www.salon.com/ (November 14, 2003), Emily Jenkins, review of *Mr. Peabody's Apples.**

* * *

LOVE, Judith Dufour
See LOVE, Judy

* * *

LOVE, Judy
(Judith Dufour Love)

Personal

Married; husband's name Alan; children: Matt, Tom.

Addresses

Home and office—Belmont, MA.

Career

Illustrator.

Writings

ILLUSTRATOR

John and Cindy Trent, *The Treasure Tree,* Word (Dallas, TX), 1992.

John Trent, *There's a Duck in My Closet!,* Word (Dallas, TX), 1993.

John Trent, *I'd Choose You!,* Word (Dallas, TX), 1994.

John Trent, *Spider Sisters,* Word (Dallas, TX), 1996.

Ivon Cecil, *Kirby Kelvin and the Not-Laughing Lessons,* Whispering Coyote (Dallas, TX), 1998.

John Trent, *The Two Trails: A Treasure Tree Adventure,* Tommy Nelson (Nashville, TN), 1998.

The Cook's Illustrated Complete Book of Poultry, C. Potter (New York, NY), 1999.

John Trent, *The Black and White Rainbow,* Waterbrook (Colorado Springs, CO), 1999.

Julie Danneberg, *First Day Jitters,* Charlesbridge (Watertown, MA), 2000.

Lois G. Grambling, *The Witch Who Wanted to Be a Princess,* Whispering Coyote (Watertown, MA), 2002.

(With Phil Bliss and Jerry Tiritilli) *Silly Songs Sing-Along,* Publications International (Lincolnwood, IL), 2002.

Matthew Gollub, *Gobble, Quack, Moon,* Tortuga (Santa Rose, CA), 2002.

Julie Dannenberg, *First Year Letters,* Charlesbridge (Watertown, MA), 2003.

Juanita Havill, *The Blue Racer,* Zaner-Bloser (Columbus, OH), 2004.

(Under name Judy Dufour Love) Larry Dane Brimner, *Calamity Jane,* Compass Point (Minneapolis, MN), 2004.

Lester L. Laminack, *Jake's 100th Day of School,* Peachtree (Atlanta, GA), 2006.

Julie Dannenberg, *Last Day Blues,* Charlesbridge (Watertown, MA), 2006.

Lois G. Grambling, *Can I Bring My Pterodactyl to School, Miss Johnson?,* Charlesbridge (Watertown, MA), 2006.

Karen Jo Shapiro, *I Must Go Down to the Beach Again, and Other Poems,* Charlesbridge (Watertown, MA), 2007.

Eve Bunting, *The Baby Shower,* Charlesbridge (Watertown, MA), 2007.

Contributor of illustrations to *Poetry Speaks to Children,* edited by Elise Paschen, Sourcebooks (Naperville, IL), 2005.

ILLUSTRATOR; UNDER NAME JUDITH DUFOUR LOVE

Carol Bershad, *The Changer and the Changed: A Working Guide to Personal Change,* Management Sciences for Health (Boston, MA), 1983.

Karl Squier, *Leapin' Lizzie,* Lady of the Lake (Winchester, MA), 1985.

Jannette Kooy, *Going Outside,* SRA School Group (Santa Rosa, CA), 1994.

Funny Songs, Publications International (Lincolnwood, IL), 1994.

Barbara Beveridge, *Honey, My Rabbit,* SRA School Group (Santa Rosa, CA), 1994.

Sarah Toast, *Duckling: At Home on the Pond,* Publications International (Lincolnwood, IL), 1995.

JoAnn Early Macken, *Cats on Judy,* Whispering Coyote (Boston, MA), 1997.

Katherine Mead, *The Missing Pet,* Steck-Vaughn (Austin, TX), 1998.

Sidelights

Judy Love (who also illustrates under the name Judith Dufour Love) has created artwork for dozens of books for children, including those by well-known authors such as Eve Bunting, Julie Danneberg, Larry Dane Brimner, and Lois G. Grambling. In Love's illustra-

tions for Grambling's *The Witch Who Wanted to Be a Princess,* the narrative's "matter-of-factness gets ratcheted up to slapstick" via Love's artwork, according to a *Publishers Weekly* contributor. Sally R. Dow, reviewing the same book for *School Library Journal,* wrote that "hilarious cartoonlike illustrations enhance this engaging story."

Love's illustrations are often noted for their comedic value. In Danneberg's *First Day Jitters,* Sarah imagines the worst things that could happen on her first day of school. Connie Fletcher wrote of the picture book in *Booklist* that "Love's ink-and-watercolor illustrations add humor to Sarah's fears." In *School Library Journal,* Adele Greenlee wrote that the book's "ink-and-watercolor illustrations are full of action and maintain the [author's] lighthearted tone." In *First Year Letters,* the teacher from *First Day Jitters* returns, charting the course for a new school year through letters from her students. "Love's uproarious illustrations are overflowing with comic touches," wrote a contributor to *Kirkus Reviews,* and in *School Library Journal* Piper L. Nyman remarked that Dannenberg's "vibrant colors and animated faces bring the barely controlled chaos to life." A further collaboration, *Last Day Blues,* prompted Carolyn Phelan to conclude in *Booklist* that the "comic exaggeration" in the book's "vivid, colorful illustration makes [*Last Day Blues*] . . . a lively choice for sharing."

Love also turns her attention to classroom activities in *Jake's 100th Day of School,* where her "richly realistic, abundantly detailed pencil, ink, and watercolor illustrations spill across the pages," according to *Booklist* critic Shelle Rosenfeld. In a review of Matthew Gollub's *Gobble, Quack, Moon* for *Publishers Weekly,* a contributor wrote that "Love's limber animal cast cavorts, squawks and munches feed with much enthusiasm," while Phelan maintained that Gollub's rhyming text is "expanded by the good-humored ink drawings, brightened with watercolor washes." In another illustration project, Eve Bunting's *The Baby Shower,* Ms. Brindle Cow and Mr. Bull receive numerous gifts from their animal neighbors in celebration of the calf the couple is expecting. Love's pictures provide "a charming complement to the gently plotted story," according to *School Library Journal* critic Maura Bresnahan.

Along with picture books, Love has contributed her artwork to adult nonfiction and poetry collections. Her work for Karen Jo Shapiro's poetry collection *I Must Go Down to the Beach Again, and Other Poems* prompted Kathleen Whalin to write in *School Library Journal* that "Love's black-and-white pen-and-ink drawings underscore the humor in each selection." Hazel Rochman, reviewing the same work for *Booklist,* similarly commented that Love's "black-and-white illustrations extend the nonsense" in Shapiro's entertaining verses.

Biographical and Critical Sources

PERIODICALS

Booklist, May 15, 1998, John Peters, review of *Kirby Kelvin and the Not-Laughing Lessons,* p. 1630; March 15, 2000, Connie Fletcher, review of *First Day Jitters,* p. 1386; June 1, 2002, Carolyn Phelan, *Gobble, Quack, Moon,* p. 1737; February 1, 2003, Diane Foote, review of *First Year Letters,* p. 1000; December 15, 2005, Hazel Rochman, review of *Can I Bring My Pterodactyl to School, Ms. Johnson?,* p. 50; January 1, 2006, Carolyn Phelan, review of *Last Day Blues,* p. 109; February 1, 2006, Shelle Rosenfeld, review of *Jake's 100th Day of School,* p. 56; February 15, 2007, Hazel Rochman, review of *I Must Go Down to the Beach Again, And Other Poems,* p. 81.

Kirkus Reviews, June 15, 2002, review of *The Witch Who Wanted to Be a Princess,* p. 881; December 15, 2002, review of *First Year Letters,* p. 1848; January 15, 2006, review of *Last Day Blues,* p. 82; December 15, 2006, review of *I Must Go Down to the Beach Again, and Other Poems,* p. 1272.

Publishers Weekly, April 1, 2002, review of *Gobble, Quack, Moon,* p. 81; June 3, 2002, review of *The Witch Who Wanted to Be a Princess,* p. 87.

School Library Journal, May, 2000, Adele Greenlee, review of *First Day Jitters,* p. 133; August, 2002, Sally R. Dow, review of *The Witch Who Wanted to Be a Princess,* p. 156; April, 2003, Piper L. Nyman, review of *First Year Letters,* p. 118; July, 2004, Lisa G. Kropp, review of *First Day Jitters,* p. 42; February, 2006, Genevieve Gallagher, review of *Last Day Blues,* p. 95; March, 2006, Marge Loch-Wouters, review of *Can I Bring My Pterodactyl to School, Ms. Johnson?,* p. 187, Grace Oliff, review of *Jake's 100th Day of School,* p. 196; February, 2007, Kathleen Whalin, review of *I Must Go Down to the Beach Again, and Other Poems,* p. 145; September, 2007, Maura Bresnahan, review of *The Baby Shower,* p. 158.

ONLINE

Charlesbridge Publisher Web site, http://www.charlesbridge.com/ (March 9, 2008), "Judy Love."
Judy Love Home Page, http://www.judyloveillustration.com (March 9, 2008).*

*   *   *

LYNE, Alison Davis

Personal

Married Frank Lyne (a farmer and sculptor).

Addresses

Home—Adairville, KY. *E-mail*—alison@lyneart.com.

Career

Illustrator.

Member

Society of Children's Book Writers and Illustrators (Mid-South chapter).

Illustrator

Alice Couvillon and Elizabeth Moore, retellers, *Evangeline for Children* (based on the poem by Henry Wadsworth Longfellow), Pelican Publishing (Gretna, LA), 2002.

Beverly Barras Vidrine, *Easter Day Alphabet,* Pelican Publishing (Gretna, LA), 2003.

Jennifer Holloway Lambe, *Kudzu Chaos,* Pelican Publishing (Gretna, LA), 2003.

Beverly Barras Vidrine, *Halloween Alphabet,* Pelican Publishing (Gretna, LA), 2004.

Sheila Hébert-Collins, *Jacques et la canne à sucre: A Cajun Jack and the Beanstalk,* Pelican Publishing (Gretna, LA), 2004.

Beverly Barras Vidrine, *Thanksgiving Day Alphabet,* Pelican Publishing (Gretna, LA), 2006.

Lynn Sheffield Simmons, *Bo and the Roaring Pines,* Pelican Publishing (Gretna, LA), 2008.

Sidelights

Illustrator Alison Davis Lyne works out of her home in rural Kentucky, where she lives on a farm with her husband, sculptor Frank Lyne. In addition to being a fine-

Alison Davis Lyne combines history and whimsy in her artwork for Beverly Barras Vidrine's **Halloween Alphabet.** (Pelican Publishing Company, 2004. Reproduced by permission.)

art painter, creating landscape studies and portraits of people and architecture, Lyne also works as a freelance illustrator, creating magazine covers and spot art. In 2002 she moved into children's-book illustration with *Evangeline for Children,* Alice Couvillon and Elizabeth Moore's retelling of Henry Wordsworth Longfellow's 1847 poem about the forcible migration of Acadian families from eastern Canada south to Louisiana during the mid-eighteenth century. The book, geared for children aged five to eight years old, is enhanced by Lyne's detailed paintings. "I had great fun doing research on the clothes, landscapes, and daily life in the mid-1750s when the story takes place," the illustrator noted on her home page. In a review of *Evangeline for Children, School Library Journal* contributor Sheilah Kosco wrote that Lyne's "bright and colorful" paintings "enhance the telling of this story" and deemed the picture book "an essential purchase for Louisiana libraries."

Other books featuring Lyne's richly toned acrylic paintings include *Kudzu Chaos,* a humorous story by Jennifer Holloway Lambe that describes the rampages of the invasive kudzu vine on a small southern town, and *Jacques et la canne à sucre: A Cajun Jack and the Beanstalk,* Sheila Hebért-Collins' regional take on a traditional story that includes a popular seafood recipe. Collaborating with Louisiana writer Beverly Barras Vidrine, Lyne has also created art for a series of holiday concept books: *Easter Day Alphabet, Halloween Alphabet,* and *Thanksgiving Day Alphabet.* Each of these alphabet books allowed Lyne to illustrate interesting historical facts about the individual holidays.

Lyne has always had a love of history, and through her art she tells visual stories of the past, in all its glorious color. In addition to her book illustration, shee has painted historical portraits of fourteen famous Kentucky women, and these now hang in a permanent display in the Kentucky State Capitol rotunda. In these pictures Lyne was able to tell, visually, a bit about each woman's life accomplishments through her detailed painting.

Biographical and Critical Sources

PERIODICALS

Booklist, June 1, 2002, Susan Dove Lempke, review of *Evangeline for Children,* p. 1721.
Kirkus Reviews, September 15, 2006, review of *Thanksgiving Day Alphabet,* p. 969.
School Library Journal, July, 2002, Sheilah Kosco, review of *Evangeline for Children,* p. 86; July, 2003, Jane Marino, review of *Easter Day Alphabet,* p. 119; December, 2004, Wendy Woodfill, review of *Halloween Alphabet,* p. 138; April, 2005, Judith Constantinides, review of *Jacques et la canne à sucre: A Cajun Jack and the Beanstalk,* p. 123; November, 2006, Mary Elam, review of *Thanksgiving Day Alphabet,* p. 126.

ONLINE

Alison Davis Lyne Home Page, http://www.lyneart.com (March 15, 2008).

M

MACKEY, Weezie Kerr
(Anne Louise Kerr)

Personal

Born in London, England; daughter of Sue Felt Kerr (an author and artist); married; children: two sons. *Education:* Trinity College (Hartford, CT), B.A. (English); American University, M.F.A. (creative writing).

Addresses

Home—Wilimette, IL.

Career

Children's author and coach. Greenhill School, Dallas, TX, physical education teacher and coach.

Awards, Honors

Best Young-Adult Book Award nomination, Texas Institute of Letters, 2007, for *Throwing like a Girl*.

Writings

Throwing like a Girl, Marshall Cavendish (New York, NY), 2007.

Sidelights

While growing up in the Midwest, Weezie Kerr Mackey's passion was sports: field hockey, basketball, softball, and badminton. Her field-hockey team's state-championship win during her senior year fueled her athleticism, and she continued to participate on college teams even while majoring in English. Mackey's first novel for young adults, *Throwing like a Girl*, reflects her love of organized sports and is based on her experiences as a gym teacher and coach at a Texas high school.

In *Throwing like a Girl* readers meet high-school sophomore Ella Kessler, who moves from Chicago to Texas and a new private school in the middle of the school year. Dealing with this upheaval is difficult for most teens, and Ella is no different. When her gym teacher suggests that she join the school softball team, the fifteen year old does so, despite the fact that she has never played competitive sports. While Ella musters up enough natural skill to catch and bat the ball, throwing is a problem, as is the defiant and competitive stance of a talented teammate. Nonetheless, support from new friends and an understanding mom, as well as the girl's can-do attitude, help Ella turn adversity to her advantage and learn the value of belonging to a team.

Throwing like a Girl earned the praise of several critics. Citing Ella's "forthright, often funny" narrative, a *Publishers Weekly* contributor deemed Mackey's fiction debut an "engaging novel" with "a satisfying finale." A *Kirkus Reviews* writer, while dubbing the story "undemanding if pleasant," recommended the novel to "teen girls, sports-minded or not." Appraising the book for *School Library Journal,* Kim Dare wrote that, with its likable protagonist and "brisk pace," *Throwing like a Girl* is "feel-good chick lit that will appeal to reluctant readers and sports fans."

Biographical and Critical Sources

PERIODICALS

Booklist, March 15, 2007, GraceAnne A. DeCandido, review of *Throwing like a Girl,* p. 42.
Kirkus Reviews, April 1, 2007, review of *Throwing like a Girl.*
Publishers Weekly, May 14, 2007, review of *Throwing like a Girl,* p. 55.
School Library Journal, May, 2007, Kim Dare, review of *Throwing like a Girl,* p. 138.

Cover of Weezie Kerr Mackey's middle-grade novel Throwing like a Girl, *featuring artwork by Alex Ferrari.* (Jacket photo illustration © by Alex Ferrari. All rights reserved. Reproduced by permission.)

Voice of Youth Advocates, June, 2007, Sherrie Williams, review of *Throwing like a Girl,* p. 147.

ONLINE

Weezie Kerr Mackey Home Page, http://www.weeziekerr mackey.com (March 28, 2008).*

*   *   *

MAKHIJANI, Pooja

Personal

Born in New York, NY; married. *Education:* Johns Hopkins University, B.S. (biomedical engineering); Sarah Lawrence College, M.F.A. *Hobbies and other interests:* Dancing, listening to Bollywood music.

Addresses

Home—New York, NY. *E-mail*—pooja@poojamakhi jani.com.

Career

Children's book author, educator, and book reviewer. Formerly worked in publishing. Western Connecticut State University, Danbury, instructor in M.F.A. program.

Awards, Honors

Society of Children's Book Writers and Illustrators Magazine Merit Award Honor in Nonfiction, 2003, for essay.

Writings

(Editor) *Under Her Skin: How Girls Experience Race in America,* Seal Press (Emeryville, CA), 2004.
Mama's Saris, illustrated by Elena Gomez, Little, Brown (New York, NY), 2007.

Contributor to periodicals, including *Writing!, Kahani, Cicada, Village Voice, Indian Express, Time Out, India Today, Weekly Reader, New York Times,* and *New Moon.* Work included in anthology *Women Who Eat: A New Generation on the Glory of Food,* Seal Press, 2003.

Sidelights

Although she initially earned a college degree in biomedical engineering, Pooja Makhijani has since shifted the trajectory of her career to something that has been a passion since childhood: writing. A freelance writer whose fiction and articles have appeared in periodicals ranging from the *New York Times* and the *Village Voice* to *Cicada* and *Weekly Reader,* she has also edited an anthology titled *Under Her Skin: How Girls Experience Race in America,* and written the picture book *Mama's Saris.*

Mama's Saris was inspired by Makhijani's Indian heritage, as well as by memories of her own childhood. "The colors, patterns, and fabrics of my mother's saris fascinated me," she explained in an online interview with Cynthia Leitich Smith for *Cynsations.* "I wrote *Mama's Saris* after realizing that my own obsession with my mother's fancy clothes was not unique. It seemed as if each of my female friends—regardless of ethnicity or age—remembers being enthralled by her own mother's 'grown-up clothes.'"

In Makhijani's story, a seven-year-old girl wants to wear a beautiful sari like the one her mother puts on for special occasions. Convincing her mother that she is old enough to manage the delicate fabrics, the girl ultimately gets her wish. Accompanying Makhijani's story are brightly hued paintings by Elena Gomez, along with a glossary containing Hindi words and phrases. Reviewing *Mama's Saris* for *Booklist,* Gillian Engberg noted that the "story's universal themes transcend cultural specifics." Margaret R. Tassia wrote in *School Library Journal* that Makhijani's story is "a pleasant offering about family traditions" as well as a "positive" intergenerational tale, and a *Publishers Weekly* contributor dubbed *Mama's Saris* a book in which "narrative and art pay satisfying tribute to a treasured tradition."

Biographical and Critical Sources

PERIODICALS

Booklist, April 15, 2007, Gillian Engberg, review of *Mama's Saris,* p. 49.

Kirkus Reviews, April 1, 2007, review of *Mama's Saris.*

Publishers Weekly, May 28, 2007, review of *Mama's Saris,* p. 60.

School Library Journal, June, 2007, Margaret R. Tassia, review of *Mama's Saris,* p. 115.

ONLINE

Cynsations Web site, http://cynthialeitichsmith.blogspot.com/ (October 30, 2007), Cynthia Leitich Smith, interview with Makhijani.

Pooja Makhijani Home Page, http://www.poojamakhijani.com (February 15, 2008).

Pooja Makhijani introduces readers to the cultural traditions of India in* Mama's Saris, *a picture book featuring art by Elena Gomez. (Illustration copyright © 2007 by Elena Gomez. Reproduced by permission of Little Brown & Company.)

MARTIN, Jacqueline Briggs 1945-

Personal

Born April 15, 1945, in Lewiston, ME; daughter of Hugh C., Jr. (a dairy farmer) and Alice (a homemaker and cook) Briggs; married Richard Martin (a college professor), June 17, 1967; children: Sarah E., Justin A. *Education:* Wellesley College, B.A., 1966; University of Minnesota Institute of Child Development, M.A., 1971. *Hobbies and other interests:* Camping, hiking, growing roses and hot peppers.

Addresses

Office—312 Second Ave. N., Mt. Vernon, IA 52314. *E-mail*—jacqueline@jacquelinebriggsmartin.com.

Career

Children's book author. Instructor in creative writing at Cornell College, University of Iowa, Loft Literary Center, and Hamlin University.

Member

Society of Children's Book Writers and Illustrators, Authors Guild.

Awards, Honors

Notable Children's Trade Book in the Field of Social Studies commendation, National Council for the Social Studies/Children's Book Council (NCSS/CBC), 1995, for *Washing the Willow Tree Loon,* and 1997, for *The Green Truck Garden Giveaway;* Notable Book citation, American Library Association (ALA), and Lupine Award, Maine Librarians, both 1996, and Children's Book of Distinction designation, *Hungry Mind Review,* all for *Grandmother Bryant's Pocket;* Lupine Award, 1998, for *Snowflake Bentley,* and 2003, for *The Water Gift and the Pig of the Pig;* Notable Book citation, ALA, Notable Social Studies Trade Book citation, NCSS/CBC, and Notable Books for Children citation, *Smithsonian* magazine, all 2001, all for *The Lamp, the Ice, and the Boat Called Fish. Snowflake Bentley,* illustrated by Mary Azarian, received the Caldecott Award, ALA, 1999; *The Lamp, the Ice, and the Boat Called Fish,* illustrated by Beth Krommes, received the Golden Kite Award for Illustration, Society of Children's Book Writers and Illustrators, 2001.

Writings

FICTION

Bizzy Bones and Uncle Ezra, illustrated by Stella Ormai, Lothrop, Lee & Shepard (New York, NY), 1984.

Jacqueline Briggs Martin (Photograph by Sharron McElmeel. Reproduced by permission of Jacqueline Briggs Martin.)

Bizzy Bones and Moosemouse, illustrated by Stella Ormai, Lothrop, Lee & Shepard (New York, NY), 1986.

Bizzy Bones and the Lost Quilt, illustrated by Stella Ormai, Lothrop, Lee & Shepard (New York, NY), 1988.

Good Times on Grandfather Mountain, illustrated by Susan Gaber, Orchard (New York, NY), 1992.

The Finest Horse in Town, illustrated by Susan Gaber, HarperCollins (New York, NY), 1992.

Washing the Willow Tree Loon, illustrated by Nancy Carpenter, Simon & Schuster (New York, NY), 1995.

The Second Street Gardens and the Green Truck Almanac, illustrated by Alec Gillman, Four Winds Press (New York, NY), 1995, published as *The Green Truck Garden Giveaway: A Neighborhood Story and Almanac,* Simon & Schuster (New York, NY), 1997.

Grandmother Bryant's Pocket, illustrated by Petra Mathers, Houghton Mifflin (Boston, MA), 1996.

Higgins Bend Song and Dance, illustrated by Brad Sneed, Houghton Mifflin (Boston, MA), 1997.

Button, Bucket, Sky, illustrated by Vicki Jo Redenbaugh, Carolrhoda (Minneapolis, MN), 1998.

Snowflake Bentley, illustrated by Mary Azarian, Houghton Mifflin (Boston, MA), 1998.

The Lamp, the Ice, and the Boat Called Fish, illustrated by Beth Krommes, Houghton Mifflin (Boston, MA), 2001.

The Water Gift and the Pig of the Pig, illustrated by Linda Wingerter, Houghton Mifflin (Boston, MA), 2003.

On Sand Island, illustrated by David Johnson, Houghton Mifflin (Boston, MA), 2003.

(With daughter Sarah Martin Busse) *Banjo Granny,* illustrated by Barry Root, Houghton Mifflin (Boston, MA), 2006.

Chicken Joy on Redbean Road: A Bayou Country Romp, illustrated by Melissa Sweet, Houghton Mifflin (Boston, MA), 2007.

Chiru in High Tibet, Houghton Mifflin (Boston, MA), 2008.

OTHER

(With Sharron L. McElmeel) *Jacqueline Briggs Martin and You,* Libraries Unlimited (Westport, CT), 2006.

Sidelights

Jacqueline Briggs Martin's award-winning books for young readers reflect both their author's love of the past and her respect for the environment. While her tales may wander as far afield as the rocky coastline of Maine or a bustling city street, and may recount events taking place as long ago as the late eighteenth century or as recently as yesterday, they are unified by their author's enthusiasm for the people and places that make up her fictional worlds and for sharing those worlds with children. "I hope readers will find friends in my stories," Martin once explained to *SATA,* "people they want to visit again and again, people who become part of their memories, and their own stories."

"Since I was a child, I have loved the sounds of words," Martin once confided. "And I have loved stories. Though writing books is not always easy, I cannot imagine doing anything else. Every day I get to work with words that tell a story." Born in Lewiston, Maine, in 1945, she was raised in the countryside, where her appreciation for nature and her interest in the history of both her family and her town grew. "As a child I spent much time wandering in the fields and forests of our farm in Maine, wondering about the generations who lived there before we did," the author once recalled.

Although Martin's first three books, featuring a character called Bizzy Bones, were inspired by her then-young-son Justin, her 1996 picture book, *Grandmother Bryant's Pocket,* reflects her own childhood. Drawn back to 1787, readers of *Grandmother Bryant's Pocket* meet eight-year-old Sarah Bryant, who is haunted by bad dreams after her dog is killed in a horrible fire. Convinced that a change of scene will help their daughter recover from her pet's tragic death, Sarah's parents send the girl to stay with her Grandmother Bryant. A woman full of wonderful stories and knowledgeable in the ways of natural medicines and healing, Grandmother Bryant carries herbs and bandages in her pocket, a drawstring pouch worn, tied around the waist, by women of the period. Describing Martin's text as "eloquent" and [with] the force of a prose poem," a *Publishers Weekly* critic hailed *Grandmother Bryant's*

Pocket as "a pleasingly timeless historical tale." Comparing the book to the "Little House" stories by Laura Ingalls Wilder, Deborah Stevenson praised the work in the *Bulletin of the Center for Children's Books,* noting that while Martin's "telling use of detail effectively creates a world very far away from now, [her] respectful and understanding treatment of Sarah's fear . . . and of her enduring grief . . . adds a timeless touch."

Good Times on Grandfather Mountain was inspired by an article Martin read concerning a man who whittled musical instruments out of wood taken from everything from fence posts to abandoned cabins. "I have always been fascinated by people who make beautiful objects out of what others might call junk," recalled Martin, "and [I] wanted to make up a story of such a person." In *Good Times on Grandfather Mountain* Old Washburn turns bad situations around with his pocket knife. When his milk cow runs away, or his vegetable garden becomes infested with insects, he gathers up whatever wood remains, applies his pocket knife, and creates something musical. Undaunted when his home is destroyed during a bad storm, Old Washburn whittles himself up a fiddle from the floorboards that remain and starts playing a jig. His jaunty melody not only calls the mischievous cow back home but draws out his neighbors as well, and the old man's affairs are soon set to

Susan Gaber creates folk-style illustrations to bring to life Martin's country-themed picture book Good Times on Grandfather Mountain.
(Illustration © 1992 by Susan Gaber. Reprinted by permission of Orchard Books, an imprint of Scholastic, Inc.)

rights with some neighborly help. Martin's "wry, nicely cadenced narration gives her tale a hearty folk-tale flavor," noted a *Kirkus Reviews* critic, the reviewer dubbing *Good Times on Grandfather Mountain* "entertaining, original, and beautifully produced."

Martin's love of music also inspired *Banjo Granny,* a story written in collaboration with her daughter, Sarah Martin Busse. Featuring warm-toned artwork by Barry Root and an original bluegrass tune titled "Owen's Song," the gentle, rhyming story focuses on a grandmother's love for her new grandchild. When Baby Owen is born, his grandmother is determined to travel the distance to see him, no matter the hot deserts, tall mountains, or fast-moving rivers that may stand in her path. The fact that the infant wiggles to the sound of bluegrass music only adds to her zeal, and Grandma packs her banjo for the trip, which finds her traveling by very unusual—and humorous—means. Briggs and Busse employ "a finely tuned bluegrass twang" in their tale-telling, according to *School Library Journal* contributor Tamara E. Richman, the critic adding that their "narrative's cadence and traditional structure make the tale feel timeless." Praising *Banjo Granny* as "lighthearted and endearing," a *Publishers Weekly* contributor dubbed the mother-daughter collaboration "a celebration of the bond between grandparent and child," and *Booklist* critic Hazel Rochman predicted that the rhyming story will be "exactly right for the lap-sitting crowd."

Also in the folk-tale/tall-tale genre is *Higgins Bend Song and Dance,* which Martin wrote because "I love rivers," as she once told *SATA.* "I like the notion of a contest between an old grouch and a smart catfish. And I love the banter between two old friends who don't always agree." *Higgins Bend Song and Dance* is the story of a single-minded fisherman named Simon Henry who vows to catch a crafty catfish named Oscar. However, Oscar proves too wily for the boastful man, until Simon Henry comes up with one last, tantalizing bait selection. In *Kirkus Reviews* a critic called the work "a meaty tale of the quest for an uncatchable fish" that is "told in folksy, irresistible language." Jody McCoy, writing in *School Library Journal,* maintained that the story would be "pure pleasure for any who are or know dedicated (obsessed) fishermen," the critic adding that Martin's "whopper of a fish tale also makes a good read-aloud."

Featuring a story that takes readers into the past, *The Finest Horse in Town* also has its roots in Martin's family history. The story involves two sisters—the author's great-aunts Stella and Cora—who owned a dry-goods and clothing store in a small Maine town. They also owned a beautiful, gray, carriage horse named Prince. Memories of Prince and the sisters are recalled years later by an elderly local watchmaker, and because the man's memories are spotty, the story's narrator speculates on what adventures the sisters might have had with their horse. A *Publishers Weekly* reviewer praised *The Finest Horse in Town,* citing the book's "nostalgic

Beth Krommes won an award for the intricate linocut artwork she contributes to Martin's **The Lamp, the Ice, and the Boat Called Fish.** (Illustration copyright © 2001 by Beth Krommes. Reprinted by permission of Houghton Mifflin Harcourt Publishing Company. All rights reserved.)

sing-song language and descriptions of village life." Deborah Abbott complimented the story in her *Booklist* review, writing that *The Finest Horse in Town* "transports readers back in history to reflect upon the joys and cares of people and a horse named Prince."

The Lamp, the Ice, and the Boat Called Fish is a partially fictionalized account of an actual Arctic maritime catastrophe: the sinking of the ship *Karluk* in the winter of 1913-14. The ship was on a research expedition and contained several Canadian scientists, as well as their Inupiaq assistants. One of the Inupiaq hunter-guides, Kurraluk, had also brought his wife, who became the expedition's seamstress, and his two daughters, Pagnasuk and Makpii. The story is told from the point of view of eight-year-old Pagnasuk, with "the scrupulous use of such words as 'perhaps' and 'I think'" indicating that Martin sometimes guesses how her young protagonist would have felt during her adventure, as a reviewer explained in *Horn Book.* Characteristically, Martin's use of language in *The Lamp, the Ice, and the Boat Called Fish* was praised by many reviewers, *Booklist* critic Gillian Engberg commenting that "the quiet, intriguing language, with a poet's attention to sound, will lull young ones into the story's drama."

Martin's inspiration for another historical book, *On Sand Island,* was her own visit to that island in Lake Superior. *On Sand Island* tells the story of ten-year-old Carl and his quest to build his own boat. For materials,

Carl scavenges driftwood boards from a nearby beach. Within his small, tight-knit Scandinavian-American community, he then trades his own labor, picking strawberries and moving rocks, in exchange for help from his neighbors in constructing the trickier parts of the vessel. Martin's story is "told in the rhythms of lapping water," a *Publishers Weekly* contributor observed, and in *Booklist* Engberg wrote that the author "deftly balances small, revealing details about the island's characters and Carl's life with the particulars of boat building."

Boats also feature in *The Water Gift and the Pig of the Pig,* the story of Isabelle, her pet pig, and her grandfather, a former captain of sailing ships. Grandfather has the "water gift," the ability to find underground water with a forked stick called a divining rod. Or at least he did; after several failures, Grandfather gives up divining. However, when Isabelle's pig goes missing, she remembers that the water gift can also be used to find animals. The formerly shy, reserved little girl eventually takes charge of the situation and convinces Grandfather to use his gifts to rescue the pig. Martin's "narration is at once the dreamy voice of a child and the detailed, imagery-laden voice of a master storyteller," noted a *Kirkus Reviews* contributor, and in *Publishers Weekly* a reviewer wrote of *The Water Gift and the Pig of the Pig* that "Martin elegantly unfurls a story filled with memorable characters and colorful details, as well as comforting images of loyalty and family ties."

Featuring a cumulative tale as colorful as the Louisiana zydeco music that inspired it, *Chicken Joy on Redbean Road: A Bayou Country Romp* focuses on a farmyard where the ruling blue-headed rooster is in a pickle: he is threatened with a future as rooster stew after he loses his voice to a case of the chicken measles. A brown hen named Miss Cleoma, the rooster's greatest fan, is determined to help her friend regain his cock-a-doodle-do. When she reckons that music is the way to do that, she undertakes an adventurous quest for Joe Beebee, the best fiddler there is. Citing the "fine turns of phrase" that highlight Martin's text, Janice Del Negro wrote in *Booklist* that the "exuberant" illustrations by Melissa Sweet add to the book's Cajun flavor. In *School Library Journal* Marge Loch-Wouters also praised the picture book, noting that Martin's "rollicking, multilayered tale is "saturated in Cajun and Creole cadences and sensibilities."

Among Martin's stories dealing with more contemporary themes is the award-winning picture book *Washing the Willow Tree Loon.* Published in 1995, the book recounts the efforts of people living along the coast of Turtle Bay to rescue a loon that had become soaked in oil leaked by a barge that hit a bridge while traversing the bay. Found hiding under a willow tree, the bird is cared for by a group of citizens who are varied in age and occupation. "The well-drawn text has a gentle rhythm and infuses an appealing story with interesting

information," wrote *Horn Book* reviewer Margaret Bush, the critic praising Martin's inclusion of endnotes describing bird rehabilitation.

As in the case of *Washing the Willow Tree Loon,* Martin is frequently inspired with an idea for a new book by something she has read. "When I read about Dan Barker building and giving away gardens in Portland, Oregon, I knew I wanted to write a children's book about giving away gardens," she once told *SATA*. "And I wanted readers to be able to make gardens for themselves, or gardens to give away." *The Green Truck Garden Giveaway: A Neighborhood Story and Almanac* was the result of Martin's interest in Barker's work. The story opens on a Saturday morning, as a strange, green truck full of soil and seeds rolls down an unkempt city street. The truck's two passengers persuade even the most reluctant residents to attempt a seed garden; they also pass out pamphlets full of gardening tips and inspiration. Soon, the entire neighborhood is transformed into a paradise as the residents become inspired to clean up yards and vacant lots and rescue untamed tangles of raspberry plants from rubbish and weeds. Martin, an avid gardener, includes a wealth of gardening lore in addition to her central story. "I wanted this book to have enough information to be the gift of a garden in itself," the author explained.

In addition to stories that mirror her family's history or deal with contemporary issues of interest, Martin has also written a series of stories in a lighter vein. In *Bizzy Bones and Uncle Ezra,* which was her first published book for children, two mice set up housekeeping in an abandoned work boot. When the younger mouse, Bizzy Bones, worries that the shoe will blow away in the brisk, whistling March winds, the elder mouse, Uncle Ezra, finds a way to calm the mouseling by constructing a colorful carousel that captures the early spring gusts and sets them spinning. Other books featuring the young Bizzy Bones include *Bizzy Bones and Moosemouse* and *Bizzy Bones and the Lost Quilt.*

"My stories often start with something that has happened to me, or to people that I love," Martin once told *SATA* in discussing her development as a children's book author. "Sometimes they start with a question. For example, *Washing the Willow Tree Loon* began when I read an article about bird washing and asked myself, 'Who would want to wash birds?' *Higgins Bend Song and Dance* began with the question 'Who wins when a crafty old fisherman vows to catch a catfish that is just as crafty?'

"Some books begin with things I love to do, such as collecting acorns to plant oak trees (*Button, Bucket, Sky*)." One of Martin's best-known books "began with a snowflake and a memory of a brief article about a man who said he 'loved snow more that anything else in the world.' I read Wilson Bentley's articles about snow, looked at some of the thousands of photographs he took

A farmyard's efforts to save a rooster who has lost his crow come to life in Martin's **Chicken Joy on Redbean Road,** *featuring art by Melissa Sweet.*

of individual snow crystals, read about his life, visited the farmhouse where he had lived, and eventually wrote *Snowflake Bentley.*

"When I am writing, I become obsessed with the world of my work and have been known to walk into shelves, or other people, because I am thinking so hard about my characters. I live with them and am always a little sad to finish a story."

Biographical and Critical Sources

BOOKS

McElmeel, Sharron, L., and Jacqueline Brigs Martin, *Jacqueline Briggs Martin and You,* Libraries Unlimited (Westport, CT), 2006.

PERIODICALS

Booklist, February 1, 1992, Hazel Rochman, review of *Good Times on Grandfather Mountain,* p. 80; June 15, 1992, Deborah Abbott, review of *The Finest Horse in Town,* pp. 1849-1850; August, 1993, Nancy McCray, review of *Celebrating Authors: Meet Jacqueline Briggs Martin,* p. 67; December 15, 1995, Leone McDermott, review of *Washing the Willow Tree Loon,* p. 709; May 15, 1996, Leone McDermott, review of *Grandmother Bryant's Pocket,* p. 1592; May 1, 1997, Carolyn Phelan, review of *Green Truck Garden Giveaway: A Neighborhood Story and Almanac,* pp. 1501-1502; October 1, 1998, Ilene Cooper, review of *Snowflake Bentley,* p. 323; March 1, 2001, Gillian Engberg, review of *The Lamp, the Ice, and the Boat Called Fish,* p. 1273; August, 2003, Gillian Engberg, review of *On Sand Island,* p. 1981; November 1, 2006, Hazel Rochman, review of *Banjo Granny,* p. 58; February 15, 2007, Janice Del Negro, review of *Chicken Joy on Redbean Road: A Bayou Country Romp,* p. 84.

Award-winning artist Mary Azarian brings to life Martin's picture-book biography of a fascinating individual in **Snowflake Bentley.** (Illustration copyright © 1998 by Mary Azarian. Reprinted by permission of Houghton Mifflin Harcourt Publishing Company. All rights reserved.)

Bulletin of the Center for Children's Books, March, 1992, review of *Good Times on Grandfather Mountain,* p. 186; July, 1992, review of *The Finest Horse in Town,* p. 300; July-August, 1996, Deborah Stevenson, review of *Grandmother Bryant's Pocket,* pp. 363-364; January, 2007, Deborah Stevenson, review of *Banjo Granny,* p. 205; April, 2007, Deborah Stevenson, review of *Chicken Joy on Redbean Road,* p. 337.

Des Moines Register (Des Moines, IA), February 7, 1999, review of *Snowflake Bentley,* p. 1; October 13, 1999, Dave DeValois, "Author Shares Writing Tips," p. 4.

Horn Book, May-June, 1992, Nancy Vasilakis, review of *Good Times on Grandfather Mountain,* pp. 332-333; September-October, 1995, Margaret Bush, review of *Washing the Willow Tree Loon,* p. 591; July-August, 1996, Hanna B. Zeiger, review of *Grandmother Bryant's Pocket,* p. 460; September-October, 1998, Elizabeth S. Watson, review of *Snowflake Bentley,* p. 622; March, 2001, review of *The Lamp, the Ice, and the Boat Called Fish,* p. 198; May-June, 2003, Anita L. Burkam, review of *The Water Gift and the Pig of the Pig,* p. 331.

Kirkus Reviews, February 1, 1992, review of *Good Times on Grandfather Mountain,* pp. 186-187; October 15, 1995, p. 1496; July 1, 1997, review of *Higgins Bend Song and Dance,* p. 1032; April 1, 2003, review of *The Water Gift and the Pig of the Pig,* p. 537; July 15, 2003, review of *On Sand Island,* p. 966; November 1,

2006, review of *Banjo Granny,* p. 1121; March 1, 2007, review of *Chicken Joy on Redbean Road,* p. 227.

New York Times Book Review, April 27, 1997, Erin St. John Kelly, review of *Grandmother Bryant's Pocket,* p. 29; April 15, 2001, Heather Vogel Frederick, review of *The Lamp, the Ice, and the Boat Called Fish,* p. 25; September 21, 2003, Stephanie Deutsch, review of *The Water Gift and the Pig of the Pig,* p. 27.

Publishers Weekly, February 12, 1988, review of *Bizzy Bones and the Lost Quilt,* pp. 84-85; February 3, 1992, review of *Good Times on Grandfather Mountain,* p. 80; June 22, 1992, review of *The Finest Horse in Town,* p. 61; February 5, 1996, review of *Grandmother Bryant's Pocket,* p. 89; April 7, 1997, review of *The Green Truck Garden Giveaway,* p. 92; June 8, 1998, review of *Button, Bucket, Sky,* p. 59; August 31, 1998, review of *Snowflake Bentley,* p. 75; December 18, 2000, review of *The Lamp, the Ice, and the Boat Called Fish,* p. 78; March 31, 2003, review of *The Water Gift and the Pig of the Pig,* p. 67; July 21, 2003, review of *On Sand Island,* p. 194; October 30, 2006, review of *Banjo Granny,* p. 60.

Reading Teacher, December-January, 1992, Lee Galda, review of *The Finest Horse in Town,* pp. 330-338.

School Library Journal, November, 1984, Susan Powers, review of *Bizzy Bones and Uncle Ezra,* p. 112; October, 1986, Cathy Woodward, review of *Bizzy Bones and Moosemouse,* p. 164; June-July, 1988, Ruth Semrau, review of *Bizzy Bones and the Lost Quilt,* p. 93; August, 1992, Charlene Strickland, review of *The Finest Horse in Town,* p. 144; October, 1993, Leah Hawkins, review of *Celebrating Authors,* p. 67; October, 1995, Ellen Fader, review of *Washing the Willow Tree Loon,* p. 108; June, 1996, Virginia Golodetz, review of *Grandmother Bryant's Pocket,* p. 105; June, 1997, John Sigwald, review of *The Green Truck Garden Giveaway,* p. 98; September 19, 1997, Jody McCoy, review of *Higgins Bend Song and Dance,* pp. 187-188; September, 1998, Tom S. Hurlburt, review of *Button, Bucket, Sky,* p. 176, and Virginia Golodetz, review of *Snowflake Bentley,* pp. 194-195; July, 2001, Sue Sherif, review of *The Lamp, the Ice, and the Boat Called Fish,* p. 96; June, 2003, Marianne Saccardi, review of *The Water Gift and the Pig of the Pig,* p. 112; November, 2003, Susannah Price, review of *On Sand Island,* p. 110; December, 2006, Tamara E. Richman, review of *Banjo Granny,* p. 95; March, 2007, Marge Loch-Wouters, review of *Chicken Joy on Redbean Road,* p. 180.

Teacher Librarian, May, 1999, Shirley Lewis, review of *Snowflake Bentley,* p. 47.

ONLINE

Houghton Mifflin Web site, http://www.houghtonmifflinbooks.com/ (November 20, 2003), "Jacqueline Briggs Martin."

Jacqueline Briggs Martin Home Page, http://www.jacquelinebriggsmartin.com (March 28, 2008).

OTHER

Celebrating Authors: Meet Jacqueline Briggs Martin (video tape), 1993.*

MENCHIN, Scott

Personal

Married Yvetta Fedorova (an artist); children: Karina. *Education:* Studied at Art Students' League; Pratt Institute, degree.

Addresses

Office—640 Broadway, Ste. 3E, New York, NY 10012. *E-mail*—s.menchin@verison.net.

Career

Illustrator. Pratt Institute, New York, NY, professor in graduate design program. *Exhibitions:* Work included in exhibition at Eric Carle Museum of Picture-Book Art, 2007.

Awards, Honors

Please Touch Museum Book Award, 2006, for *Wiggle* by Doreen Cronin; Christopher Award, 2008, for *Taking a Bath with the Dog and Other Things That Make Me Happy.*

Writings

SELF-ILLUSTRATED

Taking a Bath with the Dog and Other Things That Make Me Happy, Candlewick Press (Cambridge, MA), 2007.

ILLUSTRATOR

Eve Bunting, *The Day the Whale Came,* Harcourt (San Diego, CA), 1998.
Bob Dylan, *Man Gave Names to All the Animals,* Harcourt (San Diego, CA), 1999.
Ann Braybrooks, *Plenty of Pockets,* Harcourt (San Diego, CA), 2000.
Mat Connolley, compiler, *Butter Comes from Butterflies: When I Was a Kid I Used to Believe—,* Chronicle Books (San Francisco, CA), 2004.
Doreen Cronin, *Wiggle,* Atheneum (New York, NY), 2005.
Doreen Cronin, *Bounce,* Atheneum (New York, NY), 2007.

Contributor of illustrations to periodicals, including *Newsweek, Rolling Stone, Time,* and the *New York Times.*

Sidelights

A graduate of New York City's prestigious Pratt Institute, Scott Menchin created advertising art for several major corporations, including Intel, Toyota, and Dr. Pepper, before he began writing and illustrating children's books. Menchin's first picture-book project, Eve Bunting's text for *The Day the Whale Came*, involves a dead whale that was transported throughout the streets of a town in Illinois during the early 1900s. The illustrator's "quirky pen-and-ink pictures effectively contrast the ordinary Midwestern town with the surrealism of the event," Linda Perkins wrote in *Booklist*. As a *Publishers Weekly* contributor noted of the same book, "Menchin's unconventional pictures . . . subtly incorporate photographs with stylized drawings."

The art in Menchin's second picture book, an adaptation of a Bob Dylan song titled *Man Gave Names to All the Animals,* was highly praised in *Publishers Weekly.* Menchin turns the song into a "guessing game," the critic explained, noting that the artist reveals only part of each animal being sung about in his mixed-media collage art. Despite the lack of musical accompaniment, "Menchin makes visual the rollicking, reggae-inflected sounds" of Dylan's song, according to *Booklist* critic GraceAnne A. DeCandido.

Man Gave Names to All the Animals is not the only book in which Menchin incorporates clues into his artwork. Describing *Plenty of Pockets,* a picture book with a story by Ann Braybrooks, *Booklist* contributor Connie Fletcher concluded that "Menchin's collage illustrations . . . pack in surprises."

Menchin collaborates with writer Doreen Cronin on several books which follow an energetic spotted dog through its day, among them *Wiggle* and *Bounce.* "The delightful cartoon-style, ink-and-watercolor art is highlighted by tidbits of collage," wrote Ilene Cooper in her *Booklist* review of *Wiggle.* Noting Menchin's use of

Cover of Scott Menchin's lighthearted self-illustrated picture book **Taking a Bath with the Dog, and Other Things That Make Me Happy.**

collage, Kathy Krasniewicz commented in *School Library Journal* that photographs and other materials "are well integrated into broad, bright cartoon illustrations," while a *Publishers Weekly* critic dubbed the artist's use of "whimsical photographic images" a form of "comic punctuation." In *Bounce,* Menchin's "cartoon art is eye-catching and as playful as the text," according to *School Library Journal* critic Marge Loch-Wouters.

Menchin's first self-illustrated title, *Taking a Bath with the Dog and Other Things That Make Me Happy,* begins when a mother asks her sobbing young daughter what would make her happy. Unsure, the girl asks the dog, then the rabbit, then other people and animals what makes them happy, thereby learning how many things there are to smile about. The tale "will likely inspire youngsters who are in a funk to seek joy in the unexpected as well as in the perfectly ordinary," observed a *Publishers Weekly* critic. In *Kirkus Reviews,* a contributor wrote that, with "striking effect, [Menchin's] . . . illustrations contrast the characters painted in textured watercolors against a backdrop of one vivid color."

Biographical and Critical Sources

PERIODICALS

Booklist, April 15, 1998, Linda Perkins, review of *The Day the Whale Came,* p. 1449; December 15, 1999, GraceAnne A. DeCandido, review of *Man Gave Names to All the Animals,* p. 785; July, 2000, Connie Fletcher, review of *Plenty of Pockets,* p. 2037; May 1, 2005, Ilene Cooper, review of *Wiggle,* p. 1586.
Horn Book, September-October, 2005, review of *Wiggle,* p. 560.
Kirkus Reviews, June 1, 2005, review of *Wiggle,* p. 635; May 15, 2007, review of *Taking a Bath with the Dog and Other Things That Make Me Happy.*
Publishers Weekly, February 23, 1998, review of *The Day the Whale Came,* p. 76; November 15, 1999, review of *Man Gave Names to All the Animals,* p. 1999; May 23, 2005, review of *Wiggle,* p. 77; March 5, 2007, review of *Bounce,* p. 59; July 9, 2007, review of *Taking a Bath with the Dog and Other Things That Make Me Happy,* p. 52.
School Library Journal, May, 2000, Tina Hudak, review of *Plenty of Pockets,* p. 130; June, 2005, Kathy Krasniewicz, review of *Wiggle,* p. 107; June, 2007, Shelley B. Sutherland, review of *Taking a Bath with the Dog and Other Things That Make Me Happy,* p. 81, Marge Loch-Wouters, review of *Bounce.* p. 96.

ONLINE

Pippin Properties Web site, http://www.pippinproperties. com/ (March 9, 2008), "Scott Menchin."
Pratt Institute Web site, http://www.pratt.edu/ (March 9, 2008), *Pratt Folio Alumni Magazine,* "Scott Menchin."
Scott Menchin Home Page, http://www.scottmenchin.com (March 10, 2008).

*   *   *

MILES, Victoria 1966-

Personal
Born 1966, in Canada.

Addresses
Home—North Vancouver, British Columbia, Canada. *Agent*—Curtis Brown Ltd., 10 Astor Place, New York, NY 10003. *E-mail*—victorianunuk@telus.net.

Career
Children's author.

Member
Children's Writers and Illustrators of British Columbia.

Awards, Honors
Science in Society Book Award finalist and Red Maple Award finalist, Ontario Library Association, both 2005, both for *Wild Science;* ASPCA Henry Bergh Award for Children's Fiction, 2007, for *Old Mother Bear;* Chocolate Lily Award finalist, 2007, for *Magnifico.*

Writings

Sea Otter Pups, Orca (Vancouver, British Columbia, Canada), 1993.
Bald Eaglets, Orca (Vancouver, British Columbia, Canada), 1993.
Spotted Owlets, Orca (Vancouver, British Columbia, Canada), 1993.
Cougar Kittens, Orca (Vancouver, British Columbia, Canada), 1993.
Pup's Supper, illustrated by Andrea Tachiera, Monterey Bay Aquarium (Monterey, CA), 1999.
Wild Science: Amazing Encounters between Animals and the People Who Study Them, Raincoast Books (Vancouver, British Columbia, Canada), 2004.
City Bat, Country Bat, illustrated by George Juhasz, Tradewind (Vancouver, British Columbia, Canada), 2004.
Magnifico, Fitzhenry & Whiteside (Markham, Ontario, Canada), 2006.
The Chocolatier's Apprentice, illustrated by Lee Edward Födi, Echo Memoirs (Vancouver, British Columbia, Canada), 2006.
Old Mother Bear, illustrated by Molly Bang, Chronicle Books (San Francisco, CA), 2007.

Contributor to *Lady Bug, Wild,* and *Know: The Science Magazine for Curious Kids.*

Sidelights

Victoria Miles' nonfiction titles introduce North American children to the basic concepts of wildlife biology. From her bestselling series for Canadian publisher Orca, including *Sea Otter Pups* and *Spotted Owlets,* to her fictional biography of a bear in *Old Mother Bear,* she brings science into the homes of young readers. Along with her science writing, Miles is also the author of the novel *Magnifico* as well as of *The Chocolatier's Apprentice,* a picture book describing how chocolate is made.

Wild Science: Amazing Encounters between Animals and the People Who Study Them, which was a finalist for two awards in Miles' native Canada, is part of the respected "Scientists in the Field" series. *Wild Science* presents the work of the men and women who study animals in their natural habitats, from marine biologists helping to rescue beached whales to scientists who track bats in Arizona. Alongside the description of each scientist are interesting facts about the specific animals they study. "Miles' lively text includes visceral details of what it's really like to work outdoors," wrote Gillian Engberg in her *Booklist* review of the book. Patricia Manning, writing in *School Library Journal,* predicted that Miles' "lucid, energetic reportage will be a delight and an inspiration," and a *Kirkus Reviews* contributor maintained that *Wild Science* "should be required reading for children with an active interest in understanding the natural world." Noting that it is "beautifully designed and organized," Joan Marshall concluded in *Resource Links* that the volume's "strength . . . is that it will attract young readers to the possibility of working at a job that connects science and animals."

Miles moves to fiction in *Old Mother Bear* and provides a detailed, realistic description of the birth of three grizzly bear cubs in a wildlife sanctuary in British Columbia. The story follows the cubs from their earliest moments on earth, through their development into rambunctious, tumbling cubs. Following the cubs through their first three years, *Old Mother Bear* ends poignantly as the young bears journey off on their own while their aging mother prepares for her death. "Without anthropomorphism, the one animal's viewpoint is the drama," wrote Hazel Rochman in *Booklist.* According to June Wolfe in *School Library Journal,* by "using matter-of-fact language, the author treats her subjects with genuine respect and obvious admiration." A *Kirkus Reviews* contributor praised *Old Mother Bear* as "a beautiful introduction to these awesome animals."

An historical novel set in 1930s Vancouver, *Magnifico* introduces readers to young Mariangela. Mariangela wants to play the piano, but her Nonna insists that she learn to play the accordion. Despite the charm of her handsome accordion teacher, the girl is more interested in his stories than in learning how to play the less-desirable instrument. As Mariangela listens to the teacher's tales of Italy, she learns why her family wants her to be connected to her roots: the accordion she practices upon used to belong to her Italian grandmother. "Miles's evocation of the place and period is light-handed and persuasive, coming always from the child's eye," wrote Deirdre Baker in a review of *Magnifico* for *Quill & Quire.* Noting the depiction of the Italian immigrant experience in Canada, Margaret R. Tassia commented in *School Library Journal* that "the values and norms of the culture are clearly reflected" in Miles' story. Explaining that the author was inspired to write *Magnifico* after discovering an accordion in her garage, Nancy Kim concluded in *Booklist* that "Miles evokes a rich set of images of a particular time and place."

Along with writing, Miles also makes classroom presentations and runs a writing workshop for fourth through twelfth grades. As she wrote on her home page, her motto is: "Use your words for good."

Biographical and Critical Sources

PERIODICALS

Booklist, December 1, 2004, Gillian Engberg, review of *Wild Science: Amazing Encounters between Animals and the People Who Study Them,* p. 666; July 1, 2006, Nancy Kim, review of *Magnifico,* p. 58; April 15, 2007, Hazel Rochman, review of *Old Mother Bear,* p. 49.

Bulletin of the Center for Children's Books, December, 2004, Deborah Stevenson, review of *Wild Science,* p. 176.

Victoria Miles shares her fascination with the natural world in the intriguing **Wild Science.** (Cover by Gabi Proctor/DesignGeist. Reproduced by permission.)

Cover of Miles' middle-grade novel Magnifico, *featuring artwork by* *Tara Anderson.* (Fitzhenry & Whiteside, 2006. Reproduced by permission.)

Canadian Book Review Annual, 1995, review of *Cougar Kittens,* p. 561.

Canadian Geographic, September-October, 2004, Carol Hilton, review of *Wild Science,* p. 114.

Horn Book, July-August, 2007, Martha V. Parravano, review of *Old Mother Bear,* p. 382.

Kirkus Reviews, October 1, 2004, review of *Wild Science,* p. 965; March 1, 2007, review of *Old Mother Bear,* p. 228.

Publishers Weekly, April 2, 2007, review of *Old Mother Bear,* p. 56.

Quill & Quire, October, 1993, review of *Sea Otter Pup,* pp. 41-42; May, 2006, review of *Magnifico.*

Resource Links, October, 2004, Joan Marshall, review of *Wild Science,* p. 39.

School Library Journal, December, 2004, Patricia Manning, review of *Wild Science,* p. 164; July, 2006, Margaret R. Tassia, review of *Magnifico,* p. 108; June, 2007, June Wolfe, review of *Old Mother Bear,* p. 116.

Washington Post Book World, May 6, 2007, Elizabeth Ward, review of *Old Mother Bear,* p. 11.

ONLINE

Children's Writers and Illustrators of British Columbia Web site, http://www.cwill.bc.ca/ (March 10, 2008), "Victoria Miles."

Victoria Miles Web log, http://www.magnifico-victoria-miles.blogspot.com/ (February 22, 2008).

* * *

MOWLL, Joshua 1970(?)-

Personal

Born c. 1970, in England. *Education:* Attended art school. *Hobbies and other interests:* Sailing, restoring old Land Rovers.

Addresses

Home—London, England.

Career

Author and illustrator. *Mail on Sunday* (newspaper), London, England, graphic artist, 1994—.

Writings

"GUILD OF SPECIALISTS" NOVEL SERIES; FOR CHILDREN

Operation Red Jericho, illustrated by Benjamin Mowll, Niroot Puttapipat, and Julek Heller, Candlewick Press (Cambridge, MA), 2005.

Operation Typhoon Shore, Candlewick Press (Cambridge, MA), 2006.

Sidelights

Joshua Mowll sets up an adventurous premise in his "Guild of Specialists" novels, an old-fashioned science-fiction trilogy geared for readers aged from nine to twelve. The series is "action-packed all the way," according to London *Guardian* reviewer Philip Ardaugh, the critic adding that Mowll's work "has the feel of a B-movie from the 30s or 40s but with child protagonists, with skullduggery involving johnny-foreigners on the South China Seas." The drama involves missing parents, secret societies, murdered scientists, and sinister villains, all brought to life through the fold-out maps and diagrams, photographs, and other ephemera that fill the pages of each volume and add a tantalizing layer of realism. "Budding scientists, inventors and fans of all things nautical . . . will . . . be enraptured by this lovingly created, highly visual offering," predicted a *Kirkus Reviews* critic of the series.

Mowll begins his "Guild of Specialists" saga in *Operation Red Jericho,* which includes a preface purportedly revealing the book's source: the memoirs of Mowll's late great aunt Rebecca MacKenzie. The woman's papers, bequeathed to Mowll at her death, set forth adventures she encountered during the 1920s. Then age fifteen, Rebecca and her thirteen-year-old brother Doug

MacKenzie were living in India when their parents disappeared during a trip to China. The siblings are sent to live with their uncle, Captain Fitzroy MacKenzie, whose ship, the *Expedient,* is on an oceanographic research mission. Soon the children find themselves setting sail for the Orient aboard the *Expedient.* With boundless curiosity and rebellious natures, Becca and Doug uncover the existence of a secret society called the Honorable Guild of Specialists, the purpose of which is to fight evil in all its guises. As *Operation Red Jericho* continues, the siblings encounter pirates, strange undersea vessels, opium dens, the villainous warlord Sheng-Fat, and a rare and deadly compound called zoridium. They also learn that the trail to their missing parents leads directly into the secret depths of the mysterious Guild. "Mowll spins a heady yarn," noted *Booklist* contributor Francisca Goldsmith, the critic adding that the sketches, maps, and other illustrations "will have great appeal for readers who thrive on schematics and puzzles." "Some readers may pore over the details in this novel," asserted Diane S. Marton in *School Library Journal;* "others will simply appreciate the comic adventure."

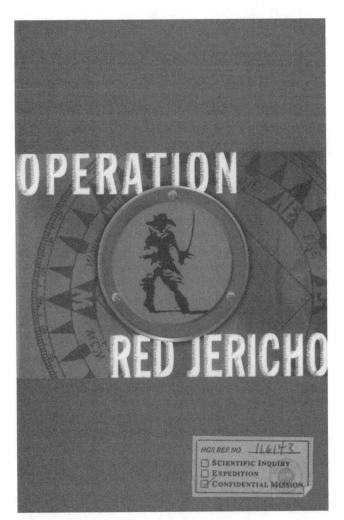

Cover of **Operation Red Jericho,** *the first installment in Joshua Mowll's "Guild of Specialists" series.* (Cover illustration copyright © 2005 by Joshua Mowll. Reproduced by permission of the publisher Candlewick Press, Inc., Cambridge, MA, on behalf of Walker Books, Ltd., London, England.)

The adventures of the MacKenzie children continue in *Operation Typhoon Shore* as Becca and Doug escape from the remote South Sea island of a ruthless pirate only to find themselves battling a powerful storm at sea that strands them on a volcanic island. While they are desperate to resume the search for their parents, their guardian, Captain MacKenzie, is more interested in tracking down a missing gyrolabe. As the story progresses, a sixteenth-century painting reveals a singular clue that may reveal Mr. and Mrs. MacKenzie's whereabouts, and the secret of the Guild as well. However, with their nemesis and his evil warrior army quickly advancing, will Becca and Doug be able to follow their new lead? In *Kirkus Reviews* a contributor observed that the "gleefully seamless mix of fact and fancy" Mowll conjures up in *Operation Typhoon Shore* sustains the "wild South Seas rumpus begun" in the first book. Noting the "ingenuity, bravery, and wit" exhibited by the novel's teen protagonists, Tasha Saecker wrote in *School Library Journal* that the second "Guild of Specialists" adventure "rolls along with plenty of action and fun."

Part of the attraction of Mowll's "Guild of Specialists" books is their design: With their heavy paper and textured, leather-like covers, they resemble old-fashioned journals. As Nicolette Jones wrote of the first book in the London *Sunday Times, Operation Red Jericho* "is not just an adventure story; it is a designer object." In fact, Mowll submitted his original manuscript to his publisher in a cardboard box secured with red sealing wax. The manuscript pages inside were supplemented with photos, maps, and other illustrations, all of which had to be sifted through and sorted. For Mowll, a graphic designer, as well as for his publisher, creating the "Guild" novels soon became an adventure in itself. Calling *Operation Red Jericho* "something of a multimedia extravaganza, London *Mail on Sunday* writer John Williams concluded that the book "adds up to a smart, effective package likely to appeal to children of all ages."

Biographical and Critical Sources

PERIODICALS

Booklist, November 15, 2005, Francisca Goldsmith, review of *Operation Red Jericho,* p. 55; January 1, 2007, Francisca Goldsmith, review of *Operation Typhoon Shore,* p. 81.

Bulletin of the Center for Children's Books, December, 2005, review of *Operation Red Jericho,* p. 196.

Guardian (London, England), November 12, 2005, Philip Ardagh, review of *Operation Red Jericho,* p. 20.

Kirkus Reviews, August 1, 2005, review of *Operation of Red Jericho,* p. 854; October 15, 2006, review of *Operation Typhoon Shore,* p. 1075.-

Kliatt, September, 2005, Michele Winship, review of *Operation Red Jericho,* p. 11.

Magpies, September, 2005, Lyn Linning, review of *Operation Red Jericho,* p. 32; November, 2006, Rayma Turton, review of *Operation Typhoon Shore,* p. 34.

Mail on Sunday (London, England), September 4, 2005, John Williams, review of *Operation Red Jericho,* p. 61.

Publishers Weekly, September 5, 2005, review of *Operation Red Jericho,* p. 63.

School Librarian, winter, 2005, Steve Hird, review of *Operation Red Jericho,* p. 215; spring, 2007, Robin Barlow, review of *Operation Typhoon Shore,* p. 34.

School Library Journal, December, 2005, Diane S. Marton, review of *Operation Red Jericho,* p. 150; March, 2007, Tasha Saecker, review of *Operation Typhoon Shore,* p. 214.

Sunday Times (London, England), September 25, 2005, Nicolette Jones, review of *Operation Red Jericho,* p. 54.

ONLINE

Walker Books Web site, http://www.walkerbooks.co.uk/ (March 25, 2008), "Joshua Mowll."*

N-O

NADIMI, Suzan

Personal
Married; children.

Addresses
Office—113 Brighton Ct., Chapel Hill, NC 27516.
E-mail—suzan@nurpublications.com.

Career
Children's author and publisher. Nur Publications, Chapel Hill, NC, founder, 2005.

Awards, Honors
Middle East Book Award honorable mention, 2007, and *Storytelling World* Resource Award Honor designation, 2008, both for *The Rich Man and the Parrot*.

Suzan Nadimi introduces readers to a traditional Persian tale in The Rich Man and the Parrot, *featuring illustrations by Ande Cook.*

Writings

The Hungry Cat (in Persian), illustrated by Christopher Downie, Nur Publications (Chapel Hill, NC), 2005.

(Reteller) Rumi, *The Rich Man and the Parrot,* illustrated by Ande Cook, Albert Whitman (Morton Grove, IL), 2007.

Sidelights

Suzan Nadimi retells a traditional Persian story in *The Rich Man and the Parrot.* Based on a work by Mevlana Jalal ad-Din Rumi, the thirteenth-century poet known as Rumi, the book focuses on a talking parrot that is owned by a wealthy merchant. Because the bird desires freedom, it asks the man to release it, but the man declines; for him, the parrot is his most prized possession. When the merchant travels to India on business, the parrot asks that he convey a message to his parrot relatives in a nearby jungle. The greeting is a special one, and when the merchant repeats it to the jungle birds, they immediately fall from the trees as if dead. When the caged parrot is informed of their response, it, too, falls down in its cage like a stone. The owner then opens the cage to remove his deceased parrot, whereupon the bird flutters back to life and soars off to freedom. Although Catherine Threadgill wrote in *School Library Journal* that she was unimpressed by the book's illustrations and turn-of-the-twentieth-century setting, she concluded of Nadimi's work that her "simple adaptation of an ancient Middle Eastern parable reads easily and sends a salient message." In *Booklist,* Hazel Rochman called *The Rich Man and the Parrot* "attractive," adding that the author's "simple" story about a "small trickster" "will have strong appeal for children." A *Kirkus Reviews* writer dubbed Nadimi's retelling "an easy-to-understand allegory," and in *Publishers Weekly* a critic described the book as "a sprightly, elegant retelling" of Rumi's classic tale.

In addition to *The Rich Man and the Parrot,* Nadimi works to help parents of Islamic heritage teach Persian to their American-born children. Toward that end, she helped found Nur Publications in 2005, and has published a Persian-language picture book titled *The Happy Cat.*

Biographical and Critical Sources

PERIODICALS

Booklist, April 1, 2007, Hazel Rochman, review of *The Rich Man and the Parrot,* p. 54.

Kirkus Reviews, March 15, 2007, review of *The Rich Man and the Parrot.*

Publishers Weekly, April 15, 2007, review of *The Rich Man and the Parrot,* p. 51.

School Library Journal, April, 2007, Catherine Threadgill, review of *The Rich Man and the Parrot,* p. 124.

ONLINE

Nur Publications Web site, http://www.nurpublications.com/ (March 28, 2008).*

NICKEL, Barbara 1966-

Personal

Born 1966, in Saskatoon, Saskatchewan, Canada; married. *Education:* University of British Columbia, M.F.A. (creative writing). *Hobbies and other interests:* Playing the violin.

Addresses

Home—Yarrow, British Columbia, Canada. *Agent*—Leona Trainer, Transatlantic Literary Agency, 2 Glengowan Rd., Toronto, Ontario M4N 1G4, Canada. *E-mail*—barbaranickel@shaw.ca.

Career

Poet and novelist. University of British Columbia, writing instructor.

Member

League of Canadian Poets, Children's Writers and Illustrators of British Columbia.

Awards, Honors

Second place, 1995 Kalamalka Press New Writers Competition; Geoffrey Bilson Award for Historical Fiction for Young People shortlist, and Canadian Children's Book Centre Choice designation, both 1996; Mr. Christie's Book Award for Best Children's Book shortlist, 1997, and Red Cedar Awards shortlist, 1998, all for *The Secret Wish of Nannerl Mozart;* Pat Lowther Memorial Award, 1997, for *The Gladys Elegies;* travel grant, Canada Council for the Arts, 1998; Canadian Library Association (CLA) Book of the Year for Children finalist, and Canadian Children's Book Centre Choice designation, both 1999, both for *From the Top of a Grain Elevator;* Governor General's Award for Children's Literature nomination, 2005, Sheila A. Egoff Award for Children's Literature, CLA Book of the Year Award honor book, Saskatchewan Young Readers' Choice Award nomination, and Chocolate Lily Young Readers Choice Award nomination, all 2006, and Manitoba Young Readers Choice Award nomination and Rocky Mountain Book Award nomination, both 2007, all for *Hannah Waters and the Daughter of Johann Sebastian Bach; Malahat Review* Long Poem Prize and *Quill & Quire* Best Books designation, both 2007, both for *Domain.*

Writings

FOR CHILDREN

The Secret Wish of Nannerl Mozart, Second Story Press (Toronto, Ontario, Canada), 1996.

Barbara Nickel (Photo by Lyla Rempel. Courtesy of Barbara Nickel.)

From the Top of a Grain Elevator, illustrated by Kathy Thiessen, Beach Holme (Vancouver, British Columbia, Canada), 1999.
Hannah Waters and the Daughter of Johann Sebastian Bach, Penguin Canada (Toronto, Ontario, Canada), 2005.

FOR ADULTS

The Gladys Elegies (poetry), Coteau Books (Regina, Saskatchewan, Canada), 1997.
SchumannBrahmsSchuman (stage play), first produced at Vancouver Fringe Festival, 1998.
Domain (poetry), Anansi (Toronto, Ontario, Canada), 2007.

Also author of chapbook *Opal's Sun: Stories and Essays from Home,* 1987. Contributor of poetry and articles to periodicals, including *Books in Canada, Canadian Notes & Queries, Malahat Review, Fiddlehead, NeWest Review, Poetry Ireland Review, Maisonneuve, Notre Dame Review, Prairie Schooner, Rhubarb,* and *Antigonish Review.*

Sidelights

Canadian writer Barbara Nickel has been honored for both her poetry for adults as well as her evocative novels for young readers. Reviewing her verse collection *From the Top of a Grain Elevator,* Evette Berry noted in *Resource Links* that "Nickel's language is sure to inspire young writers to be creative."

Nickel was born and raised in Saskatchewan, Canada, a region that has inspired the prairie landscapes that are the focus of *From the Top of a Grain Elevator.* She earned her master's degree in fine arts in creative writing at the University of British Columbia, and served as poetry editor of the school's literary magazine, *Prism International.* She remained in western Canada, writing and teaching at the University of British Columbia, for several years. Although she briefly moved east to Newfoundland, Nickel has since returned to British Columbia.

Nickel's love of music—she is a violinist—is clearly the inspiration for both of her award-winning middle-grade novels. In *The Secret Wish of Nannerl Mozart* she takes readers back to 1763 and brings attention to bear on the older sister of noted composer Wolfgang Amadeus Mozart. Set amid the world of Salzburg's court culture, Nickel's story finds twelve-year-old Nannerl as musically gifted as her younger brother. The text is framed as a series of the girl's journal entries as she describes the stresses the talented siblings must bear. Her overbearing father, a music teacher and kappelmeister to the orchestra of the Archbishop of Salzburg, nurtures and even exploits the children's talent while directing Wolfgang and Nannerl's tour of the courts of Europe. As a girl, Nannerl is also frustrated by her brother's preeminence. Ultimately, however, her dream of becoming a composer is realized when one of her symphonies is performed to a large and appreciative audience. While noting that younger children might become confused over Nickel's fictionalization of elements of Nannerl's life, a *Resource Links* contributor deemed *The Secret Wish of Nannerl Mozart* "an entertaining and accessible example" of an historical novel.

Like *The Secret Wish of Nannerl Mozart, Hannah Waters and the Daughter of Johann Sebastian Bach* is based on the life of a relative of a famous classical musician. In this case, Nickel focuses on Catharina Bach, the daughter of noted baroque musician Johann Sebastian Bach, and her story takes a jump in time from past to present. As she watches her father compose his concert for two violins, the young girl is inspired to sing. Three centuries later, violin student Hannah Waters is wrestling with the same Bach concerto. Just as Catharina felt intimidated by the vast musical talent around her, so Hannah feels out of place in her new school, and also emotionally disconnected since the death of her mother three years before. Through Bach's music, the two girls connect, and with their growing knowledge of each other's lives they learn to deal with their own challenges. Calling the novel "readable and interesting," a *Resource Links* contributor added that Nickel creates "believable" young characters "and makes the transition from Catherine's sixteenth century to Hannah's modern-day Canada with relative ease."

Biographical and Critical Sources

PERIODICALS

Canadian Book Review Annual, 2005, Dave Jenkinson, review of *Hannah Waters and the Daughter of Johann Sebastian Bach,* p. 511.
Resource Links, February, 1997, review of *The Secret Wish of Nannerl Mozart,* pp. 132-133; December, 1999, review of *From the Top of a Grain Elevator,* p. 16; February, 2006, Evelle Berry, review of *Hannah Waters and the Daughter of Johann Sebastian Bach,* p. 27.

ONLINE

Children's Writers and Illustrators of British Columbia Web site, http://www.cwill.bc.ca/ (March 22, 2008), "Barbara Nickel."
League of Canadian Poets Web site, http://www.poets.ca/ (February 15, 2008), "Barbara Nickel."
Transatlantic Literary Agency Web site, http://www.tla1.com/ (February 15, 2008), "Barbara Nickel."

*   *   *

O'CONNOR, Ian 1965-

Personal

Born 1965; married; wife's name Tracey; children: Kyle.

Addresses

Home—NJ.

Career

Author of young-adult fiction and sports columnist. Columnist for *Record,* Bergen County, NJ, 2006—; sports columnist for *USA Today* and Westchester, NY, *Journal News,* 2006.

Writings

The Jump: Sebastian Telfair and the High-Stakes Business of High School Ball, Rodale Press (Emmaus, PA), 2005.
Arnie and Jack: Palmer, Nicklaus, and Golf's Greatest Rivalry, Houghton Mifflin (Boston, MA), 2008.

Biographical and Critical Sources

PERIODICALS

Booklist, March 1, 2005, Wes Lukowsky, review of *The Jump: Sebastian Telfair and the High-Stakes Business of High School Ball,* p. 1129; March 1, 2008, Bill Ott, review of *Arnie and Jack: Palmer, Nicklaus, and Golf's Greatest Rivalry,* p. 40.
Kirkus Reviews, February 1, 2008, review of *Arnie and Jack.*
Library Journal, March 15, 2005, Larry R. Little, review of *The Jump,* p. 91.
Publishers Weekly, February 25, 2008, review of *Arnie and Jack,* p. 67.

ONLINE

Journal News Online (Westchester, NY), http://www.thejournalnews.com/ (March 28, 2008), "Ian O'Connor."*

P

PERKINS, Mitali 1963-

Personal

Born April 30, 1963, in Calcutta, West Bengal, India; immigrated to United States; daughter of Sailendra Nath (a civil engineer and port director) and Madhusree (a teacher) Bose; married Robert K. Perkins (a Presbyterian minister), August 16, 1986; children: two sons. *Education:* Stanford University, B.A. (political science), 1984; University of California, Berkeley, M.P.P., 1987. *Religion:* Christian. *Hobbies and other interests:* Tennis, travel, hiking.

Addresses

Home—Newton, MA. *E-mail*—mitaliperk@yahoo.com.

Career

Educator, homemaker, and writer. Pepperdine University, Malibu, CA, visiting professor in international relations; Chiang Mai International School, Thailand, teacher of literature and writing.

Member

PEN, Society of Children's Book Writers and Illustrators, Boston Author's Club, readergirlz.

Awards, Honors

Bank Street College Best Book for Children designation, New York Public Library Book for the Teen Age designation, and Texas/TAYSHAS Best Book for Young Adults designation, all 2004, and American Library Association (ALA) Popular Paperback for Young Adults designation, 2008, all for *Monsoon Summer;* ALA Book for Reluctant Readers designation, and Lamplighter Award, Christian Schools Association, both 2007, both for *The Not-so-Star-spangled Life of Sunita Sen;* Boston Author's Club Honor Book Award, ALA Amelia Bloomer Project citation, and Lupine Honor Book Award (ME), all 2008, all for *Rickshaw Girl.*

Writings

FOR CHILDREN

The Sunita Experiment, Joy Street Books (Boston, MA), 1993, published as *The Not-so-Star-spangled Life of Sunita Sen,* 2005.
Monsoon Summer, Delacorte Press (New York, NY), 2004.
Rickshaw Girl, illustrated by Jamie Hogan, Charlesbridge (Watertown, MA), 2007.

"FIRST DAUGHTER" NOVEL SERIES

Extreme American Makeover, Dutton (New York, NY), 2007.
White House Rules, Dutton (New York, NY), 2008.

OTHER

Islam and Christianity, Congregational Ministries/ Presbyterian Church U.S.A. (Louisville, KY), 2003.
Ambassador Families: Equipping Your Kids to Engage Popular Culture, Brazos Press (Grand Rapids, MI), 2005.

Contributor of articles to periodicals, including *Campus Life* and *Horn Book.* Member of editorial advisory board, *Kahani* magazine.

Sidelights

Mitali Perkins is the author of several young-adult novels that focus on young women coming to terms with their mixed racial and cultural identity. She addresses this topic in her first novel, *The Sunita Experiment*—also published as *The Not-so-Star-spangled Life of Sunita Sen*—as well as in her other novels for teen readers, such as *Monsoon Summer* and the books in her "First Daughter" series. In *Rickshaw Girl,* a picture book, Perkins turns to younger readers, while her nonfiction book *Ambassador Families: Equipping Your Kids to Engage Popular Culture* shares her lifelong experiences with parents working to help their children adjust to a new culture.

The topic of racial identity is one close to Perkins' heart: she was born in Calcutta, India, and her name means "friendly" in Bangla. As a child, she and her family moved frequently due to her father's work as a civil engineer, and she spent time in Ghana, Cameroon, England, and Mexico before settling in northern California in time to attend middle school. Perkins' experiences learning to accept the United States as her new home helped inspire *The Sunita Experiment.* Praised as a "gentle coming of age story" by *Voice of Youth Advocates* contributor Mary L. Adams, the novel recounts the year thirteen-year-old Sunni's Indian grandparents come to visit her family in California. Sunni leads a typical American life, complete with sports tryouts, boy trouble, and battles with her parents over clothing and makeup. These battles take a new turn after her tradition-minded grandparents arrive, as the teen gradually realizes that the subtle influence of her Indian heritage sets her apart from her Caucasian friends and classmates. Perkins' "personal experience shows," Karen Ray observed of the novel in the *New York Times Book Review,* the critic concluding that *The Sunita Experiment* contains "genuine insights."

Critics praise the warm humor of Perkins' narrative, which enlivens the troubles Sunni experiences without negating them. The teen's narration is dotted with the exaggerated expressions that typify teen speak, and her "exasperation is real but funny," according to *Bulletin of the Center for Children's Books* contributor Roger Sutton. The transformation of Sunni's mother from blue-jean-clad chemistry instructor to dutiful, sari-draped daughter adds depth to what Sutton dubbed "a perky, upbeat story." Other critics focused on Sunni's altered relationships with her friends, her family, and herself as she begins to perceive herself as both Indian and American. "Perkins refrains from lecturing," wrote Adams, "letting the reader and Sunita work out answers to simple and difficult problems." A *Kirkus Reviews* critic also noted the author's light touch, writing that, "gentle and palatable, the lessons are offered with compassion and easily absorbed insights."

In *Monsoon Summer* Perkins focuses on Jasmine Gardner, a fifteen-year-old half-Indian teen who goes by the name Jazz. When her family leaves California for Pune, India in the midst of her budding love affair with best friend Steve, Jazz is understandably frustrated. When she arrives in India and begins to help her family in their work setting up a birth clinic in the midst of the rainy season, she finds her sporty all-American persona slipping away in favor of that of a more compassionate young woman. Her efforts to help a new friend avoid an arranged marriage builds the teen's sense of self, as well as her confidence, and the "romance [she] develops even over such a long distance is . . . appealing," in the opinion of *Kliatt* contributor Claire Rosser. Noting that the novel successfully introduces readers to "India's culture and its problems," a *Publishers Weekly* critic added that in *Monsoon Summer* Perkins "sensitively traces an American girl's emotional growth." In *Booklist* Gillian Engberg cited the teen narrator for her "smart, funny, self-deprecating voice," and added that the novel's focus extends beyond cultural differences. The author's "warm, romantic story . . . shows how the deepest private discoveries often come from very public risks," the critic concluded.

In Perkins' "First Daughter" series, readers meet sixteen-year-old Sameera Righton. Adopted from Pakistan at age three, Sameera was raised in a household where politics rules. In *Extreme American Makeover* her father is running for president of the United States, and this puts the teen in the public eye. Members of her father's campaign staff push for her to acquire an all-American look, and soon the teen undergoes a total image reconstruction: wardrobe, hairstyle, posture, Web presence, and all. For Sameera, honesty is most important, however, and she manages to support her father's P.R. presence while also being true to her political viewpoint with the help of a group of South Asian students at her new school. In *White House Rules* readers follow Sameera as she morphs into "daughter of the president," and experience life in Washington, DC, as a resident of the White House. In *Publishers Weekly* a critic observed that Perkins' teen narrator is "intelligent, witty and prepossessed," adding that *Extreme American Makeover* provides a "lighthearted . . . peek at the behind-the-scenes finessing that goes on in modern politics." "Both the public and private worlds depicted" in the "First Daughter" books "will grab readers," added *Booklist* contributor Hazel Rochman, and in *School Library Journal* Kathleen E. Gruver wrote that the series successfully conveys "a sense of the demands made on those who are constantly in the public eye."

In *Rickshaw Girl,* featuring illustrations by Jamie Hogan, Perkins takes readers to Bangladesh to tell a story about challenging traditions. Ten-year-old Naima is known throughout her rural village for her skill at painting the decorative patterns called *alpanas,* but it is her younger sister's turn to get her basic education, Naima must go to work to help support her family. Because of her village's traditional culture, she must disguise herself as a boy in order to help her father in his job as a rickshaw driver. Although her scheme backfires, the girl ultimately finds a way to allow her to paint and earn money as well. Noting the "lively" nature of Perkins' tale, Rochman wrote that *Rickshaw Girl* "tells a realistic story with surprises that continue until the end." A *Kirkus Reviews* writer also praised the chapter book for presenting "a child-eye's view of Bangladesh that makes a strong and accessible statement about heritage, tradition and the changing role of women." In *Horn Book,* Norah Piehl viewed *Rickshaw Girl* in a different light, writing that Perkins ties her "vibrant plot to the economic model of microfinance—probably a first for an early chapter book!"

Although her academic studies took her into the realm of international public policy and a part-time teaching career, reading and writing have always been important to Perkins. As a writer, she also visits schools and libraries, talking about her experiences crossing cultures and the power of fiction. In an interview with Laura Atkins for *Paper Tigers* online, she discussed how writing reflects her lifelong goals. "I've always longed to help the poor and the displaced, and to inspire others to do the same . . . ," Perkins explained. "You'll find 'development' themes interwoven into many of my stories." However, she added, "When I write, I don't ask myself: 'Now I'm going to teach THIS political science lesson. . . . Hmm . . . how can I stuff it into a story?'" "I focus on character, place, plot, like most writers. But heartfelt convictions are part of who I am," she admitted, "so they are bound to come out through my writing. At least, I hope so!" "I write . . . to bring some of the excellent values that saturate good children's books from the past into the fiction I publish today," Perkins also explained to *SATA*. "Books were the ticket as this young immigrant New Yorker journeyed to the four corners, perched on a sixth-story fire escape. I write so that I can help others to fly."

Biographical and Critical Sources

PERIODICALS

Booklist, May 1, 1993, review of *The Sunita Experiment*, p. 1582; June 1, 2004, Gillian Engberg, review of *Monsoon Summer*, p. 1720; November 1, 2006, Hazel Rochman, review of *Rickshaw Girl*, p. 54; May 15, 2007, Hazel Rochman, review of *Extreme American Makeover*, p. 41.

Bulletin of the Center for Children's Books, September, 1993, Roger Sutton, review of *The Sunita Experiment*, p. 21; May, 2007, Hope Morrison, review of *Rickshaw Girl*, p. 380.

Horn Book, November-December, 2004, Jennifer M. Brabander, review of *Monsoon Summer*, p. 715; May-June, 2007, Norah Piehl, review of *Rickshaw Girl*, p. 288.

Kirkus Reviews, May 15, 1993, review of *The Sunita Experiment*, p. 67; July 15, 2004, review of *Monsoon Summer*, p. 692; December 1, 2006, review of *Rickshaw Girl*, p. 1225; May 1, 2007, review of *Extreme American Makeover*.

Kliatt, July, 1994, review of *The Sunita Experiment*, p. 11; July, 2004, Claire Rosser, review of *Monsoon Summer*, p. 12.

Los Angeles Times Book Review, June 20, 1993, review of *The Sunita Experiment*, p. 3.

New York Times Book Review, June 27, 1993, Karen Ray, review of *The Sunita Experiment*, p. 21.

Publishers Weekly, May 24, 1993, review of *The Sunita Experiment*, p. 88; August 23, 2004, review of *Monsoon Summer*, p. 55; June 25, 2007, review of *Extreme American Makeover*, p. 61.

School Library Journal, June, 1993, review of *The Sunita Experiment*, p. 132; September, 2004, Kathleen Isaacs, review of *Monsoon Summer*, p. 215; April, 2007, Susan Hepler, review of *Rickshaw Girl*, p. 115; June, 2007, Kathleen E. Gruver, review of *Extreme American Makeover*, p. 157.

Voice of Youth Advocates, October, 1993, Mary L. Adams, review of *The Sunita Experiment*, p. 218; August, 1997, review of *The Sunita Experiment*, p. 173; August, 2007, Ava Donaldson, review of *Extreme American Makeover*, p. 248.

ONLINE

Mitali Perkins Home Page, http://www.mitaliperkins.com (March 15, 2008).

Mitali Perkins Web log, http://www.mitaliblog.com (March 26, 2008).

Paper Tigers Web site, http://www.papertigers.org/ (July 1, 2005), Laura Atkins, interview with Perkins.

*   *   *

PERL, Erica S.

Personal

Married Michael P. Sewell (an architect), 1995; children: two daughters. *Education:* Hampshire College, B.A.; Tulane University, J.D.

Addresses

E-mail—erica@ericaperl.com.

Career

Attorney, picture-book author, and writer for television. Louisiana Supreme Court, New Orleans, former central-staff law clerk; Harvard Children's Initiative, attorney; Legal Aid Society, New York, NY, attorney. Television-program developer, Powderhouse Productions; WGBH, Boston, MA, writer for television series *Peep and the Big Wide World*. Writer's Center, Bethesda, MD, writing teacher; freelance writer and editor; presenter in schools.

Awards, Honors

Reuben Award for best illustrated book, Book Sense Pick, and *Slate.com* Best Books designation, all 2006, all for *Ninety-three in My Family*.

Writings

Chicken Bedtime Is Really Early, illustrated by George Bates, Harry Abrams (New York, NY), 2005.

Ninety-three in My Family, illustrated by Mike Lester, Harry Abrams (New York, NY), 2006.

Contributor to periodicals, including the *New York Times* and *Slate.*

Sidelights

Although she grew up to become an attorney, Erica S. Perl really wanted to be a writer. Her first published work, a poem, appeared in the pages of *Cricket* magazine while she was still in elementary school, and her writing destiny seemed increasingly assured after she won writing contests and was accepted into Breadloaf's New England Young Writers' Conference as a high school student. Fortunately for young readers, the birth of her first child renewed Perl's interest in writing, and entertaining picture books such as *Chicken Bedtime Is Really Early* and *Ninety-three in My Family* have been the result. In addition to her writing for preschool-and elementary-school-aged children, Perl also writes for middle-grade and teen readers, and she has contributed scripts to the Emmy award-winning animated television series *Peep and the Big Wide World.* She teaches creative writing to adults and children and has done interactive workshops and performances based on her books on stage and in school settings. Writing in *Washingtonian* magazine, Wendi Kaufman dubbed Perl "a writer to watch."

Illustrated by George Bates, *Chicken Bedtime Is Really Early* addresses the universal reluctance of children to go to bed while there are still things happening on Earth. In her rhyming text with its arch wordplay, Perl focuses on chicks, fish, hamsters, bunnies, and other creatures, all of which attempt to wrangle a few more hours of play-time from their respective parents. The rudiments of time-telling are woven into Perl's "perfectly pitched" text, resulting in a concept book that mixes "puns . . . , simple rhymes, silly words and repetition to achieve a satisfying snappiness," according to a *Publishers Weekly* critic. Describing the text as "a charming countdown to bedtime in a barnyard" recounted in "infectious, bouncing rhymes," Gillian Engberg added in her *Booklist* review that *Chicken Bedtime Is Really Early* also benefits from Bates's acrylic art, which "capture[s] the delicious chaos and tumble of toddler bedtime."

A household of pet-lovers is the focus of *Ninety-three in My Family.* In the story, Perl's young narrator is quizzed by a skeptical teacher and must describe, in detail, the menagerie that shares his family home. Brought to life in comic cartoon art by Mike Lester, the boy's household members range from five humans and various dogs and cats to gerbils, goldfish, frogs, and even owls, lions, and armadillos. Perl cleverly frames her story in such a way as to incorporate addition and subtraction, as readers keep up with the jaunty text with their own mental tally. *Ninety-three in My Family* serves as a "rib-tickling romp with many counting opportunities for young listeners," according to a *Kirkus Reviews* writer. While admitting that Perl "begins with an outlandish premise," Susan Weitz concluded in her *School* *Library Journal* review of the books that the combination of text and "visual jokes" combine to produce "a comic masterpiece."

Biographical and Critical Sources

BOOKS

Dell'Antonia, K.J., and Susan Straub, *Reading with Babies, Toddler, and Twos,* Sourcebooks, 2006.

PERIODICALS

Booklist, March 15, 2005, Gillian Engberg, review of *Chicken Bedtime Is Really Early,* p. 1287.
Kirkus Reviews, August 1, 2006, review of *Ninety-three in My Family,* p. 794.
Publishers Weekly, February 21, 2005, review of *Chicken Bedtime Is Really Early,* p. 173.
School Library Journal, April, 2005, Joy Fleishacker, review of *Chicken Bedtime Is Really Early,* p. 108; October, 2006, Susan Weitz, review of *Ninety-three in My Family,* p. 123.
Wondertime, February-March, 2007, Daniel Pinkwater, "Picture Books That Teach Numbers," p. 110.
Washingtonian, May, 2006, Wendi Kaufman, "Author, Author," p. 83.

ONLINE

Erica S. Perl Home Page, http://www.ericaperl.com (March 15, 2008).
Erica S. Perl Web log, http://ericaperl.blogspot.com (March 15, 2008).

*   *   *

PINKWATER, Jill

Personal

Married Daniel Manus Pinkwater (an author and radio commentator), October 12, 1969. *Hobbies and other interests:* Dogs.

Addresses

Home—Hyde Park, NY.

Career

Illustrator and author.

Writings

FOR CHILDREN

Cloud Horse, illustrated by Irene Brady, Lothrop, Lee & Shepard (New York, NY), 1983.

The Disappearance of Sister Perfect, Dutton (New York, NY), 1987.

Buffalo Brenda, Macmillan (New York, NY), 1989.

Tails of the Bronx: A Tale of the Bronx, Macmillan (New York, NY), 1991.

Mister Fred, Dutton (New York, NY), 1994.

ILLUSTRATOR

Daniel Pinkwater, *Wallpaper from Space,* Atheneum (New York, NY), 1996.

Daniel Pinkwater, *Young Larry,* Marshall Cavendish (New York, NY), 1997.

Jill Pinkwater brings to life two of husband Daniel Pinkwater's most popular animal characters in the book series that includes **Bad Bears in the Big City.**

Daniel Pinkwater, *At the Hotel Larry,* Marshall Cavendish (New York, NY), 1997.

Daniel Pinkwater, *Wolf Christmas,* Marshall Cavendish (New York, NY), 1998.

Daniel Pinkwater, *Second-Grade Ape,* Scholastic (New York, NY), 1998.

Daniel Pinkwater, *Bongo Larry,* Marshall Cavendish (New York, NY), 1998.

Daniel Pinkwater, *Rainy Morning,* Atheneum (New York, NY), 1998.

Daniel Pinkwater, *Big Bob and the Thanksgiving Potatoes,* Scholastic (New York, NY), 1998.

Daniel Pinkwater, *Big Bob and the Halloween Potatoes,* Scholastic (New York, NY), 1999.

Daniel Pinkwater, *Big Bob and the Magic Valentine's Day Potato,* Scholastic (New York, NY), 1999.

Daniel Pinkwater, *Big Bob and the Winter Holiday Potato,* Scholastic (New York, NY), 1999.

Daniel Pinkwater, *The Hoboken Chicken Emergency,* Aladdin Paperbacks (New York, NY), 1999.

Daniel Pinkwater, *Ice Cream Larry,* Marshall Cavendish (New York, NY), 1999.

Daniel Pinkwater, *Cone Kong: The Scary Ice Cream Giant,* Scholastic (New York, NY), 2001.

Daniel Pinkwater, *Uncle Boris in the Yukon, and Other Shaggy Dog Stories,* Simon & Schuster (New York, NY), 2001.

Daniel Pinkwater, *Mush, a Dog from Space,* Aladdin (New York, NY), 2002.

Daniel Pinkwater, *Mush's Jazz Adventure,* Aladdin (New York, NY), 2002.

Daniel Pinkwater, *Looking for Bobowicz: A Hoboken Chicken Story* (sequel to *The Hoboken Chicken Emergency*), HarperCollins (New York, NY), 2004.

Daniel Pinkwater, *The Artsy Smartsy Club* (sequel to *Looking for Bobowicz*), HarperCollins (New York, NY), 2005.

Daniel Pinkwater, *Dancing Larry,* Marshall Cavendish (New York, NY), 2006.

Daniel Pinkwater, *Sleepover Larry,* Marshall Cavendish (New York, NY), 2006.

ILLUSTRATOR; "WEREWOLF CLUB" SERIES

Daniel Pinkwater, *The Magic Pretzel,* Aladdin (New York, NY), 2000.

Daniel Pinkwater, *The Lunchroom of Doom,* Aladdin (New York, NY), 2000.

Daniel Pinkwater, *The Werewolf Club Meets Dorkula,* Aladdin (New York, NY), 2001.

Daniel Pinkwater, *The Werewolf Club Meets the Hound of the Basketballs,* Aladdin (New York, NY), 2001.

Daniel Pinkwater, *The Werewolf Club Meets Oliver Twit,* Aladdin (New York, NY), 2002.

ILLUSTRATOR; "IRVING AND MUKTUK" SERIES

Daniel Pinkwater, *Irving and Muktuk: Two Bad Bears,* Houghton (Boston, MA), 2001.

Daniel Pinkwater, *Bad Bears in the Big City,* Houghton Mifflin (Boston, MA), 2003.

Daniel Pinkwater, *Bad Bears and a Bunny,* Houghton Mifflin (Boston, MA), 2005.

Daniel Pinkwater, *Bad Bear Detectives,* Houghton Mifflin (Boston, MA), 2006.

Daniel Pinkwater, *Bad Bears Go Visiting,* Houghton Mifflin (Boston, MA), 2007.

OTHER

(With Daniel Pinkwater) *The Natural Snack Cookbook: 151 Good Things to Eat,* Four Winds Press (New York, NY), 1975.

(With D. Manus Pinkwater; and illustrator) *Superpuppy: How to Choose, Raise, and Train the Best Possible Dog for You,* Seabury Press (New York, NY), 1977, reprinted, Clarion (New York, NY), 2002.

Adaptations

Characters from the Pinkwaters' "Irving and Muktuk" and "Larry" books were included in a stage play produced by the Lifeline Theatre, Chicago, IL.

Sidelights

An author and artist, Jill Pinkwater is best known for illustrating many of the zany chapter books written by her husband, well-known author and National Public Radio commentator Daniel Pinkwater. In her art Pinkwater brings to life engaging characters such as polarbear friends Irving and Mukluk; Larry the Polar Bear, who stars in *Ice Cream Larry* and *Bongo Larry;* Phil the Gorilla, introduced in *Second-Grade Ape;* and young werewolf Bill Furball, whom readers meet in a series of books including *The Lunchroom of Doom.* "A new Pinkwater book is cause for celebration," announced *Booklist* contributor Connie Fletcher in her review of *Irving and Muktuk: Two Bad Bears.* Jill Pinkwater's "funny marker-and-ink" drawings perfectly capture her husband's quirky stories, Fletcher added, and fellow *Booklist* critic Julie Cummins characterized Pinkwater's style as featuring heavy, black "squiggly lines" that animate the characters positioned "against colorful backgrounds."

In the "Werewolf Club" books, geared for readers in the upper elementary grades, Pinkwater depicts the saga of fourth-grader Norman Gnormal. The series plays out in five volumes, including *The Magic Pretzel, The Lunchroom of Doom,* and *The Werewolf Club Meets Dorkula.* In *School Library Journal,* Kate Kohlbeck called *The Magic Pretzel* "creative and filled with zany humor," providing beginning readers with "howling good fun." Pinkwater's illustrations for *The Lunchroom of Doom* "add more fun and humor to an already entertaining title," according to Betsy Barnett in *School Library Journal,* and Martha Simpson wrote in the same periodical that the "understated humor" in *Sleepover Larry* "is perfectly matched with the bright, cheerful illustrations" depicting Larry the polar bear. Her work for the "Irving and Muktuk" books is perhaps her most popular; series installment *Bad Bears and a Bunny* benefits from Jill's "giggleworthy artwork," according to *Booklist* critic Ilene Cooper, while a *Kirkus Reviews* critic concluded of *Bad Bears in the Big City* that Pinkwater's "spare line drawings perfectly capture these strange, gratifying bear" characters.

In addition to her work as illustrator, Pinkwater has also written several novels for younger readers: *Cloud Horse, Mister Fred, The Disappearance of Sister Perfect,* and *Tails of the Bronx: A Tale of the Bronx.* In *Mister Fred,* Pinkwater leads readers to Class 6-A at My Dear Watson Elementary School, where the young students worry that their new teacher is not what he appears: human. High school freshmen India Ink and Brenda Tuna stir things up at their school in *Buffalo Brenda,* while in *The Disappearance of Sister Perfect* a teen sleuth tracks the troubling behavior of her older sister to its source in a religious cult. A group of city children hunt for some runaway cats and learn about homelessness in the process in *Tails of the Bronx,* while *Cloud Horse* is a favorite among horse lovers due to its story weaving to-gether the life of a contemporary girl with the legacy of a Viking child and the cloud horses of Iceland. Praising *Tails of the Bronx* as a "magnificent mystery" with a "spirited cast," a *Publishers Weekly* critic in particular noted the mix of humor and poignancy that treats readers of Pinkwater's "solid, thought-provoking" novel.

Biographical and Critical Sources

PERIODICALS

Booklist, October 1, 1992, review of *Tails of the Bronx: A Tale of the Bronx,* p. 341; December 15, 1994, Ilene Cooper, review of *Mister Fred,* p. 754; September 15, 2001, Todd Morning, review of *The Werewolf Club Meets Dorkula,* p. 223; September 15, 2001, Connie Fletcher, review of *Irving and Muktuk: Two Bad Bears,* p. 233; February 15, 2005, Ilene Cooper, review of *Bad Bears and a Bunny,* p. 1085; April 1, 2007, Julie Cummins, review of *Bad Bears Go Visiting,* p. 60.

Pinkwater gives shape and form to another popular ursine character created by her husband in her humorous cartoon illustrations for **Dancing Larry.** (Illustration copyright © 2006 by Jill Pinkwater. All rights reserved. Reproduced by permission of Marshall Cavendish Corporation.)

"Here is the most humane, straight-from-the-shoulder dog book around. . . . *Superpuppy* is a superbook."—*School Library Journal*

SUPERPUPPY

HOW TO CHOOSE, RAISE, AND TRAIN THE BEST POSSIBLE DOG FOR YOU

BY JILL AND D. MANUS PINKWATER

Joining with husband Daniel Pinkwater, Pinkwater translates her love of dogs into the perennially popular self-illustrated dog-training manual **Superpuppy.** (Illustration copyright © 1977 by Jill Pinkwater. Reprinted by permission of Clarion Books, an imprint of Houghton Mifflin Harcourt Publishing Company. All rights reserved.)

Bulletin of the Center for Children's Books, December, 1983, review of *Cloud Horse,* p. 76; April, 1989, review of *Buffalo Brenda,* p. 202; January, 1995, review of *Mister Fred,* p. 174.

Horn Book, July-August, 1989, Edith R. Twichell, review of *Buffalo Brenda,* p. 489; March-April, 2007, Vicky Smith, review of *Bad Bears Go Visiting,* p. 188.

Kirkus Reviews, February 15, 2004, review of *Bad Bears in the Big City,* p. 183.

Publishers Weekly, May 12, 1989, review of *Buffalo Brenda,* p. 295; May 17, 1991, review of *Tails of the Bronx,* p. 64; July 7, 1997, review of *Young Larry,* p. 67.

School Library Journal, December, 1983, review of *Cloud Horse,* p. 76; May, 1987, review of *Cloud Horse,* p. 76; December, 1989, Trev Jones, review of *Buffalo Brenda,* p. 120; May, 1987, Ruth S. Vose, review of *The Disappearance of Sister Perfect,* p. 117; June, 1991, Tatiana Castleton, review of *Tails of the Bronx,* p. 112; January, 1995, Mary Jo Drungil, review of

Mister Fred, p. 109; November, 2000, Kate Kohlbeck, review of *The Magic Pretzel,* p. 129; May, 2001, Betsy Barnett, review of *The Lunchroom of Doom,* p. 131; September, 2001, Karen J. Tannenbaum, review of *Irving and Muktuk,* p. 203; February, 2002, Kate Kohlbeck, review of *The Werewolf Club Meets the Hound of the Basketballs,* p. 110; May, 2005, Alison Follos, review of *The Artsy Smartsy Club,* p. 138; November, 2007, Martha Simpson, review of *Sleepover Larry,* p. 98.

Voice of Youth Advocates, October, 1982, review of *Superpuppy: How to Choose, Raise, and Train the Best Possible Dog for You,* p. 67; August, 1989, review of *Buffalo Brenda,* p. 160.

ONLINE

Daniel and Jill Pinkwater Home Page, http://www.pinkwater.com (March 26, 2008).*

* * *

PRINCE, Joshua

Personal

Married; children: three. *Education:* University of Vermont, B.A. (English).

Addresses

Home—CT.

Career

Writer and author of children's books. Copywriter for advertising firms; Cline, Davis & Mann (advertising agency), New York, NY, 1986—, began as copy writer, currently managing partner and chief creative officer.

Writings

I Saw an Ant on the Railroad Track, illustrated by Macky Pamintuan, Sterling Publishing (New York, NY), 2006.

I Saw an Ant in a Parking Lot, illustrated by Macky Pamintuan, Sterling Publishing (New York, NY), 2007.

Sidelights

Although Joshua Prince has established a successful career in advertising, his love of books and his belief in the importance of reading inspired him to channel some of his skill as a writer into children's books. Featuring colorful cartoon illustrations by Macky Pamintuan, Prince's books include *I Saw an Ant on the Railroad Track* and *I Saw an Ant in a Parking Lot.*

In *I Saw an Ant on the Railroad Track* Jack is a railroad switchman who is in charge of pulling the lever to shift ongoing trains from one track to another. When he spots a tiny black ant scurrying along a length of track in the path of an oncoming freight train, Jack quickly jumps to pull the switch, but the lever is stuck. The tension quickly mounts through Prince's rhyming prose as readers worry over the ant's safety. In *Booklist* Ilene Cooper found the story's "sprightly rhyme" effective, writing that "Prince's text is rhythmically perfect." "The big, bold color caricatures have a timeless feel, in keeping with the text," noted Susan E. Murray in her *School Library Journal* review of the book. Praising Pamintuan's "slick" and energetic art, a *Publishers Weekly* contributor also concluded that Prince's "percussive, theatrical text" combines with these "larger-than-life pictures" to make *I Saw an Ant on the Railroad Track* "a made-to-order read-aloud."

Presenting their story "with mock-epic flair," according to *Booklist* critic Shelle Rosenfeld, Prince and Pamintuan return in *I Saw an Ant in the Parking Lot.* Here parking-lot attendant Dorothy Mott has her work cut out for her when she spots an ant looking for crumbs in the middle of a busy parking lot. Their story is infused "with mega silliness and suspense," Rosenfeld added, citing Pamintuan's digitally enhanced, large-scale illustrations and Prince's rhyming text. While noting that parking lots do not have the "timeless appeal" of train yards, Rachel G. Payne added in *School Library Journal* that Prince's creative use of "rhyme and wordplay make [*I Saw an Ant in a Parking Lot*] . . . a buoyant read-aloud."

Biographical and Critical Sources

PERIODICALS

Booklist, February 1, 2006, Ilene Cooper, review of *I Saw an Ant on the Railroad Track,* p. 56; April 1, 2007, Shelle Rosenfeld, review of *I Saw an Ant in a Parking Lot,* p. 60.

Kirkus Reviews, March 15, 2006, review of *I Saw an Ant on the Railroad Track,* p. 299; January 15, 2007, review of *I Saw an Ant in a Parking Lot,* p. 80.

Publishers Weekly, May 22, 2006, review of *I Saw an Ant on the Railroad Track,* p. 50.

School Library Journal, July, 2006, Susan E. Murray, review of *I Saw an Ant on the Railroad Track,* p. 84; July, 2007, Rachel G. Payne, review of *I Saw an Ant in a Parking Lot,* p. 84.

ONLINE

Cline, Davis & Mann Web site, http://www.clinedavis.com/ (March 27, 2008), "Joshua Prince."

First Book Blog, http://blog.firstbook.org/ (May 19, 2006), interview with Prince.*

R

RABB, Margo 1972-
(M.E. Rabb)

Personal

Born 1972, in New York, NY; married; husband's name Marshall; children: one daughter.

Addresses

Home—Brooklyn, NY. *Agent*—c/o William Morris Agency, 1325 Avenue of the Americas, New York, NY 10019. *E-mail*—margo@margorabb.com.

Career

Author.

Awards, Honors

Best New American Voices award, 2000; Association of Jewish Libraries Notable Book selection, and Booksense Pick, both 2007, both for *Cures for Heartbreak*; grand prize, *Zoetrope* Short Story Contest; first prize, *Atlantic Monthly* Fiction Contest; first prize, American Fiction Contest; PEN Syndicated Fiction Project Award.

Writings

Cures for Heartbreak, Delacorte (New York, NY), 2007.

Contributor of short fiction to periodicals, including *Atlantic Monthly, Mademoiselle, Best New American Voices, New England Review, One Story, Chicago Review, Glimmer Train, Shenandoah,* and *Seventeen.* Work included in anthologies, such as *New Stories from the South: The Year's Best,* 2000; *Best New American Voices,* 2000; *Zoetrope II,* 2003; and *Mother Knows,* 2004.

"MISSING PERSONS" MYSTERY SERIES; UNDER NAME M.E. RABB

The Rose Queen, Speak (New York, NY), 2004.
The Chocolate Lover, Speak (New York, NY), 2004.
The Venetian Policeman, Speak (New York, NY), 2004.
The Unsuspecting Gourmet, Speak (New York, NY), 2004.

Sidelights

Although Margo Rabb began her career as a writer of literary short fiction, a suggestion from an editor turned her interest writing for young adults. As she told an interviewer for *Bookslut.com,* "young adult novels, and mysteries, were so important to me as a kid and teenager. The books that I read at that age affected me very deeply, and I remember those books more vividly than some books I read last year." Published under Rabb's pen name of M.E. Rabb, her "Missing Persons" series features Sarn and Sophie Shattenberg, New York City sisters who move to the Midwest and find themselves solving crime. Adam Langer, reviewing the series for *Book,* described the "Missing Persons" novels as "sprightly, humorous romps."

Cures for Heartbreak, a standalone novel, was more of a labor of love. Written over the course of eight years and told from the perspective of fifteen-year-old Mia Perlman, the novel follows the girl as she struggles through the grief of losing her mother. Like Mia, Rabb had also suffered the death of her mother, and after she finished the first draft of the novel her father died. To deal with her grief, the novelist read many stories featuring grieving characters, eventually returning to fiction writing but putting *Cures for Heartbreak* on hold. Several years later, she returned to the manuscript, completing the editing process.

Cures for Heartbreak records Mia's freshman year in high school and recounts her struggles to cope not with only her grief, but also with her emotionally distant father and old sister. "Readers will cherish this powerful debut," wrote Gillian Engberg in *Booklist,* while *Horn*

148

Book critic Christine M. Heppermann praised *Cures for Heartbreak* as "an artful mix of the poignant and the sometimes comically mundane." A *Publishers Weekly* contributor called Rabb's young-adult novel "keenly insightful," and went on to note that the author "balances sorrow with humor" and "writes with authority and precision."

Asked about her evolution as a writer, Rabb explained to a *Random House Web site* interviewer: "I've wanted to be a writer for as long as I can remember. I've kept a journal since I was twelve, and have written in it nearly every day since I was seventeen. The one I'm writing in now is the seventy-ninth. . . . I love capturing people and places and fleeting experiences, and reading about them again years later, long after I've forgotten them."

Biographical and Critical Sources

PERIODICALS

Book, January-February, 2003, "The New Nancy Drew: Margo Rabb," p. 49.

Booklist, December 15, 2006, Gillian Engberg, review of *Cures for Heartbreak,* p. 47.

Bulletin of the Center for Children's Books, April, 2007, Deborah Stevenson, review of *Cures for Heartbreak,* p. 342.

Horn Book, March-April, 2007, Christine M. Heppermann, review of *Cures for Heartbreak,* p. 201.

Kliatt, January, 2007, Myrna Marler, review of *Cures for Heartbreak,* p. 18.

Publishers Weekly, January 22, 2007, review of *Cures for Heartbreak,* p. 186.

School Library Journal, January, 2007, Miranda Doyle, review of *Cures for Heartbreak,* p. 136.

Voice of Youth Advocates, April, 2007, Carlisle Kraft Webber, review of *Cures for Heartbreak,* p. 55.

ONLINE

Bookslut Web site, http://www.bookslut.com/ (March 10, 2008), interview with Rabb.

Margo Rabb Home Page, http://www.margorabb.com (March 5, 2008).

Random House Web site, http://www.randomhouse.com/ (March 10, 2008), "M.E. Rabb."

Studio 2B Web site, http://www.studio2b.org/ (March 10, 2008), Judy Schoenberg, interview with Rabb.

*   *   *

RABB, M.E.
See RABB, Margo

*   *   *

REEVE, Rosie

Personal

Born in England.

Addresses

Home—London, England.

Career

Illustrator and writer.

Writings

SELF-ILLUSTRATED

Cuddle up Tight, Macmillan Children's Books (London, England), 2005.

ILLUSTRATOR

Margrit Cruickshank, *We're Going to Feed the Ducks,* Frances Lincoln (London, England), 2003.

Ian Whybrow, *Hey, I Love You!,* Macmillan Children's Books (London, England), 2004.

Ruth Louise Symes, *Mondays at Monster School,* Orion Children's Books (London, England), 2005.

Ian Whybrow, *Bella Gets Her Skates On,* Abrams Books for Young Readers (New York, NY), 2007.

ILLUSTRATOR; "ANNIE" SERIES

Tony and Jan Payne, *Not Again, Annie!,* Dolphin (London, England), 2004.

Tony and Jan Payne, *Oh No, Annie!,* Dolphin (London, England), 2004.

Tony and Jan Payne, *It's Only Annie,* Dolphin (London, England), 2005.

ILLUSTRATOR; "DELILIAH" SERIES

Jeanne Willis, *Delilah Darling Is in the Library,* Puffin (London, England), 2006, published as *Delilah D. at the Library,* Clarion Books (New York, NY), 2007.

Jeanne Willis, *Delilah Darling Is in the Classroom,* Puffin (London, England), 2007.

Biographical and Critical Sources

PERIODICALS

Booklist, February 1, 2007, Ilene Cooper, review of *Delilah D. at the Library,* p. 49; December 1, 2007, Julie Cummins, review of *Bella Gets Her Skates On,* p. 47.

Bulletin of the Center for Children's Books, April, 2007, Karen Coats, review of *Delilah D. at the Library,* p. 348.

Kirkus Reviews, March 1, 2007, review of *Delilah D. at the Library,* p. 234; October 15, 2007, review of *Bella Gets Her Skates On.*

School Library Journal, March, 2007, Grace Oliff, review of *Delilah D. at the Library,* p. 191; November, 2007, Teri Markson, review of *Bella Gets Her Skates On,* p. 103.

Washington Post Book World, May 20, 2007, Elizabeth Ward, review of *Delilah D. at the Library,* p. 12.*

*   *   *

ROCCO, John 1967-

Personal

Born 1967, in RI; married Aileen Leijten (an author/illustrator); children: Alaya Marzipan. *Education:* Attended Rhode Island School of Design and School of Visual Arts.

Addresses

Home—Brooklyn, NY. *E-mail*—john@roccoart.com.

Career

Illustrator and author. Art director for film and television, theme parks, and museums; freelance illustrator, 2004—.

Member

Society of Children's Book Writers and Illustrators.

Awards, Honors

Borders Original Voices Award for Best Picture Book of the Year, 2007, National Parenting Publication Gold Award, and *Storytelling World* Resource Award, both 2008, and Society of Illustrators (Los Angeles) Silver Medal, all for *Wolf! Wolf!*

Writings

(Illustrator) Whoopie Goldberg, *Alice,* Bantam Books (New York, NY), 1992.

Wolf! Wolf!, Hyperion Books for Children (New York, NY), 2007.

Moonpowder, Hyperion Books for Children (New York, NY), 2008.

Sidelights

John Rocco illustrated his first picture book for children, Whoopie Goldberg's *Alice,* while he was employed as a bartender. Goldberg's 1992 story was well received by critics and Rocco's illustrations were praised for their surreal depiction of the tale's contemporary urban setting. However, Rocco did not make the transition to book illustrator for over twelve years, in the meantime he worked as an art director on films such as *Shrek,* as well as on projects for television, mu-

John Rocco (Photo courtesy of John Rocco.)

seums, and theme parks. Finally, in 2004 he decided to focus on book illustration, inspired in part by his wife, illustrator Aileen Leijten, and by the birth of their daughter. His paintings bring to life his original stories in the award-winning picture book *Wolf! Wolf!* as well as in the fantasy adventure *Moonpowder.* In addition, Rocco creates cover art for numerous children's books by other writers.

Rocco grew up in a coastal community in Rhode Island and was working as a deckhand on a fishing boat by the time he was in middle school. A string of other jobs got him through high school and college, including paperboy, retail clerk, golf caddy, waiter (and later bartender), soccer coach, and carpenter. He began his art training at the prestigious Rhode Island School of Design and eventually moved to New York City to attend the School of Visual Arts. Although his career as an art director found him working in California, Hawaii, and the Philippines, Rocco has since returned to the East Coast and now makes his home in Brooklyn, New York.

In *Wolf! Wolf!* Rocco presents what *School Library Journal* contributor Genevieve Gallagher dubbed a "twisted treatment of Aesop's fable" about the boy who cried "Wolf!" Featuring a nostalgic setting that evokes a China of centuries ago, the story introduces a dapper but elderly wolf with a hearing problem. When the well-dressed creature hears a boy cry "Wolf, wolf!," he mistakenly thinks he is being summoned for lunch. He therefore feels tricked by the youngster when a group of angry villagers arrive and tag him as a menacing creature. The poor animal is, in fact, only looking for a tasty meal, possibly one of the boy's goats since his garden has fallen into disarray. In the end, the boy gives the old wolf a goat; instead of making the gift a one-time-only meal, the wolf puts the goat to work in his garden and the two become fast friends. Praising Rocco's unique take on a traditional tale, Gallagher cited the author/illustrator's "purposeful use of frames, unusual setting, and visual humor," while a *Kirkus Reviews* critic described *Wolf! Wolf!* as "good-humored fun all around."

Biographical and Critical Sources

PERIODICALS

Bulletin of the Center for Children's Books, April, 2007, Deborah Stevenson, review of *Wolf! Wolf!,* p. 343.

Kirkus Reviews, February 15, 2007, review of *Wolf! Wolf!*

Publishers Weekly, February 19, 2007, review of *Wolf! Wolf!,* p. 168.

School Library Journal, February, 2007, Genevieve Gallagher, review of *Wolf! Wolf!,* p. 94.

Rocco sets a well-known story in a traditional Chinese setting in his self-illustrated picture book **Wolf! Wolf!** (Illustration copyright © 2007 by John Rocco. All rights reserved. Reproduced by permission of Hyperion Books for Children.)

ONLINE

John Rocco Home Page, http://www.roccoart.com (March 15, 2008).

John Rocco Web log, http://roccoart.blogspot.com/ (March 15, 2008).

*   *   *

RUSSO, Marisabina 1950-

Personal

Born May 1, 1950, in New York, NY; daughter of Michele Russo (a naval architect) and Sabina Heliczer (a businesswoman); married Whitney W. Stark (a teacher), October 4, 1975; children: Hannah, Samuel, Benjamin. *Education:* Mount Holyoke College, B.A., 1971 (studio art); attended Boston Museum School and Art Students League. *Politics:* "Independent." *Hobbies and other interests:* Yoga, animation, gardening.

Addresses

Home—Yorktown Heights, NY. *E-mail*—marisabina russo@marisabinarusso.com.

Career

Author and illustrator of children's books. *Exhibitions:* Works included in exhibits, including Biennale, Bratislava, Czechoslovakia, 1989; Itabashi Art Museum, Tokyo, Japan, and on tour, 1990; Society of Illustrators' Museum of American Illustration, New York, NY, 1992, 1993; Westchester Community College Fine Arts Gallery, Westchester, NY, 1993; Rye Arts Center, Rye, NY, 1996; Society of Illustrators' Museum of American Illustration, 1997; Katonah Museum of Art, Katonah, NY, 2006; and Westchester Arts Council, White Plains, NY, 2007.

Awards, Honors

Children's Choice Award, International Reading Association (IRA), 1986, for *The Line Up Book;* Washington Irving Children's Choice Book Award, 1994, for *A Visit to Oma;* National Parenting Publications Book Award, 1994, for *Time to Wake Up!;* Children's Choice Award, IRA/Children's Book Council, 1994, for *Trade-in Mother;* Best Books of the Year citation, Bank Street College of Education, 1998, for *Under the Table;* New York Public Library 100 Titles for Reading and Sharing, 2000, for *The Big Brown Box,* and 2005, for *Always Remember Me;* Charlotte A Zolotow Award Highly Commended honor, 2002, for *Come Back, Hannah!;* Parents' Choice Foundation Silver Award, 2005, and American Library Association Notable Children's Book designation, 2006, both for *Always Remember Me.*

Writings

SELF-ILLUSTRATED

The Line Up Book, Greenwillow (New York, NY), 1986.

Marisabina Russo (Reproduced by permission of Marisabina Russo.)

Why Do Grown-Ups Have All the Fun?, Greenwillow (New York, NY), 1987.

Only Six More Days, Greenwillow (New York, NY), 1988.

Waiting for Hannah, Greenwillow (New York, NY), 1989.

Where Is Ben?, Greenwillow (New York, NY), 1990.

A Visit to Oma, Greenwillow (New York, NY), 1991.

Alex Is My Friend, Greenwillow (New York, NY), 1992.

Trade-in Mother, Greenwillow (New York, NY), 1993.

Time to Wake Up!, Greenwillow (New York, NY), 1994.

I Don't Want to Go Back to School, Greenwillow (New York, NY), 1994.

Grandpa Abe, Greenwillow (New York, NY), 1996.

Under the Table, Greenwillow (New York, NY), 1997.

When Mama Gets Home, Greenwillow (New York, NY), 1998.

Hannah's Baby Sister, Greenwillow (New York, NY), 1998.

Mama Talks Too Much, Greenwillow (New York, NY), 1999.

The Big Brown Box, Greenwillow (New York, NY), 2000.

Come Back, Hannah!, Greenwillow (New York, NY), 2001.

House of Sports (young-adult novel), Greenwillow (New York, NY), 2002.

The Trouble with Baby, Greenwillow (New York, NY), 2003.

Always Remember Me: How One Family Survived World War II, Greenwillow (New York, NY), 2003.

A Portrait of Pia, Harcourt (Orlando, FL), 2007.

The Bunnies Are Not in Their Beds, Schwartz & Wade (New York, NY), 2007.

ILLUSTRATOR

Nikki Giovanni, *Vacation Time: Poems for Children,* Morrow (New York, NY), 1980.

Elizabeth Burton Brown, *Vegetables: An Illustrated History with Recipes,* Prentice-Hall (Englewood Cliffs, NJ), 1981.

Mary and Dewey Blocksma, *Easy-to-Make Spaceships That Really Fly,* Simon & Schuster (New York, NY), 1983.

Nancy Van Laan, *The Big Fat Worm,* Knopf (New York, NY), 1987.

Helen Plotz, editor, *A Week of Lullabies,* Greenwillow Books (New York, NY), 1988.

Susi Gregg Fowler, *When Summer Ends,* Greenwillow Books (New York, NY), 1989.

Stephanie Calmenson, *It Begins with an A,* Hyperion (New York, NY), 1993.

Susan Straight, *Bear E. Bear,* Hyperion (New York, NY), 1995.

Kevin Henkes, *Good-Bye, Curtis,* Greenwillow Books (New York, NY), 1995.

Eve Rice, *Swim!,* Greenwillow Books (New York, NY), 1996.

Contributor of illustrations to periodicals, including the *New Yorker.*

Russo's books have been translated into Japanese, Korean, and French.

Sidelights

Marisabina Russo has created numerous self-illustrated picture books for young children as well as fiction for older readers. Her realistic stories for toddlers focus on common childhood situations: deciding what to do with a jumbled of blocks, counting down the days until a birthday, or confronting a sibling's worries while awaiting the birth of a new baby. Russo keeps her story lines simple and direct, pairing them with original gouache illustrations filled to the brim with color and background detail. In both illustration and writing, she deals with the familiar, imbuing books such as *Time to Wake Up!,* *The Big Brown Box,* and *The Trouble with Baby* "with a reassuring aura of love, understanding, and acceptance," according to Sandra Ray in *Children's Books and Their Creators.*

Russo grew up in Queens, New York, the daughter of a single parent raising siblings much older than she. A shy child, she spent much of her time alone where drawing and writing kept her occupied. Art lessons from a neighbor encouraged Russo's natural talent, and visits to New York City's museums introduced her to the possibilities of art and inspired her determination to become an artist. In the sixth grade, she first read *The Diary of Anne Frank,* and this experience moved her to keep her own journal. With the encouragement of a seventh-grade English teacher, Russo started writing short stories, one of which was published in her junior-high literary magazine.

After high school, Russo majored in studio art at Mount Holyoke College, then went on to study lithography at the Boston Museum School and life drawing at the Art Students League in New York City. Freelance illustrating jobs and marriage both came about in the mid-1970s. Early illustration assignments included spot drawings and covers for the *New Yorker* as well as illustrations for cookbooks, two of which were award winners. After her third child was born, Russo began writing and illustrating picture books.

Russo's first picture book, *The Line Up Book,* was published in 1986 and set the tone for much of her subsequent work. It was inspired by her son, Sam, who was obsessed with lining up objects in his own house. In the book, Sam dumps his blocks on the floor when his mother calls him to lunch. He uses objects in the house—including blocks, books, and boots—to make a line from the bedroom to kitchen. Lying down on the kitchen floor, Sam becomes the last "object" in line. "The reassurance of [the mother's] reaction and Sam's pride in his innovative route combine to create a warm, satisfying feeling," Lauralyn Persson remarked in *School Library Journal.* The illustrations are also reassuring, a *Publishers Weekly* contributor citing their "folk-art look and . . . homey touches." *Horn Book* reviewer Mary M. Burns commented on Russo's "skill in developing striking graphic patterns from the juxtaposition of ordinary household artifacts." The winner of a Children's Choice Award from the International Reading Association and the Children's Book Council, *The Line Up Book* jump-started Russo's picture-book career.

A child's fantasies about how wonderful it would be to stay up late are at the heart of *Why Do Grown-Ups Have All the Fun?* In the story, young Hannah imagines her parents eating ice cream, working with Play Dough, and building towers out of blocks. "The beauty of this

Using a simple text and child-friendly art, Russo finds an interesting way to explore basic concepts in **The Line Up Book.** (Copyright © 1986 by Marisabina Russo. Used by permission of HarperCollins Publishers.)

***Russo creates colorful acrylic painting that bring to life her family-centered picture book* When Mama Gets Home.** (Copyright © 1998 by Marisabina Russo. Used by permission of HarperCollins Publishers.)

book lies in its simple story line, in the charm of the ingenious protagonist, and in Russo's graphic illustrations," commented David Gale in a *School Library Journal* review. Again Russo pairs gouache paintings in two-dimensional blocks of color with a simple, child-centered text. In *Booklist,* Denise M. Wilms concluded that "the story's gentle handling of a child's sleep problems is nice to see and the pictures . . . echo the story's quiet sensibility."

Expectation is the theme of several of Russo's titles, including *Only Six More Days, When Mama Gets Home,* and *Hannah's Baby Sister.* A mother awaiting the birth of her child forms the plot of *Waiting for Hannah,* a "tender story that captures the love and expectancy of birth far better than most books written on the topic," according to *Booklist* contributor Ilene Cooper. Leda Schubert, writing in *School Library Journal,* noted that "children rarely tire of hearing this kind of tale; it should be particularly successful in one-on-one reading." *Hannah's Baby Sister* is something of a reprise of this idea, with young Hannah now waiting for the birth of a baby sister—which, in the event, turns out to be a baby brother. Pam Gosner remarked in *School Library Journal* that this "loving family is warmly portrayed in both text and in the cheerful childlike paintings with Russo's signature use of flat areas of color and pattern."

Expectation takes the form of waiting for a birthday in *Only Six More Days,* and Ben is the birthday boy. With only six days left until he turns five, Ben begins counting down, but older sister Molly gets tired of the whole subject and decides to boycott the party until Mother comes to the rescue. In *Booklist* Cooper concluded of the book that the "party scene featuring a multiracial group has warm appeal." Mother again intervenes in *When Mama Gets Home.* Here a little girl awaits her mother's arrival home from work so that she can tell her all about her day. *When Mama Gets Home* provides a "realistic glimpse into family life where children are often home before their parents," noted Lisa Gangemi Kropp in *School Library Journal.* "The dreamy quality of the narrative is extended in flat gouache paintings in muted colors," according to a critic in *Kirkus Reviews,* while Hazel Rochman concluded in *Booklist* that "Russo captures the drama of a small child's day with immediacy and feeling and without condescension."

Several of Russo's books deal with the relationship between young children and their grandparents. In *A Visit to Oma* Celeste visits her great-grandmother, receives a warm welcome, and listens to stories she cannot understand because Oma does not speak English. Celeste fashions her own story about Oma in a "perceptive glimpse of a child's imaginative concept of her elder's past," according to a *Kirkus Reviews* contributor. Ellen Fader remarked in *Horn Book* that "Russo's story will engage young readers with its warmth, love, and mysterious sense of personal history."

Another multigenerational tale, *Grandpa Abe* "celebrates the special connection between a grandparent and a child," Maeve Visser Knoth wrote in a *Horn Book* review. However, there is a twist to Russo's tale; Grandpa Abe is Sarah's step-grandfather. When Sarah is born, he is Sarah's grandmother's boyfriend, but from the beginning, he is there for the girl. Sarah. He lies about his relationship to Sarah to get into the hospital to visit her as a newborn. Later, when Sarah is in school and he and her grandmother have married, Abe goes to her school on Grandparents Day. Through the years, he gives Sarah plenty of love, presents, and affection, until he dies when Sarah is nine years old. "Bright, clear gouache paintings in Russo's signature style illustrate an expressive story," Hazel Rochman commented in *Booklist.*

Celeste returns in *Mama Talks Too Much.* In this tale, Celeste and her mother are trying to walk to the supermarket, but Mama has to stop and talk to the many neighbors they meet along the way. Celeste, uninterested in the grown-ups' chit-chat, becomes increasingly impatient until Mrs. Castro comes along with her new puppy. Now it is Mama's turn to be annoyed, as Celeste wants to linger and play with the dog. "The text neatly pins down Celeste's feelings," a reviewer wrote in *Publishers Weekly,* "and the artwork is equally assured." *Mama Talks Too Much* is "winsome and utterly recognizable," declared *Booklist* contributor GraceAnne A. DeCandido.

Childhood rebellion is the focus of *Trade-in Mother, Time to Wake Up!, I Don't Want to Go Back to School,* and *The Bunnies Are Not in Their Beds.* In *Trade-in Mother* Max blames Mama for his frustrating day and wishes he could trade her in, until it occurs to him that he might wind up with a mom who would trade *him* in. A *Kirkus Reviews* critic noted that Russo's "attractive illustrations . . . reinforce the realistic story's warmth and sense of security." Another little boy is gently coaxed to get out of bed and start his day in *Time to*

Wake Up, a book that shows Russo to be "a master at capturing the special times between mother and child that become cherished family memories," according to *Horn Book* contributor Ellen Fader.

I Don't Want to Go Back to School finds Ben unenthusiastic about returning to school at the end of summer. His parents offer reassurances, while his big sister Hannah tells horror stories of her own school years. Jacqueline Elsner, writing in *School Library Journal,* called *I Don't Want to Go Back to School* an "all-around superior picture book." Reoccurring characters Sam, Ben, and Hannah return for more fun in *The Big Brown Box, Hannah!,* and *The Trouble with Baby.*

Three rambunctious bunnies are the focus of *The Bunnies Are Not in Their Beds,* which finds the cottontailed sibling trio outlasting their parents in their efforts to stay up and play all night long. Russo's "colorful, folksy gouache illustrations bring real personality to the text," wrote Catherine Callegari in a *School Library Journal* review of the book, and in *Kirkus Reviews* a critic predicted that *The Bunnies Are Not in Their Beds* is "sure to spark laughter from . . . parents and children alike."

Russo captures a common childhood playtime activity in *Under the Table.* The young protagonist of this picture book brings her dolls, crayons, books, and even the dog to her special hiding place. One day, she begins to draw pictures on the underside of the table, which her

Cover of Russo's self-illustrated, multigenerational picture book **A Visit to Oma.** *(Jacket art © 1991 by Marisabina Russo Stark. Used by permission of Harper-Collins Publishers.)*

Cover of Russo's young-adult novel House of Sports, *featuring artwork by Kadir Nelson.* (Cover copyright © 1992 by Kadir Nelson. Used by permission of HarperCollins Publishers.)

parents discover upon moving the furniture. Fortunately, Mom and Dad are understanding and make things right in a gentle way. "Many kids will see themselves in this pleasing tale," predicted Cooper.

Russo turns to middle-grade readers in *House of Sports,* which focuses on the relationship between twelve-year-old Jim and his eighty-two-year-old grandmother, whom he calls Nana. Nana, a quick-witted Holocaust survivor, is appalled that her grandson prefers basketball to studying. Even though the boy is bright, he gets poor grades. Then a series of disasters, including Nana's stroke, force Jim to reevaluate his priorities in life. "Throughout, the author nicely balances the comic and the tragic, creating scenes that ring true," Todd Morning wrote in *School Library Journal. House of Sports* also received praise from a *Publishers Weekly* reviewer, who noted that "the dialogue flows spontaneously, even minor characters have complexities, and the optimism expressed flows naturally from the storytelling."

Also for older readers, *A Portrait of Pia* addresses a sibling's mental illness and how it affects his younger sister. Raised by her single mother, twelve-year-old Pia Crossley feels lost when her best friend drifts into a dif-

ferent crowd at school and her older brother exhibits the beginning symptoms of schizophrenia. As the girl's mother becomes distracted by her son's strange behaviors, as well as by her own romantic relationship, the girl turns to art, as well as to her Italian family for solace. A visit to Italy reveals several things about Pia's family that had been hidden from the girl, and she returns home to New York with a new sense of herself and her future. Noting that Russo presents a realistic middle-grade protagonist in her novel, *Booklist* contributor Kathy Isaacs added that preteen readers "will find it easy to relate to Pia's uncertainties as well as to her solutions." *A Portrait of Pia* presents a "thoughtful story of a family's troubles and triumphs," wrote a *Kirkus Reviews* writer, the critic adding that "Russo skillfully renders" her young character's revelations and "sensitively showcases the anguish of siblings of the mentally ill."

To create her picture books, Russo employs incidents from her own childhood as well as observations of her children. Indeed, the main characters of her stories often bear her children's names. *Always Remember Me: How One Family Survived World War II* is particularly personal. In what Rochman deemed a "moving picture book," the author/illustrator recalls her memories of her German Jewish grandmother, Oma, and Oma's three daughters as they lived through the Holocaust and survived the horror of the Nazi concentration camps. In the story, Oma shares her photo album with granddaughter Rachel, and while several pages had been left unturned and unexplored in the past, the girl is now old enough to learn the whole family history. Through the maps, newspaper clippings, and other objects Russo intersperses within her gouache illustrations, both Rachel and the reader come to know the trials of the women as they were separated and sent to different camps, only to be reunited at war's end. Calling the book "moving yet unsentimental," a *Publishers Weekly* reviewer added that *Always Remember Me* "presents tragedy in the context of family love and hope," and thereby introduces children to "a difficult chapter of history." In *School Library Journal,* Susan Scheps maintained that Russo's book "answers the need for appropriate Holocaust literature for young children," and a *Kirkus Reviews* critic praised *Always Remember Me* for telling an inspiring story in an "exquisitely understated text."

In reviewing Russo's books for children, critics repeatedly point to the simple, direct language she employs, and also cite her paintings, with their strong, bold colors and folk-art themes. Russo has noted that creating these paintings provides her with the most fun as a picture-book author, and on occassion she has even created art for texts by other writers. "Our lives are filled with stories beginning in early childhood," she told *SATA.* "My mother was one of the funniest storytellers I ever knew. She called me her 'best audience.' As a child I loved to draw and often made up stories to go with my pictures. In college I thought creating books for children would be the perfect life for me! I started out as a freelance illustrator, but when I met Susan Hirschman at Greenwillow Books she encouraged me to write my own story. That led to *The Line Up Book,* my first picture book, and many others. Every day when I sit down to work in my studio I feel very happy and very lucky."

Biographical and Critical Sources

BOOKS

Children's Books and Their Creators, Houghton Mifflin (Boston, MA), 1995.

PERIODICALS

Booklist, April 15, 1987, Denise M. Wilms, review of *Why Do Grown-Ups Have All the Fun?,* p. 1294; March 1, 1988, Ilene Cooper, review of *Only Six More Days,* p. 1185; September 15, 1989, Ilene Cooper, review of *Waiting for Hannah,* pp. 189-190; May 1, 1992, Stephanie Zvirin, review of *Alex Is My Friend,* p. 1610; March 1, 1993, Stephanie Zvirin, review of *Trade-in Mother,* p. 1237; June 1, 1993, Kathryn Broderick, review of *It Begins with an A,* p. 1842; June 1, 1994, Hazel Rochman, review of *Time to Wake Up!,* p. 1844; September 1, 1994, Hazel Rochman, review of *I Don't Want to Go Back to School,* p. 54; March 15, 1995, Hazel Rochman, review of *Bear E. Bear,* p. 1338; October 15, 1995, Carolyn Phelan, review of *Good-bye, Curtis,* p. 411; May 15, 1996, Hazel Rochman, review of *Grandpa Abe,* p. 1593; August, 1996, Carolyn Phelan, review of *Swim!,* p. 1908; April 1, 1997, Ilene Cooper, review of *Under the Table,* p. 1339; March 1, 1998, Hazel Rochman, review of *When Mama Gets Home,* pp. 1141-1142; December 1, 1999, GraceAnne A. DeCandido, review of *Mama Talks Too Much,* p. 714; May 1, 2000, Hazel Rochman, review of *The Big Brown Box,* p. 1679; March 1, 2005, Hazel Rochman, review of *Always Remember Me: How One Family Survived World War II,* p. 1190; February 1, 2007, Julie Cummins, review of *The Bunnies Are Not in Their Beds,* p. 49; April 1, 2007, Kathy Isaacs, review of *A Portrait of Pia,* p. 52.

Bulletin of the Center for Children's Books, January, 2007, Deborah Stevenson, review of *The Bunnies Are Not in Their Beds,* p. 228; October, 2007, Hope Morrison, review of *A Portrait of Pia,* p. 109.

Childhood Education, February, 1987, Phyllis G. Sidorsky, review of *The Line Up Book,* p. 211; June, 1988, Phyllis G. Sidorsky, review of *A Week of Lullabies,* p. 312; winter, 1988, Tina L. Burke, review of *Only Six More Days,* p. 117; mid-summer, 2002, Liane Ford, review of *Come Back, Hannah!,* p. 308.

Horn Book, November-December, 1986, Mary M. Burns, review of *The Line Up Book,* p. 739; May-June, 1987, Ethel L. Heins, review of *Why Do Grown-ups Have All the Fun?,* p. 334; September-October, 1989, Hanna B. Zeiger, review of *Waiting for Hannah,* p. 615;

November-December, 1990, Hanna B. Zeiger, review of *Where Is Ben?,* p. 100; March-April, 1991, Ellen Fader, review of *A Visit to Oma,* pp. 195-196; May-June, 1993, Nancy Vasilakis, review of *Trade-in Mother,* p. 325; July-August, 1994, Ellen Fader, review of *Time to Wake Up!,* pp. 444-445; May-June, 1996, Maeve Visser Knoth, review of *Grandpa Abe,* p. 328; March-April, 2005, Susan P. Bloom, review of *Always Remember Me,* p. 216.

Kirkus Reviews, May 1, 1991, review of *A Visit to Oma,* p. 609; February 15, 1993, review of *Trade-in Mother,* p. 233; February 15, 1998, review of *When Mama Gets Home,* p. 274; March 15, 2003, review of *The Trouble with Baby,* p. 477; March 15, 2005, review of *Always Remember Me,* p. 357; December 1, 2006, review of *The Bunnies Are Not in Their Beds,* p. 1225; June 15, 2007, review of *A Portrait of Pia.*

Language Arts, September, 1987, Janet Hickman, review of *Why Do Grown-ups Have All the Fun?,* p. 547; November, 1988, Janet Hickman, review of *A Week of Lullabies,* p. 720.

Mothering, summer, 1989, Max T. Neumeyer, review of *The Line Up Book,* p. 54.

New York Times Book Review, November 9, 1980, X.J. Kennedy, review of *Vacation Time,* p. 62; June 4, 1995, review of *Bear E. Bear,* p. 25; July 28, 1996, Judith Viorst, review of *Grandpa Abe,* p. 21.

Publishers Weekly, July 25, 1986, review of *The Line Up Book,* p. 184; November 13, 1987, review of *The Big Fat Worm,* p. 68; January 29, 1988, review of *A Week of Lullabies,* pp. 432-433; February 24, 1989, review of *When Summer Ends,* p. 232; January 25, 1993, review of *Trade-in Mother,* p. 86; April 26, 1993, review of *It Begins with an A,* p. 77; April 3, 1995, review of *Bear E. Bear,* p. 61; August 2, 1999, review of *Mama Talks Too Much,* p. 84; January 21, 2002, review of *House of Sports,* p. 90; March 21, 2005, review of *Always Remember Me,* p. 51; December 18, 2006, review of *The Bunnies Are Not in Their Beds,* p. 61.

Reading Teacher, February, 1988, Alida von Krogh Cutts, interview with Russo, pp. 540-543.

School Library Journal, November, 1986, Lauralyn Persson, review of *The Line Up Book,* p. 83; March, 1987, David Gale, review of *Why Do Grown-Ups Have All the Fun?,* p. 150; December, 1987, Lee Bock, review of *The Big Fat Worm,* p. 78; April, 1988, Barbara S. McGinn, review of *A Week of Lullabies,* p. 96; October, 1988, Nemeth McCarthy, review of *Only Six More Days,* pp. 127-128; March, 1989, Lori A. Janick, review of *When Summer Ends,* p. 162; November, 1989, Leda Schubert, review of *Waiting for Hannah,* pp. 92-93; October, 1990, Karen James, review of *Where Is Ben?,* p. 100; July, 1991, Patricia Pearl, review of *A Visit to Oma,* pp. 195-196; April, 1992, Virginia Opocensky, review of *Alex Is My Friend,* p. 100; July, 1993, Lori A. Janick, review of *Trade-in Mother,* pp. 70-71; May, 1994, Marianne Saccardi, review of *Time to Wake Up!,* p. 102; July, 1994, Jacqueline Elsner, review of *I Don't Want to Go Back to School,* p. 88; June, 1995, Rosanne Cerny, review of *Bear E. Bear,* p. 96; October, 1995, Patricia Pearl Dole, review of

Good-bye, Curtis, p. 104; July, 1996, Janet M. Blair, review of *Grandpa Abe,* p. 72; September, 1996, Sally R. Dow, review of *Swim!,* p. 189; April, 1997, Lisa Falk, review of *Under the Table,* p. 116; April, 1998, Lisa Gangemi Kropp, review of *When Mama Gets Home,* p. 108; September, 1998, Pam Gosner, review of *Hannah's Baby Sister,* p. 180; September, 1999, Sue Norris, review of *Mama Talks Too Much,* p. 202; May, 2000, Linda Ludke, review of *The Big Brown Box,* p. 153; April, 2002, Todd Morning, review of *House of Sports,* p. 156; April, 2005, Susan Scheps, review of *Always Remember Me,* p. 126; December, 2006, Catherine Callegari, review of *The Bunnies Are Not in Their Beds,* p. 114; August, 2007, Jennifer Ralston, review of *A Portrait of Pia,* p. 125.

Times Educational Supplement, October 13, 1989, Jill Bennett, review of *Only Six More Days,* p. 62.

ONLINE

Marisabina Russo Home Page, http://www.marisabina russo.com (March 20, 2008).

OTHER

Russo, Marisabina, comments in a Greenwillow Books publicity release, 1996.

S

SANTAT, Dan

Personal

Married; wife's name Leah; children: Alek. *Education:* Art Center College of Design, graduate.

Addresses

Home—Southern CA. *E-mail*—dsantat@yahoo.com.

Career

Children's book author and commercial illustrator. Disney Channel, creator of animated cartoon *The Replacements.*

Writings

SELF-ILLUSTRATED

The Guild of Geniuses, Arthur A. Levine Books (New York, NY), 2004.

Author of comic strip "The Contender."

ILLUSTRATOR

Rhea Perlman, *Born to Drive* ("Otto Undercover" series), Katherine Tegan Books (New York, NY), 2006.
Rhea Perlman, *Water Balloon Doom* ("Otto Undercover" series), Katherine Tegan Books (New York, NY), 2006.
Rhea Perlman, *Canyon Catastrophe* ("Otto Undercover" series), Katherine Tegan Books (New York, NY), 2006.
Rhea Perlman, *Toxic Taffy Takeover* ("Otto Undercover" series), Katherine Tegan Books (New York, NY), 2006.
Rhea Perlman, *The Brink of Ex-Stink-tion* ("Otto Undercover" series), Katherine Tegan Books (New York, NY), 2006.

Rhea Perlman, *Brain Freeze* ("Otto Undercover" series), Katherine Tegan Books (New York, NY), 2007.
Barbara Jean Hicks, *The Secret Life of Walter Kitty,* Alfred A. Knopf (New York, NY), 2007.
Phyllis Shalant, *The Society of Super Secret Heroes: The Great Cape Rescue,* Dutton (New York, NY), 2007.
Anne Isaacs, *The Ghosts of Luckless Gulch,* Atheneum Books for Young Readers (New York, NY), 2008.

Sidelights

Based in Southern California, Dan Santat is a commercial illustrator and cartoonist who has become well known for his work in children's books. Some children already know Santat as the creator of *The Replacements,* an animated series airing on the Disney Channel in which a brother and sister are able to replace any adult in their life with a simple phone call. With his work illustrating actress Rhea Pearlman's five-book "Otto Undercover" series, he made his first mark in children's publishing, and in *Publishers Weekly* a reviewer remarked of series opener *Born to Drive* that "Santat's brash cartoons add to the inanity" of Pearlman's high-action story. In his book illustrations, Santat uses a mixture of acrylics, pen and ink, and digital imaging. As a commercial artist, his cartoon-style art has appeared in video games, film, animation, and magazines and galleries throughout the United States.

Santat takes on the role of both author and illustrator in *The Guild of Geniuses,* a picture book that transports young readers into a futuristic 'fifties-inspired fantasy world. In Santat's story, a monkey named Mr. Pip finds the perfect gift for his best friend, Frederick Lipton. Lipton is a famous actor, however, and is used to the finer things. As Mr. Pip watches lavish gifts heaped upon his friend during the birthday celebration, he goes glum with worry that his own gift does not reflect the depth of his friendship. Meanwhile, Lipton does not understand his monkey friend's down mood, so he takes Mr. Pip to the Guild of Geniuses in order to find out what is wrong. "Inventive is the word here, especially for the artwork," wrote Ilene Cooper in her *Booklist* review of *The Guild of Geniuses.* While Blair Christolon noted in *School Library Journal* that Santat's story features an ending that children might anticipate, she nonetheless noted that his artwork, with its "varying perspectives and bold colors, keep the action moving quickly." Praising the "kitschy fifties design and appealingly drawn characters" in *The Guild of Geniuses,* a contributor to *Publishers Weekly* dubbed Santat's picture book "a promising debut."

Biographical and Critical Sources

PERIODICALS

Booklist, November 15, 2004, Ilene Cooper, review of *The Guild of Geniuses,* p. 592.

Publishers Weekly, January 10, 2005, review of *The Guild of Geniuses,* p. 55; December 19, 2005, review of *Born to Drive,* p. 65; April 23, 2007, review of *The Secret Life of Walter Kitty,* p. 50.

School Library Journal, December, 2004, Blair Christolon, review of *The Guild of Geniuses,* p. 120; January, 2007, H.H. Henderson, review of *Water Balloon Doom,* p. 100; June, 2007, Elaine E. Knight, review of *The Society of Super Secret Heroes: The Great Cape Rescue,* p. 123; July, 2007, Susan Scheps, review of *The Secret Life of Walter Kitty,* p. 77.

ONLINE

Dan Santat Home Page, http://www.dantat.com (February 15, 2008).

*   *   *

SCANNEL, John Vernon
See SCANNELL, Vernon

*   *   *

SCANNELL, Vernon 1922-2007
(John Vernon Scannel)

OBITUARY NOTICE—

See index for *SATA* sketch: Born January 23, 1922, in Spilsby, Lincolnshire, England; died November 16, 2007. Poet, novelist, critic, children's author, and memoirist. Scannell spent much of his life haunted by images of war. Memories of the horrors he witnessed during World War II reportedly inspired him to desert the British Army twice, once in Tunisia (for which he was imprisoned) and again after his experiences in Normandy (for which he was briefly remanded to a mental hospital). His wartime experiences also inspired some of his best poetry, including "Walking Wounded," which some critics regard as one of the most impressive poems to emerge from that war. Scannell was a prolific poet, publishing thirty or more collections in his long life, many of them for children. He wrote steadfastly into his eighties, almost to the moment of his death. Scannell's poems have been described as more anecdotal than abstract, and critics have commended his straightforward language and clarity of purpose. Not all of his writing concerned war and other melancholy themes. He also commented on love, marriage, fatherhood, aging, and the commonplace events of daily living, but some critics noted that elements of doubt or gloom often appear, at least fleetingly, even in these poems. Scannell worked primarily as a poet, with occasional forays into broadcasting and criticism. Not surprisingly, it was his poetry that earned him the greatest recognition, including a Heinemann Award in 1960 from the Royal Society of Literature for *The Masks of Love,* and the prestigious Cholmondeley Poetry Prize in 1974 from the British Society of Authors for *The Winter Man: New Poems.* One of his last published collections was *Of Love and War: New and Selected Poems* (2002). In addition to three volumes of memoirs, Scannell also wrote the reportedly autobiographical novels *Ring of Truth* (1983) and *Argument of Kings* (1987).

Dan Santat creates the artwork that brings to life Barbara Jean Hicks's entertaining story in **The Secret Life of Walter Kitty.** (Illustration copyright © 2007 by Dan Santat. All rights reserved. Used by permission of Alfred A. Knopf, an imprint of Random House Children's Books, a division of Random House, Inc.)

OBITUARIES AND OTHER SOURCES:

BOOKS

Contemporary Poets, 7th edition, St. James Press (Detroit, MI), 2001.
Scannell, Vernon, *The Tiger and the Rose: An Autobiography,* Hamish Hamilton (London, England), 1971.
Scannell, Vernon, *A Proper Gentleman,* Robson Books (London, England), 1977.
Scannell, Vernon, *Drums of Morning: Growing up in the Thirties,* Robson Books (London, England), 1992.
St. James Guide to Children's Writers, 5th edition, St. James Press (Detroit, MI), 1999.

PERIODICALS

Times (London, England), November 20, 2007, p. 65.

*   *   *

SHEA, Bob

Personal
Male.

Addresses
E-mail—newsocks@bobshea.com.

Career
Author, illustrator, and graphic artist.

Writings

New Socks, Little, Brown (New York, NY), 2007.

New Socks was adapted as an animated film with voiceover by Shea.

Biographical and Critical Sources

PERIODICALS

Kirkus Reviews, March 1, 2007, review of *New Socks,* p. 231.
Publishers Weekly, March 5, 2007, review of *New Socks,* p. 59.
School Library Journal, April, 2007, Joy Fleischhacker, review of *New Socks,* p. 116.

ONLINE

Bob Shea Home Page, http://www.bobshea.com (March 5, 2008).*

SOLOMON, Heather M.

Personal
Married; children: Kelen (daughter), one son. *Education:* Brigham Young University, B.A. (illustration)/ B.S. (molecular biology), 1999.

Addresses
Home—Albuquerque, NM. *Agent*—Meryl Jones, Craven Designs, 1202 Lexington Ave., Box 242, New York, NY 10028.

Career
Illustrator. *Exhibitions:* Work included in Society of Illustrators Original Art Show, and exhibited at Albuquerque Children's Museum, Albuquerque, NM.

Awards, Honors
Horn Book Honor designation, and Charlotte Zolotow Award, both 2002, both for *Clever Beatrice* by Margaret Willey.

Illustrator
Margaret Willey, *Clever Beatrice: An Upper Peninsula Conte,* Atheneum (New York, NY), 2001.
Margaret Willey, *Clever Beatrice and the Best Little Pony,* Atheneum (New York, NY), 2004.
Sarah Weeks, *If I Were a Lion,* Atheneum (New York, NY), 2004.
Janice M. Del Negro, reteller, *Willa and the Wind,* Marshall Cavendish (New York, NY), 2005.
Kate Coombs, *The Secret-Keeper,* Atheneum (New York, NY), 2006.
Margaret Willey, *A Clever Beatrice Christmas,* Atheneum (New York, NY), 2006.
Margaret Willey, *Three Bears and Goldilocks,* Atheneum (New York, NY), 2008.

Sidelights
Although Heather M. Solomon focused much of her college study on molecular biology, her love of art eventually won out. Doing the extra coursework necessary to achieve a double major, she ultimately pursued the illustration career that has rewarded her with both critical acclaim and several rewards for her work. Describing Solomon's multi-media art, Carolyn Phelan wrote in her *Booklist* review of *A Clever Beatrice Christmas* that the artist incorporates "acrylic and oil painting with fluid watercolors and collage elements," injecting "unexpected textures" into her "appealing" art.

Solomon's first illustration project was creating art for Margaret Willey's *Clever Beatrice: An Upper Peninsula Conte.* Based on a folktale hailing from the French-trapper culture of northern Michigan, the tale focuses on a quick-thinking young girl who, to help her poor family, outsmarts a giant and acquires his stores of gold. Willey's spunky and clever heroine returns in *Clever Beatrice and the Best Little Pony* and *A Clever Beatrice Christmas,* both which feature Solomon's watercolor and collage art. Praising Solomon's "impressive debut," a *Publishers Weekly* contributor noted that the detailed art in *Clever Beatrice* brings to life "a world in which realism blends with fantasy images to magical effect." In *Horn Book,* Martha V. Parravano wrote that the book's "remarkable" illustrations "have unusual texture and depth," and bring to life Willey's colorful characters. In portraying the French-Canadian holiday traditions at the heart of *A Clever Beatrice Christmas,* Solomon creates "homey, convivial illustrations" that feature highlights of rich reds and purples, Parravano noted, while in *Clever Beatrice and the Best Little Pony* Solomon's "art is as vivid as ever."

Other books featuring artwork by Solomon include the award-winning picture book *If I Were a Lion,* featuring a rhyming text by Sarah Weeks. In this gently amusing story, in which a toddler sitting in a time-out-chair imagines the bad behavior of a menagerie of wild creatures, Solomon creates what a *Publishers Weekly* critic described as "trippy, beguiling" collages done in shades of aqua, pink, and light purple, in which "bold gouaches incorporate computer-altered snips of animal fur and scales." The art features "meticulous precision and ratchets up the sense of chaos with dizzying perspectives," according to *Booklist* critic Jennifer Mattson, while Laurie Edwards wrote in *School Library Journal* that Solomon reflects the humor in Weeks's text by creating a "cartoonlike" child character with "oversized features" and setting her within a background rendered "with a painterly touch just shy of realistic."

Willa and the Wind, Janice M. Del Negro's retelling of a story about a blustery old North Wind who helps a young girl keep her magic gifts from an unscrupulous innkeeper, features what *School Library Journal* contributor Kathie Meizner described as "big-boned, big-eyed elongated" characters imbued by Solomon with "a delicious energy" that is in keeping with the animated story. The artist's work in bringing to life Kate Coombs' *The Secret-Keeper,* a magical tale about a woman who carries the burden of many secrets, "is buoyed by Solomon's gorgeous illustrations," according to *Booklist* contributor Abby Nolan. Praising the artwork as "an intriguing blend of paint and collage that exude[s] texture and depth," Kristen Cutler deemed *The Secret-Keeper* "an uplifting modern fairy tale" in her *School Library Journal* review.

Biographical and Critical Sources

PERIODICALS

Booklist, March 15, 2004, Jennifer Mattson, review of *If I Were a Lion,* p. 1311; September 1, 2005, Shelle Rosenfeld, review of *Willa and the Wind,* p. 143; June 1, 2006, Abby Nolan, review of *The Secret-Keeper,* p. 80; October 15, 2006, Carolyn Phelan, review of *A Clever Beatrice Christmas,* p. 55.

Horn Book, November-December, 2001, Martha V. Parravano, review of *Clever Beatrice: An Upper Peninsula Conte,* p. 763; September-October, 2004, Martha V. Parravano, review of *Clever Beatrice and the Best Little Pony,* p. 577; November-December, 2006, Martha V. Parravano, review of *A Clever Beatrice Christmas,* p. 694.

Kirkus Reviews, September 1, 2001, review of *Clever Beatrice,* p. 1303; February 1, 2004, review of *If I Were a Lion,* p. 139; August 1, 2004, review of *Clever Beatrice and the Best Little Pony,* p. 750; August 15, 2005, review of *Willa and the Wind,* p. 912; June 1, 2006, review of *The Secret-Keeper,* p. 570; November 1, 2006, review of *A Clever Beatrice Christmas,* p. 1135.

Publishers Weekly, July 30, 2001, review of *Clever Beatrice,* p. 84; December 24, 2001, Shannon Maughan, "Flying Starts," p. 30; February 9, 2004, review of *If I Were a Lion,* p. 79; November 7, 2005, review of *Willa and the Wind,* p. 73; July 10, 2006, review of *The Secret-Keeper,* p. 81.

School Library Journal, April, 2004, Laurie Edwards, review of *If I Were a Lion,* p. 126; November, 2004, Linda M. Kenton, review of *Clever Beatrice and the Best Little Pony,* p. 132; December, 2005, Kathie Meizner, review of *Willa and the Wind,* p. 110; July, 2006, Kirsten Cutler, review of *The Secret-Keeper,* p. 70; October, 2006, Lisa Falk, review of *A Clever Beatrice Christmas,* p. 101.

ONLINE

Directory of Illustration Web site, http://www.directory ofillustration.com/ (March 28, 2008), "Heather Solomon."*

*   *   *

STEAD, Rebecca 1968(?)-

Personal

Born c. 1968, in New York, NY; married; children: two sons. *Education:* Vassar College, bachelor's degree, 1989; New York University, J.D., 1994.

Addresses

E-mail—rebecca@firstlightbook.com; rebecca.stead@ gmail.com.

Career

Children's author. Formerly worked as an attorney and public defender.

Writings

First Light, Wendy Lamb Books (New York, NY), 2007.
You Are Here, Wendy Lamb Books (New York, NY), 2009.

Sidelights

Rebecca Stead, a former public defender, revisited her interest in writing while raising her two sons and produced the young-adult novel *First Light*. In addition to tapping current concerns about global climate change, the novel also engages children's love of fantasy and adventure and "rests on an intriguing premise" about a secret world, according to a *Publishers Weekly* contributor.

First Light focuses on twelve-year-old Peter, the son of a glaciologist whose focus is global warming. When he accompanies his parents to Greenland, where his father is studying the ice shield, Peter is excited about the potential for cold-weather adventures in an exotic location. He is also increasingly plagued by the same unusual headaches that trouble his genetic scientist mom. Then he meets Thea, a fourteen-year-old young woman who is the descendent of an Englishwoman who established a secret commune called Gracehope, located deep within the Greenland icecap. Thea is Grace's last direct female descendent, and she comes to believe that it is time for her community to rejoin the rest of mankind. She meets Peter just as she reaches Earth's surface and sees the sun for the first time. As Stead's story unfolds, Peter and Thea discover a surprising bond as they grapple with the secrets of past generations. The *Publishers Weekly* critic called it "a testament to [Stead's] . . . storytelling" that this alternate world and the story's adventurous young protagonists "are both credible and absorbing." "Gracehope itself is sketched with sure strokes, its icy setting and its matriarchal social structure fresh and believable," wrote Vicky Smith in her *Horn Book* review of *First Light*. *School Library Journal* contributor Connie Tyrrell Burns deemed the novel "an exciting, engaging mix of science fiction, mystery, and adventure." While Jennifer Hubert noted several "gaps in Gracehope's invented mythology," her *Booklist* review dubbed *First Light* a "solid-well-meaning fantasy," and a *Kirkus Reviews* critic described Stead's novel as a "compelling contemporary ice-age mystery."

Biographical and Critical Sources

PERIODICALS

Booklist, April 15, 2007, Jennifer Hubert, review of *First Light,* p. 45.
Bulletin of the Center for Children's Books, September, 2007, April Spisak, review of *First Light,* p. 56.
Horn Book, July-August, 2007, Vicky Smith, review of *First Light,* p. 405.
Kirkus Reviews, June 1, 2007, review of *First Light.*
Publishers Weekly, June 18, 2007, review of *First Light,* p. 54.
School Library Journal, August, 2007, Connie Tyrrell Burns, review of *First Light,* p. 126.
Voice of Youth Advocates, June, 2007, Ruth Cox Clark, review of *First Light,* p. 168.

ONLINE

Class of 2k7 Web site, http://classof2k7.com/ (March 18, 2008), "Rebecca Stead."
First Light Web site, http://www.firstlightbook.com (March 18, 2008).
Random House Web site, http://www.randomhouse.com/ (March 28, 2008), "Rebecca Stead."

*　　*　　*

SWINBURNE, Stephen R. 1952-

Personal

Born November 8, 1952, in London, England; son of William Walter and Lillian Swinburne; married May 19, 1984; wife's name Heather; children: Hayley, Devon. *Education:* Castleton State College, B.A. *Hobbies and other interests:* Gardening, bird watching, canoeing.

Cover of Rebecca Stead's middle-grade novel **First Light,** *which combines fantasy with environmental science.* (Jacket illustration copyright © 2007 by Ericka O'Rourke; image of ring © by Andy Potts. All rights reserved. Used by permission of Wendy Lamb Books, an imprint of Random House Children's Books, a division of Random House, Inc.)

Addresses

Home and office—P.O. Box 2005, Main St., South Londonderry, VT 05155. *E-mail*—swinny@sover.net.

Career

Writer, photographer, and naturalist. Has also worked as a park ranger for National Park Service.

Member

Society of Children's Book Writers and Illustrators, Children's Book Insider.

Writings

AND PHOTOGRAPHER, UNLESS OTHERWISE NOTED

Guide to Cumberland Island National Seashore, illustrated by Casey French Alexander, Eastern Acorn Press (New York, NY), 1984.

Swallows in the Birdhouse, illustrated by Robin Brickman, Millbrook Press (Brookfield, CT), 1996.

Water for One, Water for Everyone: A Counting Book of African Animals, illustrated by Melinda Levine, Millbrook Press (Brookfield, CT), 1998.

Moon in Bear's Eyes, illustrated by Crista Forest, Millbrook Press (Brookfield, CT), 1998.

Lots and Lots of Zebra Stripes: Patterns in Nature, Boyds Mills Press (Honesdale, PA), 1998.

In Good Hands: Behind the Scenes at a Center for Orphaned and Injured Birds, Sierra Club Books for Children (San Francisco, CA), 1998.

Coyote: North America's Dog, Boyds Mills Press (Honesdale, PA), 1999.

Safe, Warm, and Snug (poems), illustrated by José Aruego and Ariane Dewey, Harcourt (San Diego, CA), 1999.

Once a Wolf: How Wildlife Biologists Fought to Bring Back the Gray Wolf ("Scientists in the Field" series), photographs by Jim Brandenburg, Houghton Mifflin (Boston, MA), 1999.

Guess Whose Shadow?, Boyds Mills Press (Honesdale, PA), 1999.

Unbeatable Beaks (poems), illustrated by Joan Paley, Henry Holt (New York, NY), 1999.

What's Opposite?, Boyds Mills Press (Honesdale, PA), 2000.

What's a Pair? What's a Dozen?, Boyds Mills Press (Honesdale, PA), 2001.

Stephen R. Swinburne's photographs, taken during his many travels around the world, are featured in picture books such as Guess Whose Shadow?
(Photograph copyright © 1999 by Stephen R. Swinburne. Reproduced by permission.)

Bobcat: North America's Cat, Boyds Mills Press (Honesdale, PA), 2001.

Boxing Rabbits, Bellowing Alligators, and Other Animal Showoffs, Millbrook Press (Brookfield, CT), 2002.

Go, Go, Go!: Kids on the Move, Boyds Mills Press (Honesdale, PA), 2002.

What Color Is Nature?, Boyds Mills Press (Honesdale, PA), 2002.

The Woods Scientist ("Scientists in the Field" series), photographs by Susan C. Moore, Houghton Mifflin (Boston, MA), 2003.

Black Bear: North America's Bear, Boyds Mills Press (Honesdale, PA), 2003.

Turtle Tide: The Way of Sea Turtles, illustrated by Bruce Hiscock, Boyds Mills Press (Honesdale, PA), 2005.

Saving Manatees, Boyds Mills Press (Honesdale, PA), 2006.

Wings of Light: The Migration of the Yellow Butterfly, illustrated by Bruce Hiscock, Boyds Mills Press (Honesdale, PA), 2006.

Sidelights

Writer, photographer, and naturalist Stephen R. Swinburne shares his love of nature in his many books for children. The adventures to be experienced within the pages of his books include stalking elusive bobcats through their range in North America, learning about the innovative ways animals protect their offspring, watching a field biologist studying animals in the wild, and witnessing a lumbering sea turtle's laborious journey to land and her efforts to battle predators in order to hatch at least one of her hundred eggs. Swinburne's books often feature his imaginative photographs, which are geared to help very young children visualize concepts such as "a pair," "a dozen," "shadows," and "opposites." In a *Booklist* review of Swinburne's *The Woods Scientist,* Gillian Engberg described his writing as "immediate, clear, and filled with moment-by-moment observations," and Margaret Bush wrote in her *School Library Journal* review that Swinburne's books "offer many invitations for personal involvement in studying wildlife."

Swallows in the Birdhouse, one of Swinburne's early picture books, finds a brother and sister building a birdhouse. Through the text, readers then explore what happens when a pair of tree swallows finds the birdhouse, builds a nest, and successfully hatches a brood of chicks. At the end of the book, the swallows amass in great numbers for a communal flight. In *Booklist,* Lauren Peterson commended *Swallows in the Birdhouse* for its "lovely descriptive language" and for including helpful facts on swallow biology and birdhouse building.

In his nonfiction works, Swinburne's focus is primarily on those creatures native to North America, and in *Moon in Bear's Eyes* and *Black Bear: North America's Bear* he introduces readers to the grizzly bear common to the American West and the more-common black bear

Swinburne works with nature photographer Jim Brandenburg in several of his nonfiction titles, among them Once a Wolf. (Photograph copyright © 1999 by Jim Brandenburg. Reprinted by permission of Houghton Mifflin Harcourt Publishing Company. All rights reserved.)

respectively. April Judge wrote in *Booklist* that *Moon in Bear's Eyes* "reads like an adventure story" in its focus on a family of grizzlies while also covering the essential biology and ecology of the species. *Black Bear* introduces a species that is finding its way into suburban backyards as its numbers increase and the Eastern forests return. While presenting an overview of the species and teaching readers to spot bear signs, Swinburne also "counters some common misconceptions" and shares "his own brief encounters with black bears," according to *Booklist* critic John Peters. In *School Library Journal,* Nancy Call praised the author's color photographs and "lively text," adding that *Black Bear* provides readers with an "intriguing introduction to these fascinating animals.

In the course of his travels Swinburne frequently works alongside wildlife biologists, both professional and amateur. In *In Good Hands: Behind the Scenes at a Center for Orphaned and Injured Birds* he introduces sixteen-year-old Hannah, a volunteer who is nursing an injured baby owl until it can be released into the wild. Sally Margolis, reviewing the book for *School Library Journal,* cited the "immediacy" imparted by Hannah's personal interactions with the owl and with human visitors to the shelter. In *Booklist,* Kathleen Squires wrote that the "bittersweet" ending "will tug on the heartstrings."

Swinburne has contributed several books to Houghton Mifflin's respected "Scientists in the Field" series, which is geared for older readers. In *The Woods Scientist,* he profiles the work of Susan C. Morse, a fourth-generation wildlife biologist and forester who lives and works in Vermont. Illustrated with Morse's own photographs, the book focuses on the many creatures that make their home in the boreal forests of the New England region: bears, deer, bobcats, raccoons, foxes, deer, among many others. In his narrative, Swinburne "brings young readers close to the excitement of scientific discovery," according to Engberg in *Booklist.*

Also part of the "Scientist in the Field" series, *Once a Wolf: How Wildlife Biologists Fought to Bring Back the Gray Wolf* pairs Swinburne's text with photographs by noted nature photographer Jim Brandenburg. Donna Beales, writing in *Booklist,* declared that the work "packs a lot of information" about a species that has been reviled by the farmers and ranchers invading its habitat while also demonstrating a keen intelligence. *Once a Wolf* focuses in particular on the efforts to reintroduce gray wolves to Yellowstone National Park and its environs, despite the objections of neighboring farmers and ranchers. Swinburne presents both sides of the controversy: the wolves' crucial role in the region's ecology as well as the economic impact of this predator on area ranches. A *Horn Book* critic deemed *Once a Wolf* "bracingly journalistic," and Ruth S. Vose in *School Library Journal* praised "the excitement of science in action" to be found in its pages.

Bears, coyotes, and bobcats are among the illusive large predators prowling the North America wilderness. In *Bobcat: North America's Cat,* Swinburne goes in search of the beautiful predator, accompanied by professional trackers as well as by a class of curious sixth graders. Interspersing the account of this trek, he shares with readers information regarding the bobcat's survival skills and its passion for privacy. In *School Library Journal,* Margaret Bush wrote that Swinburne's personal anecdotes "lend an inviting immediacy" to the narrative. *Booklist* contributor Ilene Cooper predicted that *Bobcat* will encourage readers to contemplate "the relationship between animals and their prey." Swinburne takes a similar approach in *Saving Manatees,* as he joins a class of fourth graders on a ranger-guided visit to a Florida wildlife refuge known for its giant manatee population. The author's "enthusiastic descriptions of his experiences with the animals are contagious and will draw children right into the subject," predicted Engberg of the large-format work.

Realizing the opportunities Nature provides for teaching useful concepts, Swinburne has created several well-received picture books that feature his original full-color photographs. *Lots and Lots of Zebra Stripes: Patterns in Nature* uses living examples to teach preschoolers about pattern, while the questions he poses in *What's Opposite?, What's a Pair? What's a Dozen?,* and *What Color Is Nature?* are answered in vivid images of objects that young children will recognize, even if they have never seen them so vividly presented. Lauren Peterson, writing in *Booklist,* called *Lots and Lots of Zebra Stripes* a "gorgeous photo-essay," and *Booklist* correspondent Carolyn Phelan dubbed *What's Opposite?* a "handsome book of photographs." In *School Library Journal* Kristina Aaronson described *What's a Pair? What's a Dozen?* as a good introduction to mathematical concepts, as well as a "well-designed picture book" featuring "clear, engaging photographs." *What*

Swinburne collaborates with noted illustrators José Aruego and Ariane Dewey in the nature-centered picture book **Safe, Warm, and Snug.** (Illustration copyright © 1999 by José Aruego and Ariane Dewey. In the U.S. reproduced by permission of Harcourt Inc. In the U.K., used by permission of the illustrators' agent, Sheldon Fogelman Agency, Inc. All rights reserved.)

Swinburne's skill as a photographer is one of the attractions of his evocative children's book **Coyote: North American's Dog.** (Photograph copyright © 1999 by Stephen R. Swinburne and photographers credited. All rights reserved. Reproduced by permission.)

Color Is Nature? drew additional praise from Phelan, the critic describing Swinburne's "jewel-bright photos" as "clear and well composed."

Featuring a theme designed to appeal to younger children, Swinburne's *Safe, Warm, and Snug* uses rhyming verses to offer glimpses into the many ways that animals protect their babies. From toads to penguins to marsupials, the book covers some of the most bizarre parental behavior on the planet. In her *School Library Journal* review of the work, Marian Drabkin called *Safe, Warm, and Snug* "a celebration of the animal world" that offers the added attraction of giving children "reassurance that parents are protectors."

The natural world is not always a kind world, and Swinburne illustrates this fact in several of his books for slightly older children. *Turtle Tide: The Ways of Sea Turtles* is one of several collaborations between Swinburne and watercolor artist Bruce Hiscock. In this pic-

ture book, author and illustrator follow a large Loggerhead turtle as she clambers from the Atlantic Ocean onto a sandy beach and digs the nest in which she lays the many eggs that, after her departure, will be vulnerable to gulls, raccoons, crabs, and sand sharks as they mature. Noting that the sea turtle is one of the oldest creatures on Earth, Bush wrote in *Horn Book* that the "spare prose and fine paintings" in *Turtle Tide* reveal the drama of Nature, as "animal encounters . . . reduce the eggs and hatchlings to one lone survivor."

Praised by Phelan as "a well-written and beautifully illustrated picture book," *Wings of Light: The Migration of the Yellow Butterfly* again pair the talents of Swinburne and Hiscock, this time as they follow a flock of cloudless sulfur butterflies on its daunting one-way migration from Mexico's Yucatan rain forest north along the east coast of North America to its destination in northern New England. Noting the book's ability to inspire, a *Kirkus Reviews* writer commented of *Wings of*

Light that "young readers will come away with a sense of wonder and admiration for the frail creature's remarkable flight."

Biographical and Critical Sources

PERIODICALS

Booklist, June 1, 1996, Lauren Peterson, review of *Swallows in the Birdhouse,* p. 1729; May 1, 1998, April Judge, review of *Moon in Bear's Eyes,* p. 1520; July, 1998, Kathleen Squires, review of *In Good Hands: Behind the Scenes at a Center for Orphaned and Injured Birds,* p. 1880; September 15, 1998, Lauren Peterson, review of *Lots and Lots of Zebra Stripes: Patterns in Nature,* p. 233; March 1, 1999, Stephanie Zvirin, review of *Once a Wolf: How Wildlife Biologists Fought to Bring Back the Gray Wolf,* p. 1211; June 1, 1999, Kay Weisman, review of *Safe, Warm, and Snug,* p. 1835; October 15, 1999, Donna Beales, review of *Coyote: North America's Dog,* p. 440; March 15, 2000, Shelle Rosenfeld, review of *What's a Pair? What's a Dozen?,* p. 1384; September 1, 2000, Carolyn Phelan, review of *What's Opposite?,* p. 120; April 1, 2001, Ilene Cooper, review of *Bobcat: North America's Cat,* p. 1468; June 1, 2002, Carolyn Phelan, review of *What Color Is Nature?,* p. 1732; March 15, 2003, Gillian Engberg, review of *The Woods Scientist,* p. 1326; January 1, 2004, John Peters, review of *Black Bear: North America's Bear,* p. 851; April 1, 2005, John Peters, review of *Turtle Tide: The Ways of Sea Turtles,* p. 1362; April 1, 2006, Carolyn Phelan, review of *Wings of Light: The Migration of the Yellow Butterfly,* p. 46; September 1, 2006, Gillian Engberg, review of *Saving Manatees,* p. 123.

Horn Book, July, 1999, review of *Once a Wolf,* p. 487; May-June, 2005, Margaret A. Bush, review of *Turtle Tide,* p. 351.

Kirkus Reviews, September 1, 2003, review of *North America's Bear,* p. 1131; March 15, 2005, review of *Turtle Tide,* p. 358; April 1, 2006, review of *Wings of Light,* p. 358; September 15, 2006, review of *Saving Manatees,* p. 969.

Publishers Weekly, May 3, 1999, review of *Safe, Warm, and Snug,* p. 75; April 8, 2002, review of *Safe, Warm, and Snug,* p. 230.

School Library Journal, June, 1996, Helen Rosenberg, review of *Swallows in the Birdhouse,* p. 118; August, 1998, Ruth S. Vose, review of *In Good Hands,* p. 184; January, 1999, Arwen Marshall, review of *Lots and Lots of Zebra Stripes,* p. 122; May, 1999, Ruth S. Vose, review of *Once a Wolf,* p. 140; June, 1999, Marian Drabkin, review of *Safe, Warm, and Snug,* p. 122; April, 2000, Kristina Aaronson, review of *What's a Pair? What's a Dozen?,* p. 126; October, 2000, Lucinda Snyder Whitehurst, review of *What's Opposite?,* p. 154; August, 2001, Margaret Bush, review of *Bobcat,* p. 205; April, 2003, Margaret Bush, review of *The Woods Scientist,* p. 193; August, 2003, Kathy Piehl, review of *Once a Wolf,* p. 117; November, 2003, Nancy Call, review of *Black Bear,* p. 132; September, 2004, Janet Dawson Hamilton, review of *What's a Pair? What's a Dozen?,* p. 59; March, 2005, Patricia Manning, review of *Turtle Tide,* p. 204; May, 2006, Margaret Bush, review of *Wings of Light,* p. 118; November, 2006, Christine Markley, review of *Saving Manatees,* p. 165.

ONLINE

Stephen R. Swinburne Home Page, http://www.steveswinburne.com (March 3, 2008).*

T

TINKHAM, Kelly A.

Personal
Born in MI; married Mark Tinkham, May, 1987; children: Justin, Jared. *Education:* Valley Forge Christian College, degree (missions); studied writing at Institute of Children's Literature. *Religion:* Christian. *Hobbies and other interests:* Collecting cobalt Depression glass, reading children's books, spending time with family and friends.

Addresses
Home—Newaygo, MI. *E-mail*—kellyatinkham@att.net.

Career
Children's author and librarian. Newaygo Area District Library, Newaygo, MI, librarian. Presenter at schools and libraries.

Member
Society of Children's Book Writers and Illustrators.

Awards, Honors
Notable Social Studies Trade Book for Young People, National Council for the Social Studies/Children's Book Council, Bank Street College Best Book designation, and Cooperative Children's Book Center Choice, all 2008, all for *Hair for Mama*.

Writings

Hair for Mama, illustrated by Amy June Bates, Dial Books for Young Readers (New York, NY), 2007.

Sidelights
Kelly A. Tinkham is a children's author whose favorite place to spend time is the local library where she works as a librarian. "I have always loved reading books," she

Kelly A. Tinkham (Photo courtesy of Kelly A. Tinkham.)

told *SATA*. "To step into that imaginary world with the main characters and to see the world through their eyes is cool! Some of my favorite books are *The Mouse and the Motorcycle, Blue Willow,* and *Pippi Longstocking.* As an author, I love to create the magical world for my readers to dive into and enjoy."

Hair for Mama, Tinkham's first book for young readers, has been praised by reviewers for addressing a difficult subject with warmth and sensitivity. "The idea for *Hair for Mama* came from my son, Justin," the author

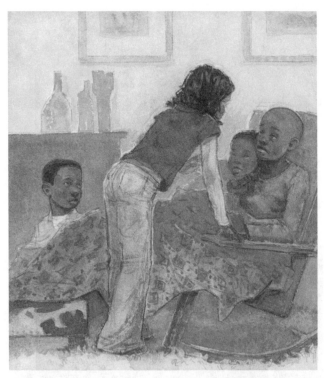

Tinkham depicts a strong, supportive family in Hair for Mama, *a picture book featuring illustrations by Amy June Bates.* (Illustration copyright © 2007 by Amy June Bates. All rights reserved. Reproduced by permission of Dial Books for Young Readers, a division of Penguin Young Readers Group.)

explained. "When I was explaining to him that I would lose my hair from chemotherapy, he promised to give me his hair. Eventually he and the other important guys in my life all shaved their heads for me! It is my hope that *Hair for Mama* will help other families experiencing cancer to open the lines of communication and pull together to face the future in hope."

In *Hair for Mama* readers meet Marcus Carter, an eight-year-old boy whose mother has cancer. Because she is being treated through chemotherapy, Marcus's mama loses her hair. When October comes and the family looks forward to taking their annual family photograph to share with friends, Mama feels self-conscious and does not want to be included in the picture. At first Markus tries to help his mother by finding her a wig, but when this doesn't work he makes a personal sacrifice that helps everyone in the Carter family recognize how important it is to participate in the family picture and preserve the tradition it represents. Praising the watercolor-and-pencil illustrations contributed by artist Amy June Bates for "matching the depth of emotions perfectly," a *Kirkus Reviews* writer described *Hair for Mama* as "a realistic look at a strong family facing cancer." Judith Constantinides, reviewing Tinkham's story in *School Library Journal,* noted that the "beautifully written" text provides readers with "a simple, sensitive, and articulate look at an illness through the eyes of a [loving] child," while in *Booklist* GraceAnne A. De-Candido observed that, while "straightforward and sweet," *Hair for Mama* is also "heart-wrenching" in its realism and lack of sentimentality.

Tinkham's advice for anyone who wants to become a writer: "Read many good books and try to see how the writers drew you into their stories; write about what you are interested in because your enthusiasm will shine; don't be afraid to revise your stories—the greatest part of writing is revising!"

Biographical and Critical Sources

PERIODICALS

Booklist, April 1, 2007, GraceAnne A. DeCandido, review of *Hair for Mama,* p. 61.
Horn Book, July-August, 2007, Robin Smith, review of *Hair for Mama,* p. 387.
Kirkus Reviews, April 1, 2007, review of *Hair for Mama.*
School Library Journal, July, 2007, Judith Constantinides, review of *Hair for Mama,* p. 86.

ONLINE

Kelly A. Tinkham Home Page, http://www.kellyatinkham.com (March 15, 2008).

*   *   *

TONG, Paul

Personal
Male.

Addresses
Home—Berkeley, CA. *E-mail*—ptong@att.net.

Career
Illustrator.

Writings

*Cynthia Cotten, *Some Babies Sleep,* Philomel Books (New York, NY), 2007.
*Stephen Krensky, adaptor, *Pecos Bill,* Millbrook Press (Minneapolis, MN), 2007.

Biographical and Critical Sources

PERIODICALS

Kirkus Reviews, December 1, 2006, review of *Some Babies Sleep,* p. 1218.

Paul Tong Home Page, http://www.paultong.com (March 15, 2008).*

*   *   *

TRIPP, Jenny

Personal

Female.

Addresses

Home—Essex, CT.

Career

Children's author, screenwriter, and librarian. Essex Library, Essex, CT, member of staff.

Writings

FOR CHILDREN

The Man Who Was Left for Dead, illustrated by Charles Shaw, Raintree Publishers (Milwaukee, WI), 1980.
One Was Left Alive, illustrated by John Burgoyne, Raintree Publishers (Milwaukee, WI), 1980.
Pete and Fremont, illustrated by John Manders, Harcourt (Orlando, FL), 2007.
Pete's Disappearing Act, illustrated by John Manders, Harcourt (Orlando, FL), 2008.

SCREENPLAYS

The Online Adventures of Ozzie the Elf (television film), 1997.
'Twas the Night (television film), 2001.
Here Comes Peter Cottontail, 2005.

Contributor to Disney-produced screenplays, including *The Prince and the Pauper,* 1990, and *The Lion King,* 1994. Contributor to periodicals, including *Los Angeles Times, Family Life,* and *FamilyFun.*

Sidelights

Jenny Tripp turned to writing books for children after working for several years working in film, where her credits include work on Disney's animated *The Prince and the Pauper* and *The Lion King.* Illustrated by John Manders, Tripp tells an amusing story in *Pete and Fremont.* In the story, Pete is an elderly poodle who had been the star of a small traveling circus for several years. When he misses the mark and singes his tale during a jump through a flaming hoop, Pete gets recast as a canine cannonball by circus owner Moliere. The poodle's hopes to return to the limelight look dim until a friendship with Fremont the wild grizzly bear results in a new show-stopping act and an act of kindness. According to *School Library Journal* contributor Adrienne Furness, "Tripp's strength" in *Pete and Fremont* comes from her ability to "keep . . . the plot moving along while revealing interesting behind-the-scenes details of circus life." In *Booklist,* Todd Morning predicted that "young readers will enjoy this story of a circus in which the animals . . . actually run the show." Furness also had praise for Manders' "freewheeling" cartoon illustrations, while a *Kirkus Reviews* writer called Tripp's story a "heartwarming tale of interspecies bonding."

Other books by Tripp include two works of nonfiction. Based on a true story, *The Man Who Was Left for Dead* takes place in the early 1800s and focuses on Hugh Glass, who survived an attack by a grizzly bear during a trek into the American frontier during which he was abandoned by his companions. A similar tale of survival is captured by Tripp in *One Was Left Alive,* which described the ordeal faced by seventeen-year-old Juliane Koepcke as the sole survivor of a commercial plane crash in the Peruvian jungle in December of 1971.

In cartoon art, illustrator John Manders brings to life Jenny Tripp's entertaining, circus-themed story in **Pete and Fremont.** (Illustration copyright © 2007 by John Manders. Reproduced by permission of Houghton Mifflin Harcourt Publishing Company. This material may not be reproduced in any form or by any means without the prior written permission of the publisher.)

Biographical and Critical Sources

PERIODICALS

Booklist, March 15, 2007, Todd Morning, review of *Pete and Fremont,* p. 49.
Kirkus Reviews, April 1, 2007, review of *Pete and Fremont.*
School Library Journal, June, 2007, Adrienne Furness, review of *Pete and Fremont,* p. 126.*

* * *

TURNER, Ann 1945-
(Ann Warren Turner)

Personal

Born December 10, 1945, in Northampton, MA; daughter of Richard (a printer) and Marion (an artist) Warren; married Richard E. Turner, June 3, 1967; children: Benjamin, Charlotte. *Education:* Bates College, B.A., 1967; attended Oxford University, received certificate of study; University of Massachusetts, M.A.T., 1968. *Politics:* "Liberal Democrat." *Religion:* Protestant. *Hobbies and other interests:* Gardening, tennis, cooking, sailing, reading.

Addresses

Home and office—Williamsburg, MA. *Agent*—Marilyn E. Marlow, Curtis Brown Ltd., 10 Astor Place, New York, NY 10003. *E-mail*—annwturner@aol.com.

Career

Author and educator. High school English teacher in Great Barrington, MA, 1968-69; writer, 1971—; Antioch University, Northampton, MA, assistant director, 1978-80. Affiliated with Friends of Meekins Library, 1986-87; instructor of writing at University of Massachusetts.

Member

Society of Children's Book Writers and Illustrators.

Awards, Honors

First prize, *Atlantic Monthly* college creative writing contest, 1967; New York Academy of Sciences Honor Book citation, 1976, for *Vultures;* American Library Association (ALA) Notable Children's Book citations, 1980, for *A Hunter Comes Home,* and 1985, for *Dakota Dugout;* International Reading Association (IRA)/ Children's Book Council (CBC) Children's Choice, 1988, for *Nettie's Trip South;* National Council for the Social Studies (NCSS) Notable Book citations, 1989, for *Heron Street* and *Grasshopper Summer,* 1990, for *Through Moon and Stars and Night Skies,* 1991, for *Stars for Sarah,* and 2000, for *Abe Lincoln Remembers;*

Ann Turner (Photo by Ellen Augarten. Courtesy of the photographer.)

School Library Journal Best Books selection, 1991, for *Rosemary's Witch;* Pick of the List selection, American Booksellers Association (ABA), 1993, for *Katie's Trunk,* and 1996, for *Shaker Hearts;* Books for the Teen Age designation, New York Public Library, 1994, for *Grass Songs; Smithsonian* magazine Notable Books for Children designation, 1997, for *Finding Walter;* Best Books for Young Adults and Quick Picks for Reluctant Readers designations, Young Adult Library Service Association, both 1999, both for *A Lion's Hunger;* Willa Literary Award, children's/YA category, Women Writing the West, 2000, for *Red Flower Goes West;* Best Books for Young Adults selection, ALA, 2000, Book Sense 76 selection, ABA, 2000, and Young Adult Honor Book designation, Massachusetts Book Award, 2001, all for *Learning to Swim.*

Writings

FOR CHILDREN

Vultures (nonfiction), illustrated by Marion Gray Warren, McKay (New York, NY), 1976.
Houses for the Dead (nonfiction), McKay (New York, NY), 1976.
Rituals of Birth: From Prehistory to the Present (nonfiction) McKay (New York, NY), 1978.
A Hunter Comes Home (young-adult novel), Crown (New York, NY), 1980.
The Way Home (historical fiction), Crown (New York, NY), 1982.
Dakota Dugout (historical poem), illustrated by Ronald Himler, Macmillan (New York, NY), 1985.
Tickle a Pickle (poems), illustrated by Karen Ann Weinhaus, Macmillan (New York, NY), 1986.
Street Talk (poems), illustrated by Catherine Stock, Houghton, Mifflin (Boston, MA), 1986.
Third Girl from the Left (young-adult novel), Macmillan (New York, NY), 1986.
Nettie's Trip South (historical poem), illustrated by Ronald Himler, Macmillan (New York, NY), 1987.
Time of the Bison (fiction), illustrated by Beth Peck, Macmillan (New York, NY), 1987.
Grasshopper Summer (young-adult novel), Macmillan (New York, NY), 1989.

Hedgehog for Breakfast (picture book), illustrated by Lisa McCue, Macmillan (New York, NY), 1989.

Heron Street (picture book), illustrated by Lisa Desimini, Harper (New York, NY), 1989.

Through Moon and Stars and Night Skies (picture book), illustrated by James Graham Hale, Harper (New York, NY), 1990.

Stars for Sarah (picture book), illustrated by Mary Teichman, Harper (New York, NY), 1991.

Rosemary's Witch (fiction), Harper (New York, NY), 1991.

Rainflowers (picture book), illustrated by Robert J. Blake, HarperCollins (New York, NY), 1992.

Katie's Trunk, illustrated by Ron Himler, Macmillan (New York, NY), 1992.

Grass Songs: Poems, illustrated by Barry Moser, Harcourt (New York, NY), 1993.

Apple Valley Year, illustrated by Sandi Wickersham Resnick, Macmillan (New York, NY), 1993.

Swing Quilts (picture book), illustrated by Thomas B. Allen, Macmillan (New York, NY), 1994.

A Moon for Seasons (picture book), illustrated by Robert Noreika, Macmillan (New York, NY), 1994.

The Christmas House (poems), illustrated by Nancy Edwards Calder, HarperCollins (New York, NY), 1994.

Dust for Dinner (fiction), illustrated by Robert Barrett, HarperCollins (New York, NY), 1995.

One Brave Summer (novel), HarperCollins (New York, NY), 1995.

Elfsong (novel), Harcourt (New York, NY), 1995.

Mississippi Mud: Three Prairie Journals (historical poems), illustrated by Robert J. Blake, HarperCollins (New York, NY), 1997.

Shaker Hearts (picture book), illustrated by Wendell Minor, HarperCollins (New York, NY), 1997.

Finding Walter (novel), Harcourt (New York, NY), 1997.

Drummer Boy: Marching to the Civil War (historical picture book), illustrated by Mark Hess, HarperCollins (New York, NY), 1998.

Angel Hide and Seek (picture book), illustrated by Lois Ehlert, HarperCollins (New York, NY), 1998.

Let's Be Animals (picture book), illustrated by Rick Brown, HarperFestival (New York, NY), 1998.

Secrets from the Dollhouse (picture book), illustrated by Raúl Colon, HarperCollins (New York, NY), 1999.

A Lion's Hunger (poetry), Marshall Cavendish (New York, NY), 1999.

Red Flower Goes West (picture book), illustrated by Dennis Nolan, Hyperion (New York, NY), 1999.

The Girl Who Chased away Sorrow: The Diary of Sara Nita, a Navajo Girl, Scholastic (New York, NY), 1999.

What Did I Know of Freedom?, illustrated by Mark Hess, HarperCollins (New York, NY), 2000.

Learning to Swim: A Memoir (verse), Scholastic (New York, NY), 2000.

In the Heart (picture book), illustrated by Salley Mavor, HarperCollins (New York, NY), 2001.

Abe Lincoln Remembers (historical picture book), illustrated by Wendell Minor, HarperCollins (New York, NY), 2001.

Shaker Hearts, illustrated by Wendell Minor, David R. Godine (Boston, MA), 2002.

When Mr. Jefferson Came to Philadelphia: What I Learned of Freedom, 1776 (historical novel), HarperCollins (New York, NY), 2003.

Love Thy Neighbor: The Tory Diary of Prudence Emerson, Scholastic (New York, NY), 2003.

Pumpkin Cat (picture book), illustrated by Amy June Bates, Hyperion (New York, NY), 2004.

Maia of Thebes: 1463 B.C., Scholastic (New York, NY), 2005.

Hard Hit (young-adult novel), Scholastic (New York, NY), 2006.

Sitting Bull Remembers (historical picture book), illustrated by Wendell Minor, HarperCollins (New York, NY), 2007.

Sidelights

The books of Ann Turner reflect her wide-ranging interests as well as her talent; her treatment of historical material in fiction, nonfiction, and poetry for children and young adults has earned her a special reputation along with many awards. A versatile writer, Turner has penned works ranging from picture books such as *Pumpkin Cat, In the Heart,* and *Angel Hide and Seek* to middle-grade and young-adult novels such as *Hard Hit.* Often working in verse, Turner draws a variety of themes into her work, from U.S. Civil War history to a teen's first love to sexual abuse to the challenge of international adoption. "My upbringing influenced my writing," Turner once commented. "Possibly because my liberal family was somewhat 'different' from the New Englanders of our town, I grew up being interested in different people and cultures. Living in the country and having an artist for a mother gave me a certain way of seeing, an eye for beauty and interest in what others might think ugly or dull."

Turner's first book was a family collaboration: *Vultures* features illustrations by Turner's mother, artist Marion Gray Warren. The book, published in 1976, is a scientific yet accessible study of a species of bird that has gained a bad reputation. She continues in the nonfiction vein with *Houses for the Dead,* a book that employs fictional dialogues in detailing burial rites across cultures and through the centuries, and *Rituals of Birth: From Prehistory to the Present,* which examines the other end of the life continuum. Turner has more recently turned to another form of nonfiction—her own life—in *Learning to Swim: A Memoir,* which softens her recollections of being sexually abused at age six through the filter of free verse. The purpose of sharing her experiences is made plain at the book's end, as the author encourages readers not to be afraid of telling caring adults about similar experiences. Calling Turner's text "spare, direct, and . . . laced with strong, immediate feelings," John Peters wrote in *Booklist* that *Learning to Swim* is "a courageous, moving acknowledgment as well as a call to action for readers nursing secrets of their own."

Turner's first work of fiction, the young-adult novel *A Hunter Comes Home,* introduces Jonas, a fifteen-year-old Inuit who returns to his village after a year away at a boarding school. Jonas has had his fill of white culture; now, he wants to go hunting with his grandfather and learn the ways of the Inuit. Making the transition from modern to traditional does not come easily to the young man, however. In the novel, Turner "shows extraordinary sensitivity in revealing the feelings of schoolboys surrounded by a totally unfamiliar atmosphere," according to *Horn Book* contributor Virginia Haviland. By the end of the story, "Jonas has come to terms with himself by coming to terms with his imposing, demanding grandfather," concluded a *Kirkus Reviews* writer, the critic adding that Jonas's decision to "not . . . flatly reject . . . the new for the old" prevents *A Hunter Comes Home* "from being still another polemical exercise."

The theme of survival emerges in several of Turner's historical novels, among them *The Way Home, Grasshopper Summer, Third Girl from the Left, Maia of Thebes, The Girl Who Chased away Sorrow: The Diary of Sarah Nita, a Navajo Girl,* and *Love Thy Neighbor: The Tory Diary of Prudence Emerson,* the last two part of the "Dear America" series for middle-grade readers. In *The Way Home* Turner focuses on Anne, a teen with a cleft lip living in fourteenth-century England who is forced to flee from her village after publicly cursing a local tyrant. After hiding in a marsh and living off the land for a summer, Ann returns, only to find that everyone in her village has died from the Black Plague. A thirteen year old, the niece of a temple priest in ancient Egypt, risks her safety to tell the truth in *Maia of Thebes,* a middle-grade novel that is rich with information on everyday life in a fascinating place and time. According to a reviewer for the *Bulletin of the Center for Children's Books, The Way Home* features "vivid details . . . , good dialogue and adequate characterization, a focused development, and a strong sense of narrative," while *Booklist* reviewer Carolyn Phelan predicted that readers of *Maia of Thebes* "will want to follow" Turner's brave heroine "to the end."

Praised by *Booklist* contributor Anne O'Malley as "a solid tale about interesting characters," *Love Thy Neighbor* transports readers to Massachusetts and the years leading up to the American Revolution as Prudence and her family side with the British against those agitating for independence. Moving closer to the present, *Grasshopper Summer* follows twelve-year-old Sam who, along with his younger brother and parents, makes the move from his grandfather's orderly Kentucky farm to the undeveloped Dakota prairie. "Both a family story and an account of pioneer living, the book is accessible as well as informative," noted Mary M. Burns in a *Horn Book* review of *Love Thy Neighbor.*

Another historical novel by Turner, *Third Girl from the Left,* finds eighteen-year-old Sarah becoming a mail-order bride as a way of escaping the boring Maine community where she was raised. After a move to Montana, the young woman learns, too late, that there are things

worse than boredom. A *Kirkus Reviews* contributor called *Third Girl from the Left* a "compelling story about a strong-willed 19th-century woman forging her own life without conventional expectations of love and happiness." Turner also presents the fictionalized biography of one of America's most beloved presidents in *Abe Lincoln Remembers,* an "insightful" work that features "stately, lifelike" oil paintings by acclaimed New England artist Wendell Minor, according to a *Publishers Weekly* critic.

Mixing the past with the present, *Rosemary's Witch* follows nine-year-old Rosemary as she discovers a 150-year-old witch named Mathilda hiding in the woods near the old New England house her parents have just bought. The witch was unloved as a child and was driven away by villagers. Longing for affection, she now plays pranks on Rosemary, even stealing the girl's bike to gain attention. Eventually, Rosemary comes to empathize with this childish, lonely, and sometimes malevolent creature. In his review for the *Bulletin of the Center for Children's Books,* Roger Sutton noted that Turner's technique of alternating "Rosemary's and Mathilda's point of view" is "intensely effective." Also reviewing the book, a *Kirkus Reviews* contributor wrote that "Turner thoughtfully explores the idea of home and how it can be shared" in *Rosemary's Witch,* calling the work "skillfully written" and "entertaining."

Turner incorporates a heavy dose of magic into *Elfsong.* In this novel, ten-year-old Maddy Trevor spends her annual summer vacation at the home of her grandfather. When the resident cat, Sabrina, goes missing, the girl searches for her in the nearby woods. There Maddy discovers a magical world when she finds an elf riding on her cat. Soon Maddy and her grandfather are enlisted to help the Eastern Clan of elves battle an evil creature called the Horned One. Sutton remarked in the *Bulletin of the Center for Children's Books* that *Elfsong* serves as "an easy entree into a lyrically drawn landscape of nature and magic."

A lighter magical touch is also apparent in Turner's intergenerational novel *Finding Walter,* in which nine-year-old Emily and her sister Rose are visiting their grandmother. Somehow, the two sisters are able to sense the thoughts of the dolls at their grandmother's house, and they agree to join in the dolls' search for Walter, a doll baby who has been missing for some time. "Turner does a particularly good job of integrating the world of dolls and the world of children," noted *Booklist* reviewer Ilene Cooper, the critic adding that "the dolls' ability to communicate their thoughts never seems forced."

In addition to prose fiction, Turner has also created numerous works of verse, both collections of individual poems such as *Grass Songs, Mississippi Mud,* and *A Lion's Hunger: Poems of First Love* and the verse novels *Learning to Swim* and *Hard Hit. Grass Songs* collects seventeen poems inspired by the correspondence and diaries of pioneer women, treating subjects such as marriage, childbirth, Indian raids, and death. A *Kirkus Reviews* contributor found the work "even more vivid and personalized" than Turner's other historical work, while *Bulletin of the Center for Children's Books* reviewer Betsy Hearne maintained that "Turner has matched the intensity" of the womens' "struggle with a poetic intensity of her own, spare and plainspoken." *Mississippi Mud* features a series of poems based on the journals of three pioneer children on their family's journey from Kentucky to Oregon, while *A Lion's Hunger* brings to life the pangs of a young woman's first crush, "captur[ing] . . . the emotions, insecurities, and rituals that define first love and its powerful impact," according to *Booklist* reviewer Shelle Rosenfeld.

In *Hard Hit* readers meet popular high school sophomore Mark Warren, who seems to have the best of everything: the prettiest girlfriend, close friends, and a promising career as a baseball pitcher. When his father is diagnosed with pancreatic cancer, however, Mark watches as his family falls apart and his own disillusionment and grief cause him to question all he had once trusted and relied on. In what *School Library Journal* writer Kathryn Childs dubbed a "profound novel," Turner poignantly "conveys the absence of all the family has known and its emptiness" without Mark's father at its core, explained *Booklist* reviewer Frances Bradburn. The use of verse to describe dying and its aftermath "is a powerful means of conveying the intensity of feelings," Claire Rosser maintained in *Kliatt*, the critic going on to cite *Hard Hit* as "a helpful resource" for teens coping with the death of a loved one.

Geared for younger, elementary-aged readers, *Dakota Dugout* finds a grandmother sharing her memories of life with her husband in a sod house on the Dakota prairie in the late nineteenth century. The woman's recollections, shared with her granddaughter, bring to life the loneliness, the slow spring, the heat of a summer drought, and finally a successful crop and the building of a clapboard house. Turner's "spare text, like poetry pruned of any excess words but rich in emotional impact, is perfectly attuned to the splendid black-and-white drawings" by Ronald Himler, wrote Mary M. Burns in a review of the work for *Horn Book,* while *New York Times Book Review* contributor Mark Jonathan Harris noted of *Dakota Dugout* that "the impressionistic pictures combine with the vivid prose to create a moving memoir."

Noting that writing poetry is her "first love," Turner once admitted: "I like writing silly poems, such as the ones in *Tickle a Pickle*." As its title implies, *Tickle a Pickle* is a collection of mostly nonsense poems in which, as a *Kirkus Reviews* critic wrote, "the images and rhythms are energetic and unusual, and the sheer nonsensical and offbeat aspects will delight some readers." Among Turner's other poetry volumes is *Street Talk,* a collection of free verse, and *The Christmas House,* thirteen poems expressing the spirit of Christ-

mas through the varying perspectives of several members of a family. A *Bulletin of the Center for Children's Books* contributor wrote of *Street Talk* that "what [Turner] sees, the way she sees it, and the way she makes readers see it are full of fresh flashes." Another verse collection for younger readers, *Secrets from the Dollhouse,* describes the lives of a family of dolls and their servants as they share the dollhouse in a young girl's bedroom.

Turner is especially well known for her many picture books, which range widely in subject. In *Katie's Trunk* and *Nettie's Trip South* she draws on personal anecdotes from her own family history. Echoing the theme of *Love Thy Neighbor, Katie's Trunk* finds a girl in a staunchly loyal Tory family confused by the enmity of her former friends and neighbors as the American colonies begin their war for independence. *Bulletin of the Center for Children's Books* reviewer Deborah Stevenson explained that *Katie's Trunk* "hints at the complexities of rebellion and dissent in a way that should provoke thought and discussion." *Nettie's Trip South* was inspired by the author's great-grandmother's diary entries about a journey made in 1859 and describes a ten-year-old northern girl's encounter with slavery. *School Library Journal* contributor Elizabeth M. Reardon called the "compelling and thought-provoking" picture book "sure to arouse readers' sympathies."

History also figures in *Red Flower Goes West,* in which a family heads west with a red geranium that reminds them of their old home, while a darker history is the focus of *Drummer Boy: Marching to the Civil War.* The story of a thirteen-year-old boy who comes of age during the bloody battles of the U.S. Civil War, *Drummer Boy* recounts what a *Kirkus Reviews* writer called "an unforgettably sad story, of youth wasted," as the teen marches into a bloody battle and experiences the grim realities of war. Another *Kirkus Reviews* writer noted of *Red Flower Goes West* that "Turner makes a red flower . . . a symbol of a young boy's journey to California that, in turn, becomes a testimony to the pioneers of westward expansion."

Another picture book for young readers, *Heron Street* charts the changes in a New England marsh from the colonial era to the present. "Unlike other books on the topic, this implies an appreciation of progress—a refreshing change—as well as dismay over the loss of nature," commented Cooper in *Booklist*. In *Through Moon and Stars and Night Skies* Turner focuses on the cross-cultural adoption by an American family of a young Asian boy. The boy retells the story of his adoption and his fear at first of what he encounters before the love of his new family gradually draws him in. *Horn Book* contributor Ellen Fader found that the story "illuminates in a lyrical and compassionate way" the process of adapting faced by a child from a faraway country.

Domestic matters fill the pages of several picture books by Turner. *Stars for Sarah* concerns a young child's fears of moving to a new house, while *Apple Valley*

Year chronicles a year in the life of an apple farm, from winter pruning to spring pollination and fall harvest. A child's-eye view of her cozy neighborhood is brought to life in the pages of Turner's *In the Heart,* a "sweetly sentimental" work that features what *Booklist* critic John Peters described as highly detailed illustrations by Salley Mavor. "The seasons in the Clark family orchard turn poetically in Turner's competent hands," commented Lee Bock in a *School Library Journal* review of *Apple Valley Year.* Featuring a poetic text, *Angel Hide and Seek* imagines the possible angels that may be found in the oddest places: the faces of sunflowers, for instance, or in the pattern of old wood in a barn. A *Kirkus Reviews* writer remarked that Turner's "words are simple and limpidly clear as they trace angels through the seasons," while a *Publishers Weekly* writer dubbed *Angel Hide and Seek* an "imagination-stretching look at nature."

Biographical and Critical Sources

PERIODICALS

Booklist, May 15, 1989, Ilene Cooper, review of *Heron Street,* p. 1657; January 1, 1995, review of *Rosemary's Witch,* p. 831; October 15, 1997, Ilene Cooper, review of *Finding Walter,* pp. 406-407; September 15, 1998, Carolyn Phelan, review of *Drummer Boy: Marching to the Civil War,* p. 232; March 1, 1999, Shelle Rosenfeld, review of *A Lion's Hunger: Poems of First Love,* p. 1202; November 15, 1999, Karen Hutt, review of *The Girl Who Chased Away Sorrow: The Diary of Sarah Nita, a Navajo Girl,* p. 629; January 1, 2000, Ilene Cooper, review of *Secrets from the Dollhouse,* p. 913; October 1, 2000, John Peters, review of *Learning to Swim: A Memoir,* p. 329; January 1, 2001, Carolyn Phelan, review of *Abe Lincoln Remembers,* p. 964; August, 2001, John Peters, review of *In the Heart,* p. 2133; July, 2003, Anne O'Malley, review of *Love Thy Neighbor: The Tory Diary of Prudence Emerson,* p. 1892; August, 2004, Ilene Cooper, review of *Pumpkin Cat,* p. 1946; June 1, 2005, Carolyn Phelan, review of *Maia of Thebes,* p. 1814; February 1, 2006, Frances Bradburn, review of *Hard Hit,* p. 46.

Bulletin of the Center for Children's Books, February, 1983, review of *The Way Home,* p. 118; June, 1986, review of *Street Talk,* p. 197; May, 1991, Roger Sutton, review of *Rosemary's Witch,* p. 230; December, 1992, Deborah Stevenson, review of *Katie's Trunk,* p. 123; June, 1993, Betsy Hearne, review of *Grass Songs,* p. 331; July, 1995, review of *One Brave Summer,* p. 399; September, 1995, review of *Dust for Dinner,* p. 31; December, 1995, Roger Sutton, review of *Elfsong,* pp. 141-142; July, 1999, review of *Red Flower Goes West,* p. 404; November, 2000, review of *Learning to Swim,* p. 123; September, 2004, Deborah Sullivan, review of *Pumpkin Cat,* p. 42; March, 2006, Loretta Gaffney, review of *Hard Hit,* p. 329.

Horn Book, October, 1980, Virginia Haviland, review of *A Hunter Comes Home,* p. 529; January, 1986, Mary M. Burns, review of *Dakota Dugout,* p. 52; September,

1989, Mary M. Burns, review of *Grasshopper Summer,* p. 624; May 6, 1990, Ellen Fader, review of *Through Moon and Stars and Night Skies,* p. 330; June, 1999, Martha A. Brabander, review of *Red Flower Goes West,* p. 602.

Kirkus Reviews, September 15, 1980, review of *A Hunter Comes Home,* p. 1237; March 15, 1986, review of *Tickle a Pickle;* June 1, 1986, review of *Third Girl from the Left,* p. 872; March 15, 1991, review of *Rosemary's Witch,* p. 400; February 15, 1993, review of *Grass Songs,* p. 235; May 15, 1998, review of *Angel Hide and Seek,* p. 745; June 15, 1999, review of *Red Flower Goes West,* p. 971; December 15, 2003, review of *When Mr. Jefferson Came to Philadelphia: What I Learned of Freedom, 1776,* p. 1455; July 1, 2004, review of *Pumpkin Cat,* p. 639; February 1, 2006, review of *Hard Hit,* p. 138.

Kliatt, January, 2006, Claire Rosser, review of *Hard Hit,* p. 13.

New York Times Book Review, January 12, 1986, Mark Jonathan Harris, review of *Dakota Dugout,* p. 25.

Publishers Weekly, September 19, 1994, review of *The Christmas House,* p. 31; June 15, 1998, review of *Angel Hide and Seek,* p. 59; August 17, 1998, review of *Drummer Boy,* p. 71; June 14, 1999, review of *Red Flower Goes West,* p. 69; January 24, 2000, review of *Secrets from the Dollhouse,* p. 311; October 30, 2000, review of *Learning to Swim,* p. 77; December 4, 2000, review of *Abe Lincoln Remembers,* p. 73; June 4, 2001, review of *In the Heart,* p. 80; November 11, 2002, review of *Abe Lincoln Remembers,* p. 67.

School Library Journal, July-August, 1987, Elizabeth M. Reardon, review of *Nettie's Trip South,* p. 88; February, 1992, Jane Marino, review of *Stars for Sarah,* p. 79; November, 1993, Lee Bock, review of *Apple Valley Year,* p. 95; September, 1998, Patricia Lothrop-Green, review of *Angel Hide and Seek,* p. 184; June, 1999, Steven Engelfried, review of *Red Flower Goes West,* p. 108; November, 2000, Sharon Korbeck, review of *Learning to Swim,* p. 177; February, 2001, Mary Ann Carich, review of *Abe Lincoln Remembers,* p. 116; August, 2003, Kristen Oravec, review of *Love Thy Neighbor,* p. 168; February, 2004, Beth Tegart, review of *When Mr. Jefferson Came to Philadelphia,* p. 124; August, 2004, Catherine Threadgill, review of *Pumpkin Cat,* p. 97; February, 2006, Kathryn Childs, review of *Hard Hit,* p. 138.

Voice of Youth Advocates, February, 1999, review of *A Lion's Hunger,* p. 460; December, 2000, review of *Learning to Swim,* p. 372; April, 2006, Nancy Zachary, review of *Hard Hit,* p. 54.

Washington Post Book World, March 14, 2004, Elizabeth Ward, review of *When Mr. Jefferson Came to Philadelphia,* p. 11.

ONLINE

Ann Turner Home Page, http://www.annturnerbooks.com (April 15, 2007).

OTHER

Turner, Ann, Macmillan publicity brochure, 1989.

Autobiography Feature

Ann Turner

Ann Turner contributed the following autobiographical essay to *SATA:*

I was born into a family that loved books. In *A Hole Is to Dig,* by Ruth Krauss, which Dad read to us as children, there is picture of a boy kneeling on a book, nose pressed to its pages, inhaling its smell. I was like that. My entire extended family on both sides was passionate about books as well. One story was told of my aunt Lucy, who used to return from school and sink into a chair in the hallway to read her book, not even taking off her coat.

With such a background, how could I *not* become a writer? My dad was a printer and ran a business housed in a long, low brick building, with a shed attached out back. Entering his business was like entering the gates of heaven. The sharp almost greasy smell of ink—the sounds of the presses shunting back and forth with a deafening sound, the stacks of colored paper on the shelves in the shed—all of these spoke of a world that revered books: how they were written, how they were printed, and even the paper they were printed on.

My mother was an artist and taught us to draw and paint at an early age. We were always doing some project at the dining room table: cutting out linoleum blocks, making collages out of the colored paper brought home from my dad's shop, gluing yarn into the shape of a cat, and painting horses over and over. For, along with being crazy about books, I was also crazy about horses. But more about that later. For now we are going to look at the early years of my growing up: what happened, how did it effect me, who shaped me, and when did I begin to think that becoming a writer would be a seriously wonderful thing to do?

My family was also devoted to libraries, which is no surprise, because when you are as passionate about books as we all were, libraries are where the goods are. It's like the story about someone asking a famous bank robber, "Why do you rob banks?" "Because that's where the money is!" the man replied. Anyone could see that, couldn't they?

In the town where I spent my earliest years, Northampton, Massachusetts, we would travel to the library in my dad's big black Dodge car. In those days (the end of the 1940s–early 1950s) cars were big and roomy and smelled like living-room couches. The roofs were high and domed so there would be enough room for men and women to wear their hats. And, of course, there were no such things as seat belts in those days. We just racketed about happily in the back, sitting on the sometimes scratchy material of the seat, eager to get to the library.

And when we did, I—along with my two brothers (one older, Nick, and one younger, Peter) would swarm up the long stairway to the Children's Room. Clearly the Children's Room was the best place in the library. It had books by Margaret Wise Brown—*Goodnight Moon* and *Runaway Bunny*—which my dad read to us when we were quite young. I strongly suspect that the musi-

Ann, nearly two years old, 1948 (Photo courtesy of Ann Turner.)

cal repetition of hearing "goodnight" to the room and the moon in *Goodnight Moon* was part of my formation as poet.

We would load up on books and take them back to our big brick house on the hill where we lived with my comfortable, plump grandmother and my scholarly, plump grandfather. Each night Dad would sit us down on the rug and read to us. I sometimes thought of him as a daddy bird, plucking out a new book each day and popping it into the gaping beaks of his children—me, Nick, and Peter.

What do I remember of the books he read to us? I remember hearing *The Moffats,* and being delighted by the messiness of Rufus. How I loved their family—the bravery of the mother in bringing them up alone, the comfy chaos of their family life, and the security of the world they lived in where everyone down the street was known to them, and each child was known by every adult nearby. Sadly, that world has been lost to children now.

I can recall my father reading the "Homer Price" books by Robert McClosky to us; the one where he keeps a skunk in a basket ("How could he *do* that, Dad? Wouldn't it stink up his house?" we'd shriek), and the picture book *Lentil,* where a cranky man sits on the roof of a building, sucking a lemon to confound the band down below in the square, while they try to play a rousing tune for some famous person coming in on the train.

I loved it that this guy could totally disrupt the band's self-important rhum-pahing by sucking this lemon, thus making every musician down below pucker up his lips and be unable to play. I liked mischievous people, being one myself, and you can see that in an early book of poetry I wrote for children, called *Tickle a Pickle.* In this collection—as in real life in my grandmother's house—we kids would make "toilet soup" in the toilet, pouring in talcum powder, a sprinkle of Mom's perfume, and the last finishing touch, one of Dad's shoes. We were very young—that is my only excuse!

When I was seven years old, my family moved from the big brick house in Northampton to a yellow clapboard house in Williamsburg, about ten miles away. Although I missed my grandparents, I was excited to be out in the country. We had meadows. Two of them! We had an old, fallen-down apple orchard with bright blossoms in the spring and twisted branches which were perfect for climbing and perching on. There were several acres of woods stretching out back, with dense stands of pines and more open land with green myrtle on the ground running down to a stream.

Grapevines hung in thick, tangled clusters from some of the trees, and I remember how we would pull on them, swinging back and forth, bellowing out, "Aia— yahhhh!" the way Johnny Weismuller did in his incarnation as Tarzan in the movies.

Once my older brother sharpened a set of sticks along the stream, perhaps to represent some wartime scene? Peter and I had to swing over the stream and not wound ourselves on the vicious stakes below. Childhood was a continual series of surviving things that were almost fatal, as I remember, or at least limb-threatening.

There was a magnificent, slightly tilted red barn behind the house, with actual hay in the loft and a huge wooden machine downstairs that had once held chicken eggs— for our old 1756 house had at one time been a chicken farm.

There were little shallow trays inset in the big round drum, which I gather someone could rotate around under the warmth of some lights so the eggs would hatch. We took the trays out, of course, and, wedging ourselves into the big drum, would shout to one of our siblings, "Turn, turn the drum!"

And round and round we would rocket, our hair hanging down, knees bent, all enveloped in this delightful, dangerous racket. I don't know if my parents, especially my mom, ever quite knew what we got up to in that barn. In the days when I was growing up, children had more freedom. We simply exited the kitchen door at a certain sunny time of the morning, went out to play (while Mom did her thing inside), and didn't come inside until it was either time to eat or the light was going.

On that same barn was a wonderful slate roof, covered with thin slate shingles. We would go up to the top floor in the barn and hoist ourselves out of one window onto the roof, scrabbling up to the top, using our fingers to steady ourselves. You had to have sneakers on for this, and shorts were okay to wear too.

Then, at the very top ridge of the roof, we'd launch ourselves downwards, screaming mightily, to the bottom of the roof, which ended in a low shed roofed with tar paper. It felt as if we were going to fall off the edge, but, actually, was probably not all that dangerous. But it felt dangerous. And foolhardy. And we loved it. I went through a lot of pairs of jeans and shorts that way, and it is a testimony to my mom that she never fussed about our clothes. This early love of danger and pushing the limits can be seen in many of the kids in my books: Rosemary in *Rosemary's Witch,* Prudence in *Love Thy Neighbor,* and the boy who goes off to war in *Drummer Boy.*

At the end of a day of adventuring, sliding down roofs and being rotated in the wooden incubator, the three of us children would come inside to be read to. I particularly remember my mom reading Laura Ingalls Wilder to me on the bed in my parents' bedroom, curled up on the pink-and-green quilt. When I listened to *The Long Winter,* both my mom and I had to snuggle under the quilt, even in July, for Laura's descriptions were so strong and visual that we felt we were there in the tiny house on the prairie, blizzard winds howling outside and scouring the roof. Even then layers were being laid down for me inside: *Wouldn't it be wonderful to make people feel this way, too? To describe things with such power that your world would come alive for your readers?*

Laura Ingalls Wilder was also a favorite role model for me. I wanted to be like her: resourceful, brave, able to withstand terrible blizzards without complaining, a good friend, a loyal family member, and not above leading the loathsome Nellie into the dark creek waters where the leeches lived.

I had already learned to read by the time we moved to Williamsburg and the wonderful old house with the meadows, grapevines, shambling barns, and dangerous play things. But my younger brother, Peter, was learning to read soon after we made this move, and I was moved to pity for him because he was stuck with the "Dick and Jane" books. I know it is fashionable now to look back on those books fondly: that snotty little dog, the little girl in her dreadfully pressed dress, the little boy so horribly clean that *he* certainly would never climb into a chicken-hatching machine and have his brothers whirl him round and round until he was so dizzy he could not walk. None of these children—none of the animals or the people in those books—looked as if they ever got dirty, said a bad word, or misbehaved, and they certainly did not suck lemons on top of a roof to mess up the town band!

And those slow little words, measured as a funeral cadence—one after another—I thought Peter would die of boredom trying to learn to read from them. *Look, Jane, look.* At what, I'd want to scream wildly? *Go, Spot, go.* Go where, you foolish dog?

Ann with her brothers, Nick (right) and Pete, playing dress up, about 1950 (Photo courtesy of Ann Turner.)

Dad continued to read to us in our new, old house, where we three children would get into our pajamas and sit on the flowered rug to listen. He read *Pippi Longstocking* to us, and I adored how naughty Pippi was. I wished I could have a horse on *my* porch and a monkey for a friend. He also read all of the Edgar Eager books to us. I particularly liked the humor in *Half Magic,* how the magic coin the four children found on the pavement never quite got them what they wished for. When they wished to be on a desert island, they got the desert; when they asked for their cat to talk, it could—but only sometimes, and often with a whole lot of *xxxxyyymmmm*'s mixed up in the words.

I was beginning to think that writing was something that I wanted to do for myself. In my mind I held onto that image of the little boy kneeling on the book, sniffing its heavenly smell; I had embedded in me images from Laura Ingalls Wilder's books, and I began to write my own stories. At the age of eight I wrote my first short story, called "The Puckity." It had all the elements of a classic short story: a main character, tension and conflict, a wish line (what the character most wants to happen), a beginning, a middle, and an end. It even had spelling errors.

Once upon a time there lived a little man and his name was Puckity. He lived in a little house in the woods. Well this little man however wanted adventure and he got it. Well one day a dragon was walking and thinking how tasty a dwarf would taste. Well then puckity got his wish. Just then the dragon saw puckity and puckity didn't see him! The dragon kept on coming and puckity kept on cleaning his house and the dragon said, "What's going on here? He's supposed to see me and run away from me but puckity kept on cleaning his house." Well puckity at last saw the dragon and the dragon roared and said, "I'm going to eat you up!" Puckity was so afraid and neves that he didn't mean to say it but he did say it and he said, "Oh go away I'm too busy cleaning my house!" The dragon was never in his life so surprised that he made a funny sound like this erglupplup. The nois sounded so funny that Puckity laughed and laughed. The dragon was so ashamed that he went away and hid in his cave and nevercame out again. The forest once again was in peace. The end.

Perhaps the mechanical parts of the story are a bit weak—such as spelling and punctuation and non-repetition of words—but it is a story, nonetheless. And for me, at that young age, it felt like a triumph. I had put words down on paper that created images, told about some actions, and had an ending and a resolution. I was hooked. Writing was the thing for me!

My second experience with the exhilaration of writing came in fifth grade, several years after writing my first story. We were studying the Civil War with a marvelous teacher of rather strict demeanor, of Scots origin. She had a delightfully different accent, rolling her r's in such a way that we were always impressed by the importance of her words. When we studied the U.S. Civil War, Mrs. Breckenridge asked us to write a little essay or piece about the time.

At home, my parents had a book of photographs of the U.S. Civil War by a photographer called Matthew Brady, some of the earliest war photography in history. (Brady actually had a group of photographers who went out onto the battlefields, and he supervised them.) The scenes of the battles were eerily still—dead men lying in heaps on the meadows of the South; some with their arms flung out, others with their hats slung over their eyes. Some of the scenes showed battle lines massed against each other, soldiers standing still with their rifles at the ready.

These grim and graphic photographs sent a message to me—of the horror of battle, the smoke covering the battlefield, the sound of voices and horses neighing, and of utter chaos. They affected me deeply.

In my fifth-grade essay I wrote as if I were a bystander on a hill, looking over the battle—much as the photographer himself was. I talked about the smoke and noise and confusion of battle as if I had experienced it myself, as if I actually knew what I was talking about. And, in a sense, I did.

I was not a true bystander, but because I could *imagine* being there, my words had a kind of authenticity and truth to them. I was much taken with my story, as were my parents. I can still remember my mom's delighted grin, "Annie, you did this?" In a family where achievement was honored and education was worshipped, I felt I had accomplished something wonderful. And I learned another lesson about writing: words have the power to move people, words have the power to take your readers on time travel to other places and eras. I was doubly hooked.

This was my first "you are there" story, and it is a style of writing I have used often when crafting historical narratives from a child's point of view, as I did with the girl, Katy, in *Katie's Trunk* and the boy in *Drummer Boy*, about the U.S. Civil War. In fact that story can be traced directly back to that essay written in the fifth-grade so many years ago.

While I was being hooked by the idea of writing my own stories—inspired by the wonderful books my parents read to me—I was also living in a household with people who had many stories to tell. Indeed, I come from a family of storytellers. It is no accident that I grew up to be a writer—it was as if some "writer gene" (a tiny, tiny little piece of genetic material, holding a tiny, tiny pen) had been born with me.

My great-grandmother, Henrietta Chapin, lived in Albany, New York, in the mid-1800s and was an abolitionist, meaning she was a person who favored the freeing of the slaves in the South and in the North. (Let us not forget that people were slave-owners up North as well as in the South, and in New York State there were quite a number of slaves.) In 1859 she and some of her family went down South to visit relatives who lived in Virginia. She kept a journal of her travels, a meticulous recording of each day's events: how she felt about them, what the weather was like, and other musings.

With her older brother and cousin, she visited a slave auction one day, to see how it actually happened. There was a red flag outside the slave auction, notifying people of the "prime gang" within. Nettie and her companions went in to take their seats, and the sale began. The auctioneer was drunk and "disgusting," she wrote in her diary, and she painfully recorded what it was like to see a young woman jump and run and show her muscles up on the platform, while someone held her six-month-old baby.

Henrietta noted that often babies that young were separated from their mothers during such a sale. But all the while she was getting angrier and more disturbed, finding it impossible to sit still. Back at the hotel they talked together about the horrors they had seen and resolved to work harder once they were home to help free the slaves.

I took my great-grandmother's firsthand account of a real slave auction and made it into a story, an illustrated historical picture book called *Nettie's Trip South*. First written on the backs of old envelopes as I sat one night on the couch—riveted by her account of this auction and knowing I must write about it somehow—the story took me twenty separate revisions until I finally got it "right."

I tried different narrative voices; I tried different ways of telling the story; and it wasn't until I made Henrietta into a ten-year-old child—with all the innocence and wide eyes of a girl that age—that I finally had a story that worked. My friend Jane Yolen (Jane and I have been members of the same writer's group for over thiry years) suggested that I write the story as if it were a letter home. This was a fine idea, and I took her advice, also putting in several other "true" things in the writing of this poetic narrative.

I included my great-grandmother's real-life cousin Addie, who lived in Oneida, New York, making her the recipient of the fictional letter Nettie wrote home about her visit to the South just before the war. I wove in the kind of response to evil that I still have to this day—it makes me physically ill. I also included a piece of real history from my own childhood, when Nettie tells Addie, *"When you come in June / we will climb the apple tree to our perch / and I will tell you all I saw."*

For at my grandmother's summer house—where all of the cousins, aunts, and uncles used to gather—there was a tangled, tall apple tree on which some uncle had nailed a series of small boards as footholds up the trunk.

Ann, eight years old, "playing the violin with great seriousness" (Photo courtesy of Ann Turner.)

Out on separate limbs were little wooden platforms nailed down, perfect for perching and reading or for having a secret conversation with a cousin.

In the wonderful way of picture books, the illustrator—Ronald Himler—sketched a young Addie and Nettie sitting up in the apple tree, reading a book together. It is always one of the delights of writing a picture book, to see how your words, your story, and your characters are drawn and made real by an artist. I send off the words and they come back with astonishing and beautiful pictures! How wonderful is that?

But there were other people in my family who contributed to our collection of stories and who gave me a sense of the magic of history. My grandfather, William D. Gray, who married the second Henrietta—daughter of my great-grandmother of the trip South—was a professor of classics at Smith College and traveled abroad with his family, acquiring several interesting objects as he did so. Some found their way onto the top of the green-painted bookcase in my childhood home in Williamsburg.

There was a flaked stone knife that may have been from the Neolithic period or even older. I used to run my finger gingerly along its edge, wondering who had made it, how it had been used, and where it really came from.

You can see right here that I asked a lot of questions, and indeed, it is one of the things that makes a writer a writer—insatiable curiosity and asking unending questions.

I also had a golden Greek coin made into a necklace on a black ribbon which my mother gave me. A rather musty box held some treasures from abroad: a series of Roman coins, dense and heavy and ancient-looking, an Egyptian scarab, and a small statue of some goddess, probably one that protected women in childbirth.

The reason for mentioning these treasures is that they affected me; they gave me a key to other cultures and times and a desire to learn more about them. Did writing *Maia of Thebes,* about a girl who wished to be a scribe in the time of Hatshepsut in Egypt, grow from those two Egyptian treasures at home? Possibly. Just knowing that I could hold an authentic scarab made in ancient Egypt made that land come closer to me and seem more real. A human being, long ago, had actually *held* that scarab in his or her hand!

Other stories came from different family members, one important one from my dear and sometimes eccentric aunt Lucy, my mom's middle sister. Aunt Lucy had married a brilliant mathematician from Arkansas whose voice engaged me when I was young. It definitely was not a Massachusetts voice, but something sharp and twangy, with an abrupt and yet slower cadence which I could listen to all day. And it was my aunt Lou, as we called her, who one day asked me, "Annie, what ever happened to that big black trunk that used to be in the Northampton house?"

I had no idea and, in fact, no recollection of it, but Lou did, and proceeded to tell me two stories about this high-domed trunk: one, that some of our ancestors hid from the Native Americans in it; and two, that some of our ancestors hid from the Patriots in it.

I was aghast. "You mean, we had Tories in our family?" Those were the people who were loyal to King George and who did not want the colonies to set up on their own but to stay linked to British government and control. From this conversation *Katie's Trunk* was born. (I was later to write a novel called *Love Thy Neighbor,* for the "Dear America" series, telling the story of the beginning of the American Revolution through the eyes of a Tory girl called Prudence, who never *was* prudent.)

I wanted to experience what it felt like to be on the wrong side of a war, to be inside a Tory girl, and to see friends falling away from their family. What was it like to endure insults and persecution from the Patriots, as many Tories did before and during the Revolution? We seldom read of this in our history classes in school, but when I found an account of one dignified Tory man being "smoked" out of his house by angry Patriots (they set fire to his house, waiting for him to escape), I began to get a sense of how people felt, being on the wrong side of that war.

In the beginning of *Katie's Trunk,* the ten-year-old girl is not sure what is wrong, but she senses the coming

war and conflict: *"I couldn't tell it with a name / though I felt it inside / the way a horse knows a storm is near."* I wanted to write this story as a child experiencing a civil war—for that is what the American Revolution was in many ways; it tore families apart, separated neighbors, and set one part of a town against another.

In this book, as in so many others, I imagined myself as "other." This is a theme that runs throughout my work—what it is like to be on the outside, to feel that you are different and set apart in some way. This comes directly from my childhood experience of growing up in a family that was quite, quite different from the other families in our small New England village in the safe and sedate 1950s.

My clothes were different. I remember being teased for some argyle socks I wore in fourth grade. I played the violin and everyone in my family played an instrument so that we sometimes had small, rather badly played concerts at night: Mom on the piano, Dad and Nick on cellos, Pete on the flute, and I on my violin.

I was not the only one who was different in my family. My mother was an artist. She wore jeans, flat shoes, and tied her hair back in a day when women tended to curl their hair, wear dresses, stockings, and heels. She wandered into our meadows with an easel and a set of pens, sketching dried weeds and old apple trees leaning against the fields. She saw beauty in things others often did not—dead birds, dried weeds, tangles of briars and bittersweet. Once she kept a dead starling in our freezer for a week so that she could draw him more perfectly. I thought all moms were like this and was greatly surprised to discover that this was not so.

My dad was a printer, as I mentioned earlier, who smoked a pipe and was definitely a liberal. In those days it was not considered a terrible thing to be a "liberal." It meant, for us, that you looked out for disadvantaged people; that you wanted a fair wage for workers; that in, general, you did not support war unless no other course was left open to you; that you worked for world peace; and that you took care of creation.

These are all good values and ones which permeate my writing and my life. So being different informs most of my books, as well as my love for stories which comes from my family. But it wasn't just my family who had stories to tell—which enriched my life and got knitted up in me so that I could never separate myself from them. I also lived in a house built in 1756 that was full of tales.

Dad told us our house had once been part of the Underground Railroad, where escaped slaves made their way North, staying at safe places.

"Ours was one of them," he told us. "And our neighbor told me there used to be a tunnel going between this house and his on the other side of the meadow."

The author's parents, Richard and Marion Warren, in 1967 (Photo courtesy of Ann Turner.)

We wondered greatly about that tunnel: was it still there under the grass? Had people really used it to escape detection, crouching low as they hurried from one safe hiding place to another? My brother Peter decided it was up to him to discover the truth about this tunnel and started digging in the lawn. We never found it, and the hole my brother dug became a fort covered with boards where he took a hurricane lantern and books to escape the family.

But we three children continued searching for where the slaves might have been hidden, swarming upstairs to the attic, poking into every nook and cranny.

One day we found an old bundle of rolled up cloth tacked above a small entrance. A little room with no real floor in it, just cross beams above the ceiling below, was on the other side of this dark entrance. "It must be it!" we exclaimed.

Was it the real secret place? I rather doubt it, as the room was part of the house which had been added on later. But the sense that we lived in a house where history had happened—where injustice had been thwarted—excited me. It still does.

It also gave me a feeling that the whole world was soaked in history, soaked in stories, and if only I looked hard enough, I could discover secrets and tales.

I used my childhood house in my novel *Rosemary's Witch,* written in 1990. In it, the father is based somewhat on the writer Patricia MacLachlan's husband, Bob, a retired professor, mixed in with my own dad. In one passage Rosemary is describing to her mother how she sees her father, who is a professor of history: "He has, you know, categories for everything, like signs in a supermarket. Pet food—soda—gum. Dad has names for them, like Kindness to Older People, and Being Nice to New Babies, and Never Kicking Your Dog."

In this house I finally found what I had been looking for—a true home. My home. Not my grandparents', much as I loved it, but something belonging just to us, just for us. In *Rosemary's Witch,* when the family (Mom, Dad, Nicholas, and Rosemary) first sees the house, each one has a dream of what a real home should be.

From the open porch Mother wants to "watch thunderstorms . . . and shooting stars. We can catch fireflies in the meadow and make up ghost stories in the dark."

Except Rosemary (who is me) does not want to make up ghost stories, as she hates scary things. Rosemary likes it that the house "felt like a favorite armchair in a corner waiting for someone to curl up in it. Beyond the porch a lawn ran down to the road, shaded by a huge maple."

"My childhood home in Williamsburg, said to be on the Underground Railway" (Photo courtesy of Ann Turner.)

Nicholas wants a room for all of his fossils, and Dad wants a place to store all of his Abraham Lincoln books, a man whom he admires and almost worships. Dad lives by the famous words of Abe: "We cannot escape history!"

You will see when you read my historical books how much this theme is woven through. It is actually a foundation for my books, a bedrock for them.

But this wonderful, very old house had more than stories in it. It was a place that cradled my soul. A ways beyond the house the woods began, and near the entrance to the woods stood a giant pine. When I was about ten years old, I would climb steadily up the rough bark of that tree, then scrooge out along a long, massive branch to the very end. Where the branch turned into smaller branches and the thick weavings of pine needles, I would lie face down. When the wind blew, I would ride the branch up and down, up and down, as if riding an ocean of wind in my pine boat. I didn't even particularly dream in this special place of mine, I just *was*. I felt myself to be part of something larger and wider and more beautiful than anything I knew or could imagine.

What I learned from the pines and the rich, dense woods, and the tangles of grapevines was that beauty is throughout the world and that it upholds us, just as the pine branch held my weight when the wind blew. It is one of the reasons that my books have so much description in them.

Once a child reader asked me, "Why do you describe so many things in your books?" And I my answer was, "Because that is how I see the world—full of beauty, full of detail, and deeply interesting."

One of the other big influences in my life when a child was the camps I went to in the summer. It amazes me now to think that my mother and dad sent us off to an eight-week camp soon after school was let out, and we didn't return until almost the end of August. Heaven for them and heaven for us.

At the first camp I went to, Camp Windigo (of course they all had those dreadful names which are disrespectful to Native Americans, but people were just not aware of that then), most of our time was spent outdoors—riding horses (my passion), canoeing, swimming, camping out, picking blueberries, and only coming inside when it rained or it was time to sleep.

Our counselor read to us each and every night, sometimes with rain drumming on the tin roof overhead. I remember listening to *The Secret Garden,* a book by Frances Hodges Burnett that is full of mystery and a secret, of course, and a sense that children have the power to change each others' lives. I liked stories where children are powerful and go off on their own without adults to help them.

When we camped out at night, we would set up our sleeping bags on mounds of soft moss and go to sleep with the stars shining overhead. In the morning, once, I awoke before anyone else to see a light so golden it was almost unbelievable. It was a light that surrounded everything—every twig, every leaf on the bushes nearby, every bird in the trees. It was a light composed of birdsong and music, wonder and awe, and I guess its name was God, although I did not know that at the time.

In my books the characters I create tend to be strongminded, as I was, although sometimes shy, as I was. They solve problems—as Rose and Emily do in *Finding Walter,* searching for the missing doll in the dollhouse family. That search reunites the fighting sisters in a way nothing else could. The way those sisters quarreled is reminiscent of the way in which my older brother, Nick, and I fought when children—often and hard.

In *Rosemary's Witch,* Rosemary must learn how to deal with the witch, Matilda, who lives in their woods, finding out what she likes and cares about so that she—Rosemary—can persuade the witch to leave the woods and their house alone. It is only at the end, through an act of loving generosity, that Rosemary succeeds, when she gives the witch a knapsack full of presents: a sweater for warmth, a ceramic cat (the witch loves cats, although the girl does not know that), a bar of chocolate—which the witch devours, wrapper and all—a book, and the ultimate sacrifice, Freddy, her old stuffed bear.

Like all writers, I use events from my past, my children's lives, and the lives of people I love, The bear, Freddy, came from my husband's childhood when Rick had accidentally dropped his teddy bear into a grubby stream by the side of the road. His mother decided it had gotten too dirty to save and threw the bear away. Rick's anguish at the loss of his beloved bear features in my novel, for Rosemary is still devoted to this stuffed animal, even though she is ten years old.

Of course, none of my children held onto their stuffed animals into their teens. No sir!

But, like the gentle wind moving the feathery pine branch up and down, time flowed past our family, and I began to leave the world of childhood. I entered seventh grade in the brick schoolhouse of our small village in 1957. It was a cozy, undemanding sort of school; even now I have lists of spelling words from that grade with the reassuring C's marking my words correct. How I loved to get things right! Our teacher, Mrs. Milanesi, read *Mr. Popper's Penguins* to us sometimes during class, and that is a mark of how things have changed. We eagerly looked forward to each day's reading, but such a book would be considered far beneath any seventh grader today; it would be more appropriate for second graders.

I made the leap from reading children's books to investigating adult books; back then, we didn't have a category called "young adult." I had a great liking for the long novels of Charles Dickens and Jane Austen, my favorites at the time. I remember visiting my cousin at her rugged camp on Squam Lake in New Hampshire, sleeping in the bottom bunk of the narrow room. My cousin Jean and I would share the books we were reading and tell each other stories, always stories, like the air we breathed.

Eighth grade was unremarkable in most ways, except for a gorgeous dress I had for my first dance and my first kiss from a boy. Truly, that is all I can recall of that year. I expect we did things in school, but they have left no lasting mark on my brain. Life continued its secure and cozy round of family, school, and friends. It was almost like a life out of time, for during those years I knew no one who was divorced, no girl who was on a diet, no one who had an eating disorder. Drugs were unheard of in our town, although some of the older high school kids might drink, as the gossip told us.

In high school I discovered boys and the delights of flirting. I spent incredible amounts of time on my hair, which, to my great despair, curled wildly and frizzed when I was out on a date on a humid night. I used that hair—and my hatred of its willful independence—in *Rosemary's Witch* when Matilda, the witch, "patted her hair and it sprang off to one side. 'Quiet!' she shouted. The hair lay flat for a moment and then hissed behind her."

I joined the choir of our local church, partly because I liked to sing and partly because the boys I liked were also members of the choir. Whatever the reasons, it proved to be a good place to be. We had a wonderful new minister who formed a youth group, then called Pilgrim Fellowship, and we did a number of interesting things, one of which was visiting the state hospital, whose inmates suffered from various mental disorders.

Now, of course, you would not be allowed to do that, as it violates the laws of privacy, but things were different in 1960. A group of us, along with our minister, would drive down to the state hospital (now vacant, all its inmates gone, either released onto the streets or into the inadequate community homes) and be let inside one of the wards by an attendant who unlocked the doors.

With a mixture of fear and anticipation, I would walk in a huddle with my friends into the blasting heat of the ward, where women sat dully on beds or walked about. I think they were happy to see us, happy for a break in the routine, and eager to accept the cigarettes we brought, which they stuffed inside their sweaters. We would talk a little to the people on the wards, and it was an important learning experience for me.

I learned an invaluable lesson from these visits, at first thinking that the folks in the hospital were "not like us" and were "different." But after a time, I realized they were not "other" but could be our relatives, our sisters, our brothers, or our cousins. I call this an education for an understanding heart, something that we writers need if we are to create sympathetic characters who may be very different indeed from the people we think ourselves to be.

I couldn't create a fourteen-year-old boy in *Drummer Boy* who flees his harsh father to join the Union Army if I didn't already have practice in imagining myself inside the lives of others. I couldn't create a girl called Sarah Nita in my book about the Long Walk (*The Girl Who Chased away Sorrow*), where Navajos were cruelly marched across the entire state of Arizona in wintertime, without the practice of imagining myself inside another's life, another's body.

A part of this education for an understanding heart continued with the books I read in high school. I read widely and deeply: many novels by Thomas Hardy, books by Emile Zola, Dostoevsky, Tolstoy, and others. In my sophomore year I had a marvelous English teacher who had us read *The Red Badge of Courage,* by Stephen Crane. Being the good little grind that I was, I read the introduction, which told me that the initials for the main character, J.C., were the same as those for Jesus Christ. I waved my hand madly in class, eager to share my knowledge, and I well remember how dampened I felt when the teacher squashed my enthusiastic contribution about the significance of the character's name. Apparently, I had leapt ahead to something we weren't meant to talk about for another few days or so. This is one reason why I can identify with Hermione Granger in the "Harry Potter" books and movies. I, too, studied overly hard; I, too, always had my hand in the

Ann (right), in the eighth grade, with her cousin Jean, "in seriously nerdy Bermuda shorts," 1959 (Photo courtesy of Ann Turner.)

air in class; I, too, was determined to do well in school and get good grades. I even had bushy hair, like her, but my teeth did not, thankfully, stick out.

I was always jumping ahead in English class, reading towards the back in the anthology when the class sometimes seemed to move too slowly for me. Actually, it often felt far too slow for me. As my own daughter said to us once when we were sauntering through the woods, running back to us, "Pick up the pace, guys, pick up the pace!"

On one occasion when I read past where our class was in the anthology, I discovered a poet who has remained a favorite of mine through my adult years—Walt Whitman. His way of writing was completely fresh to me, modern, and I could sense the breezes blowing through his poems when I read "Out of the Cradle Endlessly Rocking." I didn't always understand his words, but their power and rhythm took me far away from the over-heated classroom.

I was beginning to experiment with writing poetry by this time as well, even as I was learning to love reading poetry. My English teacher for sophomore year encouraged me to enter a high-school writing contest, which I did.

It was very odd being the only student in the library writing away while she stayed as monitor, probably to make sure I didn't cheat, although I would no more have cheated than I would have cut off my index finger. At any rate, I wrote a number of poems that day, one of them being about the cold war between the United States and the USSR and how governments were more interested in sending up missiles instead of talking about

As a freshman in high school, "dressed to kill to go to New York City," *1960* (Photo courtesy of Ann Turner.)

peace. I was much impressed with this early poetic effort, and became hooked on writing words in short lines which sometimes rhymed but more often did not. I was encouraged that another adult in my life—this marvelous English teacher—paid attention to the words I wrote and thought that I had some talent.

When I went to Bates College in Lewiston, Maine, I majored in English, to my great delight. One of my professors was quite famous in the college, a rather wizened, elderly man who would point a knobby finger at our class saying, "Messy notebook, messy mind!" I did not agree with that, of course, and have never been known for my neat notebooks. Patty MacLachlan declares that my handwriting is "unreadable!"

Another English professor taught both American and British novels brilliantly, and was so passionate about the meaning of these novels that one day he actually thrust his leg into the wastebasket as he strode about the room! I liked the idea of people being passionate about books—it spoke to me.

I had the great good fortune to spend my junior year abroad in Oxford, England, studying and staying at a tiny place called Manchester College. We could take any of the lectures British students took at the various colleges, and I soaked up learning about early English writers like Chaucer and Spencer. We were close enough to London to hop on a train and go in to the theater, returning to our college after midnight. I thought this all very dashing and romantic and adored the plays, music, and dance that we could see.

On spring vacation, I rode by train with a friend all the way to Athens, Greece, and promptly fell in love with that country and its citizens. The temples still surviving

from ancient Greece, the old theater at Epidaurus, the temple at Delphi, the Greek Islands, including Crete and the ruins of the Minoan palace where, legend said, the minotaur lived—all this fed my imagination. And when I returned to college at the end of my year abroad, I wrote an essay called "Athenai" for an *Atlantic Monthly* writing contest, which won first prize nationwide. In it I wrote of my love for the sharp air of Greece, the men dancing with their arms over each other's shoulders, the wonderful food and wine, and the turquoise sea lapping against the sides of a boat.

I remember calling my mother to tell her I had won this contest and her astonished response: "Annie? You won out of *all* the seniors in the country?" It was gratifying in some ways but her surprise also made me wonder about her faith in me.

I wondered what winning this contest might mean for me: did it mean I was meant to be a writer? Should I go on to train as a teacher, as planned, with my husband-to-be, or should I go to the Bread Loaf Writer's Conference as part of the prize? I chose to take the money instead of going to the conference, as it came at a time when I was to be married. But winning that contest planted a strong seed in me that perhaps I had a small measure of talent—and that others recognized it. This was a happy thought, even if it was tucked away for awhile.

After graduation, my husband and I attended the University of Massachusetts in 1967, studying to get our Master's of Art in Education, which would allow us to teach.

When we were done with graduate studies, we both taught English at a regional high school in Great Barrington for a year, but while there were parts of teaching I really liked, I loathed the routine and following a clock. I was not a terrific disciplinarian, but enjoyed teaching *Les Miserables, Catcher in the Rye,* and "The Love Song of J. Alfred Prufrock." As an admirer of the Beatles, I used some of their songs to teach poetry in my classes. Teaching gave me enormous respect for the job of teachers—how diligently they work, how they struggle to be creative and engage their students, and how what looks like "time off" is usually filled with correcting papers and planning classes for weeks to come. I believe teachers are some of America's heroes and heroines and are neither appreciated the way they should be nor paid enough for their important work.

The idea of being a writer tugged at me, becoming stronger and stronger as I went through my first year of teaching. I wanted to *write* books, not discuss them. Sometime in early spring I read a magazine that had a glorious two-page spread on the Aran Islands, off the west coast of Ireland, a place I had visited during my year abroad, and a place important in the great Irish literary revival in the early twentieth century. I asked Rick, "Why couldn't we go there, honey? Let's be writers and live abroad for a year!"

With the reckless abandon of youth and the courage to do things differently, we began to save much of our paychecks and prepared to live abroad for a year. Through friends we rented a small cottage in Devon, England, near the sea, having decided that the Aran Islands were a bit too remote for us.

With great excitement we shipped our goods abroad, thinking then that we would even become British citizens. In that small cottage where roses bloomed into December and where cows grazed and lowed in the green meadows nearby, I began my first fantasy novel, along with my husband. It was an odd and engaging way to write; we would sit in chairs near the coal fire (for there was no central heating then in 1969), notebooks open on our lap, talking about plot and character and what would happen next. I'd write some lines, read them out loud, and Rick would write some lines and read them out loud. Somehow chapters got written and a plot developed, over lots of creamy hot chocolate and Cadbury biscuits.

Although the novel was never completed, it was my first attempt at writing something that "big," and gave me good training in figuring out a plot line and the wishes of the characters. When we weren't writing, we would drive down to the shore and watch birds, hike on the Devon land, and visit old manor houses. It was a marvelous life.

When we returned to the United States, our funds depleted, my husband went back to teaching while I settled down to truly become a writer, or so I thought. I sat at my desk from eight in the morning until three in the afternoon, either reading poetry, writing it, or revising it. It was very arduous and a wonderful discipline. But it was also lonely. I didn't know any other writers at the time and did not have the support of a writer's group as I do now. At the end of two years writing, I actually had one poem published in the *Christian Science Monitor*! I was ecstatic, and promptly went out to spend the princely sum of twenty-five dollars on fabric to make clothes for my husband and me.

We also experimented with communal living, joining a small commune in a village in the hills of Ashfield, Massachusetts, in 1970. The rambling white farmhouse sat on what had been a dairy farm, with a huge three-storied red barn, over two hundred acres of woods and meadows, and a chilly pond where we swam in summer.

I continued to write mostly poetry at the time, sitting at a desk overlooking a meadow stretching to the woods, where crashing thunderstorms would pound the grass in the field, rain slamming against my window. And here I wrote my first published book called *Vultures,* illustrated by my mother, Marion Gray Warren.

It was a natural-history book—nonfiction—about vultures, who, it turns out, are nature's custodians. They clean up road kill, take care of animal corpses in the

woods, and while we joke about moving so the vultures won't circle us, I found them fascinating. My husband and I traveled to Florida with my parents, where Rick took scores of pictures of vultures for my mother to draw.

We would get a package of suet at a Piggly-Wiggly store, take it out to some parking lot where we had seen vultures, and put down the bait on the tar as we waited in the car. Rick's camera would click away madly, taking shot after shot of the vultures landing, taking off, and squabbling with each other.

For the book I researched old myths about vultures and folktales about them, along with scientific facts. It was wonderful to work on a book with my mother who was a fine graphic artist. This book was her memorial, as she died of cancer before its actual publication, but she did manage to finish all of the fine pen-and-ink drawings. She even used my father as a model for a Greek man in one of the pictures, showing a vulture dropping a turtle on this man's head. Illustrators, like writers, also use their family in their work.

My husband and I settled into a small white clapboard house with green shutters in the village of Haydenville,

"Not looking terribly happy as a first-year teacher," 1969 (Photo courtesy of Ann Turner.)

not far from my childhood home. While my husband taught in an alternative school, I focused on becoming a real writer—sitting at my desk in a small study, researching and writing. There I wrote my second book, *Houses for the Dead,* a survey of burial and mourning customs across time and cultures. I loved doing the research and taking facts and presenting them in story form—almost a kind of fictionalized nonfiction. I would read so many books about a period and take down so many notes, that the time period became "mine" in my imagination. I could imagine myself a character in it and write stories about a different age as if I lived there.

When I was not writing, I was learning building skills as we restored this house: blow-torching wood, sanding floors, putting up Sheetrock, painting, and more. I just liked making things, whether they were books, clothes, or a house.

We began building a passive solar house on a ridge not far away, up in the woods on a dirt road. This is where I live now and where we had our family—two children, Ben (now in college) and Charlotte (now in high school). My study has large glass windows up above the tree line, overlooking a beaver pond down the road. Hawks fly by my window; bears come padding out of the woods; and once two turkey vultures even landed on a huge glacial rock outside the house, spreading their wings in the sun.

In my journal I wrote, "The beauty of the world upholds me," and it is true. As a writer, I am fed and nourished by this landscape—the trees, pond, birds, and animals.

Perhaps because my husband and I did a form of homesteading, I wrote a book called *Dakota Dugout,* about a man who went West, built a sod dugout, and invited his bride to join him. In the book I expressed my belief that "sometimes the things we start with are best," that a simple life, well lived, has much to give us. I still believe that.

The research was fascinating: how settlers used a special plough to cut a long strip of sod from the land, then cut it into "bricks" to use in building; how they fashioned roofs out of willow boughs and straw, then put more sod over the top. Remember how the runaway oxen plunged his hoof through the roof of the dugout in Laura Ingalls Wilder's *On the Banks of Plum Creek?* I'm sure that all of this became part of my historical picture book, honoring the settlers in our country—their courage and stamina.

In our solar house on the ridge I also wrote *Nettie's Trip South,* based on my great-grandmother's diary of her trip South in 1859. I've spoken of that earlier in this essay. In fact, most of the books I'm known for have been created at this desk near the big window, overlooking the trees and the pond shimmering through the trees.

I continued to love doing research for my historical picture books, writing one called *Abe Lincoln Remembers,* where I looked at the early, formative years of that great president. I was surprised to learn how shy he was, especially with women; how he sometimes suffered from deep depression, particularly during the war. He grieved over the deaths of the soldiers and kept a joke book in the drawer of his desk to take out and try and cheer himself. In so many ways, he was a tragic figure—losing two of his sons whom he adored. Yet, somehow, he managed to lead this country through the terrible and bloody Civil War, almost to the end.

I was struck by Lincon's compassion for deserters. He made one comment that expressed his sympathy—it's not their fault they have "cowardly legs." Although he was not the true radical many portray him to be, he was a man of integrity and courage who still stands head and shoulders over many other presidents.

I also researched another president I admire, Thomas Jefferson, for my book *When Mr. Jefferson Came to Philadelphia.* (Originally it was called, "What Did I Know of Freedom?" but that title sadly did not survive the editing process.) He was, far more than Abe, a true radical. When I write one of these historical picture books, which wind up being about four-and-a-half typewritten pages, I have to read scores of books. I probably spend over four to five months just reading books and doing research, taking copious notes and scribbling things in the margins of the books I read.

I search for telling details, things that reveal character. For example, with Thomas Jefferson (whom I named T.J.), he always sang or hummed to himself when driving his carriage or curricle. He was passionate about horses, riding them up until his death. He loved once—his wife Martha—and probably never quite loved again, although we now know that he had a slave mistress, Sally Hemmings, with whom he had a number of children. This fact has been shocking to many and is part of the complexity and contradictions of Thomas Jefferson. He thought the slaves should be freed, and yet he refused to free his own slaves.

And at the end of this process of researching and investigating? I receive the gift of understanding important historical figures; somehow, through the process of reading and writing, they become "mine" in a way, part of an inner family as if they were my ancestors.

My most recent historical picture book is called *Sitting Bull Remembers,* the third in a study of great leaders—Abe Lincoln, Thomas Jefferson, and now Sitting Bull, the powerful leader of the Hunkpapa Sioux at the end of the nineteenth century. Using that format, of a historical figure remembering back, allows me to pick and choose events from his or her life, central events that show character or that have influenced the course of our country.

The Turner children: Ben, at fifteen, and Charlotte, at twelve, with two young friends, 2002 (Photo courtesy of Ann Turner.)

In this book you see the inevitable and deadly conflict between white settlers and Native Americans coming to a head in the famous Battle of Little Bighorn, where General George Custer and his soldiers were horribly outnumbered by the large force of Sioux and other tribes gathered by the river. It is a lesson in arrogance, for Custer thought he could surprise the Native Americans and beat them, small though his force was. Sadly, the decisive victory over Custer and his soldiers became a death knell for Sitting Bull and many other tribes and their leaders. Soon, they would be captured and herded and imprisoned on reservations, their way of life gone, their freedom finished. It is a sad and bloody story.

Two more historical picture books, this time about great women leaders, will be coming out in the future: one, "My Name Is Truth," is about the charismatic ex-slave Sojourner Truth, her journey to freedom and to finding her own voice; the other is about the visionary leader for women's suffrage, Susan B. Anthony. It is tentatively called "Stir up the World!"

But I haven't written books just about history and great leaders. Recently I have been branching out into writing what we call books for young adults, or YA books. In 1999 I started writing poetry and in a blast of creative energy, wrote twenty-two poems over two days, which became the core of the collection *Learning to*

Swim, about the sexual abuse I suffered as a young girl from a neighboring teenage boy. It was excruciating to write, more painful than anything I've ever done, but it was like lancing a boil—it hurt at first but it let out all the bad stuff that was hiding inside. In other words, it was cathartic.

I used the real-time, real Annie of six years old, as I was then, trying to learn to swim in Dresser's Pond up the road from our summer house—recalling how the swimming ring would help, how my daddy held me up. But once the abuse started, any courage I had in the water disappeared. This became one of those wonderful, unlooked-for metaphors which carried the book—something that came out of the creative process and was also part of a dialogue with my wonderful editor at Scholastic, Tracy Mack.

When the abuse finally stops, Annie finds it possible to go on with her life and to actually learn to swim—which I remember. Here is Annie with her dad beside her, helping her, but she has to do this on her own.

> . . . I let go of his hand.
> "I am learning to swim."
> I chanted
> and when the bottom
> fell away

I bobbed on the top,
my face like a white flower
before me.

If we are lucky, a writer will find one or two editors in her lifetime who help bring out the best in her—and in her works. Certainly, Charlotte Zolotow did that for me with my early picture book *Through Moon and Stars and Night Skies,* about adopting an Asian boy. She cherished her writers and nurtured them through a relationship based on dialogue, asking gentle questions to push them towards their best writing. Toni Markiet did that for me with so many of my historical picture books at HarperCollins, talking to me on the phone, asking questions like, "Yes, but what makes Sitting Bull great?" And later, Tracy Mack at Scholastic pushed me harder than probably any other editor has done to look at my poems, to rewrite them and rewrite them and rewrite them until I sometimes wanted to set fire to the book in my driveway.

"Now, are you *sure* about the ending here, Ann?" she would ask of a poem in *Learning to Swim* or *Hard Hit.* "Does it really say what you mean it to say? Could we have some more about the dad's relationship with Mark before Dad gets sick?"

The author with her husband, *Rick* (Photo by Ellen Augarten. Courtesy of the photographer.)

Then I'd go back to the computer, sipping a cup of tea, saying a few prayers to the patron saint of writers, trying to get to the meat of the poem in a way that would speak to me but also satisfy my editor. It is a complicated relationship but a necessary one. Editors ask for our best, but they also support their writers, encouraging them—"I know you can do this! You can do it!" And we need that, for, as I have said before, writing is a lonely profession.

With Tracy, I worked on *Hard Hit,* my most recent book of poems that tells a story—we now like to call it a "novel in poems." It is about a sixteen-year-old boy, Mark, a star pitcher on his high school's team, whose dad (an amateur astronomer) suddenly falls ill with deadly, rapidly spreading pancreatic cancer. How Mark deals with this news, how his mom and sister face this crisis, how Dad faces his coming death are all part of the story.

One poem is based on my ten year-old son's response to his grandpa's impending death. Ben spent hours on the porch playing video games, killing raiders and crossing the River of Fire, announcing at the end, "I feel like I helped Baba." So, too, Mark plays video games and feels that he is keeping evil at bay.

It is probably my most religious book, reflecting my own deep faith; there is a priest who appears at various times in some of the poems, helping the family and Mark to survive this great loss, and Mark prays and attends church with his family. All of this helps, but in the end, it is the strength in Mark and the warmth of his family and friendships (with Eddie and Diane, his girlfriend) that carry him through.

I used my own recent experience of my father's death when I began writing this collection: the stages of grief, the anger and denial, the wish to turn back the clock, the hope that somehow we can heal our ill parent, all of that comes from my own life.

When I write a "novel in poems" I create characters, just as I would in a prose novel. I fashion what are called "wish lines" for each person in the story: what that person most wants from his or her life. How does he plan on getting it? How do these wish lines cross and conflict or reinforce each other?

For example, Mom wishes Dad to live, as does Dad and Josie and Mark. But Dad wants Mark to be a star pitcher. Mark wants this too, but not in the same way his father does. When Dad falls ill, Mark makes a sort of bargain with God, that if he can pitch a no-hitter—when no one on the opposing team scores, extremely hard to do—that will somehow help his dad to get better.

But no one's efforts can keep Dad from dying, and Mark has to accept the inevitable with all the pain he'd wished to avoid. After his dad dies, he looks up at the sky and sees stars shining overhead.

One star gleamed
and sparked
like Dad's eyes
it seemed he was there
loving me
his dust his bones his voice
part of a star.

What's ahead of me as I write this essay? I think we writers are changed by the books we write, and sometimes, after one is finished, we know we'll never quite write the same kind of book again. We are different. So, after completing these two collections of poems, I am changed, and my writing has changed—to something deeper, harder, and probably darker.

The book I am currently working on is called *The Father of Lies,* about an unusual girl, Libby, who was alive during the time of the Salem Witch trials in 1692. Her experiences and the way she sees the fear and horror are radically different from other stories written about this gruesome time. Only she knows the accusing girls are lying, for only Libby has her own internal demon.

What is true for me is also true for you; I am as surprised by what comes out of my fingers flying over the keyboard as you may be reading it. I want to know how the story turns out just as you, my reader, do. I never know the ending to my stories when I begin. I have to figure it out, step by step, as I move through the writing process. There is a wonderful poem by Theodore Roetke called "Waking to Sleep," which perfectly describes my writing process: I only learn where I am going by taking one step forward at a time until I reach the end of the book.

What I know about my writing is that it comes from many deep places within me and my life: my childhood, its joys and its wounds; the strengths of my family and the love that surrounded us and surrounds us still; the deep faith I have in God and how that has changed me and the way I view the world (as full of meaning, as not ultimately tragic).

My work also is influenced deeply by: having my own children and watching them grow up, which has brought me more joy and sorrow than I thought possible; my profound interest in the history of this country, who shaped it, and how past events inform the present; my own sense of humor: I love to laugh and see the humor in most situations; my love of animals (you will see dogs and cats in many of my books, twining their way around the family); my desire for a home and searching for a secure home, a theme that winds throughout my work; my belief that in the end love brings us home, no matter who we are, no matter our situation (it is Rosemary's compassion toward the witch that frees the family from her awful presence).

Finally, my writing springs from a profound gratefulness that I get to sit down at my computer, turn it on, and let the musings of my mind and heart flow out onto the page. I know I will work on those pages until I sweat, but it is still a blessing. How lucky I am.

*   *   *

TURNER, Ann Warren
See TURNER, Ann

U-V

UMANSKY, Kaye 1946-

Personal
Born December 6, 1946, in Plymouth, England; married; husband's name Moe; children: Ella; (stepchildren) Dave, Dan, Zoe. *Education:* Attended teachers' training college. *Hobbies and other interests:* Travel, reading, music.

Addresses
Home—Crouch End, North London, England.

Career
Writer, actor, musician, and educator. Teacher of music and drama in London, England.

Awards, Honors
Nottinghamshire Book Award, 1993, for *Pongwiffy and the Spell of the Year; Times Educational Supplement* Junior Music Book Award, 1999, for *Three Rapping Rats.*

Writings

Bandybones, illustrated by Maggie Read, Macmillan Education (Basingstoke, England), 1986.

Little Sister, illustrated by David Dowland and Joyce Smith, Macmillan Education (Basingstoke, England), 1986.

The Toymaker's Birthday, illustrated by Ken Morton, Macmillan Educational (Basingstoke, England), 1986.

Big Iggy, illustrated by Katie Thomas, A. & C. Black (London, England), 1987, reprinted, 2004.

Litterbugs (play), Macmillan Educational (Basingstoke, England), 1987.

Phantasmagoria: Thirty-three Songs, Story Lines, and Sound Adventures (song book), music by Andy Jackson, A. & C. Black (London, England), 1988.

Witches in Stitches, illustrated by Judy Brown, Puffin (London, England), 1988.

The Fwog Pwince, illustrated by Gwyneth Williamson, A. & C. Black (London, England), 1989.

King Keith and the Nasty Case of Dragonitis, illustrated by Ainslie Macleod, Viking (London, England), 1990.

Tin Can Hero, illustrated by John Dyke, Hodder & Stoughton (London, England), 1990.

Tiger and Me, illustrated by Susie Jenkin-Pearce, Red Fox (London, England), 1991.

Trash Hits, illustrated by Judy Brown, Puffin (London, England), 1991.

King Keith and the Jolly Lodger, illustrated by Ainslie Macleod, Viking (London, England), 1991.

Sir Quinton Quest Hunts the Yeti, illustrated by Judy Brown, A. & C. Black (London, England), 1992.

The Misfortunes of Captain Cadaverous, illustrated by Judy Brown, BBC Books (London, England), 1992.

Pass the Jam, Jim, illustrated by Margaret Chamberlain, Red Fox (London, England), 1993.

Do Not Open before Christmas Day!, illustrated by Garry Davies, Puffin (London, England), 1993.

Sir Quinton Quest Hunts the Jewel, illustrated by Judy Brown, Young Lions (London, England), 1994.

Three Singing Pigs: Making Music with Traditional Stories, illustrated by Michael Evans, A. & C. Black (London, England), 1994.

(Author of text) Annabel Collis, *Dobbin,* Bodley Head (London, England), 1994.

Sophie and Abigail, illustrated by Anna Currey, Gollancz (London, England), 1995, Good Books (Intercourse, PA), 2004.

A Ruby, a Rug, and a Prince Called Doug, illustrated by Chris Fisher, Young Lions (London, England), 1995.

The Empty Suit of Armour, illustrated by Keren Ludlow, Orion (London, England), 1995.

Sophie in Charge, illustrated by Anna Currey, Gollancz (London, England), 1995, Good Books (Intercourse, PA), 2005.

Sophie and the Mother's Day Card, illustrated by Anna Currey, Gollancz (London, England), 1995, Good Books (Intercourse, PA), 2005.

Sophie and the Wonderful Picture, illustrated by Anna Currey, Gollancz (London, England), 1995, Good Books (Intercourse, PA), 2004.

The Night I Was Chased by a Vampire, illustrated by Keren Ludlow, Orion (London, England), 1995.

Cinderella (play), illustrated by Caroline Crossland, A. & C. Black (London, England), 1996.

The Jealous Giant, illustrated by Doffy Weir, Hamish Hamilton (London, England), 1997.

Noah's Ark (play), illustrated by Tessa Richardson-Jones, A. & C. Black (London, England), 1997.

The Emperor's New Clothes (play), illustrated by Caroline Crossland, A. & C. Black (London, England), 1997.

The Romantic Giant, illustrated by Doffy Weir, Puffin (London, England), 1997.

The Spooks Step Out, illustrated by Keren Ludlow, Orion (London, England), 1997.

The Bogey Men and the Trolls Next Door, illustrated by Keren Ludlow, Orion (London, England), 1997.

Cover of Kaye Umansky's amusing picture book I Don't Like Gloria!, ***featuring artwork by Margaret Chamberlain.*** (Illustration copyright © 2007 by Margaret Chamberlain. Reproduced by permission of the publisher Candlewick Press, Inc., Cambridge, MA on behalf of Walker Books, Ltd., London, England.)

Beyond the Beanstalk, illustrated by Chris Fisher, Hodder Children's (London, England), 1997.

Hammy House of Horror, illustrated by Chris Fisher, Hodder Children's (London, England), 1998.

You Can Swim, Jim, illustrated by Margaret Chamberlain, Bodley Head (London, England), 1998.

Three Rapping Rats: Making Music with Traditional Stories, illustrated by Stephen Chadwick and Katie Buchanan, A. & C. Black (London, England), 1998.

Never Meddle with Magic Mirrors, illustrated by Stella Voce, Cambridge University Press (Cambridge, England), 1998.

Tickle My Nose, and Other Action Rhymes, illustrated by Nick Sharratt, Puffin (New York, NY), 1999.

Donkey Ride to Disaster, illustrated by Chris Fisher, Hodder Children's (London, England), 1999.

Madness in the Mountains, illustrated by Chris Fisher, Hodder Children's (London, England), 1999.

Nonsense Counting Rhymes, illustrated by Chris Fisher, Oxford University Press (Oxford, England), 1999.

Need a Trim, Jim, illustrated by Margaret Chamberlain, Bodley Head (London, England), 1999.

Moon Adventure, illustrated by Steve Smallman, Longman (Harlow, England), 2000.

Strange Days at Sea, illustrated by Chris Fisher, Hodder Children's (London, England), 2000.

Sleeping Beauty (play), illustrated by Caroline Crossland, A. & C. Black (London, England), 2000.

Three Tapping Teddies: Musical Stories and Chants for the Very Young, A. & C. Black (London, England), 2000.

The Rubbish Monster, illustrated by Ken Stott, Pearson Education (Harlow, England), 2000.

I Am Miss Cherry, illustrated by Tom Clayton, Pearson Education (Harlow, England), 2000.

The Carnival, illustrated by Steve Smallman, Pearson Education (Harlow, England), 2000.

Rope That Cow!, illustrated by Steve Smallman, Pearson Education (Harlow, England), 2000.

What a Mess! (play), illustrated by Tom Clayton and Steve Smallman, Pearson Education (Harlow, England), 2000.

Poor Sam (play), illustrated by Tom Clayton, Pearson Education (Harlow, England), 2000.

Pirates Ahoy!, illustrated by Steve Smallman, Pearson Education (Harlow, England), 2000.

Wilma's Wicked Revenge, illustrated by Tony Blundell, Puffin (London, England), 2000.

No More Master Niceguy, illustrated by Chris Fisher, Hodder Children's (London, England), 2000.

Beyond Strange Street, illustrated by Steve Smallman, Pearson Education (Harlow, England), 2001.

Soup with Obby, illustrated by Steve Smallman, Pearson Education (Harlow, England), 2001.

Down the Rushing River, illustrated by Steve Smallman, Pearson Education (Harlow, England), 2001.

Wizard Wagoo, illustrated by Steve Smallman, Pearson Education (Harlow, England), 2001.

Up the Dizzy Mountain, illustrated by Steve Smallman, Pearson Education (Harlow, England), 2001.

Gong!, illustrated by Steve Smallman, Pearson Education (Harlow, England), 2001.

Nonsense Animal Rhymes, illustrated by Chris Fisher, Oxford University Press (Oxford, England), 2001.

Big Iggy, A. & C. Black (London, England), 2001.

The Dressed-up Giant, illustrated by Doffy Weir, Penguin (London, England), 2001.

Three Days with Jim, illustrated by Judy Brown, Red Fox (London, England), 2001.

Prince Dandypants and the Masked Avenger, illustrated by Trevor Dunton, Puffin (London, England), 2001.

Cruel Times: A Victorian Play, illustrated by Martin Ursell, Hodder Wayland (London, England), 2002.

Goblinz!, illustrated by Andi Good, Puffin (London, England), 2002.

This Is Jane, Jim, illustrated by Margaret Chamberlain, Red Fox (London, England), 2002.

Wiggle My Toes, illustrated by Nick Sharratt, Puffin (London, England), 2002.

Wilma's Wicked Spell, illustrated by Tony Blundell, Penguin (London, England), 2002.

Humble Tom's Big Trip (play), illustrated by Chris Mould, Hodder Wayland (London, England), 2003.

Meet the Weirds, illustrated by Chris Mould, Barrington Stoke (Edinburgh, Scotland), 2003.

Buster's Big Surprise, illustrated by Leo Broadley, Scholastic (London, England), 2003.

The Big Mix up, Scholastic (London, England), 2003.

The Snow Queen (musical), A. & C. Black (London, England), 2003.

Mick McMenace, Ghost Detective, illustrated by Ian Cunliffe, Puffin (London, England), 2003.

The Romantic Giant, illustrated by Doffy Weir, Barn Owl Books, 2004.

The Jealous Giant, illustrated by Doffy Weir, Barn Owl Books, 2004.

The Night I Was Chased by a Vampire, and Other Stories, illustrated by Chris Mould, Orion (London, England), 2004.

A Chair for Baby Bear, illustrated by Chris Fisher, Barrons Educational (Hauppauge, NY), 2004.

The Time the Play Went Wrong, illustrated by Kelly Waldek, Pearson Education (Harlow, England), 2004.

My Very First Joke Book, Puffin (London, England), 2004.

The Silver Spoon of Solomon Snow, Puffin (London, England), 2004, Candlewick Press (Cambridge, MA), 2005.

Goblinz: Detectives, Inc., illustrated by Andi Good, Puffin (London, England), 2004.

Solomon Snow and the Stolen Jewel, Puffin (London, England), 2004, Candlewick Press (Cambridge, MA), 2006.

Weird Happenings, illustrated by Chris Mould, Barrington Stoke (London, England), 2004.

Horses' Holiday, illustrated by Ainslie Macleod, Collins (London, England), 2005.

I Want a Pet!, illustrated by Sarah Horne, Collins (London, England), 2005.

Goblinz and the Witch, illustrated by Andi Good, Puffin (London, England), 2005.

Wildly Weird, illustrated by Chris Mould, Barrington Stoke (Edinburgh, Scotland), 2006.

I Am a Tree, illustrated by Kate Sheppard, A. & C. Black (London, England), 2006.

I Don't Like Gloria!, illustrated by Margaret Chamberlain, Candlewick Press (Cambridge, MA), 2007.

I Live in a Mad House, illustrated by Kate Sheppard, A. & C. Black (London, England), 2007.

Umansky presents a wacky story in **A Chair for Baby Bear,** *an off-beat version of the Goldilocks story that features illustrations by Chris Fisher.* (Illustration copyright © 2004 by Chris Fisher. Reproduced by permission.)

Let's Go to London!, illustrated by Adrienne Salgado, A. & C. Black (London, England), 2007.

Clover Twig and the Incredible Flying Cottage, Bloomsbury (London, England), 2008.

Yo Ho Ho, a Pirating We'll Go, illustrated by Nick Sharratt, Puffin (London, England), 2008.

Contributor to books, including *Bingo Lingo: Supporting Language Development through Songs,* by Helen MacGregor, A. & C. Black (London, England), 1999.

"PONGWIFFY"SERIES; FOR CHILDREN

Pongwiffy: A Witch of Dirty Habits, illustrated by Chris Smedley, A. & C. Black (London, England), 1988, Pocket Books (New York, NY), 2001.

Broomnapped, illustrated by Chris Smedley, A. & C. Black (London, England), 1991.

Pongwiffy, a Witch of Dirty Habits, and the Spell of the Year, illustrated by Chris Smedley, Viking (London, England), 1992.

Pongwiffy and the Goblins' Revenge, illustrated by Chris Smedley, Puffin (London, England), 1992.

Pongwiffy and the Holiday of Doom, illustrated by David Roberts, Puffin (London, England), 1996.

Pongwiffy and the Pantomime, illustrated by Chris Smedley, Puffin (London, England), 1997.

The Spellovision Song Contest, illustrated by David Roberts, Puffin (London, England), 2003.

Adaptations

The "Pongwiffy" books were adapted by Telemagination as television programs airing on British and Australian television, c. 2004; many of Umansky's books were adapted as audiobooks by Chivers Children's Audio, including the "Pongwiffy" books, which are narrated by Prunella Scales.

Sidelights

A music teacher and actress, Kaye Umansky is also a popular author who has channeled her creativity and quirky humor into a long list of books for younger readers. Her creation of the unkempt witch Pongwiffy, who made her introduction to readers in 1988's *Pongwiffy: A Witch of Dirty Habits,* has made Umansky well known in her native Great Britain as well as in Australia, while her other humor-filled works have gained her a large following as far away as North America, where many have been published. Reviewing Umansky's picture book *A Chair for Baby Bear,* a sequel to the story of Goldilocks and the three bears in which the young cub goes shopping for a new chair, *School Library Journal* critic Catherine Callegari described the author's "lighhearted" story as "just right for . . . one-on-one sharing." Youngsters left with questions at the close of

Cover of Umansky's engaging middle-grade mystery **Solomon Snow and the Stolen Jewel,** *featuring artwork by Scott Nash.* (Cover illustration copyright © by Scott Nash. Reproduced by permission of the publisher Candlewick Press, Inc., Cambridge, MA.)

the traditional tale will find that Umansky and illustrator Chris Fisher do "a nifty job of tying up the loose ends," according to a *Publishers Weekly* contributor. Other picture books featuring Umansky's unique humor include *I Don't Like Gloria!,* a tale about a disgruntled bulldog whose family has adopted a fluffy Persian cat that is humorously brought to life in Margaret Chamberlain's cartoon art.

Born in Devon, England, in 1946, Umansky started her writing career in the mid-1980s, after she left teaching to stay home and raise her just-about-to-be-born daughter. "I always thought authors must be special people—not ordinary, like me," she explained on the Penguin UK Web site. "In fact, there is no magic to it. You just need to enjoy it and be prepared to work hard." Her advice to beginning writers includes keeping a paper and pencil handy to write down ideas, as well as her number-one suggestion: "Read, read and read again. It is by reading that you learn how to become a good writer."

Since her introduction, the witch called Pongwiffy has reappeared in several books by Umansky, and has proved so popular with British readers that the "Pongwiffy" books were adapted for television. In *Pongwiffy and the Spell of the Year* the witch is keen to enter a local Spell of the Year contest, and when she locates a highly touted recipe by spellmeister Granny Malodour, Pongwiffy assumes that the win will be hers. However a search for the necessary ingredients—the spell includes wild cat whiskers, quicksand, a vulture's feather, and the hair of a princess, cut during a full moon to ensure maximum potency—proves problematic. *Pongwiffy and the Pantomime* finds the resilient sorceress penning a play for members of her local coven to perform. However, in typical Umansky fashion, things quickly degenerate into humorous chaos.

As she does in the "Pongwiffy" books, Umansky enjoys creating stories that feature supernatural and ghostly elements, and she makes scary characters comical—and far less scary!—in the process. In *Goblinz!,* for example, a lone goblin named Shy has aspirations of being part of a gaggle. Unfortunately, coming up with the six other members to make the seven goblins required for official gaggle status is hard when you don't have any friends. However, once Shy decides to take action and find a way to attract members, Tuf, Wheels, and Oggy sign up for his group and thus form the core of the Goblinz.

Having assembled her cast of quirky ghouls, Umansky continues their story in *Goblinz: Detectives, Inc.,* which finds the gaggle all outfitted in super-spy gear and ready to go sleuthing, and *Goblinz and the Witch,* in which the gruesome gang hit a rough spot with a local witch when they attempt to take their new go-cart for a trial run down Gaspup Hill. She balances such fantastic fictions with down-to-earth stories such as *The Carnival* and *Sophie and the Wonderful Picture,* the latter in which a frog and rabbit attempt to create an impressive work of art for presentation at their school. In a *School Arts* review, Ken Marantz predicted that beginning readers will get a "smiling boost" from *Sophie and the Wonderful Picture,* and praised the "light-hearted illustrations" created for the book by Anna Currey.

Umansky turns to fantasy in the mock-Victorian melodrama *The Silver Spoon of Solomon Snow.* Solomon is the quintessential foundling: he was discovered on the doorstep of laundress Ma Stubbins teething on the proverbial silver spoon. Raised in the rough-and-tumble Stubbins household, where Mr. Stubbins' drinking keeps things on an uneven keel, Solomon exhibits unusual good manners. When the boy turns ten, he goes in search of his actual parents, helped by loyal friends Prudence Pidy, Freddy the chimney sweep's son, a pet rabbit named Mr. Skippy, and Rosabella, a young prodigy who has escaped from a traveling circus. Readers reunite with the troupe in *Solomon Snow and the Stolen Jewel,* as Solomon and Prudence attempt to save Prudence's poacher father from being imprisoned on a convict ship. Divided into short chapters, Umansky's fast-moving plot thickens when the evil Dr. Casimir Calimari enters the picture, involving the travelers in his theft of a huge but cursed ruby. Reviewing *The Silver Spoon of Solomon Snow,* Ilene Cooper wrote in *Booklist* that the novel features "enough Dickensian moments and clever characters" to capture children's imaginations, and *School Library Journal* contributor Steven Engelfried cited the story's "quirky characters and funny moments." A *Kirkus Reviews* writer dubbed Umansky's "over-the-top parody of Oliver Twist-type adventures . . . a good giggle." In her *Booklist* review of *Solomon Snow and the Stolen Jewel* Kathleen Isaacs praised the sequel's "gently humorous third-person narrative" and "satisfying end." Commending both books as attractive to reluctant readers, Carly B. Wiskoff wrote of *Solomon Snow and the Stolen Jewel* that Umansky's "fast-paced read" trades "character development . . . for some Victorian-tinted atmosphere and humor."

Biographical and Critical Sources

PERIODICALS

Booklist, November 1, 2005, Ilene Cooper, review of *The Silver Spoon of Solomon Snow,* p. 48; April 15, 2007, Kathleen Isaacs, review of *Solomon Snow and the Stolen Jewel,* p. 45.

Horn Book, January-February, 2006, Joanna Rudge Long, review of *The Silver Spoon of Solomon Snow,* p. 90; May-June, 2007, Joanna Rudge Long, review of *Solomon Snow and the Stolen Jewel,* p. 292.

Kirkus Reviews, March 15, 2005, review of *Sophie and the Mother's Day Card,* p. 360; October 1, 2005, review of *The Silver Spoon of Solomon Snow,* p. 1091; April 1, 2007, review of *Solomon Snow and the Stolen Jewel.*

Publishers Weekly, July 5, 1999, review of *Tickle My Nose and Other Action Rhymes,* p. 73; November 15, 2004, review of *A Chair for Baby Bear,* p. 58; February 12, 2007, review of *I Don't Like Gloria!,* p. 84.

School Arts, October, 2004, Ken Marantz, review of *Sophie and the Wonderful Picture,* p. 66.

School Library Journal, August, 2002, Ronni Krasnow, review of *Sleeping Beauty,* p. 179; February, 2005, Catherine Callegari, review of *A Chair for Baby Bear,* p. 110; December, 2005, Steven Engelfried, review of *The Silver Spoon of Solomon Snow,* p. 156; July, 2007, Carly B. Wiskoff, review of *Solomon Snow and the Stolen Jewel,* p. 86.

ONLINE

Kaye Umansky Home Page, http://kayeumansky.com (March 26, 2008).

Puffin UK Web site, http://www.penguin.co.uk/ (March 26, 2008), "Kaye Umansky."

Story Street Web site, http://www.storystreet.co.uk/ (March 14, 2005), "Kaye Umansky."*

*   *   *

VIDRINE, Beverly Barras 1938-

Personal

Born September 30, 1938, in New Iberia, LA; daughter of Charles (a building contractor) and Estelle Barras; married Dennis J. Vidrine (an attorney), July 22, 1961; children: Denise Vidrine Torian, William, Kenneth. *Education:* University of Southwestern Louisiana (now University of Louisiana at Lafayette), B.A. (elementary education); attended Lamar State College of Technology (now Lamar University) and Institute of Children's Literature. *Religion:* Roman Catholic. *Hobbies and other interests:* Classical music, playing piano.

Addresses

Home—Lafayette, LA.

Career

Educator and writer. Elementary school teacher in Lafayette, LA, 1960-61, 1973, 1988-91, Beaumont, TX, 1961-62, 1964-65, Baton Rouge, LA, 1970-72, and Broussard, LA, 1973-76; law office of Dennis J. Vidrine, Lafayette, office manager, legal secretary, and bookkeeper, 1976-88.

Member

Writers Guild of Acadiana (historian, beginning 1991), Society of Children's Book Writers and Illustrators.

Writings

A Mardi Gras Dictionary, illustrated by Patrick Soper, Sunflower Press (Lafayette, LA), 1994.

A Christmas Dictionary, illustrated by Patrick Soper, Pelican Publishing (Gretna, LA), 1997.

St. Patrick's Day Alphabet, illustrated by Patrick Soper, Pelican Publishing (Gretna, LA), 2001.

Easter Day Alphabet, illustrated by Alison Davis Lyne, Pelican Publishing (Gretna, LA), 2003.

Halloween Alphabet, illustrated by Alison Davis Lyne, Pelican Publishing (Gretna, LA), 2004.

Thanksgiving Day Alphabet, illustrated by Alison Davis Lyne, Pelican Publishing (Gretna, LA), 2006.

Contributor of short fiction to magazines, including *U.S. Kids.*

Sidelights

A Louisiana native, Barbara Barras Vidrine worked for many years as an elementary-school teacher before turning to writing for children. Her first two books, *A Mardi Gras Dictionary* and *A Christmas Dictionary,* introduce young children to the sights, sounds, traditions, and history of two holidays with both Christian and secular significance. New Orleans' lavish Mardi Gras carnival ushers in Shrove Tuesday or "Fat Tuesday," the day before Ash Wednesday and the start of the period of fasting known as Lent. More familiar to non-Louisiana readers is Christmas, in which the arrival of Santa Claus and the birth of Jesus Christ both figure in the day's history and traditions. Vidrine's books are especially

Beverly Barras Vidrine weaves history and cultural tradition within a familiar concept-book format in **Thanksgiving Alphabet.** (Pelican Publishing Company, 2006. Republished by permission.)

significant to her family; her eight grandchildren are featured in the colorful illustrations that artists create to accompany her texts.

Other holidays are explored by Vidrine in her series of illustrated concept books. *St. Patrick's Day Alphabet* explains twenty-six Irish traditions surrounding the Irish-born saint and the holiday that honors him. *Easter Day Alphabet* explores the history of another Christian holiday that has become a favorite of children, and in keeping with Easter traditions readers can search for the golden egg concealed in the artwork on each page. Turning from Easter bunnies to ghouls, *Halloween Alphabet* bring to life the sights, sounds, and general spookiness of another child-friendly holiday, while the history of a uniquely North American day of thankfulness and celebration is presented in *Thanksgiving Day Alphabet.* Praising *Thanksgiving Alphabet,* which focuses on the original 1621 harvest festival in the Massachusetts colony, Mary Elam wrote in *School Library Journal* that Vidrine's text "informs with unusual words and names . . . , creating a useful teaching tool" for elementary-grade readers.

Biographical and Critical Sources

PERIODICALS

Kirkus Reviews, September 15, 2006, review of *Thanksgiving Day Alphabet,* p. 969.

School Library Journal, July, 2003, Jane Marino, review of *Easter Day Alphabet,* p. 119; December, 2004, Wendy Woodfill, review of *Halloween Alphabet,* p. 138; November, 2006, Mary Elam, review of *Thanksgiving Day Alphabet,* p. 126.

ONLINE

Pelican Publishing Web site, http://www.pelicanpub.com/ (February 6, 2006), "Beverly Barras Vidrine."*

*   *   *

VINCENT, Erin 1969-

Personal

Born 1969, in Sydney, New South Wales, Australia; married. *Education:* Graduated from college.

Addresses

Home—Australia; United States. *E-mail*—erin@griefgirl.com.

Career

Author and actor.

Writings

Grief Girl: My True Story, Delacorte Press (New York, NY), 2007.

Sidelights

The title of Erin Vincent's memoir *Grief Girl: My True Story* reflects the extent to which a tragic incident can affect and overwhelm a young person's life. In her book, Vincent returns readers to the year she was fourteen and living in Sydney, New South Wales, Australia. She describes the death of, first, her mother and then her father, as the result of an automobile accident. Dealing with the grief of this dual loss affected much of Vincent's teen years and continued to shadow her for many years thereafter. Finally, with the encouragement of her husband, Vincent was able to reflect on her feelings. Six years in the writing, *Grief Girl* recounts this painful experience and provides teen readers with "a gripping memoir" and a work that "will resonate" with teens in the opinion of *School Library Journal* contributor Rebecca M. Jones.

With the death of her parents in 1983, Vincent's life changed forever. Because her older sister, Tracy, had turned eighteen, Vincent and her three-year-old brother, Trent, were able to remain together, but the lack of a parent left each of the children emotionally isolated. Over the next two years, Vincent insulated herself from friends, family, and teachers who tried to help, and other misfortunes followed, such as the breakdown of the relationship among the siblings, abandonment by extended family, a loss of personal faith, and unwanted sexual advances. "I became such an angry person, and I thought the world was just a horrible place," Vincent revealed to Richard Fidler in a profile posted on the Australian Broadcasting Corporation—Queensland Web site. "I stopped washing, I stopped washing my hair . . . ," she added. "I didn't wear my school uniform. . . . I became very 'eff you'."

Vincent narrates her story in the present tense, using the "gritty language" and adolescent perspective that gives *Grief Girl* a "palpable immediacy," in Jones' view. A *Publishers Weekly* reviewer cited the book's "unadorned, journalistic style" and noted that Vincent's "intimate, honest narrative captures both . . . strength and vulnerability." "Any adolescent going through the grieving process will tearfully embrace" *Grief Girl,* concluded Jennifer Hubert, the critic dubbing Vincent's memoir "poignant" in her *Booklist* review.

Biographical and Critical Sources

BOOKS

Vincent, Erin, *Grief Girl: My True Story,* Delacorte (New York, NY), 2007.

PERIODICALS

Booklist, February 1, 2007, Jennifer Hubert, review of *Grief Girl: My True Story,* p. 41.

Cover of Erin Vincent's poignant autobiographical novel **Grief Girl,** *in which a teen's future is overshadowed by a parent's death.* (Jacket design by Angela Carlino. Used by permission of Random House Children's Books, a division of Random House, Inc.)

Bulletin of the Center for Children's Books, April, 2007, Deborah Stevenson, review of *Grief Girl,* p. 347.

Kirkus Reviews, February 1, 2007, review of *Grief Girl,* p. 130.

Publishers Weekly, April 2, 2007, review of *Grief Girl,* p. 59.

School Library Journal, February, 2007, Rebecca M. Jones, review of *Grief Girl,* p. 146.

Voice of Youth Advocates, April, 2007, Mary E. Helsin, review of *Grief Girl,* p. 82.

ONLINE

Australian Broadcasting Corporation—Queensland Web site, http://www.abc.net.au/queensland/ (April 20, 2007), Richard Fidler, profile of Vincent.

Blurb, http://www.theblurb.com.au/ (February 1, 2008), Karin van Heerwaarden, interview with Vincent.

Erin Vincent Home Page, http://www.griefgirl.com (February 18, 2008).

Random House Web site, http://www.randomnhouse.com/ (March 28, 2008), "Erin Vincent."

W-Y

WALDEN, Mark 1952-

Personal

Born 1952, in England; married; wife's name Sarah; children: Megan. *Education:* Newcastle University, B.A. (English literature), M.A. (twentieth-century literature, film, and television).

Addresses

Home—England.

Career

Children's author. Formerly worked as a video-game designer.

Writings

"H.I.V.E." NOVEL SERIES

H.I.V.E.: Higher Institution of Villainous Education, Bloomsbury (London, England), 2006, Simon & Schuster (New York, NY), 2007.
The Overlord Protocol, Bloomsbury (London, England), 2007, Simon & Schuster (New York, NY), 2008.
Escape Velocity, Bloomsbury (London, England), 2008.

Sidelights

Mark Walden's work as a video-game designer came in handy when he decided to change careers and become a writer. His novels in the "H.I.V.E." series feature many of the same qualities that make certain games more popular among teen players: likable characters, an extraordinarily villainous villain, cool superheroes with unusual skills, and the mission of fighting a threat posed by a cabal of conspiratorial, control-seeking adults.

In Walden's series opener, *H.I.V.E.: Higher Institution of Villainous Education,* readers meet thirteen-year-old Otto Malpense. An orphan, Otto is kidnaped along with dozens of other misbehaving teens. Having demonstrated a penchant for vice, these young people are transported to a secret school located on a remote island and forcibly enrolled in a six-year program designed to produce an alumni roster of successful criminals. Together with martial artist Wing Fanchu, computer geek Laura Brand, and jewel-thief prodigy Shelby Trinity, Otto hatches a scheme to thwart the aims of H.I.V.E. mastermind Dr. Nero and break free from the perverted and authoritarian boarding school. Although remarking that some of the villains in *H.I.V.E.* are "cartoonish" renditions of the fictional nemeses of James Bond, a *Publishers Weekly* contributor wrote that "Walden's characters are memorable." Reflecting a similar view, a *Kirkus Reviews* writer noted that "well-developed characters" and "a world that isn't as far-fetched as one might first surmise" are combined with Walden's "irreverent humor" to produce a fast-moving middle-grade adventure.

Dubbed "fast-moving fun" by *Kliatt* reviewer Paula Rohrlick, *The Overlord Protocol* finds Otto and company still trapped at the institute and beginning their second year. When he and Wing are allowed temporary leave to attend Wing's father's funeral, the boys cross the path of Cypher, a vicious supervillain who commands an army of talented and ruthless ninjas. Tragedy strikes after Otto and Wing are forced to be part of Cypher's efforts to obtain a computer intelligence that aids world domination, and Otto must join with Dr. Nero in order to stop the threat to mankind. In *Booklist* Diana Tixier Herald dubbed *The Overlord Protocol* "a real page turner" featuring "a wickedly compelling adventure," and *School Library Journal* critic Eric Norton cited the novel's "plot twists and startling revelations" as the root of its "appeal to [fans of] . . . action and intrigue."

Biographical and Critical Sources

PERIODICALS

Booklist, April 1, 2007, Francisca Goldsmith, review of *H.I.V.E.: Higher Institution of Villainous Education,* p.

53; March 1, 2008, Diana Tixier Herald, review of *The Overlord Protocol*, p. 70.

Bulletin of the Center for Children's Books, July-August, 2007, April Spisak, review of *H.I.V.E.,* p. 488.

Kirkus Reviews, May 1, 2007, review of *H.I.V.E.;* December 1, 2007, review of *The Overlord Protocol.*

Kliatt, January, 2008, Paula Rohrlick, review of *The Overlord Protocol,* p. 13.

Publishers Weekly, April 23, 2007, review of *H.I.V.E.,* p. 52.

School Library Journal, June, 2007, Walter Minkel, review of *H.I.V.E.,* p. 164; March, 2008, Eric Norton, review of *The Overlord Protocol,* p. 213.

Voice of Youth Advocates, June, 2007, David Goodale, review of *H.I.V.E.,* p. 169.

ONLINE

Bloomsbury Web site, http://www.bloomsbury.com/ (March 28, 2008), "Mark Walden."*

*   *   *

WALLACE, Karen 1951-

Personal

Born April 1, 1951, in Ottawa, Ontario, Canada; immigrated to England, 1962; daughter of David (a diplomat) and Margaret (an architect); married Sam Llewellyn (a writer), February, 1975; children: William, Martin. *Education:* University of London, B.A. (with honors); University of Grenoble (France), received diploma. *Politics:* Liberal. *Religion:* Church of England (Anglican).

Addresses

Agent—Pat White, Rogers, Coleridge & White, 20 Powis Mews, London W11 1JN, England.

Career

Children's book author and writer for television. Worked in editorial and promotions departments in publishing companies in England and Canada, 1974-78; freelance writer. Formerly worked as a cabaret and bluegrass singer.

Awards, Honors

Times Educational Supplement Junior Prize, Kurt Maschler Award, and Parent's Choice Gold Award, all for *Think of an Eel;* London *Guardian* Children's Fiction Prize shortlist, 2002, for *Raspberries on the Yangtze;* British Academy of Film and Television Arts Award, 2001, for *The Hoobs;* British Book Trust Teenage Prize shortlist, 2005, for *The Unrivalled Spangles.*

Writings

FOR CHILDREN

The Battle for Gold Diggers' Forest, Simon & Schuster (London, England), 1989.

Fearless Fiona and the Mothproof Hall Mystery, Young Lion (London, England), 1992.

Zizz Bear, Walker (London, England), 1992, Candlewick Press (Cambridge, MA), 1995.

Zizz Bear, Busy Bear, Walker (London, England), 1993, Candlewick Press (Cambridge, MA), 1995.

Fearless Fiona and the Mystery of the Great Stone Haggis, Young Lion (London, England), 1993.

Fearless Fiona and the Rolls-Royce Racket Mystery, Young Lion (London, England), 1993.

Why Count Sheep?, illustrated by Patrice Aggs, Hyperion (New York, NY), 1993.

Think of an Eel, illustrated by Mike Bostock, Candlewick Press (Cambridge, MA), 1993.

Think of a Beaver, illustrated by Mick Manning, Candlewick Press (Cambridge, MA), 1993.

My Hen Is Dancing, illustrated by Anita Jeram, Walker (London, England), 1993, Candlewick Press (Cambridge, MA), 1994.

Fearless Fiona and the Purple Poodle Mystery, Young Lion (London, England), 1994.

Red Fox, illustrated by Peter Melnyczuk, Candlewick Press (Cambridge, MA), 1994.

Bears in the Forest, illustrated by Barbara Firth, Candlewick Press (Cambridge, MA), 1994.

Gorgonzola's Revenge, illustrated by Judy Brown, Collins (London, England), 1995, Barron's (Hauppauge, NY), 1996.

Thunder and Lightning, illustrated by Judy Brown, Collins (London, England), 1995, Barron's (Hauppauge, NY), 1996, published in *Karen Wallace's Spooky Beasts,* 2007.

Snapper Bites Back, Collins (London, England), 1995, published in *Karen Wallace's Spooky Beasts,* 2007.

King Henry VIII's Shoes, illustrated by Chris Fisher, Collins (London, England), 1995.

Flash Harriet and the Giant Vegetable Monster Mystery, illustrated by Judy Brown, Hodder (London, England), 1995.

Flash Harriet and the Most Peculiar Moustache Mystery, illustrated by Judy Brown, Hodder (London, England), 1995.

A Pig Called Henry, Franklin Watts (London, England), 1995.

Flash Harriet and the Outrageous Ostrich Egg Mystery, illustrated by Judy Brown, Hodder (London, England), 1995.

Flash Harriet and the Fiendishly Wicked Whistle Mystery, illustrated by Judy Brown, Hodder (London, England), 1995.

The GrumbleRug Gang and the Day the Mums Disappeared, illustrated by Kim Blundell, Collins (London, England), 1996.

The GrumbleRug Gang and the Great-Hairy-Thing, illustrated by Kim Blundell, Collins (London, England), 1996.

Queen Victoria's Swing, illustrated by Chris Fisher, Collins (London, England), 1996.

Birthdays Are a Serious Business, illustrated by Martin Remphry, Franklin Watts (London, England), 1996.

Dancing for Captain Drake, illustrated by Martin Remphry, Franklin Watts (London, England), 1996.

Imagine You Are a Tiger, illustrated by Peter Melynszuk, Holt (New York, NY), 1996.

Imagine You Are a Crocodile, illustrated by Mike Bostock, Hodder (London, England), 1996, Holt (New York, NY), 1997.

Imagine You Are a Dolphin, illustrated by Mike Bostock, Franklin Watts (London, England), 1996.

Ace Ghosts, illustrated by Tony Ross, Hamish Hamilton (London, England), 1996.

Ghouls Rule, illustrated by Tony Ross, Hamish Hamilton (London, England), 1996.

All Aboard for the Milky Way, Hodder (London, England), 1997.

Never Say No to a Martian, Hodder (London, England), 1997.

It Takes Two, illustrated by Ross Collins, Franklin Watts (New York, NY), 1997.

Blue Eyes, illustrated by Bee Willy, Hodder (London, England), 1997.

Rollerblading Royals, illustrated by Russell Ayto, Hodder (London, England), 1997.

Captain Drake's Orders, illustrated by Martin Remphry, Franklin Watts (London, England), 1997.

A Horse Called Deathblow, illustrated by Martin Remphry, Franklin Watts (London, England), 1997.

Louis Pasteur, illustrated by Lesley Bisseker, Franklin Watts (London, England), 1997.

Thomas Edison, illustrated by Peter Kent, Franklin Watts (London, England), 1997.

London's Burning, illustrated by Jamie Smith, Franklin Watts (London, England), 1997.

Star Spooks, illustrated by Tony Ross, Puffin (London, England), 1998.

Tutankhamun's Arrow, illustrated by Chris Fisher, Collins (London, England), 1998.

Marie Curie, illustrated by Nick Ward, Franklin Watts (London, England), 1998.

Funky Phantoms, illustrated by Tony Ross, Puffin (London, England), 1998.

Tale of a Tadpole, Dorling Kindersley (New York, NY), 1998.

(With Russell Ayto) *A Hiccup on the High Seas,* A. & C. Black (London, England), 1998.

Hiding, illustrated by Charles Fuge, Franklin Watts (London, England), 1998.

Viking Raiders, illustrated by Richard Morgan, Franklin Watts (London, England), 1998.

Giant Gentle Octopus, illustrated by Mike Bostock, Candlewick Press (Cambridge, MA), 1998.

Imagine You Are an Orangutan, illustrated by Adrienne Kennaway, Hodder (London, England), 1998.

Great-Aunt Iris Goes Hunting ("Freaky Families" series), illustrated by Colin Paine, Puffin (London, England), 1998.

Switched On!, illustrated by Martin Remphry and Karen Hiscock, Ginn (Aylesbury, England), 1998.

Fight for the Vote, illustrated by Martin Remphy, Franklin Watts (London, England), 1998.

Duckling Days, Dorling Kindersley (New York, NY), 1999.

Penny Post Boy, illustrated by Greg Gormley, Franklin Watts (London, England), 1999.

Cousin Cedric Goes Bananas ("Freaky Families" series), illustrated by Colin Paine, Puffin (London, England), 1999.

Uncle Douglas and Aunt Doris Go Loopy ("Freaky Families" series), illustrated by Colin Paine, Puffin (London, England), 1999.

Stop, Thief!, illustrated by Greg Gormsley, Franklin Watts (London, England), 1999.

Scarlette Beane, illustrated by Jon Berkeley, Dial (New York, NY), 1999.

Madeleine the City Pig, illustrated by Lydia Monks, Macmillan (London, England), 1999, published as *City Pig,* Orchard (New York, NY), 2000.

A Day at Seagull Beach, Dorling Kindersley (New York, NY), 1999.

The Peanut Prankster, illustrated by Judy Brown, A. & C. Black (London, England), 1999, Picture Window Books (Minneapolis, MN), 2007.

The Minestrone Mob, illustrated by Judy Brown, A. & C. Black (London, England), 1999, Picture Window Books (Minneapolis, MN), 2007.

The Sandwich Scam, illustrated by Judy Brown, A. & C. Black (London, England), 1999.

The Stuff-It-In Specials, illustrated by Judy Brown, A. & C. Black (London, England), 1999.

Whatever the Weather, Dorling Kindersley (New York, NY), 1999.

Erik's New Home, illustrated by Richard Morgan, Franklin Watts (London, England), 1999.

Crook Catchers, A. & C. Black (London, England), 1999.

Busy Buzzy Bee, Dorling Kindersley (New York, NY), 1999.

Chomp! Munch! Chew!, illustrated by Ross Collins, Franklin Watts (London, England), 1999.

Dr Barnardo's Boys, illustrated by Martin Remphry, Franklin Watts (London, England), 1999.

Rockets, illustrated by Paul Collicutt, Oxford University Press (Oxford, England), 1999.

Police Cat Fuzz, illustrated by Trevor Dunton, Puffin (London, England), 2000.

Esmerelda, illustrated by Lydia Monks, Macmillan (London, England), 2000.

Cleopatra's Carpet, illustrated by Alan Wade, Collins (London, England), 2000.

Born to Be a Butterfly, Dorling Kindersley (New York, NY), 2000.

Big Machines, Dorling Kindersley (London, England, and New York, NY), 2000.

Sir Walter's Last Chance, illustrated by Jane Cope, Franklin Watts (London, England), 2000.

Lord Roderick's Romance, illustrated by Jane Cope, Franklin Watts (London, England), 2000.

Earl Inkblot's Big Night, illustrated by Jane Cope, Franklin Watts (London, England), 2000.

The Queen's Bed, illustrated by Jane Cope, Franklin Watts (London, England), 2000.

Wild Baby Animals, Dorling Kindersley (New York, NY), 2000.

A Bed for the Winter, Dorling Kindersley (New York, NY), 2000.

Granny and Grandpa Go Diving ("Freaky Families" series), illustrated by Colin Paine, Puffin (London, England), 2000.

Wolves, Oxford University Press (Oxford, England), 2000.

The Poisoned Pudding Plot, illustrated by Jane Cope, Franklin Watts (London, England), 2001.

Tartan Means Trouble, illustrated by Jane Cope, Franklin Watts (London, England), 2001.

Rockets and Spaceships, Dorling Kindersley (New York, NY), 2001.

Essex Wants It All, illustrated by Jane Cope, Franklin Watts (London, England), 2001.

Drake's Special Delivery, illustrated by Jane Cope, Franklin Watts (London, England), 2001.

Diving Dolphin, Dorling Kindersley (New York, NY), 2001.

Police Cat Fuzz Rides Again!, illustrated by Trevor Dunton, Puffin (London, England), 2001.

Dilly the Dancing Duck, illustrated by Barbara Nascimbeni, Campbell (London, England), 2001.

Archie Hates Pink, Macmillan (London, England), 2001.

Patrick the Pirate Pig, Macmillan (London, England), 2001.

Yikes! It's a Yeti!, illustrated by Michael Reid, A. & C. Black (London, England), 2001, Stone Arch Books (Minneapolis, MN), 2008.

Albert's Raccoon, illustrated by Graham Percy, Kingfisher (Boston, MA), 2001.

Max the Monster Mole, illustrated by Barbara Nascimbeni, Campbell (London, England), 2001.

Sylvester the Singing Sheep, illustrated by Barbara Nascimbeni, Campbell (London, England), 2001.

My Cat's Secret, Dorling Kindersley (New York, NY), 2001.

Mothers Are Everywhere, illustrated by David Axtell, Oxford University Press (Oxford, England), 2001.

The Case of the Howling Armour, illustrated by Emma Damon, Scholastic (London, England), 2002, Scholastic (New York, NY), 2004.

Something Slimy on Primrose Drive, illustrated by Helen Flook, A. & C. Black (London, England), 2002, Stone Arch Books (Minneapolis, MN), 2007.

Marvin, the Blue Pig, illustrated by Lisa Williams, Franklin Franklin Watts (London, England), 2002, Picture Window Books (Minneapolis, MN), 2005.

The Case of the Fiendishly Dancing Footsteps, illustrated by Emma Damon, Scholastic (London, England), 2002.

The Case of the Giant Gulping Bluebells, illustrated by Emma Damon, Scholastic (London, England), 2002.

The Case of the Disappearing Necklace, illustrated by Emma Damon, Scholastic (London, England), 2002.

Ella's New Friend, Macmillan (London, England), 2002.

Cheer Up Ella, Macmillan (London, England), 2002.

Bedtime for Ella, Macmillan (London, England), 2002.

Who Is Haunting Howling Hall?, illustrated by Mike Phillips, Scholastic (London, England), 2003.

Where Are My Shoes?, illustrated by Deborah Allwright, Franklin Franklin Watts (London, England), 2003, Sea-to-Sea Publications (N. Mankato, MN), 2006.

Clever Cat, illustrated by Anni Axworthy, Franklin Franklin Watts (London, England), 2003, Picture Window Books (Minneapolis, MN), 2005.

I Am a Tyrannosaurus, illustrated by Mike Bostock, Hodder (London, England), 2003, Atheneum (New York, NY), 2004.

A Trip to the Zoo, Dorling Kindersley (New York, NY), 2003.

I Am an Ankylosaurus, illustrated by Mike Bostock, Hodder (London, England), 2003, Atheneum (New York, NY), 2004.

Aargh, It's an Alien! (graphic novel), illustrated by Michael Reid, A. & C. Black (London, England), 2003, Stone Arch Books (Minneapolis, MN), 2006.

Quirky Times at Quagmire Castle, illustrated by Helen Flook, A. & C. Black (London, England), 2003, Stone Arch Books (Minneapolis, MN), 2007.

Ooh La La, Lottie!, illustrated by Garry Parsons, Kingfisher (Boston, MA), 2004.

I Can Swim!, Dorling Kindersley (New York, NY), 2004.

I Am a Diplodocus, illustrated by Mike Bostock, Hodder (London, England), 2004.

I Am a Quetzalcoatlus, illustrated by Mike Bostock, Hodder (London, England), 2004.

The Secret of the Crocodiles ("Lady Violet Winters" series), illustrated by Mike Bostock, Simon & Schuster (London, England), 2005.

(Reteller) *The Emperor's New Clothes,* illustrated by François Hall, Franklin Franklin Watts (London, England), 2005, Sea-to-Sea Publications (N. Mankato, MN), 2007.

Alice Goes to Hollywood, illustrated by Bob Dewar, Picture Window Books (Minneapolis, MN), 2006.

(Reteller) *The Elves and the Shoemaker,* Franklin Franklin Watts (London, England), 2006.

Alice Goes North, illustrated by Bob Dewar, A. & C. Black (London, England), 2006.

Arthur the King, illustrated by Neil Chapman, Franklin Franklin Watts (London, England), 2006.

(Reteller) *The Sword in the Stone,* illustrated by Neil Chapman, Franklin Franklin Watts (London, England), 2006.

Princess Gusty Ox's Strange Change, illustrated by Helen Flook, A. & C. Black (London, England), 2006, Picture Window Books (Minneapolis, MN), 2008.

The Man with Tiger Eyes ("Lady Violet Winters" series), illustrated by Mike Bostock, Simon & Schuster (London, England), 2006.

Prince Marvin's Great Moment, illustrated by Helen Flook, A. & C. Black (London, England), 2006, published as *Prince Marvin's Greatest Moment,* Picture Window Books (Minneapolis, MN), 2007.

King Cudgel's Challenge, illustrated by Helen Flook, A. & C. Black (London, England), 2006, Picture Window Books (Minneapolis, MN), 2008.

The Mothproof Hall Mystery; and, The Purple Poodle Mystery, illustrated by Judy Brown, Happy Cat (London, England), 2007.

Diamond Takers, Simon & Schuster (London, England), 2007.

Ma Moosejaw Means Business, illustrated by Nigel Baines, A. & C. Black (London, England), 2007.

Zigzag Rat, illustrated by Andy Catling, Franklin Franklin Watts (London, England), 2007.

Karen Wallace's Spooky Beasts: Two Gripping Ghostly Stories! (includes *Thunder and Lightning* and *Snapper Bites Back*), illustrated by Judy Brown, Happy Cat (London, England), 2007.

Thunderbelle's Bad Mood, illustrated by Guy Parker-Rees, Orchard (London, England), 2007.

Thunderbelle's Spooky Night, illustrated by Guy Parker-Rees, Orchard (London, England), 2007.

Thunderbelle's New Home, illustrated by Guy Parker-Rees, Orchard (London, England), 2007.

Thunderbelle's Party, illustrated by Guy Parker-Rees, Orchard (London, England), 2007.

Whiff Eric and the Great Green Thing, illustrated by Nigel Baines, A. & C. Black (London, England), 2007.

Li Fu's Great Aim: The Inside Story of the Terracotta Archer, illustrated by Helen Flook, A. & C. Black (London, England), 2007.

Cover of British writer Karen Wallace's A Trip to the Zoo, *a nonfiction book designed to entertain young animal lovers.* (Jacket image © Dorling Kindersley. All rights reserved. Reprinted by permission of DK Publishing, a member of Penguin Group (USA), Inc.)

Queen Carrion's Big Bear Hug, illustrated by Helen Flook, Picture Window Books (Minneapolis, MN), 2008.

NOVELS

Raspberries on the Yangtze, Simon & Schuster (London, England), Delacorte (New York, NY), 2002.

Climbing a Monkey Puzzle Tree, Simon & Schuster (London, England), 2002.

Wendy (based on the character from *Peter Pan* by J.M. Barrie), Simon & Schuster (London, England), 2003, Simon & Schuster (New York, NY), 2004.

The Unrivalled Spangles, Simon & Schuster (London, England), 2005, Atheneum (New York, NY), 2006.

OTHER

Also author of *Quest for the Golden See-Saw,* 1999. Author of television scripts, including *Wizadora,* for Workhouse Productions, 1996-97; *Make Believe Moments,* for Disney, 1997; *Teddybears,* for Meridian, 1997; *Wild Islands,* for Performance Films, 1998; *Mopatop's Shop,* for Carleton/Henson, 1998; *Timothy Goes to School,* for Nelvana, 1999-2000; *The Hoobs,* for Henson/BBC Channel 4, 2000; *Planet Cook,* 2004; *Peter Pan* (documentary), Divers Productions, 2005; and *Police Cat Fuzz* (based on the book of the same name), for Pepper's Ghost Productions.

Sidelights

Boasting published works ranging from television plays and beginning readers to middle-grade and teen novels, and from nonfiction to fiction, Karen Wallace is a prolific author who lives and works in England. Her books include the nature-oriented titles such as *I Am a Diplodocus* and *Think of an Eel,* the novels in the "Lady Violet Winters" series for older elementary-grade readers, and numerous lighthearted chapter books for beginning and younger readers, with titles ranging from *Whiff Eric and the Great Green Thing* to *The Case of the Howling Armor.*

"I write the books I would like to have read [as a child]," Wallace explained on her home page. "If I wasn't a writer, I would want to be a zoologist. It's all about looking at things and trying to understand how they work." Her nonfiction titles *Think of an Eel* and *Think of a Beaver* present factual information about these creatures in an easily accessible, illustrated format. While some young readers might seek out a book about beavers on their own, writing about the rather-less-attractive eel might seem an unusual topic for an author. "Even their greatest fans could hardly call them beautiful," Wallace readily admitted to *SATA.* "Nor could they be described as cuddly or even remotely friendly. In a boat off Bermuda, I once saw the head of a moray eel—and I do mean the head—chase a party of terrified fishermen from bow to stern and back again." It was Wallace's personal experiences with eels that inspired her

Wallace's award-winning Think of an Eel *features compelling artwork by frequent collaborator Mike Bostock.* (Illustration copyright © 1993 by Mike Bostock. Reproduced by permission of the publisher Candlewick Press, Inc., Cambridge, MA on behalf of Walker Books, Ltd., London, England.)

book on that creature's life and habits. When she discovered that very little was actually known about eels, she decided to write about them.

In order to make her subject as fascinating to young readers as it was to her, Wallace decided to write *Think of an Eel* "to be read out loud" as in the ancient English oral tradition. "Literature was part of an oral tradition—wonderful tales were told and retold," she once explained in *SATA*. "They passed from one storyteller to the next, from one generation to the next. These poems and stories, written when the world was a wild and fearful place, have a resonance all of their own. This

resonance was in the back of my mind when I first sat down and began to write *Think of an Eel*."

Reviewers were appreciative of Wallace's approach. *Bulletin of the Center for Children's Books* contributor Betsy Hearne wrote that the book demonstrates "an important point: information is power only when it's presented in a powerful way. . . . Other elements (clarity, accuracy, organization . . .) are all important, but without voice, nonfiction too often goes unheard." Hearne added that Wallace's text in *Think of an Eel* "features a distinctive blend of verbal and artistic styles that shapes the subject."

Wallace has found continued success in her nonfiction books for beginning readers. Employing the same elements that make for a successful fictional story—including repetition, limited vocabulary, compelling illustrations, and plenty of white space to encourage the timid—books such as *Duckling Days, Wild Baby Animals,* and *I Am a Tyrannosaurus* make science concepts appealing and build reader independence, according to reviewers. In *Gentle Giant Octopus,* Wallace seamlessly interweaves facts about the mysterious sea creature and a story about a female octopus that seeks a safe place to lay its eggs, fend off predators, and protect its newly hatched young. Wallace and frequent collaborator and illustrator Mike Bostock "create ocean magic in their presentation of tantalizing information with simple elegance and beauty," according to Susan P. Bloom in *Horn Book. I Am an Ankylosaurus,* in which a mother dinosaur helps her young to survive the dangers of the prehistoric word, features what *Horn Book* contributor Danielle J. Ford called an "unflinchingly realistic" third-person narrative "that neither sugarcoats animal survival nor anthropomorphizes animal parenting." According to *Booklist* critic Carolyn Phelan, "Bostock's contribution of clear, simple drawings . . . offer an imaginative vision" of the sometimes-dangerous and often-beautiful prehistoric world. A companion volume, *I Am a Tyrannosaurus,* was praised by a *Kirkus Reviews* writer as a "dramatic" and "compelling introduction to dinosaur life [that] will whet new fans' appetites."

Turning to fiction, Wallace entertains young readers with books that feature magical elements and gently silly plots. In *Madeleine the City Pig* (published in the United States as *City Pig*) Wallace's porky protagonist finds that her important job and many expensive possessions do not bring her the happiness she seeks. However, when Madeleine travels to the country and learns how other pigs live, she knows she has found what she was looking for. In *Scarlette Beane* a girl is born with a red face and green fingertips, and when her parents give her a garden of her own to plant, she grows the largest vegetables anyone has ever seen. In the story's climax, Scarlette creates a vegetable castle with her giant harvest and moves her family from its humble abode into the edible palace. *Alice Goes to Hollywood* features another amusing animal character, in this case a spunky anteater who decides to become a film star.

Frivolity and fun abound in Wallace's chapter books as well. In *Rollerblading Royals* the author reworks Mark Twain's *The Prince and the Pauper* and its story about trading places. Here King Clement and Queen Clementina are tired of doing their royal duty when they meet up with Kevin and Ricky, two circus folks who are ready for a vacation from their lives as well. A contributor to *Books for Keeps* outlined the elements in Wallace's recipe for success: "plenty of laughs, a simple but satisfying plot and an inevitable happy ending." Wallace relies on the same recipe in *Star Spooks* and *Funky Phantoms,* two mysteries that take place in an old house where the modern-day inhabitants run a hotel with the help of the ghosts of their seventeenth-century relatives. In *Aargh, It's an Alien!* Wallace presents a modern take on the well-known story about the boy who cried wolf, while in *Something Slimy on Primrose Drive* a normal-looking boy is the weird one in a family of ghoulish relatives. In *Booklist* Stephanie Zvirin called *Something Slimy on Primrose Drive* "fun, with enough yucky details" to entrance young readers and "a worthy message to seal the deal."

Tutankhamun's Arrow, a time-travel adventure, is for slightly older readers, preferably those with "a lively imagination, a receptive mind and a sense of humour," according to Ethel E. Ashworth in *School Librarian.* Other books for older elementary-grade readers include *The Secret of the Crocodiles* and *The Man with Tiger Eyes,* two Edwardian mysteries that follow the amateur sleuthing of Lady Violet Winters.

Wallace addresses middle-school readers and young teens in novels such as *Wendy, The Unrivalled Spangles,* and *Climbing a Monkey Puzzle Tree.* She incorporates a favorite character from J.M. Barrie's classic story *Peter Pan* in *Wendy,* which finds nine-year-old Wendy Darling and younger brother Peter coping with disinterested parents and a nanny who rules through intimidation while growing up in Edwardian London. Because Peter Pan has not yet entered Wendy's life, the girl must find real-world ways to cope when she uncovers a secret that threatens her family. Noting that Wallace's story diverges from the magic of *Peter Pan, Horn Book* contributor Roger Sutton called *Wendy* "a sometimes fierce exposition of the dark side of Edwardian decorum." "Twisted but ultimately comforting," the novel also expresses "the poignancy of Wendy's coming-of-age," in the opinion of a *Kirkus Reviews* writer, while in *School Library Journal* Connie Tyrell Burns dubbed the book "an interesting portrait of the world of the privileged classes in early-20th-century London." "Wallace is a supremely adept writer," maintained Ilene Cooper in *Booklist,* the critic adding that *Wendy* is likely to attract middle-grade readers "who can understand the . . . complexities" that confuse its nine-year-old heroine.

Moving slightly further back in time, *The Unrivalled Spangles* focuses on a circus family performing in London's East End during the late 1800s. Ellen Spangle is sixteen and sister Lucy is two years younger; together they star as the Amazing Scarletta Sisters in their father's circus, where their horseback-riding skills impress audiences. When a series of romantic entanglements threatens the sisters' loyalty to both their profession and each other, hearts are broken and tragedies erupt. While Michael Cart noted in *Booklist* that the novel verges on melodrama, he added that Wallace's "inside look at [Victorian] circus life . . . will keep readers' attention." In *School Library Journal* Janet Hilbun noted Wallace's "calm narrative style," and recommended *The Unrivalled Spangles* for its likeable protagonists, "fast-moving plot," salting of authentic Victorian colloquialisms, and "satisfying ending."

Based on the author's own childhood, *Raspberries on the Yangtze* brings to life a childhood summer in rural Canada during the 1950s as the backdrop for a coming-of-age story. Young Nancy, her brother Andrew, and their friends Amy and Clare are still children although they imagine themselves very knowledgeable about the adult world. Their eavesdropping on wealthier neighbors sheds new light on the world around them, however, and helps the four friends grow up. Wallace transforms other childhood memories in *Climbing a Monkey Puzzle Tree,* which focuses on a Canadian girl's sometimes difficult experiences at a British boarding school. Although the young characters in these novels may seem more naive than modern children of the same age, a *Kirkus Reviews* writer wrote of *Raspberries on the Yangtze* that Wallace's "portrayal of small-town gossip and snobbery are well done," as are her depictions of childhood friendships and sibling relations. Margaret Mackey, writing in *Resource Links,* contended that *Raspberries on the Yangtze* "conveys the joys and frustrations of childhood very evocatively," and *Horn Book* contributor Joanna Rudge Long deemed the novel "a thought-provoking look at family dynamics in any era, as well as a fast, funny, and enjoyable read."

Biographical and Critical Sources

PERIODICALS

Appraisal, spring, 2000, review of *A Day at Seagull Beach,* p. 112.

Booklist, May 15, 1993, Carolyn Phelan, review of *Think of a Beaver* and *Think of an Eel,* p. 1695; November 1, 1994, Mary Harris Veeder, review of *Bears in the Forest,* p. 504; December 1, 1994, Carolyn Phelan, review of *Red Fox,* p. 675; December 1, 1996, Susan Dove Lempke, review of *Imagine You Are a Tiger,* p. 663; May 1, 1997, Carolyn Phelan, review of *Imagine You Are a Crocodile,* p. 1497; November 15, 1998, Helen Rosenberg, review of *Gentle Giant Octopus,* p. 594; May 15, 1999, Hazel Rochman, review of *Duckling Days,* p. 1705; January 1, 2000, Todd Morning, review of *Scarlette Beane,* p. 938; February 15, 2000, Michael Cart, review of *City Pig,* p. 1123; July, 2000, Gillian Engberg, review of *Wild Baby Animals,* p. 2045; January 1, 2004, Ilene Cooper, review of *Wendy,* p. 848; April 1, 2005, Carolyn Phelan, review of *I Am an Ankylosaurus,* p. 1362; November 15, 2006, Stephanie Zvirin, review of *Something Slimy on Primrose Drive,* p. 55; December 1, 2006, Michael Cart, review of *The Unrivalled Spangles,* p. 39.

Books for Keeps, July, 1996, review of *Imagine You Are a Tiger,* p. 9; September, 1997, review of *It Takes Two,* p. 106; January, 1998, review of *Rollerblading Royals,* p. 17; May, 1998, review of *Star Spooks* and *Funky Phantoms,* p. 23; July, 1998, review of *A Hiccup on the High Seas,* p. 22; January, 1999, Margaret Mallett, review of *Think of an Eel,* p. 22; September, 2001, Andrew Kidd, review of *Police Cat Fuzz Rides Again!,* p. 23.

Bulletin of the Center for Children's Books, May 21, 1993, Betsy Hearne, reviews of *Think of a Beaver* and *Think of an Eel,* pp. 273-274; March, 2000, review of *Scarlette Beane,* p. 258; March, 2004, Deborah Stevenson, review of *Wendy,* p. 300; December, 2006, Elizabeth Bush, review of *The Unrivalled Spangles,* p. 193.

Horn Book, July-August, 1993, Ellen Fader, review of *Think of a Beaver,* pp. 478-479; November, 1998, Susan P. Bloom, review of *Gentle Giant Octopus,* p. 757; September-October, 2002, Joanna Rudge Long, review of *Raspberries on the Yangtze,* p. 583; March-April, 2004, Roger Sutton, review of *Wendy,* p. 190; July-August, 2005, Danielle J. Ford, review of *I Am an Ankylosaurus,* p. 492.

Journal of Adolescent and Adult Literacy, March, 2003, Nick Hart, review of *Raspberries on the Yangtze,* p. 530.

Kirkus Reviews, November 15, 1999, review of *Busy Buzzy Bee,* p. 1817; December 15, 1999, review of *Scarlette Beane,* pp. 1964-1965; May 15, 2002, review of *Raspberries on the Yangtze,* p. 743; December 15, 2003, review of *Wendy,* p. 1455; November 1, 2004, review of *I Am a Tyrannosaurus,* p. 1046; April 1, 2005, review of *I Am an Ankylosaurus,* p. 428; September 15, 2006, review of *The Unrivalled Spangles,* p. 969.

Magpies, March, 2001, Chloe Mauger, review of *Chomp! Munch! Chew!,* p. 43; May, 2002, review of *Marvin the Blue Pig,* p. 29.

Nature, November 30, 2000, Andrew Berry, reviews of *Chomp! Munch! Chew!* and *It Takes Two,* p. 517.

Publishers Weekly, November 30, 1998, review of *Gentle Giant Octopus,* p. 70; July 5, 1999, review of *A Day at Seagull Beach,* p. 73; February 7, 2000, review of *City Pig,* p. 84; February 28, 2000, review of *Scarlette Beane,* p. 79; June 11, 2001, review of *Think of an Eel,* p. 87.

Resource Links, October, 2001, Margaret Mackey, review of *Raspberries on the Yangtze,* p. 56.

School Librarian, February, 1997, John Feltwell, review of *Imagine You Are a Crocodile,* p. 22; November, 1997, Andrea Rayner, review of *Rollerblading Royals,* p. 202; spring, 1998, Hazel Townson, review of *Blue Eyes,* p. 22; summer, 1998, Andrea Rayner, review of *Star Spooks* and *Funky Phantoms,* p. 90; spring, 1999, Kathy Lemaire, review of *Great-Aunt Irish Goes Hunting,* p. 35; summer, 1999, Ethel E. Ashworth, review of *Tutankhamun's Arrow,* p. 91; winter, 1999, Angela Redfern, review of *A Day at Seagull Beach,* p. 188; autumn, 2001, Hazel Townson, review of *Yikes, It's a Yeti!,* p. 161; spring, 2003, review of *Something Slimy on Primrose Lane,* p. 36; winter, 2003, review of *Aargh, It's an Alien!,* p. 185; autumn, 2006, Susan Elkin, review of *The Man with Tiger Eyes,* p. 146.

School Library Journal, November, 1993, Ruth K. McDonald, review of *Why Count Sheep?,* p. 96; December, 1993, Susan Scheps, review of *Think of an Eel,* p. 110; July, 1994, Eldon Younce, review of *My Hen Is*

Dancing, p. 98; July, 1997, Lauralyn Persson, review of *Imagine You Are a Crocodile,* p. 78; January, 1999, Adele Greenlee, review of *Gentle Giant Octopus,* p. 122; April, 1999, Stephanie Bianchi, review of *Tale of a Tadpole,* p. 128; March, 2000, Kathleen Kelly M. MacMillan, review of *Scarlette Beane,* p. 219; March, 2000, Carol Ann Wilson, review of *City Pig,* p. 219; July, 2000, John Sigwald, review of *Big Machines,* p. 99; January, 2001, Debbie Whitbeck, review of *A Bed for Winter,* p. 124; July, 2002, Gerry Larson, review of *Raspberries on the Yangtze,* p. 127; March, 2004, Connie Tyrell Burns, review of *Wendy,* p. 222; May, 2005, Patricia Manning, review of *I Am an Ankylosaurus,* p. 103; December, 2006, Janet Hilbun, review of *The Unrivalled Spangles,* p. 157.

Times Educational Supplement, September 19, 1997, Gerald Haigh, review of *Louis Pasteur* and *Thomas Edison;* November 14, 1997, Michael Thorn, review of *All Aboard for the Milky Way;* October 15, 1999, Jane Doonan, review of *Scarlette Beane* and *Madeleine the City Pig,* p. 23; June 15, 2001, Michael Thorn, review of *Police Cat Fuzz Rides Again!,* pp. 20-21.

Voice of Youth Advocates, April, 2004, Brenda Moses-Allen, review of *Wendy,* p. 52.

ONLINE

Karen Wallace Home Page, http://www.karenwallace.co.uk (March 30, 2008).*

*   *   *

WELDIN, Frauke 1969-

Personal

Born 1969, in Berlin, Germany. *Education:* Hochschul für Angewandte Wissenschaften, degree (illustration), 2002.

Addresses

Home—Germany.

Career

Illustrator, beginning 2002. Creator of cover illustrations for publishers, including Loewe Verlag.

Awards, Honors

Illustration included in Bologna Exhibition, 1995.

Illustrator

(With Daniela Pohl) Claudie Weinhapl, *Ponygeschichten,* Carl Ueberreuter Verlag, 2006.

(With Ines Markowski) Andreas Seiller, *Piratengeschichten,* Carl Ueberreuter Verlag, 2006.

Christa Kempter, *Liebes kleines Schaf,* NordSüd Verlag (Zurich, Switzerland), 2006, translated by Michelle Maczka as *Dear Little Lamb,* NorthSouth Books (New York, NY), 2006.

Paul Maar and Erik Dorrmann, *Alle meine Entchen . . . lustig weitergereimt,* Oetinger (Hamburg, Germany), 2007.

Heinz Janisch, *Lili und die Dshungelbande,* NordSüd Verlag (Zurich, Switzerland), 2007.

Sabine Praml, *Weil du mein liebes Mäuschen bist,* Oetinger (Hamburg, Germany), 2008.

Biographical and Critical Sources

ONLINE

Loewe Verlag Web site, http://www.loewe-verlag.de/ (March 21, 2008), "Frauke Weldin."*

*   *   *

YAMADA, Utako 1963-

Personal

Born 1963, in Tokyo, Japan; married; children: two.

Addresses

Home—Tokyo, Japan.

Career

Author and illustrator of children's books, and restaurateur. Karen Čapek (tea house), Tokyo, Japan, founder, 1987; founder of a desert shop, 2001. Designer of prints, toys, and housewares.

Writings

SELF-ILLUSTRATED

The Story of Cherry the Pig (originally published in Japanese), Kane/Miller (La Jolla, CA), 2007.

Author and illustrator of over 20 other children's books published in Japan, include *Buzzy the Honeybee* and *Little Rabbit Pipin's Birthday.*

Biographical and Critical Sources

PERIODICALS

Booklist, February 15, 2007, Ilene Cooper, review of *The Story of Cherry the Pig,* p. 86.

School Library Journal, March, 2007, Susan Moorhead, review of *The Story of Cherry the Pig,* p. 192.

ONLINE

Kane/Miller Web site, http://www.kanemiller.com/ (March 21, 2008), "Utako Yamada."

Utako Yamada Home Page, http://www.karelcapek.co.jp (March 21, 2008).*

*   *   *

YOUNG, Janet 1957-
(Janet Ruth Young)

Personal

Born 1957. *Education:* Salem State College, B.A. (English), 1979; Boston University, M.A. (creative writing), 1987.

Addresses

Home—Gloucester, MA.

Career

Author and editor. *Stet* (literary magazine), former coeditor.

Member

PEN New England.

Awards, Honors

Children's Book Discovery Award, PEN New England, 2007, for *The Opposite of Music.*

Writings

The Opposite of Music, Atheneum (New York, NY), 2007.

Contributor of travel articles and reviews to periodicals, including the *Boston Globe.*

Sidelights

Janet Young lives in Massachusetts, on the Atlantic coast, where she works as a freelance editor while also pursuing her career as an author. Her first novel, *The Opposite of Music,* was awarded the PEN New England Children's Book Discovery Award in 2007.

Geared for teen readers, Young's story centers on a fifteen-year-old boy who is trying to cope with the effect of his father's severe depression on his household. Billy's dad has stopped working, stopped sleeping, and stopped interacting with everyone in the family. Things start to look up after the man is diagnosed with depression, but the family's hopes are dashed when the medication required to combat Dad's condition proves worse than the disease itself. As his father's illness consumes all the family's energy, Billy finds his school work and social life starting to suffer. More than that, he worries that his father's disease will one day affect him as well. Noting that readers will identify with Billy's reaction and his wry take on several alternative therapies, *School Library Journal* contributor Vicki Reutter concluded of *The Opposite of Music* that Young's "attention to medical detail and advocacy for counseling will definitely put this title on bibliotherapy lists." Noting that the author "captures the reality" of serious mental illness, Frances Bradburn wrote in *Booklist* that *The Opposite of Music* offers teen readers "a well-written, starkly honest, important story."

Biographical and Critical Sources

PERIODICALS

Booklist, March 1, 2007, Frances Bradburn, review of *The Opposite of Music,* p. 80.

Bulletin of the Center for Children's Books, April, 2007, Deborah Stevenson, review of *The Opposite of Music,* p. 349.

School Library Journal, March, 2007, Vicki Reutter, review of *The Opposite of Music,* p. 222.

Voice of Youth Advocates, April, 2007, Robyn Guedel, review of *The Opposite of Music,* p. 59.

ONLINE

Pulse Blogfest Web site, http://www.pulseblogfest.com/ (March 28, 2008).*

*   *   *

YOUNG, Janet Ruth
See YOUNG, Janet